AKANTHINA 7
COLLECTION DIRIGÉE PAR N. V. SEKUNDA

Armées grecques et romaines dans le nord des Balkans

Edité par Aliénor Rufin Solas
En collaboration avec Marie-Gabrielle Parissaki et Elpida Kosmidou

FONDATION TRADITIO EUROPAE
GDAŃSK - TORUŃ 2013

FONDATION TRADITIO EUROPAE

OUVRAGE PUBLIÉ AVEC LE CONCOURS DU CENTRE
«MÉDITERRANÉE ANTIQUE : CIVILISATION ET CHRISTIANISME ANCIEN»,
DE L'ECOLE DOCTORALE «MONDES ANCIENS ET MÉDIÉVAUX»
ET DU CONSEIL SCIENTIFIQUE DE L'UNIVERSITÉ PARIS-SORBONNE (PARIS IV).

AKANTHINA 7
COLLECTION DIRIGÉE PAR N. V. SEKUNDA

Table des matières

Auteur	Titre	Page
Aliénor Rufin Solas	Introduction	9
Elpida Kosmidou	Further thoughts on the coinage and politics of Alexander I.	15
Aliénor Rufin Solas	L'or et l'argent des aristocraties thraces. Contribution de l'étude des trésors contenant des vases en métal précieux à l'histoire de la région aux IVe et IIIe siècles avant J.-C.	29
Nicholas Victor Sekunda	The 'Victory' coinage of Patraos of Paionia.	53
Adrian Dumitru	Les Séleucides et les Balkans : les Thraces dans les armées séleucides.	69
Peter Delev	The burning of the temple at Delphi, the Roman governor L. Scipio and the rout of the Scordisci.	91
Maria-Gabriella Parissaki	Thrace under Roman sway (146 BC – AD 46). Between warfare and diplomacy.	105
Albana Meta	Guerre et circulation monétaire : le cas des drachmes de Dyrrachion.	117
Saimir Shpuza	Illyriens et Romains. Du conflit à l'intégration.	133
Danijel Dzino	The impact of Roman imperialism on the formation of group identities in some indigenous societies from the eastern Adriatic hinterland.	145
Katherine Low	Tacitus and thrace. Balkan auxiliaries from an historian's perspective.	171
Ivo Topalilov	The veterans and their descendants in the elite of Philippopolis, Thrace.	185
Oleg Alexandrov	Ethnic and social composition of the roman army in Moesia inferior : soldiers from Asia Minor and the eastern provinces of the Roman Empire.	199
Constantina Katsari	Roman army and the monetisation of Dacia.	209
	Index. Termes géographiques et ethniques	224

Introduction

C'est avec l'ambition de contribuer au renouvellement des connaissances portant sur l'histoire des peuples guerriers installés dans le nord des Balkans qui, Illyriens, Péoniens, Thraces, Celtes, Daces et autres peuples de la vallée du Danube, sont parmi les moins connus du monde antique, qu'un groupe de travail européen s'est constitué en 2009 : ce livre est le résultat de cette collaboration[1].

Strabon, dans le livre VII de sa *Géographie*, distinguait comme un ensemble géographique cohérent ces régions qui „*entre l'Adriatique et la partie gauche du Pont-Euxin, sont séparées des premières* [c'est à dire les autres régions du nord et de l'est de l'Europe] *par l'Istros et vont en direction du sud jusqu'à la Grèce et la Propontide*"[2]. Du point de vue de l'historien du XXIe siècle, les peuples habitant ces contrées dans l'Antiquité, qui n'ont laissé que très peu de témoignages écrits, ont en commun d'avoir été évoqués par des auteurs grecs puis romains principalement en lien avec les conflits militaires. Ceux-ci furent en effet nombreux et souvent difficiles pour les armées qui s'aventurèrent dans leurs pays. L'angle des relations militaires avec les puissances extérieures à la région s'imposait donc. L'originalité du sujet retenu ici tient cependant au fait que ces relations qui, de la fin de l'époque archaïque à la domination romaine, ont oscillé entre guerre et collaboration, sont étudiées sous deux aspects : celui du conflit, de la conquête ou des raids de pillage, mais aussi celui des recrutements et de l'intégration des communautés guerrières locales dans les armées grecques, puis romaines. Ce point de vue, ainsi que l'étude des échanges qui ont accompagné ces relations, en particulier les transferts d'hommes et de richesses, peuvent en effet nous renseigner non seulement sur l'histoire des rapports politiques et militaires de ces peuples avec les Grecs et les Romains, mais aussi sur leurs structures sociales et guerrières ainsi que sur leur histoire propre.

---

[1] Le projet «Structures guerrières et échanges entre peuples des Balkans», financé par l'Université Paris-Sorbonne IV et le Centre Lenain de Tillemont (UMR 8167 Orient et Méditerranée), a bénéficié du soutien généreux de la Bibliothèque Métropolitaine de Bucarest, qui nous a réservé, par deux fois, une section dans le cadre de son colloque annuel. Ce recueil constitue une nouvelle édition revue et augmentée d'articles ayant fait l'objet d'une publication préliminaire dans les actes des colloques de la Bibliothèque Métropolitaine de Bucarest (*Symposium International La Roumanie, Le livre, l'Europe*, Bucarest, 20-22 septembre 2010 et Sinaia, 19-21 septembre 2011). La fructueuse collaboration qui a eu lieu pendant et après ces rencontres ont amené les auteurs à vouloir reprendre leurs manuscrits pour développer des problématiques communes, ce qui explique, en plus du souhait de diffuser nos résultats à un public de spécialistes, le choix de cette nouvelle édition. Nous remercions Monsieur Florin Rotaru d'avoir apporté son soutien à cette initiative et, avec notre collègue et ami Adrian Dumitru, de nous avoir offert, en plus d'un accueil chaleureux, d'excellentes conditions de travail en Roumanie.
Toute notre reconnaissance va aux Professeurs Zoé Petre, Olivier Picard et Nicholas V. Sekunda pour leur soutien et leur participation à ce projet. Nous remercions très chaleureusement Nicholas V. Sekunda de la confiance et de la latitude dont il nous a fait bénéficier afin d'éditer cet ouvrage dans la collection Akanthina. Merci enfin à tous les auteurs pour leur enthousiasme et l'originalité de leurs contributions.
[2] Strabon 7.1.1: ὅσα μεταξὺ τοῦ Ἀδρίου καὶ τῶν ἀριστερῶν τῆς Ποντικῆς θαλάττης μερῶν ἀπολαμβάνει πρὸς νότον μέχρι τῆς Ἑλλάδος καὶ τῆς Προποντίδος ὁ Ἴστρος.

Le relatif déficit documentaire au sujet des peuples guerriers du nord des Balkans rend indispensable le recours aux diverses sources disponibles, textuelles, archéologiques et numismatiques.

L'apport possible de la numismatique au suivi des opérations militaires dans la région nord-balkanique, ainsi qu'à la connaissance des rapports conflictuels ou de collaboration avec les Grecs puis avec les Romains est démontré par plusieurs exposés, qui illustrent deux différents types d'approche de la monnaie comme source documentaire : d'une part, l'étude iconographique des types monétaires (E. Kosmidou, N. V. Sekunda) et, d'autre part, celle de la circulation des monnaies, qui se base sur les trésors (A. Meta, C. Katsari).

La comparaison des types monétaires macédoniens et des tribus de la région du Pangée permet à E. Kosmidou d'éclairer de manière originale les rapports conflictuels ou de collaboration entre Alexandre Ier de Macédoine et les tribus du sud-ouest de la Thrace, puisque ces relations semblent avoir eu des effets sur les monnayages des uns et des autres. S'intéressant aux costumes militaires représentés sur les monnaies de Patraos, N. V. Sekunda émet quant à lui l'hypothèse nouvelle de la participation de ce roi péonien, à la tête de ses hommes, aux guerres des Diadoques en Asie.

C. Katsari étudie la circulation monétaire en Dacie et cherche à en comprendre les ressorts, en prenant en compte l'urbanisation, le commerce et les traditions locales qui montrent en effet un rapport particulier à la monnaie, caractérisé par de nombreuses frappes d'imitations de monnaies extérieures à la région : l'auteur prend donc le contre-pied de l'opinion selon laquelle la présence de l'armée romaine suffirait à expliquer la monétarisation dans cette province aux IIe et IIIe siècles après J.-C.

Il n'en reste pas moins que la pénétration des monnaies extérieures, qui ne suivirent pas toujours les routes du commerce[3], ainsi que la prise en compte des échanges effectués dans un contexte guerrier invitent à réinterpréter certains phénomènes de circulation monétaire que l'on pouvait croire liés au commerce, mais qui s'expliquent d'abord par la guerre. C'est la conclusion de l'étude d'A. Meta sur la circulation des drachmes de Dyrrachion dans le nord des Balkans, liée aux guerres romaines en Thrace, confirmant le rôle des rapports militaires avec les puissances extérieures dans la monétarisation des régions considérées ou, au minimum, dans l'intensification de ce phénomène. La circulation des monnaies est donc susceptible de nous informer sur les opérations guerrières menées par les armées extérieures à la région et sur les relations d'hostilité, de soumission ou de coopération qu'elles ont établies avec des tribus locales.

La méthodologie des études de la circulation monétaire peut en outre être appliquée aux vases en métal précieux qui, en Thrace, ont été échangés et thésaurisés,

---

[3] Comme le montre, dans le cas de Thasos, la confrontation de la circulation des monnaies à celles des anses d'amphores thasiennes, cf. O. Picard, «*Monaies de fouilles et histoire grecque : l'exemple de Thasos*», *Numismatic Archaeology, Archaeological Numismatics*, Oxbow Monograph 75 (1997) 29-39, pl. 5-6 et, du même auteur, «La circulation monétaire dans le monde grec : le cas de Thasos», dans Th. Faucher, M.-C. Marcellesi et O. Picard (éd.), *Nomisma - La circulation monétaire dans le monde grec antique*, Actes du colloque international, Athènes, 14-17 avril 2010, *Bulletin de Correspondance Hellénique*, Supplément 53 (2011) 79-109.

afin de contribuer à l'histoire des aristocraties de la région et de leurs relations avec les Grecs aux époques classique et hellénistique (A. Rufin Solas).

Notons ici que les phénomènes de circulation monétaire (comme de la circulation des vases en métal précieux, objets 'presque monétaires') ignoraient la frontière que le Danube représentait pourtant pour les auteurs anciens.

Les possibilités d'exploitation des sources littéraires n'ont cependant pas encore été épuisées. Il est intéressant de relever à cet égard que les auteurs anciens ont certes insisté sur l'aspect conflictuel des relations entre les peuples guerriers considérés ici et les armées grecques, puis romaines, mais que les historiens modernes ont très largement négligé les relations de coopération, qui sont pourtant évoquées çà et là dans les sources ou qui peuvent être déduites de celles-ci.

La contribution de P. Delev, qui revient sur la chronologie des opérations militaires romaines dans la vallée du Danube, et propose une nouvelle datation pour le sac de Delphes par les Scordisques, démontre que la documentation littéraire et épigraphique doit continuer d'être exploitée pour contribuer à l'histoire de la région, vue sous l'angle des conflits.

Cependant il s'avère très fructueux, toujours sur le plan de la connaissance historique, de s'intéresser aussi aux relations de collaboration. Ainsi, bien que les 'guerres thraces' aient été remarquables par leur durée et leur violence, M.-G. Parissaki souligne-t-elle les efforts diplomatiques qu'ont déployé les Romains dans la région : l'auteur démontre, en particulier, le rôle méconnu de ces derniers dans la création du royaume-client de Thrace.

Les recrutements de soldats de la région dans les armées grecques puis romaines sont évoqués par les auteurs anciens, et le phénomène a été relevé depuis longtemps par les Modernes. Toutefois, et même depuis la monumentale synthèse de Marcel Launey[4], beaucoup d'incertitudes demeurent. À partir d'une documentation littéraire et épigraphique très éparse, fragmentaire et qui a fait l'objet d'interprétations divergentes, A. Dumitru fait ainsi le point sur ce qu'il est possible ou non de déduire sur la présence des Thraces dans les armées séleucides. Les sources épigraphiques peuvent en effet nous renseigner sur les recrutements de guerriers de la région et leur intégration dans les royaumes hellénistique. Leur interprétation est néanmoins difficile, tout particulièrement en ce qui concerne les données onomastiques (A. Dumitru, O. Alexandrov, I. Topalilov).

O. Alexandrov s'intéresse, pour la province romaine de Moesie inférieure, aux dédicaces de militaires qui, plus encore que les stèles funéraires (puisqu'elles mentionnent outre le nom, le rang et l'unité du soldat, le nom et l'épiclèse de la divinité honorée), sont en mesure de nous informer sur l'origine des dédicants et de nous donner une idée de l'hétérogénéité ethnique de l'armée romaine stationnée dans cette province aux IIe et IIIe siècles après J.-C.

Les études onomastiques peuvent en outre, mais là encore avec la prudence méthodologique qui s'impose, nous apporter des informations sur les aristocraties locales, sur lesquelles nous sommes peu renseignés par ailleurs. Partant de l'hypo-

---

[4] Marcel Launey, *Recherches sur les armées hellénistiques* (Paris, 1949-1950).

thèse de l'identification possible des vétérans par leurs noms, I. Topalilov étudie ainsi, d'après la documentation épigraphique, la présence des vétérans et de leurs descendants dans les plus hautes fonctions à Philippopolis à l'époque de la domination romaine. Il en ressort des conclusions originales qui pourraient confirmer la singularité, parmi les autres provinces romaines, d'une Thrace où la guerre apparaît comme facteur principal d'intégration et de promotion sociale.

Le cas, très différent, de l'intégration des aristocraties illyriennes dans l'Empire romain est présenté par S. Shpuza, à partir de la documentation épigraphique et littéraire. L'auteur étudie ce processus sur la longue durée, puisqu'il estime qu'il a débuté dès l'époque de la pénétration romaine en Grèce, au IIIe siècle avant J.-C.

Dans une autre perspective, les relations avec les puissances extérieures depuis le IVe siècle avant J.-C., mais particulièrement depuis l'irruption des Romains et les premières manifestations de leur impérialisme, sont étudiées par D. Dzino comme facteur clé de changements dans les sociétés locales et, surtout, de la construction des identités ethniques parmi les multiples groupes sociaux que l'on qualifie d'Illyriens, mais qui nous sont en fait fort mal connus.

En outre, les auteurs antiques nous ont transmis des peuples guerriers du monde nord-balkanique des images littéraires, qu'il convient de mettre en évidence afin de porter sur elles un regard critique. K. Low analyse les représentations des Thraces dans les Annales de Tacite, où ils apparaissent en relation avec les Romains, à la fois comme soldats à leur service et comme sujets qui, à trois reprises dans le récit de Tacite, s'opposent à la domination romaine. La représentation des Thraces est ici étudiée dans son aspect littéraire, l'auteur démontrant que les épisodes dans lesquels ils sont mis en scène constituent des éléments clé du récit tacitéen de l'histoire romaine.

Les articles de ce recueil offrent donc des pistes de réflexion nouvelles pour l'histoire des peuples qui ont occupé cette région dans l'Antiquité, que l'on ne peut dissocier de celle des Grecs et des Romains.

Aliénor Rufin Solas

Pour les sources anciennes (noms des auteurs et titres de leurs œuvres), les abréviations sont tirées de l'*Oxford Classical Dictionary* (Oxford University Press, 3ᵉ éd., 1996).

Celles des périodiques sont conformes aux usages de l'*Année philologique*.

Enfin, les recueils d'inscriptions sont donnés sous la forme retenue dans le *Guide de l'épigraphiste. Bibliographie choisie des épigraphies antiques et médiévales* (Presses de l'école normale supérieure, Paris, 3ᵉ éd., 2000).

FURTHER THOUGHTS ON THE COINAGE AND POLITICS OF ALEXANDER I.[1]

Elpida KOSMIDOU

This paper examines whether military elements in the iconography of coins of Alexander I and certain Thracian groups bear upon what is known or can be reconstructed about intergroup relations after the Persian wars. Attention is drawn to aspects of coin production and use pertinent to iconographic choices as well as to the state of external and military affairs from a Macedonian point of view. Secure production dates for Alexander's coinage are needed for us to construct robust links between its content and context. I have argued elsewhere for an early commencement (c. 480/479) of the coinage struck in the name of Alexander and an uninterrupted metal supply during his reign on the basis of various conditions, such as his possible joint use of the mines with the Bisaltai after 480/79 and the Edones after 465/4 or his military involvement in the Thracian campaigns against the Persians and the Athenians. Such conditions must have facilitated the royal coin production in terms of metal supply and partly affected the choice of royal coin types, which were in tune with but consistently differentiated from others in the region. These observations need not be repeated here[2], but are taken into account when assessing how coin types and their intended meaning may have fitted with the purposes of coin production and circulation or how coin data can in turn help us understand pragmatic aspects of Macedonian policies. I refrain from discussing here the well treated subject of the horseman type save for a few comments and briefly explore instead representations of a helmet or helmeted head on the reverses of tetradrachms, tetrobols and diobols of Alexander, which have received less attention.

Raymond saw the helmet as a sign of tribal subjection to Alexander, whose coinage assimilated pre-existing tribal issues[3]. Her view can no longer stand since it presupposes that Alexander's activity east of the Axios entailed annexation of native populations, which may have not been the case[4], and takes no account of the differences in the type of helmets between Thracian and royal Macedonian coins. It is usually accepted without question that the helmets on coins of Alexander and the Thracians are similar[5]. Coins struck in the name of tribes, cities or individuals in the wider area, such as the Derrones, Laeaei, Oreskioi, Ichnaioi, Lete, Mosses, Spara-

---

[1] I would like to thank Alan W. Johnston, Hans van Wees, François de Callataÿ, Riet van Bremen, Nicholas V. Sekunda, Sofia Kremmidi and Alienor Rufin Solas for helpful comments on the topic. Coin types and related issues are fully treated in my forthcoming PhD thesis (University College London), to which I refer the reader for further information. This paper draws from and expands on aspects discussed in Kosmidou 2011. All dates are BC.

[2] See Kosmidou 2011.

[3] Raymond 1953, 88-9.

[4] Kosmidou 2011, esp. 441-3.

[5] See Tatcheva 1992, 66 (his attribution of coins to the same mint on account of shared helmet types has been criticised by Tripodi (Prestianni-Giallombardo and Tripodi 1996, 324, footnote 76), who, however, does not note differences in typology); also Price 1987, 44; Hammond and Griffith 1979, 110. *Contra* the orthodox view: Moustaka 2000, 402, 404.

dokos and Dokimos, bear helmets as minor symbols or main reverse designs, but almost all are of Corinthian type. To the best of my knowledge, only one coin of Derrones now at the museum of Belgrade preserves what is clearly seen as an Illyrian helmet, but its authenticity is a matter of discussion[6]. A few tetradrachms and didrachms of Bastareus with types Illyrian helmet/bull, which had been identified as fourth-century issues of a Paionian king, are now dated in the fifth century, but secure dates and attribution are lacking[7]. The style of known dies of Bastareus is more advanced than that of royal and tribal issues of the first quarter of the fifth century and the shape of represented Illyrian helmets can support a date after the middle of the fifth century judging from actual pieces. Yet, any conclusions based on style alone in the absence of a die study are precarious. The identity of Bastareus also needs addressing since it bears upon a view of the Illyrian helmet as peculiar only to Alexander's coinage among others for the period under discussion in the region. If Bastareus was Paionian, with which of the Paionian subgroups[8] can he and his coinage be connected, i.e. those located in the lower Strymon or those between the upper Strymon and Axios? In both cases, the Illyrian helmet on coins of Bastareus must have been related to its use, which was common among ethnically diverse armies in the region. Yet, the degree of geographical and chronological proximity of Bastareus to Alexander or Perdikkas affects the extent to which any numismatic or other links between them were feasible. If coins of Bastareus and Alexander were contemporary and struck in the south, the depiction of Illyrian helmets only on coins of Bastareus among tribal issues could point to a particular occasion of tribal and royal co-operation along the lines I have discussed elsewhere[9]. If, however, coins of Bastareus were struck around or after the middle of the century further north, where Hammond places the bulk of the Paionians[10], as I believe was the case, since no coins of his have been found in the south and the shape of the helmet matches actual pieces from contexts dated to c. 450-400[11], any links with coinages in the south seem rather difficult to establish.

Limits of space here do not allow a discussion of my results from the typological analysis of helmets on known dies[12]. For the purpose of a general comparison, howe-

---

[6] Popović 1979.

[7] Hammond (Hammond and Griffith 1979, 111) has identified Bastareus as a king of Laeaei and dated his coinage in the later years of Alexander's grandson Philip II. However, neither the metrological association with Alexander's coins nor the single coin he mentions can safely point to a place of origin or production dates. On early publications see Muret 1881, 329-30; *HN*, 237. On the variant of the depicted helmet and recent references see Blečić 2007, 91-2 and my PhD thesis. Blečić identifies the variant of the helmet as IIIA1, but no distinction is visually feasible between variants IIIA1 and IIIA2, i.e. between helmets of Type IIIA with actual rivets along the edge and those with a punched, bead-like border in imitation of the former. Relevant representations should thereby be better placed under both categories (IIIA1/2).

[8] On Paionian sub-groups see Delev 2007; Theodossiev 2000, 185-7; Theodossiev 1998, 348-9, 354.

[9] Kosmidou 2011.

[10] Hammond and Griffith 1979, 55-68, Maps 1-3.

[11] For example, compare with Teleaga 2008, Cat. nos. 914, 915, Tafs.176.1-4, 147.1-4 (Type IIIA2).

[12] See brief preliminary remarks in Kosmidou 2011 and a full study of helmets on 63 collected dies in my PhD thesis.

ver, it is necessary to note that all helmets on coins of Alexander apart from a small minority are of Illyrian type, which suggests that the helmet in his coinage was consistently differentiated through its type from other representations of helmets in the region. With respect to the H-series of tetrobols, I have shown that there are good grounds for accepting a royal Macedonian rather than a Thracian issuing authority and southern Greek instead of Thracian influences in the design of certain helmets. If Alexander shared mines and mints with the Thracians in the same way in which he probably joined his military forces with them against the Persians and the Athenians, his choice of the Illyrian, not Corinthian, helmet shows that he may have been in tune with relevant designs in the region, but that his types were peculiar to the royal house. Thus, the helmet functioned in a way similar to that noted by Tripodi for the horseman type in Alexander's coinage, i.e. it was compatible with general identifiable forms, but at the same time exclusive in its use of distinct elements and its conformity with Macedonian interests[13].

Moustaka has recently suggested a political symbolism, in which the helmet functions as an emblem of royal descent and Greek ethnicity. Her main argument is the link between Alexander's intention to promote his Argive origins and the Peloponnesian origins of the helmet[14]. Her view has much to recommend it, but presupposes that the Argive origins of the Illyrian helmet were known to the users of the coins at a time when this type was specific to local workshops[15]; otherwise the association would be intelligible.

A surprising feature of current theories is their disregard of the most essential connotation which images of a helmet or helmeted head may bear: reference to the army[16]. The helmets on coins of Groups I and II are invariably represented as worn by warriors and it is this blend of the human and military elements that encourages one to seek the original symbolism in the helmeted head, i.e. the armed forces, and not in the helmet itself. The helmet as a single emblem in Group III clearly derives from the helmeted head and there is no reason to assume a difference of meaning between the two. Their only difference is in the visual means by which the same meaning is conveyed, i.e. the transition from animate to inanimate forms for encoding the concept of the army. Since there are no represented helmets that can be safely identified as decorated and therefore of special production, there is no visual hint to officer ranks or wealthy militiamen rather than to the Macedonian mass army.

Assessing whether representations of a helmet or helmeted head on coins of Alexander visually signified a specific military corps, i.e. either infantry or cavalry, is not only difficult, but it also runs the risk of crediting the design with a confined meaning, when it may have been in fact employed as a nonspecific military symbol.

---

[13] On the horseman type see Prestiani Giallombardo and Tripodi 1996, 327-8.
[14] Moustaka 2000, 401-2, 409-10.
[15] On workshops see Pflug 1988, 57-8, 61-3; Themelis 2000, esp. 503-9.
[16] Brief notes such as those in Psôma 2009, 33 and Prestianni-Giallombardo and Tripodi 1996, 325 are exceptions. A commentary of the religious and heroic connotations suggested by Hammond (Hammond and Griffith 1979, 110, 165) can be found in my PhD thesis.

However, the matter is worth pursuing in order to test the extent to which any military conditions at the time that the coins were struck help in distinguishing which army force was the most likely to have been conceived or perceived as a point of reference. There is some evidence from the cemetery of Archontiko for a distinct class of warriors armed with hoplite shields and Illyrian helmets[17]. If burial evidence reflects what the deceased wore in battle, as I believe is the case here since variations of weapon configuration appear consistent between the warrior classes listed by the excavators, the small number of deceased in full panoply of defensive and offensive weapons compared to that of the lighter equipped is inconclusive about the presence of organized heavy-armed infantry in Macedonia proper. A few literary references to Alexander's army are of equally little help in resolving the matter. The passing Herodotean note to Macedonian troops alongside various ethne on the Persian side at Plataea (Hdt 9.31.5) does not allow any solid judgments about the kind of troops or their manner of fighting[18]. There is also the questionable attribution of infantry reforms by Anaximenes of Lampsakos to an Alexander, who, however, may or may not have been Alexander I[19]. I refrain from discussing the fragment here, but I note that even if it was Alexander I who named and organised the infantry, information on military technology is lacking. The conditions for developing a hoplite force were certainly more favourable under Alexander than under Perdikkas in terms of resources and political stability. However, one can hardly see how a hoplite force could have operated effectively within the Persian army or together with the Thracians against the Persians and the Athenians or even if it was necessary for the expansion of Alexander east of the Axios. If one accepts that the Macedonians «πεζῷ μὲν οὐδὲ διενοοῦντο ἀμύνεσθαι», as Thucydides later noted (2.100.5), which seems to summarise the orthodox view that effective infantry, when needed, was drawn from the Greek colonies, while the infantry from within the early Macedonian kingdom was lightly equipped, unable to fight in hoplite formation and ill-trained, it would be odd at best for Alexander to promote a non-Macedonian or a second-rate local force on his coins. On the other hand, the Macedonian cavalry was highly esteemed and comparable only to the Thessalian and Boeotian[20]. The exclusive association of helmets with horses and horsemen on the obverses of light tetrobols and tetradrachms respectively shows a link with horsemanship, even if the horsemen on all denominations are represented in a petasos. Yet, the petasos was not necessarily the only type of headgear used by cavalrymen and good evidence exists for linking the «Illyrian» helmet with the cavalry[21].

---

[17] On classes of warriors identified by the excavators see A. Chrysostomou & P. Chrysostomou 2007.

[18] It is usually assumed they were light-armed. See Hammond and Griffith 1979, 100-1; Borza 1990, 125; Brunt 1976, 152, note 8.

[19] On Anaximenes and different attributions of the named Alexander see Develin 1985 with bibliography; now Bosworth 2010, 97-9 (Alexander II); Sekunda 2010, 447-8 (Alexander I).

[20] Hammond 1994, 14; Hammond and Griffith 1979, 114, 147, Spence 1993, 164, 176, Borza 1990, 125-6, Brunt 1976. Recently Noguera Borel 2007, 100-1 (emphasis on Perdikkas's reign).

[21] On the variety of cavalry equipment see Spence 1993, 49-65; Stevenson 2003, esp. 631. On links between the Illyrian helmet and cavalry I list here only Kottaridi 1999, 638 (Illyrian helmet found

The helmeted head and helmet were exclusive reverse types of light tetrobols in all groups. Their choice for early dies of tetradrachms in Group I was rapidly discontinued and their occurrence on diobols was rather sporadic and complementary to other types. If their meaning was indeed military as I discuss above, their choice would have been most appropriate for coins struck to meet military needs, especially payments to troops. However, apart from the early Eretrian and Athenian evidence for military payments in coins[22], there is no reference to such a practice in the north for the period in question or to any military occasions that categorically point to specific purposes and recipients of the payments.

The heavy minting of light tetrobols from the first two groups[23] and their exclusive circulation within Macedonia[24] show that the demand was local and more pressing until c.460. If the tetrobols were intended for military payments, one can rule out the Athenians as possible recipients. Notwithstanding the friendly relations between Macedonia and Athens until the early 460s, which may have involved the supply of Macedonian timber[25], Alexander and the Athenians never co-operated on a military basis. An urgent need for big sums of money would have arisen for the bribery of Kimon or his troops, but the historicity of the incident has been challenged on good grounds[26]. One can also dismiss the Thracians as recipients of the tetrobols. Even though the specifics of their joint military operations with the Macedonians are not known, it is difficult to see how they could have involved provision of services to Alexander in the 470s and 460s, which would require their payment in coins. If Alexander's role in the clash with the Persians was so instrumental as to have involved payments for Thracian assistance, his association with the event would have certainly not escaped notice by Herodotus. With respect to the Thracian opposition to Athenian colonization, it was mostly local Thracian populations who were concerned with the defense of their lands, while Alexander's role, if he was indeed involved, must have

---

together with horse paraphernalia in a funeral pyre from Aigai); Hockey et al. 1992, 286-7 (Illyrian helmets of Type IIIA with inlaid motifs of horsemen); Blečić 2007, 88-92 (representations of Illyrian helmets associated with fighting horsemen on Thracian belt buckles); graves from Archontiko (Chrysostomou and Chrysostomou 2005, 439, 446, fig. 6 (Tomb 443); Chrysostomou and Chrysostomou 2007, 126-7, 132, fig. 7 [Tomb 145]), which contained Illyrian helmets, small shields, swords, spears and decorative elements of corslets, and could have belonged to cavalrymen, since shields of this size could have easily been carried on horseback.

[22] See recently van Wees 2010.

[23] New dies added to Raymond's corpus (Chrysostomou 1993; Hersh 1991) show only a slight increase of volume of dies in Group II compared to Group I, while Group III remains proportionally smaller. Compare with Raymond 1953, 65-6, 122 (based on the number of dies available to her, she recognised a peak of production in Group II).

[24] CH VIII 88 (Chrysostomou 1993, Pella); CH VIII 87 (Hersh 1991, Eastern Macedonia). The provenance of CH VIII 87 from Eastern Macedonia is not certain.

[25] Loukopoulou and Psôma 2007, 144-5.

[26] Borza 1990, 122-3. Equally doubtful is any kind of financial assistance to Kimon by Alexander. Raymond (1953, 109-10, 117, 120) suggested the minting of octadrachms to cover supply provisions for Kimon and questioned the idea of Athenian payroll in royal Macedonian tetrobols on account of unknown rates of pay, not of Macedonian intentions. However, Alexander was not aware of Kimon's plans until the fleet arrived in 476/5 and there is no reason to assume that he perceived Athenian activity in an area of particular interest to him as potentially beneficial rather than dubious.

been auxiliary. It is reasonable to assume that if any agreement between them existed, it would certainly not require payments to Thracians by Alexander in order to defend their lands, but the reverse, i.e. his payment for rendering assistance, which seems highly unlikely, or his later compensation in other ways i.e. access to local resources, as I suggested earlier. Likely recipients of payments would seem to be the Greek colonies and regions outside the kingdom, who supplied the royal Macedonian army with hoplites and additional cavalry units when the need arose. However, if such payments were made, heavy tetrobols would have been preferred as in the case of Perdikkas[27]; otherwise one would expect to find some quantities of light tetrobols in those areas, which is not the case so far. A scenario that remains to be considered is state payments to Macedonian troops. The link is perhaps tenuous, but worth considering in place of Raymond's suggestion that the light tetrobols were struck to accommodate local transactions for Athenian troops[28].

Heinrichs and Müller have convincingly argued for the use of earlier tetrobols by Alexander for the financing of his military assistance to Xerxes before and during his campaign[29] and it makes sense that he later continued the practice of financing himself his military exploits east of the Axios. The early minting of northern coinages for military purposes, such as within the context of Xerxes' campaign, was not unprecedented as Tselekas has shown[30]. Callataÿ has estimated an original number of 40 obverse dies of light tetrobols based on the known number of 29 obverse dies, which were recorded by Raymond in her die study[31]. The range of weights from 1.39 to 2.75 with most pieces being closer to 2.10 plus or minus 0.10, which have been listed by Raymond and Hersh, allows an approximate equation of 1 light tetrobol of Alexander with 1 Attic triobol[32]. Thus, 40 obverse dies of light tetrobols of Alexander were approximately equivalent with at least 17 obverse dies of Attic drachms. If each die is accepted to have struck an average number of 20000 coins[33] and a maximum allowance of 6 obols is estimated per man per day, then 17 obverse dies would have produced 340000 Attic drachms, which in turn would translate into daily wages for up to 1000 soldiers for almost a year. If half the daily allowance is assumed, one has to double either the number of soldiers or the number of days. Since the original number of obverse dies was calculated by Callataÿ on the basis of the number of dies known to Raymond, one has to allow this number to increase given the new additions to Raymond's corpus[34]. I note here that these calculations do not take account concurrent differences in the rate of daily pay between different kinds of troops or fluctuations of daily wages over the years. Since there was no standing army and the units were recruited on a territorial basis when the need arose, the

---

[27] „On the tetrobols of Perdikkas see Psôma 2001, 175-9."
[28] Raymond 1953, 110 (Group II).
[29] See Heinrichs and Müller 2008.
[30] See recently Tselekas 2011, 171ff with references.
[31] Callataÿ 2003, 141.
[32] Raymond 1953, 39-41, 97, 109, 134; Hersh 1991, 9-11.
[33] On the average productivity per obverse die see Callataÿ 2005, 77-8.
[34] See footnote 24 here.

above estimated sums per year should be broken down into a number of single or consecutive months in order to cover seasonal needs.

A problem inherent in the use of coins for understanding the history of the area after the Persian retreat or vice versa is that both processes are interrelated and in part mutually explanatory. For example, the early use of local mines by Alexander can explain the beginning of his coinage c. 480/79, while the latter can in turn point to his metal supply through early mining. Accordingly, the use of tetrobols for military purposes by Alexander reinforces and is in turn reinforced by a view of his coin types as military. Such co-dependent arguments give a false sense of circularity only if both parameters are considered independent of others within the same framework. For example, a meaning of the helmet type has been primarily deduced here through a process of elimination, in which the option left, i.e. a military meaning, when other possible alternatives are dismissed, i.e. political, religious or other meanings, has increased probability of being valid before taking into account other factors, such as possible recipients.

The above consideration of the volume and purpose of Alexander's tetrobols makes use of a number of assumptions, which fall into such two-way deductive schemes. From a historical point of view, it is assumed that military units received payment in coins by the king, which presupposes a level of organisation of the early Macedonian army difficult to assess without further evidence. If the need for military payments arose, one has to seek for military occasions that necessitated the mobilisation of troops by Alexander. There is no firm evidence for such occasions, but assuming that such occasions existed is no less safe than assuming the opposite. The only recorded military encounter in the area after the Persian retreat, in which Alexander may have taken part, was the Thracian campaign against the Athenians at Drabeskos. However, Alexander must have needed military support for his occupation of Amphipolis and generally for his expansive endeavors east of the Axios, even if the latter did not result in direct conflict[35]. From a numismatic point of view, one could object to an attempt to quantify the production of tetrobols and translate these figures into rates of pay since coin output per die varies and fluctuations of die volume do not necessarily echo fluctuations of coin volume[36] Factors that may prolong or shorten the lifetime of a die have been treated in length elsewhere and need not be repeated here. However, it has been effectively demonstrated that die volume does reflect issue size especially in hoards and the variability of coin productivity of dies is not so random or extensive as to impede estimations of an average value[37]. A more precise estimation of the original number of dies or coins that

---

[35] On Alexander's eastern activity see Kosmidou 2011.
[36] Callataÿ 1999; Butcher 1996; Callataÿ 1995, 296-8; Buttrey 1994, 342-6; Buttrey 1993, 342-3; Esty and Carter 1992, 165,169; Howgego 1990, 7-11; Esty 1990, 207-8, 217-21; Callataÿ 1987, esp. 88-92. Normally, more or fewer dies reflect a bigger or smaller coinage respectively (contra Buttrey 1994, 346 and Buttrey 1993, 342, but see Esty 1986, 186).
[37] Callataÿ 2005 and Callataÿ 1995, 296-302, 305-6 with bibliography.

takes into account new additions to Raymond's numbers falls beyond the scope of this paper[38].

What is typically called the horseman or rider in the absence of consensus on a more precise identification is depicted in two variants on coins in the name of Alexander: a) horseman walking by his horse (octadrachms and octobols of Group II), and b) horseman riding (tetradrachms of all Groups, octadrachms and heavy tetrobols of Groups I and III)[39]. I have argued elsewhere against any Thracian influences in the design of horsemen or connotations other than military in view of coin dates and concurrent events[40]. I am concerned here only with the potential uses of coins bearing the horseman type in the light of my remarks above about the suitability of military iconography for coinage struck for military purposes.

The minting pattern and circulation of tetradrachms in particular show an urgent need for cash after 475, which fits more with a military emergency than with a commercial purpose. What the particular occasion may have been one can only speculate. With respect to octadrachms, which have been found in small numbers in eastern hoards dating from the second quarter of the fifth to the fourth centuries[41], no single pattern or purpose for their movement can be identified. The individual octadrachms in the contemporary Asyut and Jordan hoards certainly argue against the targeting of these areas by Alexander for commercial purposes. I find intriguing the inclusion of five octadrachms in a hoard from Asia Minor (c.460), which was on the commercial route to the East, but also on a route taken by armies[42]. It is tempting to see a connection with the Persians leaving Eion after Kimon's attack in 476/5[43], but the possession of such a big sum by a Persian soldier(s), who needed not be the owner(s) of the hoard, raises questions about the relationship between the remaining Persian garrison at Eion and Alexander after the retreat of the Persian army. I argued earlier that Alexander co-operated at various times and for various reasons with the Thracians or the Athenians, but one cannot exclude that he remained guarded against their policies. If he secretly funded the Persians at Eion to act as a counterbalance against neighbouring expansive plans, he would certainly not be the only one to have used money to buy allies[44].

---

[38] On formulae for estimating the size of a coinage see Callataÿ 2005, Callataÿ 1997, 53-7, Esty 1997 and Callataÿ 1995 with bibliography.

[39] Raymond 1953, 68. Caccamo-Caltabiano (Caccamo-Caltabiano 2007, 763, 765) has set apart the riding horseman accompanied by a dog in Group III as a third variant on the basis of his younger age and the addition of the dog. However, there are no visible signs of age differentiation between horsemen throughout Alexander's coinage. On the contrary, their beardlessness or clean-shaven look suggests a common, broad age group covering ephebeia or early adulthood. The smaller limbs of horsemen on some dies in Group III, which signify a younger age according to Caccamo-Caltabiano, could denote artistic variation or actual physical differences; surely not all males of a certain age group were of the same height. Furthermore, the dog is an irregular feature on octadrachms and tetradrachms of Group III and cannot characterize the horsemen of the group as a whole. See further comments in my PhD thesis.

[40] See brief preliminary remarks in Kosmidou 2011 and a full analysis in my PhD thesis.

[41] *IGCH* 1644/*CH* IX 680 (Asyut), *IGCH* 1182 (Asia Minor), *IGCH* 1482/*CH* IX 355 (Jordan), *IGCH* 1790 (Malayer) and Mitrović 2008 (Vranje).

[42] Thompson et al 1973, 200; Rutter 1981, 4.

[43] Recently Sprawski 2010,140.

[44] Cf. Bosworth 1988, 8-9 (on Philip II).

I have previously concluded that positive evidence about any interactions between certain Thracian groups and Alexander points rather to co-operation with different interests in view and less to what was considered for a long time as a constant struggle for power. The more I consider the matter the more inclined I am to believe that Macedonian and Thracian relations cannot be sufficiently explained through the simple oppositional schema of confrontation versus co-operation. Relational models based on such a theoretical opposition, which approaches both terms and corresponding contexts as stable, absolute and logically opposite, i.e. mutually exclusive, are not only misleading, but they also do not allow a flexibility of interpretations in different contexts. Any form of military collaboration between Alexander and the Thracians discussed in this paper was sporadic and served different political agendas for different parties, even if short-term interests at times overlapped in the face of common enemies such as the Persians and Athenians. Antagonism must have existed and there is no reason to assume that any expansive plans Alexander may have had in the region of Strymon were easily abandoned after his brief occupation of Ennea Odoi because of his occasional co-operation with the Thracians. A view of the helmet and horseman types on coins of Alexander discussed here supports a similar view of monetary relations, i.e. co-operation within an antagonistic framework. Alexander's helmet type was thematically akin to others in the region, but iconographically distinct and his horseman type was similar with that of the Bisaltai only to a certain degree. If common metal resources and/or mints were used by Alexander and the Thracians, such iconographic differences show that some concern by Alexander for differentiation within a co-operative monetary network must have existed.

Elpida KOSMIDOU
University College London

Abbreviations

For abbreviations not included in L'Année philologique see the Numismatic Chronicle. Otherwise, the following abbreviations are used:

Ancient Macedonia V	Αρχαία Μακεδονία V. Ανακοινώσεις κατά το πέμπτο διεθνές συμπόσιο, Θεσσαλονίκη 10-15 Οκτωβρίου 1989. Στη μνήμη του Μανόλη Ανδρόνικου. Thessaloniki: Institute for Balkan Studies, Series 240, 1993.
Ancient Macedonia VI	Αρχαία Μακεδονία VI. Ανακοινώσεις κατά το έκτο διεθνές συμπόσιο, Θεσσαλονίκη 15-19 Οκτωβρίου 1996. Στη μνήμη της Ιουλίας Βοκοτοπούλου. Thessaloniki: Institute for Balkan Studies, Series 272, 1999.
Ancient Macedonia VII	Αρχαία Μακεδονία VII. Η Μακεδονία από την εποχή του Σιδήρου έως τον θάνατο του Φιλίππου Β'. Ανακοινώσεις κατά το

	έβδομο διεθνές συμπόσιο, Θεσσαλονίκη, 14-18 Οκτωβρίου 2002. Thessaloniki: Institute for Balkan Studies, Series 280, 2007.
HN	Historia Numorum (www.snible.org/coins/hn/).
Thrace X	A. Iakovidou, (ed), 2007. *Thrace in the Graeco-Roman world, proceedings of the 10th international congress of thracology, Komotini-Alexandroupolis, 18-23 October 2005.* Athens: National Hellenic research foundation, Recearch centre for Greek and Roman antiquity, Hellenic ministry of culture, XVIII ephorate of Prehistoric and Classical antiquities.

Works cited

Blečić 2007 = M. Blečić, «The diverse meanings of Illyrian helmets», *VAMZ* 40 (2007) 73-116.

Borza 1990 = E.N. Borza, *In the shadow of Olympus. The emergence of Macedon* (Princeton N.J. 1990).

Bosworth 2010 = A.B. Bosworth, «The Argeads and the phalanx» in E. Carney and D. Ogden, (eds), *Philip II and Alexander the Great: father and son, lives and afterlives.* (Oxford 2010) 91-102.

Brunt 1976 = P.A. Brunt, «Anaximenes and King Alexander I of Macedon», *JHS* 96 (1976) 151-153.

Butcher 1996 = K. Butcher, K., «Evidence for ancient repairs to dies» in R. Ashton (ed), *Studies in ancient coinage from Turkey.* Royal Numismatic Society, Special Publication 29. British Institute of Archaeology at Ankara, Monograph 17 (1996) 97-98.

Buttrey 1994 = T.V. Buttrey, «Calculating ancient coin production II: why it cannot be done» *NC* 154 (1994) 341-352.

Buttrey 1993 = T.V. Buttrey, T.V. «Calculating ancient coin production: facts and fantasies» *NC* 153 (1993) 335-351.

Caccamo-Caltabiano 2007 = M. Caccamo-Caltabiano, «The "knights" on the coins of Alexander I: from "adventus" to dynastic succession» in *Ancient Macedonia* VII (2007) 756-72.

Callataÿ 2005 = Fr. de Callataÿ «A quantitative survey of Hellenistic coinages: recent achievements» in Z.H. Archibald, J.K. Davies and V. Gabrielsen (eds), *Making, moving and managing: The New World of Ancien economies,323-31 BC* (Oxford 2005) 74-91.
Callataÿ 2005 = Fr. de Callataÿ, *Recueil quantitatif des émissions monétaires archaïques et classiques* (Wetteren 2003).

Callataÿ 2005 = Fr. de Callataÿ «Etude de technique monétaire: le rapport «nombre de coins de revers/nombre de coins de droit» a l'époque Hellénistique» *RALouvain* 32 (1999) 91-102.

Callataÿ 2005 = Fr. de Callataÿ, «Le volume des émissions monétaires dans l'antiquité» *AIIN* 44 (1997) 53-62.

Callataÿ 2005 = Fr. de Callataÿ, «Calculating ancient coin production. Seeking a balance» *NC* 155 (1995) 289-311.

Callataÿ 2005 = Fr. de Callataÿ, «Statistique et numismatique: les limites d'un apport» *RALouvain* 20 (1987) 76-95.

Chrysostomou & Chrysostomou 2007 = A. Chrysostomou and P. Chrysostomou, «Τάφοι πολεμιστών των Αρχαϊκών χρόνων από τη δυτική νεκρόπολη του Αρχοντικού Πέλλας» in *Ancient Macedonia VII* (2007) 113-32.

Chrysostomou & Chrysostomou 2005 = A. Chrysostomou and P. Chrysostomou, «Ανασκαφή στη δυτική νεκρόπολη του Αρχοντικού Πέλλας κατά το 2005», *AEMTH* 19 (2005) 435-47.

Chrysostomou 1993 = P. Chrysostomou, «Θησαυρός πρώιμων Μακεδονικών αργυρών νομισμάτων από την Πέλλα» in *Ancient Macedonia V* (1993) 621-44.

Delev 2007 = P. Delev, «Tribes, poleis and imperial aggression in the lower Strymon area in the 5th c. BC. - the evidence of Herodotus», *Thrace X* (2007) 110-9.

Develin 1985= R. Develin, «Anaximenes (F GR HIST 72) F4», *Historia* 34 (1985) 493-6.

Esty 1997 = W.W. Esty, «Statistics in numismatics.» in Morrison, C., Kluge, B., Burnett, A., Ilisch, L. and Steguweit, W. (eds), *A survey of numismatic research*, 1990-1995 (Berlin 1997) 817-823.

Esty 1990 = W.W. Esty, «The theory of linkage.» *NC* 150 (1990) 205-221.

Esty & Carter 1992 = W.W. Esty, G.F. Carter, «The distribution of the Numbers of Coins Struck by Dies» *AJN* series II 3-4 (1992) 165-186.

Esty 1986 = W.W. Esty, «Estimation of the size of a coinage: A survey and comparison of methods.» *NC* 146 (1986) 185-215.

Hammond & Griffith 1979 = N.G.L. Hammond, G.T. Griffith, *A history of Macedonia*, Vol. II, *550-336 BC* (Oxford 1979).

Hersh 1991 = C.A. Hersh, «A fifth century circulation hoard of Macedonian tetrobols» in W.E. Metcalf (ed), *Mnemata: papers in memory of Nancy M. Waggoner* (New York 1991) 3-19.

Hockey et al 1992 = M. Hockey, A.W. Johnston, S. La Niece, A. Middleton, J. Swaddling, «An Illyrian Helmet in the British Museum» *BSA* 87 (1992) 281-91.

Kosmidou 2011 = E. Kosmidou, «Macedonian and Thracian relations in northern Greece after the Persian wars with particular reference to the coinage and politics of Alexander I», Travaux de symposium international le livre, la Roumanie, l'Europe (Bucharest 2011) 439-452.

Kottaridi 1999 = A. Kottaridi, «Βασιλικές πυρές στη νεκρόπολη των Αιγών» in *Ancient Macedonia VI* 1999 631-40.

Loukopoulou & Psoma 2007 = L.D. Loukopoulou, S.E. Psoma, «The Thracian policy of the Temenids» in *Ancient Macedonia VII* 2007, 144-51.

Mitrović 2008 = G. Mitrović, *The Vranje Hoard of the Derrones Silver Coins. Collection of the National Museum in Vranje* (Vranje 2008).

Moustaka 2000 = A. Moustaka, «Πελοπόννησος και Μακεδονία. Παρατηρήσεις στα λεγόμενα κράνη Ιλλυρικού τύπου» in P. Adam-Veleni (ed), *Μύρτος. Μνήμη Ιουλίας Βοκοτοπούλου*, (Thessaloniki 2000) 393-410.

Muret 1881 = F. Muret, «Monnaies inédites: Bastarcus, dynaste de Péonie; Orsoaltios, dynaste de Thrace» *BCH* 5.1 (1881) 329-31.

Noguera Borel 2007 = A. Noguera Borel, « L'armée macédonienne avant Philippe II » in *Ancient Macedonia VII* 2007, 97-111.

Pflug 1988 = H. Pflug, «Illyrische Helme». In Bottini, A., Egg, M., von Hase, F.-W., Pflug, H., Schaaff, U., Schauer, P., and Waurick, G., *Antike Helme. Sammlung Lipperheide und andere Bestände des Antikenmuseums Berlin*. Römisch-Germanisches Zentralmuseum, Monographien 14. (Mainz 1988) 42-64.

Prestiani-Giallombardo & Tripodi 1996 = A.M. Prestiani-Giallombardo, B. Tripodi, «Iconografia monetale e ideologia reale Macedone: i tipi del cavaliere nella monetazione di Alessandro I e di Filippo II» *RÉA* 98.3-4 (1996) 311-55.

Price 1987 = M.J. Price, «The coinages of the northern Aegean» in I. Carradice (ed.), *Coinage and administration in the Athenian and Persian empires. The ninth Oxford symposium on coinage and monetary history, BAR International Series* 343 (1987) 43-7.

Psôma 2009 = S. Psôma, «Tas sitarchias kai tous misthous ([Arist.], Oec. 1351b): bronze currencies and cash-allowances in mainland Greece, Thrace and the kingdom of Macedonia». *RBN* 155 (2009) 3-38.

Raymond 1953 = D. Raymond, *Macedonian regal coinage to 413 BC. ANS NNM* 126 (1953).

Rutter 1981 = K. Rutter, «Early Greek coinage and the influence of the Athenian state.» In B. Gunliffe (ed). *Coinage and society in Britain and Gaul. Some current problems* (London 1981) 1-9.

Sekunda 2010 = N.V. Sekunda, «The Macedonian army» in J. Roisman and I. Worthington (eds), *A companion to ancient Macedonia* (Chichester 2010) 446-71.

Spence 1993 = I.G. Spence, *The cavalry of Classical Greece. A social and military history with particular reference to Athens* (Oxford 1993).

Sprawski 2010 = S. Sprawski, «The early Temenid kings to Alexander I» in J. Roisman and I. Worthington (eds), *A companion to ancient Macedonia* (Chichester 2010) 127-44.

Stevenson 2003 = T. Stevenson, «Cavalry uniforms on the Parthenon frieze?» *AJA* 107 (2003) 629-54.

Tatcheva 1992 = M. Tatcheva, «On the problems of the coinages of Alexander I, Sparadokos and the so-called Thraco-Macedonian tribes» *Historia* 41.1 (1992) 58-74.

Teleaga 2008 = E. Teleaga, *Griechische Importe in den Nekropolen an der unteren Donau 6. Jh. - Anfang des 3. Jhs. v. Chr.* Marburger Studien zur Vor- und Frühgeschichte 23 (Rahden, Westf. 2008).

Themelis 2000 = P.G. Themelis, «Μεταλλοτεχνία Μακεδονική» in P. Adam-Veleni (ed.), *Μύρτος. Μνήμη Ιουλίας Βοκοτοπούλου* (Thessaloniki 2000) 495-517.

Theodossiev 1998 = N. Theodossiev, «The Dead with Golden Faces: Dasaretian, Pelagonian, Mygdonian and Boeotian Funeral Masks» *OJA* 17.3 (1998) 345-67.

Theodossiev 2000 = N. Theodossiev, «The Dead with Golden Faces: II Other Evidence and Connections» *OJA* 19.2 (2000) 175-210.

Thompson et al 1973 = M. Thompson, O. Morkholm and C. M. Kraay (eds), *An Inventory of Greek Coin Hoards* (New York 1973).

Van Wees 2010 = H. Van Wees, «Those who sail are to receive a wage: Naval warfare and finance in archaic Eretria» in G.G. Fagan and M. Trundle (eds), *New perspectives on ancient warfare.* History of Warfare 59 (Leiden 2010) 205-26.

L'OR ET L'ARGENT DES ARISTOCRATIES THRACES. CONTRIBUTION DE L'ÉTUDE DES TRÉSORS CONTENANT DES VASES EN MÉTAL PRÉCIEUX À L'HISTOIRE DE LA RÉGION AUX IVE ET IIIE SIÈCLES AVANT J.-C.[1]

Aliénor RUFIN SOLAS

Parmi les très nombreux objets en métal précieux datés du Ve au IIIe siècle avant J.-C. mis au jour dans le monde thrace, les pièces de vaisselle en or et en argent constituent une source documentaire riche, qui se prête à des études typologiques, stylistiques, iconographiques, épigraphiques ou encore métrologiques. Elles ne peuvent donc que susciter l'intérêt de l'historien d'une région caractérisée par un lourd déficit documentaire, celui-ci tenant principalement au fait que les Thraces n'ont laissé que très peu de témoignages écrits.

Or, dans un corpus qui n'a cessé de s'agrandir au cours des dernières décennies[2], certaines découvertes semblent particulièrement significatives des usages que les sociétés thraces ont pu avoir de ces pièces d'orfèvrerie : en 2004, deux vases en argent portant des inscriptions donnant leur poids en tétradrachmes d'Alexandre ont ainsi été découverts dans la tombe du tumulus dit Golyama Kosmatka, dans le village de Šipka, au cœur de 'la vallée des rois thraces'. Cette découverte est venue attester de manière certaine la mesure de la valeur des vases avec un étalon monétaire. En outre, on peut établir qu'une partie au moins des vases en or et en argent découverts en Thrace ont été enfouis longtemps après et loin de leur lieu de fabrication, ce qui témoigne de leur circulation[3]. Objets de thésaurisation, les vases en métal précieux ont en effet aussi été utilisés dans les échanges : ils ont donc constitué, en Thrace, des instruments 'presque monétaires'[4].

Constatant les résultats stimulants des études sur les trésors monétaires dans le monde grec antique et dans ses marges, notamment en Thrace[5], nous nous sommes demandé s'il était possible d'étudier les trésors contenant des vases en or

---

[1] J'adresse tous mes remerciements à Olivier Picard et à Marie-Christine Marcellesi pour l'aide qu'ils m'ont apportée dans la préparation de cette étude. Celle-ci n'aurait pu être réalisée sans l'accueil de l'Ecole Française d'Athènes et le soutien de l'Université Paris Sorbonne (Paris IV) qui m'a permis d'effectuer plusieurs séjours de recherche en Bulgarie dans le cadre du projet «Structures guerrières et échanges entre peuples des Balkans».

[2] On peut partir du très utile catalogue des pièces de vaisselle métalliques découvertes en Thrace établi par S. Z. Archibald (1998) et y ajouter les trouvailles récentes, en particulier dans les tombes de la vallée de la Toundja ('la vallée des rois thraces') et dans celles de la Sredna Gora à partir des années 1990, qui sont présentées dans les catalogues des expositions des pièces d'orfèvrerie thraces, par ex. celui du musée Jacquemart André, Paris (V. Fol, 2006).

[3] C'est le cas des vases du trésor découvert à Panagjuriste, fabriqués vraisemblablement dans la région des Détroits, et des nombreux « vases inscrits des Odryses » qui semblent provenir du sud-est de la Thrace mais qui ont été trouvés en divers lieux au nord de la chaîne des Balkans, cf. *infra*.

[4] Gill 1988, 735 *sqq.*; M. Vickers dans Cook 1989, 101-111; Lorber 2008, 1.

[5] Cf. les actes du colloque « Nomisma - La circulation monétaire dans le monde grec antique », Athènes, 14-17 avril 2010, parus en 2011 dans les *Suppléments du Bulletin de Correspondance Hellénique*, particulièrement la contribution de S. Psôma sur la circulation monétaire dans la Thrace de l'intérieur.

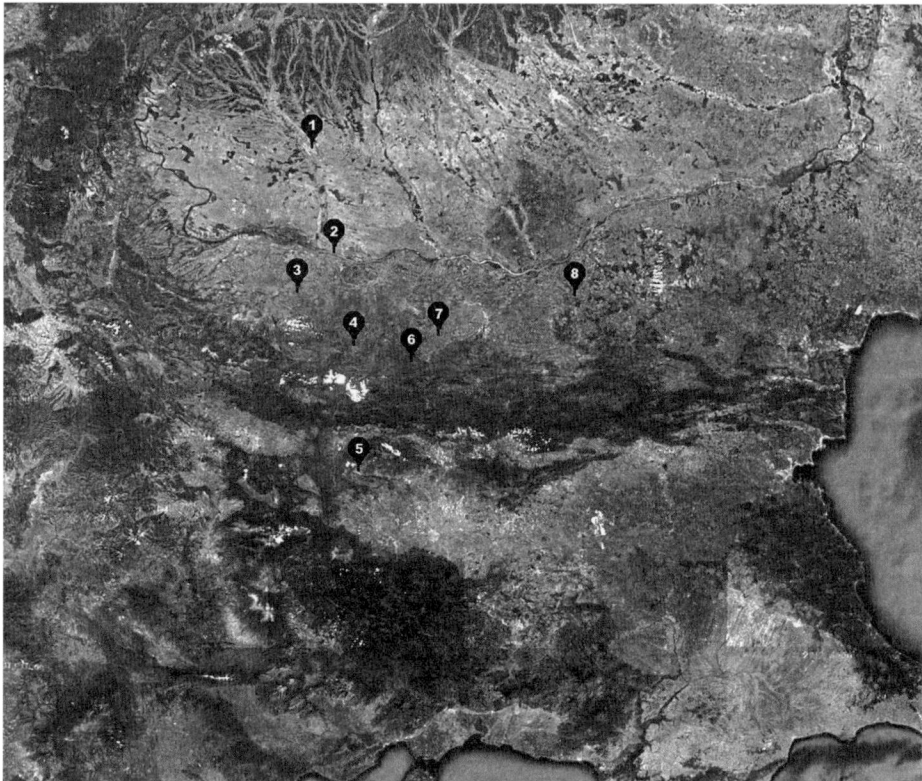

Fig. 1 *Trésors thraces contenant des vases en métal précieux (IVe – IIIe s. avant J.-C.)*
1.Craiova, 2.Orjahovo, 3.Rogozen, 4.Lukovit, 5.Panagjurište, 6.Stojanovo, 7.Vladinja, 8.Borovo.

et en argent en empruntant à la méthodologie numismatique. Certes, les usages de ces pièces d'orfèvrerie furent plus variés que ceux de la monnaie, et il convient de distinguer plusieurs types de trouvailles, en fonction du contexte de leur découverte : n'ayant pas été abandonnés dans le sol pour les même raisons, les vases trouvés dans des tombes ne nous apportent pas les mêmes informations que les trouvailles isolées et les trésors, sur lesquels cette étude s'appuiera surtout[6]. Ces derniers étant peu nombreux[7], on peut en outre s'interroger sur la faisabilité d'une étude de la circulation de ces pièces d'orfèvrerie. Cependant la chronologie et la distribution des trésors semblent répondre à une logique, puisqu'elles font apparaître un pic d'abandon de vases en métal précieux enfouis dans le sol, essentiellement au nord des monts Balkans, dans la moyenne vallée du Danube (**fig.1**).

---

[6] Quelques objets découverts en contexte funéraire mais qui paraissent significatifs des usages liés à ces vases en métal précieux seront cependant évoqués.

[7] Huit trésors sur la cinquantaine d'ensembles considérés (celle-ci incluant, outre les trésors, les trouvailles en contexte funéraire et les trouvailles isolées).

Ce phénomène est difficile à dater mais il semble avoir concerné la seconde moitié du IVe et le IIIe siècle avant J.-C. : il paraît donc avoir accompagné un phénomène d'abandons de nombreux trésors de monnaies en or et en argent dans la Thrace de l'intérieur à la même période[8]. L'hypothèse selon laquelle ces trésors de vases en métal précieux auraient été enfouis rituellement, en lien avec des pratiques religieuses[9], ne sera donc pas retenue ici : on considérera, en s'appuyant sur le parallèle avec les monnaies d'or et d'argent enfouies aux mêmes périodes et dans les mêmes régions, que ces quelques très riches trésors de vaisselles précieuses avaient été enterrés par sécurité, qu'il s'agisse d'un mode normal de protection des richesses ou d'enfouissements d'urgence[10], et qu'ils ont été abandonnés par des propriétaires qui n'étaient plus en mesure de les récupérer. Notre connaissance de ces trésors résultant du hasard des découvertes - et de l'honnêteté de ceux qui les ont faites -, nos conclusions ne peuvent être que partielles, notamment celles tirées de la répartition des découvertes, qui révèle des disparités régionales importantes lorsque l'on considère l'ensemble des pays thraces. La question de la représentativité de ces trouvailles se pose surtout en ce qui concerne les trésors et les découvertes fortuites, mais elle concerne aussi le matériel découvert dans les tombes, parce que toutes n'ont pas été fouillées et qu'un très grand nombre d'entre elles ont été pillées. Les objets considérés ici sont situés chronologiquement entre le Ve et le IIIe siècle avant J.-C., bien que les dates et les lieux de fabrication de la plupart des vases en or et en argent découverts en Thrace n'ont pu être précisés ou font l'objet de controverses, du fait d'un certain nombre de problèmes méthodologiques.

Compte tenu de ces incertitudes, il convient de rester prudent. L'étude des trésors d'orfèvrerie est cependant susceptible de contribuer à l'histoire de la région, particulièrement à la suite des campagnes de Philippe II et de la défaite des rois odryses, vers le milieu du IVe siècle avant J.-C.

Une première partie présentera les vases en métal précieux des trésors thraces, en mettant l'accent sur les problèmes méthodologiques : on s'interrogera en particulier sur les critères de datation des vases, d'enfouissement des trésors et de localisation des ateliers de fabrication. Une deuxième partie abordera la question des inscriptions de poids sur des vases qui, en or ou en argent, ont été utilisés comme des instruments d'échange presque équivalents à la monnaie. Cela nous conduira à formuler quelques hypothèses sur la circulation de ces pièces de vaisselle en métal précieux, puis, dans une quatrième et dernière partie, sur l'enfouissement et l'abandon des trésors.

---

[8] A partir du IVe siècle avant J.-C., les trésors de monnaies d'or et d'argent sont localisés en partie dans cette région, alors qu'ils ne dépassaient pas jusqu'alors la haute vallée du Strymon et la vallée de la Maritsa ; cf. les cartes des trésors monétaires de l'intérieur de la Thrace dans Psôma 2011, 162-166 (cf. supra, note 4).

[9] Par exemple Marazov 1996, Gergova 1993, 478 et S. Z. Archibald 1998, 264. L'hypothèse n'est de toute façon prouvée ni par des éléments matériels ni par aucune source littéraire.

[10] B. Nikolov a par exemple conclu que le trésor de Rogozen avait été caché soudainement, à un moment de grand danger (dans A. Fol 1989 b, 15).

Les vases en métal précieux des trésors thraces

Les vases des principaux trésors thraces sont visibles au musée d'histoire de Sofia, où une salle les réunit[11]. Ils ont en outre été présentés dans le cadre d'expositions itinérantes dans les grandes capitales occidentales. Deux trésors sont particulièrement remarquables par la quantité de métal précieux qu'ils contenaient : Panagjurište et Rogozen. Découvert en 1949, celui de Panagjurište se distingue des autres trésors par sa localisation, puisqu'il est le seul à avoir été découvert au sud des monts Balkans, et par sa composition, puisqu'il ne contenait pas d'argent : il s'agit d'un service de vaisselle en or, pesant au total plus de 6 kg. La forme des vases, rythons, amphore-rython et phiale, ainsi que leurs décors, indiquent une influence à la fois grecque et perse[12]. On peut d'ailleurs faire la même constatation à propos des vases en argent, en partie dorés, du trésor de Borovo par exemple. Le trésor de Rogozen présente aussi ces influences, mais certains des vases qui le composent portent des représentations figurées manifestement thraces. Nous avons donc affaire à un art hybride, dont l'iconographie se rattache tantôt à ce qui semble être des légendes locales, tantôt à des scènes de la mythologie grecque, qui sont d'ailleurs parfois accompagnées de légendes en grec[13]. La découverte en 1985-1986[14] du trésor de Rogozen, composé de 165 pièces de vaisselle en argent, a attiré l'attention de la communauté scientifique : celle-ci s'est notamment intéressée aux différents types d'inscriptions gravées sur les vases, particulièrement celles indiquant un nom de propriétaire et une provenance, qui semblent en effet significatives des usages qui ont pu être faits de ces objets.

L'interprétation de cette documentation est toutefois difficile, car un certain nombre de problèmes méthodologiques sont associés à la datation et à la localisation de la fabrication des vases en métal précieux.

L'absence de contexte archéologique pour les trouvailles isolées et les trésors rend leur datation d'autant plus difficile que les trésors considérés, qui comportaient parfois d'autres objets en or et en argent, ne renfermaient pas, à notre connaissance, de monnaies. En outre, la chronologie des vases en or ou en argent établie à partir des découvertes funéraires doit être utilisée avec précaution, parce que nous ne disposons pas de toutes les données nécessaires concernant les fouilles réalisées en Bulgarie, et que, de fait, la chronologie des tombes thraces semble devoir être en partie revue[15]. Il faut donc le plus souvent s'en remettre aux datations proposées à

---

[11] Parfois sous forme de copies, mais il est impossible d'en donner la liste car ces trésors voyagent régulièrement de musées en musées. La carte présentée à la fin de cet article donne les lieux de découverte des trésors contenant des pièces de vaisselle en or et en argent.
[12] Cf. *Thracian Treasures*, n° 360 à 368.
[13] Par exemple sur la phiale no 4 du trésor de Rogozen, représentant Augè et Héraklès.
[14] Un premier ensemble de vases a été découvert accidentellement en 1985; le second a été mis au jour l'année suivante par les archéologues bulgares.
[15] Nous avons proposé ailleurs de descendre la chronologie des tombes de 'la vallée des rois thraces', entre les monts Balkans et la Sredna Gora, pour ne pas les placer avant la seconde moitié du IVe siècle, cf. Rufin Solas, à paraître.

partir de l'étude du style des objets considérés, avec une part d'incertitude qui tient à la situation périphérique de cette région par rapport aux centres artistiques grecs et orientaux voisins. D'autre part, en l'absence d'autres éléments, l'étude des formes, des décors et de l'iconographie de nos vases n'a pas permis de déterminer avec certitude le lieu de leur fabrication et encore moins l'origine, grecque ou thrace, des orfèvres qui les ont réalisés[16]. Nous en sommes réduits, le plus souvent, à souligner le type grec ou perse de tel ou tel vase, en considérant la possibilité que des artisans thraces ont pu s'inspirer de modèles extérieurs grecs, perses ou encore scythes[17]. On peut d'ailleurs appliquer aux vases et aux représentations figurées que certains portent les conclusions formulées par M. B. Hatzopoulos au sujet de l'inscription de Seuthopolis, dans un article intitulé significativement « la Thrace au carrefour de deux mondes »[18] : les Thraces empruntent des formules, non seulement épigraphiques, mais aussi iconographiques ou simplement décoratives aux cultures extérieures. Or certaines évolutions stylistiques ont pu suivre avec un décalage chronologique celles qui ont eu lieu ailleurs, en particulier dans le monde grec, et que nous datons plus ou moins exactement, un phénomène que L. D. Loukopoulou a souligné au sujet de la langue des inscriptions sur les vases qui nous intéressent[19].

Il est parfois possible, à partir d'observations attentives au style, à la forme et à la décoration mais aussi aux techniques de fabrication, de repérer des ateliers dont sont issus des vases retrouvés à différents endroits[20]. Les ateliers ainsi identifiés restent toutefois à localiser, et si l'existence d'artisans itinérants n'est pas impossible, elle ne peut être le seul élément d'explication de la distance géographique entre les trouvailles issues d'un même atelier. Cette interprétation part en effet du postulat que ces pièces d'orfèvrerie ont été fabriquées là où elles ont été enfouies, sans tenir compte de leur circulation; or les vases en or et en argent sont des objets de grande valeur, dont on peut établir, en croisant les données stylistiques, métrologiques et épigraphiques, qu'ils ont au contraire beaucoup circulé.

Les vases, objets presque monétaires

Les sources littéraires, toutes extérieures à la région, ne nous font connaître qu'une partie des échanges de métaux précieux dans cette région riche en or et en argent. Elles évoquent, au sujet du royaume odryse, le paiement du tribut ainsi que les cadeaux qu'il fallait offrir aux rois et aux nobles pour obtenir leur bienveillance ou une

---

[16] On s'accorde cependant à reconnaître dans certains vases des pièces d'importation depuis le monde perse, par exemple le vase no 97 de Rogozen, cf. la *Grove encyclopedia*, s.v. « Thracian and Dacian Art », p. 696.

[17] Pour compliquer les choses, rappelons que ces cultures empruntent de toute façon les unes aux autres. Si le rython, par exemple, est un type de vase d'origine proche-orientale, il apparaît en Grèce dès le VIe et il y devient fréquent au Ve siècle avant J.-C.

[18] Hatzopoulos 2002.

[19] L.D. Loukopoulou (2008, 146-147) évoque ainsi 'la phase de transition et d'indécision caractéristique de l'évolution du ionien au Ve siècle' qui aurait été inaugurée avec un grand retard en Thrace.

[20] Alexandrescu 1983, 51, n. 25 ; Alexandrescu 1993.

faveur[21] ; elles permettent également d'établir que les relations militaires avec les Grecs se sont accompagnées de transferts d'or et d'argent dans le cadre de relations conflictuelles (raids de pillage, paiement de rançons) ou diplomatiques et d'alliances militaires, avec des échanges liés à l'intégration de guerriers thraces dans les armées grecques (cadeaux offerts aux chefs thraces, versement des soldes, partage du butin et sans doute remise de récompenses honorifiques). Les auteurs anciens ne précisent pas toujours sous quelle forme circulaient en Thrace les métaux précieux qui accompagnaient ces relations[22], mais les paiements en pièces d'orfèvrerie semblent avoir côtoyé les versements en monnaies pendant toute la période.

Le fait, démontré par les données métrologiques, que tel type de vase correspond à tel poids ou à telle somme, fait d'ailleurs du vase en argent ou en or un instrument d'échange presque équivalent à la monnaie, puisqu'il permet de mesurer une quantité d'or ou d'argent non plus en la pesant, mais en la comptant[23]. Cela pose la question de la plus-value que pouvait apporter le travail de l'orfèvre au métal qui aurait pu circuler, parallèlement aux monnaies, par exemple sous forme de lingots[24] : autant qu'on puisse le dire, en se basant sur les inscriptions de poids que l'on a retrouvées ou cru retrouver sur certaines pièces de vaisselle, il semble qu'un vase en métal précieux restait en fait échangeable avec la même quantité de métal à partir de laquelle il avait été fabriqué, qu'elle se présentât sous forme de lingots, de paillettes ou d'autres encore. La plus-value apportée au métal par le travail de l'orfèvre, par exemple par l'application, par touches, de feuilles d'or sur l'argent[25], se mesure cependant, en terme social, au prestige que de tels pièces et services devaient apporter à leurs propriétaires. Ces objets constituent en effet des cadeaux d'exception et des éléments de la magnificence royale ou aristocratique. Ils expriment en outre, par leur forme et leur iconographie, la culture de leurs propriétaires et celles auxquelles ils aspiraient : une partie de ces vases témoigne en effet de l'hellénisation, au moins partielle, des élites locales.

Il est possible que les aristocraties de cette région, alors même qu'elles étaient familiarisées avec l'instrument monétaire, aient eu longtemps tendance à privilégier les pièces d'orfèvrerie comme objet de thésaurisation et d'échange. Par exemple, après l'arrêt dans les années 460 des frappes des monnaies thraco-macédoniennes dont O. Picard a montré qu'elles étaient liées à la domination perse[26], les riches mines de la région ont continué, selon toute vraisemblance, d'être exploitées : le métal a probablement été utilisé autrement, l'or et l'argent

---

[21] Cf. Thuc. 2.97.4; Xen., Anab., livre 7.

[22] Xénophon rapporte par exemple dans l'Anabase (7.3.27) que Timasion de Dardanos a offert une phiale en argent à Seuthès.

[23] Dans plusieurs cas, en effet, la corrélation est bien établie entre certains poids standards et tels types de vases, cf. les analyses métrologiques réalisées par M. Vickers sur les vases de Rogozen (Vickers 1987), et par C.C. Lorber (Lorber 2008, tableau p. 22-29).

[24] Babelon 2000, 876. Sur ce phénomène en dehors des limites géographiques et chronologiques du monde grec : Frolow 1966, 296. On ne sait rien cependant sur une éventuelle utilisation de lingots en Thrace.

[25] C'est le cas d'une partie des vases de Rogozen, et de ceux du trésor de Borovo par exemple.

[26] Picard 2000.

du Pangée étant transformés en vases et autres objets de luxe, voire en lingot[27]. On a insisté sur une semblable utilisation des mines d'or du Pangée par Philippe II lui-même quand il a fait la conquête de la région, parce qu'il a attendu quelques années après avoir pris le contrôle de ces mines pour frapper des monnaies avec ce métal[28].

Le fait que, à notre connaissance, les vases et les monnaies en or et en argent n'ont pas été associés dans les trésors conduit à s'interroger sur un usage différencié de ces deux catégories d'objets, en ce qui concerne la thésaurisation et peut-être aussi les échanges – un problème que nous ne prétendons pas pouvoir régler ici. L'association plusieurs fois constatée entre un certain type de vase et un poids donné prouve en tout cas de manière certaine que le métal était pesé et compté selon un étalon donné avant que l'orfèvre ne le transforme[29]. Les vases ont été réalisés selon un certain nombre de poids standards et nous avons la preuve, grâce aux inscriptions, que dans certains cas au moins ils suivaient un étalon monétaire, que les monnaies aient été utilisées avant ou après la fabrication de l'objet[30].

Il faut toutefois souligner que la méthode qui consiste à peser l'objet, puis à diviser son poids par tel ou tel étalon monétaire afin de voir si cela correspond à un chiffre « rond », ne permet pas, lorsqu'il n'y a pas d'inscription de poids sur le vase, de tirer des conclusions définitives[31]. Les inventaires des sanctuaires grecs nous font d'ailleurs savoir que le poids des vases en métal précieux était souvent légèrement inférieur à un poids « rond », ce qui s'expliquerait par le recours aux monnaies pour peser le métal[32]. Une étude récente de C. C. Lorber révèle les incertitudes de la méthode. La numismate a souligné avec raison la multiplicité des étalons thraco-macédoniens pour la période allant du VIe au IVe siècle avant J.-C., distinguant dix-sept unités métrologiques différentes auxquelles elle cherche à rattacher le poids des vases en métaux précieux de cette époque, entre autres objets en or et en argent découverts en Thrace et en Macédoine. Pourtant, malgré le nombre important d'étalons considérés, elle obtient des résultats décevants – puisque près de 40% des vases étudiés ne rentrent pas dans ce schéma –, qui sont d'ailleurs à peine supérieurs à ceux obtenus, à des fins de contrôle et avec les mêmes étalons, avec des

---

[27] Voir *supra*, n. 23.
[28] Philippe II prend le contrôle des mines d'or de Crénidès dès 357 mais ses premières monnaies frappées dans ce métal ne sont attestées qu'en 352, cf. Hatzopoulos 1991. Montgomery (1985, 42-43) a insisté sur le fait que l'or du Pangée aurait dans un premier temps été exploité pour la fabrication d'objets funéraires et autres produits de luxe. Dans le même sens, voir Le Rider 1992, 52.
[29] Cf. *supra*, n. 22. Il s'agissait probablement d'étalons monétaires, cf. infra n. 31.
[30] Il est en effet possible que des monnaies aient été fondues pour fabriquer des vases, par exemple la phiale de Golyama Kosmatka, cf. *infra* n.39.
[31] C'est la méthode appliquée par M. Vickers, qui n'hésite cependant pas lui-même à comparer la métrologie de l'or et de l'argent aux spéculations sur les dimensions du temple de Salomon (Vickers 1991, 31).
[32] M.-C. Marcellesi (1998 et 2004, 5-26). Cependant A. Bresson s'est opposé à cette hypothèse et explique le phénomène par la perte de poids qu'impliquait la transformation du métal en vase (Bresson 2000, chapitre X, «Unités de pesée et poids des offrandes dans les sanctuaires grecs», 211-242).

vases en métal précieux originaires du Pérou et d'époque précolombienne (50%)[33]. L'application de la méthode aux vases du trésor de Vulchitran, daté du milieu du second millénaire avant J.-C., menant à la conclusion que trois étalons de poids thraco-macédoniens pourraient avoir été en usage dès cette date, ne convainc pas davantage[34] et inviterait plutôt à conclure qu'il est aventureux de chercher à déterminer l'étalon par lequel la valeur d'un vase était comptée à partir de la seule mesure du poids[35].

Il convient donc de s'intéresser de préférence aux vases portant des inscriptions de poids pour déterminer les étalons utilisés. Mentionnons d'abord l'existence d'inscriptions présentant des signes non déchiffrés, qui correspondent peut-être à la notation d'un poids selon un système de numération primitive, fait de points et de bâtons[36]. D'autres inscriptions, utilisant les lettres de l'alphabet grec, indiquent manifestement un nombre, mais leur interprétation est difficile[37]. Il faut en effet déterminer à la fois lequel des deux systèmes concurrents de numération a été utilisé, alphabétique ou acrophonique[38], et l'étalon utilisé. Il faudrait en outre savoir si le poids est bien celui de l'objet seul et non d'une paire ou d'un groupe de vases[39].

Les deux vases inscrits découverts en 2004 dans la tombe de Golyama Kosmatka, dans 'la vallée des rois thraces', font figure d'exception, puisque l'étalon est précisé: le poids est exprimé en tétradrachmes d'Alexandre, dont les trésors de monnaies montrent qu'ils ont beaucoup circulé dans la région. On lit ainsi, sur l'extérieur du col de la phiale en argent ΣΕΥΘΟΥ ΟΛΚΗ ΤΕΤΡΑΔΡΑΧΜΑ ΑΛΕΞΑΝΔΡΕΙΑ ΔΙΙΙ[40]. Cette découverte a permis de confirmer l'utilisation d'un étalon monétaire pour exprimer le poids d'un vase en argent sans que l'on puisse dire si, dans ce cas précis, des tétradrachmes d'Alexandre ont servi comme instruments de pesée du métal, ou si le vase a été réalisé après la refonte des monnaies.

La démarche comptable que ces inscriptions révèlent suppose un pouvoir ou une administration parfaitement consciente de la valeur de ces vases, qui fait peut-être l'inventaire de ses biens. Cette pratique est bien attestée en Grèce par les inventaires des trésoreries de sanctuaires, et P. Bernard et I. Hajime en ont ainsi souligné

---

[33] Lorber 2008, 18-19.

[34] Lorber 2008, 16-17: tout en reconnaissant que la moitié seulement des vases de ce trésor correspondent à un poids dont le chiffre tombe 'rond' avec un étalon monétaire identifiable, elle identifie parmi les autres trois étalons différents, avec les mêmes variations que celles repérées avec les monnaies dites thraco-macédoniennes.

[35] Ajoutons que certains auteurs ont également proposé de réunir plusieurs vases pour obtenir un chiffre rond avec tel ou tel étalon monétaire, une méthode apportant des résultats incertains, cf. *infra* n. 38, ainsi que D.W. Gill (2008, 340-341) à propos des vases de Dalboki et de Rogozen et H.A. Cahn (1960).

[36] Le 'groupe c' de G. Mihailov (1988, 9-40).

[37] Un exemple des controverses auxquelles cette question peut donner lieu est fourni par le trésor de Panagjurište. Voir par exemple Youroukova 1997, qui s'oppose aux arguments de Cahn 1960 et de Vickers 1991.

[38] Tod 1936/37 ; Tod 1950; Dow 1952 ; Lang 1956; Verdan 2007.

[39] Par exemple, Bernard & Inaki 2000, 1437, n. 145. Voir aussi *supra*, n. 34.

[40] Kitov 2005, 81, fig. 125 et 90, fig. 144 ; pour l'inscription sur l'anse de la cruche en argent, cf. Kitov, *op. cit.*, 91, fig. 145 et 81, fig. 124 ainsi que Manov 2006.

l'intérêt : '*La notation du poids sur un objet en métal précieux permet de s'assurer que le dit objet n'a subi aucune soustraction de son métal ni aucune substitution. Elle est donc liée à la conservation de l'objet dans une réserve familiale d'objets précieux ou dans une trésorerie d'Etat ou dans un trésor de sanctuaire (..)*'[41]. L'inscription peut en effet avoir accompagné l'entrée de l'objet dans une trésorerie, ce qui suppose une forme d'administration, avec une intendance. Dans la tombe du tumulus Golyama Kosmatka, l'inscription du nom du propriétaire, en même temps et par la même main que celle du poids du vase, témoigne sans doute de l'introduction de l'objet dans le trésor de Seuthès. Le cas de la phiale en or de Panagjurište est particulièrement intéressant car celle-ci porte deux inscriptions de poids, qui témoignent peut-être de l'entrée de cet objet dans une nouvelle comptabilité, faisant usage d'un étalon différent. On ne peut pas affirmer avec certitude, toutefois, que la notation du poids sur les vases était exclusivement liée à leur conservation à long terme dans une réserve familiale ou dans le trésor d'un sanctuaire. Cette pratique aurait pu viser par exemple, dès la fabrication du vase ou à partir de son entrée dans un trésor, la facilitation de futurs échanges.

Cadeaux, pillages, paiements ? Hypothèses sur la circulation des vases en métal précieux

La découverte du trésor de Rogozen a constitué une étape majeure dans la connaissance de l'origine de tout un groupe de vases, qui a pu être réinterprété grâce à la quantité de matériel nouveau apporté. Ce groupe est constitué d'objets retrouvés, de manière très dispersée, dans le nord de la Thrace et caractérisés par la présence d'inscriptions suivant une même formule, du type nom du propriétaire (au nominatif ou au génitif) et nom de lieu introduit par les prépositions εξ, εκ, ou ες, qui expriment la provenance[42]. Il est clair que lorsque ces vases furent enfouis, leurs propriétaires n'étaient plus ceux qui les possédaient au moment où la gravure a été réalisée, puisqu'on a retrouvé des inscriptions identiques sur des vases, de type ΚΟΤΥΣ ΕΞ ΒΕΟ, dans plusieurs tombes et trésors[43]. On s'accorde aujourd'hui à voir dans ce groupe 'les épaves du trésor royal des Odryses': nous reprenons ici l'expression de L. D. Loukopoulou qui, pour expliquer l'éclectisme de cet ensemble, a rappelé avec justesse les caractéristiques d'un trésor dynastique, assemblage tout à fait hétéroclite de cadeaux, tributs, taxes, pillages ou héritages. Si ce groupe de vases est associé aux Odryses, ce n'est pas seulement du fait des noms de personnes inscrits sur les vases, qui furent portés par des rois odryses

---

[41] Bernard & Inaki 2000, 1422 ; voir aussi Marcellesi 2004, 5-26.
[42] Sur les inscriptions des vases du trésor de Rogozen, voir dans Cook 1989, les contributions de J. Hind, A. Fol et K. Painter ; voir également Mihailov 1989, Nikolov 1989 et Byvanck-Quarles van Ufford 1990.
[43] Ainsi, avant la découverte de Rogozen, avait-on déjà connaissance de plusieurs pièces de vaisselle sur lesquelles était inscrit le nom de Kotys : les vases d'Alexandrovo, de Moghilanska, d'Agighiol, ainsi que les *rytha* et un petit pichet de Borovo.

(en particulier Kotys, Kersebleptès et Térès), mais parce que quatre toponymes, sur les cinq répertoriés, sont identifiés et localisés dans le sud-est de la Thrace, c'est à dire dans l'actuelle Turquie européenne[44]. Les différents commentateurs de ces inscriptions ont bien relevé que ces lieux étaient en territoire odryse, mais ils n'expliquent pas pourquoi nous n'avons pas d'autres lieux de provenance, en dehors de ce territoire limité dans le Sud-Est. En fait, cette région semble avoir été le cœur du territoire des Odryses, une conclusion suggérée par les sources littéraires et que confirmerait ici le témoignage des vases[45]. Nos informations sur les revenus des Odryses remontent au Ve siècle, lorsque leur royaume était à son plus haut niveau de puissance et d'extension territoriale. Thucydide écrit ainsi que sous le règne de Seuthès, ils auraient été constitués de 400 talents d'argent prélevés de manière régulière sur l'ensemble du pays barbare et des cités grecques, et d'une somme équivalente en présents, fournis en or et en argent[46]. Dans le cadre de ces versements, des quantités d'or et d'argent peuvent avoir été remises sous forme non monnayée (par exemple des pièces de vaisselle), le métal étant ensuite travaillé dans des ateliers royaux : la question est discutée[47]. A. Zournatzi a proposé une interprétation originale des inscriptions sur le groupe des vases inscrits retrouvés dans le nord de la Thrace, à partir d'un parallèle avec une pratique des rois achéménides. Celle-ci aurait consisté à faire fondre l'or et l'argent qui leur étaient versés pour en vérifier la teneur en métal précieux; une partie du métal était peut-être frappée en monnaie, le reste ayant pu être converti en pièces de vaisselle, sur lesquelles figurait, comme sur la monnaie, une garantie légale: l'inscription du nom du roi et du lieu de provenance de l'objet, peut-être en lien avec le trésor royal[48]. Cette interprétation pourrait renforcer l'hypothèse d'une fabrication dans des ateliers royaux odryses[49]. On a pu cependant lui opposer un argument à travers le fait que les inscriptions de type nom du propriétaire et provenance auraient été gravées avec assez peu de soin, ce qui signifierait qu'elles n'ont pas été réalisées dans l'atelier même de fabrication du vase, mais cela est de toute façon contredit par l'une des inscriptions du trésor de Rogozen. Celle-ci, plus longue que les autres, mentionne en effet l'orfèvre qui a fabriqué le vase : ΚΟΤΥΟΣ ΕΞ ΒΕΟ ΔΙΣΛΟΙΑΣ ΕΠΟΙΗΣΕ. Il faut donc accepter qu'une partie au moins des vases inscrits des Odryses ont été fabriqués dans le cœur du territoire des Odryses, dans l'arrière pays de la Propontide.

---

[44] Beos, Ergiske/Argiske, Geistoi/-a apparaissent chacun trois fois, Apros deux fois, et Sauthaba, qui n'est pas identifié, une seule fois. Cf. Hind 1989, 40 et carte p. 41 ; Loukopoulou 2008, 167, carte 1.
[45] Sur l'étendue de la domination des Odryses au IVe s, cf. Rufin Solas, à paraître.
[46] Thuc. 2.97. Donner l'équivalent en talent d'argent est une chose courante chez les auteurs grecs pour exprimer la valeur d'un objet en métal précieux, en or ou en argent (par exemple chez Hdt 1.50).
[47] Pour S.Z. Archibald (1998, 195), suivie par L.D. Loukopoulou (2008), les communautés tributaires versaient une quantité déterminée de métal, qui était travaillée dans un atelier d'orfèvrerie avant d'être remise au roi.
[48] Zournatzi 2000, particulièrement p. 695-701.
[49] Déjà K. Painter (1989) suggérait que ces vases, propriétés des Odryses, avaient pu être fabriqués à partir de lingots versés pour le roi dans des ateliers royaux itinérants, qui suivaient la cour.

L'exemple des vases inscrits des Odryses montre que les pièces de vaisselle en métal précieux ont bien circulé en Thrace, fût-ce avec leurs propriétaires, ou parce qu'ils avaient été cédés à un tiers sous forme de paiement, de cadeau ou d'héritage, ou encore du fait des pillages qui étaient en effet une spécialité des tribus guerrières de la région et un mode normal d'acquisition des richesses. Les raisons exactes et les voies de la circulation des vases en or et en argent resteront sans doute totalement inconnues pour la plupart d'entre eux, mais la dispersion du trésor odryse a fait l'objet de plusieurs tentatives d'explication. L'hypothèse initialement formulée, et souvent retenue encore, voudrait que ces vases furent distribués par des Odryses à des princes du nord de la Thrace, gètes et triballes[50]. Mentionnons encore celle de St. Yordanov, qui suggère que les noms inscrits sur les phiales découvertes dans les trésors du nord-ouest et du nord-est de la Bulgarie furent ceux de paradynastes odryses de la région au nord des monts Balkans[51]. Ces deux hypothèses ne sont pas étayées par les sources littéraires, la seconde étant même contredite par celles-ci, puisque les Odryses n'ont jamais étendu leur domination aussi loin et qu'ils furent vaincus par Philippe II dans les années 340. On tend désormais à s'accorder sur le fait que la dispersion de ces vases odryses a dû se produire au moment des campagnes menées par Philippe II en Thrace dans les années 340, après que le Macédonien a pillé le trésor odryse au moment de la prise de Hiéron Oros en 341[52]. Plus précisément, l'hypothèse qui semble être retenue aujourd'hui est que ce trésor, tombé aux mains de Philippe II, aurait été transporté avec les armées macédoniennes dans le nord du pays, où il aurait été pillé par les Triballes[53]. Il faut y opposer deux arguments. Le premier est que chez Justin, c'est le butin fait sur les Scythes qui est pillé par les Triballes. L'historien romain précise d'ailleurs qu'il ne contenait rien en fait d'or et d'argent[54]. Le second est qu'on comprend mal pourquoi Philippe se serait aventuré avec un butin si précieux dans cette région dan-

---

[50] L'hypothèse formulée par A. Fol dans Cook 1989, 33-37, à propos du trésor de Rogozen était que ce dernier faisait partie du trésor royal des Triballes, composé en partie de vases offerts, comme cadeaux diplomatiques, par les rois odryses. Pour Sofia Z. Archibald (1998, 242-244) ou St. Yordanov (2002, 558), comme pour Ivan Mazarov, une partie au moins des pièces de vaisselles inscrites du nord de la Thrace témoigneraient de l'amitié qui a uni Kotys et les rois gètes et triballes.
[51] Yordanov 2002, 557-558.
[52] Eschine 2.90; Dem. *Halon.*, 37, mais nos sources ne parlent pas directement d'un trésor odryse à Hiéron Oros et il faut admettre qu'il a pu être pillé en d'autres lieux.
[53] L'hypothèse que le trésor de Rogozen aurait été constitué à partir du pillage du butin transporté par Philippe II au retour de sa campagne en Thrace, en 339, a été formulée par: M. Tatcheva, (1987, 2). Voir aussi Hatzopoulos 1987, et Loukopoulou 2008, 161 : « *tous les objets inscrits des trésors nord-balkaniques – et la majorité peut-être des objets précieux non inscrits – ne sont que les épaves du Trésor royal des Odryses : arrachés à Philippe II et partagés entre les chefs des tribus de la plaine danubienne.* »
[54] Justin, 9.2; 9.3 : *Sed reverlenti a Scythia Triballi Philippo occurrunt ; negant se transitum daturos, ni portionem praedae accipiant. Hinc iurgium et mox proelium ; in quo ita in femore vulneratus est Philippus, ut per corpus eius equus interficeretur. Cum omnes occisum putarent, praeda amissa est. Ita Scythica velut devota spolia paene luctuosa Macedonibus fuere.* (Traduction M.-P. Arnaud-Lindet : « *Cependant les Triballes marchent contre Philippe, à son retour de Scythie ; ils refusent de lui livrer passage s'ils ne reçoivent pas une part du butin. De là une altercation, puis un combat au cours duquel Philippe fut blessé à la cuisse de telle façon que le coup traversa son corps et que son cheval fut tué. Alors que tous le croyaient mort, le butin fut abandonné. Ainsi les biens des Scythes, comme des dépouilles maudites, faillirent être cause de deuil pour les Macédoniens.* »)

gereuse, avant d'avoir pu en soumettre les différentes tribus guerrières[55], s'il n'avait pas eu plutôt l'intention de le redistribuer[56]. Difficile à prouver en l'absence de témoignage littéraire, cette hypothèse s'accorderait toutefois avec la réputation de Philippe[57] et la politique de recrutement de guerriers thraces qu'il a mise en œuvre grâce à la collaboration des chefs locaux. Entre le moment où ces vases ont quitté le trésor royal des Odryses et leur enfouissement par leur dernier propriétaire, l'histoire de ces vases nous échappe en grande partie, et nous n'ignorons pas que s'ils ont pu être distribués comme cadeaux, ils peuvent aussi avoir été par la suite pillés, partagés comme butin, offerts, volés de nouveau, etc. Il est cependant incontestable qu'une partie des richesses des Odryses est revenue à des Thraces de la plaine danubienne. Ces trésors renforcent donc, par leur composition et leur répartition, les conclusions qui doivent être tirées de l'existence de riches tombes aristocratiques loin de l'ancien centre du pouvoir odryse après le milieu du IVe siècle : ont émergé, dans l'intérieur de la Thrace, des aristocraties qui semblent avoir profité, au moins pour un temps, de la guerre que Philippe II a menée, peut-être avec leur aide, contre les Odryses.

Cette redistribution des richesses conduit en effet à s'interroger sur les rapports entretenus entre les aristocraties locales et le pouvoir macédonien. Il peut être aventureux de faire un parallèle entre le somptueux service de Panagjurište et la grande quantité d'or qui, manifestement entre les mains des guerriers thraces qui ont servi Alexandre en Asie, a circulé sous la forme de statères depuis les ateliers de Lampsaque et d'Abydos vers l'intérieur du pays[58]. Force est toutefois de constater que, constitué du même métal, il a suivi le même type de chemin que ces monnaies, vers la même période[59].

Enfouissements et abandons de trésors

La carte des trésors et trouvailles isolées ne se superpose pas à celle des découvertes en contexte funéraire et, surtout, elle n'apporte pas le même type d'informations. Les enfouissements volontaires de type « trésors » correspondent manifestement à une mise en sécurité de biens. Cette pratique, que l'on connaît bien pour la monnaie, s'explique d'autant mieux pour des objets d'une telle valeur et dans une région où les raids de pillages sont une pratique commune, et même un mode normal

---

[55] St. Yordanov (2002) a souligné le fait que Philippe ne se serait pas encombré de la trésorerie odryse dans sa campagne contre Athéas. Ajoutons que la maîtrise de la voie royale au sud - future Via Egnatia - fut sans doute une de ses priorités, avant qu'il ne s'enfonce vers l'intérieur de la Thrace.

[56] Déjà, M. Tatcheva (1986) considérait qu'une partie des trésors odryses pillés par Philippe II avaient dû rester dans le nord de la Bulgarie, et que les trésors d'Agighiol et de Borovo contenaient probablement des cadeaux envoyés par Philippe II à ses nouveaux alliés.

[57] Cf. Diodore 16.8.8, à propos de l'utilisation qu'il fit de l'or extrait des mines de Crénidès.

[58] Cf. Thompson 1984, qui a mis en relation la frappe de ces monnaies avec le paiement des mercenaires d'Alexandre démobilisés, et Callataÿ 1994 et 1999.

[59] Si D.E. Strong (1966, 102) la situait plus généralement dans «l'Orient grec», on localise désormais la fabrication des vases en or du trésor de Panagjurište dans une cité grecque de la région des Détroits, à partir des données stylistiques et métrologiques, cf. supra, n. 36 et Y. Youroukova (1997), qui propose Lampsaque, ainsi que M. Tonkova (2005), qui a aussi argumenté en faveur d'une cité de l'Hellespont.

d'enrichissement pour un grand nombre de guerriers. Ces trésors se localisent dans le nord-ouest de la Thrace. Tous ont été enfouis dans la moyenne vallée du Danube, à l'exception du trésor de Panagjurište, de l'autre côté des monts Balkans. En ce qui concerne la chronologie, on situe leur enfouissement, sans pouvoir préciser davantage, entre le milieu du IVe siècle et les premières décennies du IIIe siècle. Quant à leur abandon, il est impossible de l'associer, faute de datations plus précises, avec un événement en particulier. En outre, F. Duyrat a montré, pour le cas de la Syrie hellénistique, que toutes les guerres ne produisaient pas de pics d'abandons de trésors monétaires[60] : nous en retirons que l'entreprise de datation de l'abandon des trésors thraces à partir de la chronologie des événements militaires que nous connaissons est bien aventureuse. En revanche, nous expliquons la nette augmentation des trésors d'orfèvrerie thraces par les troubles durables qui, au cours de la seconde moitié du IVe et au IIIe siècle avant J.-C., ont empêché les propriétaires de retrouver leurs biens. Les pays thraces sont en effet, au cours de cette période, traversés à de nombreuses reprises par les armées macédoniennes, sous Philippe, Alexandre et Lysimaque, puis par des tribus celtes, qui s'installent même dans le sud-est du pays au cours des années 270[61]. Les guerres endémiques entre les peuples de la région ont également pu avoir une part de responsabilité[62]. Il faut peut-être encore ajouter le fait qu'une partie des aristocraties de cavaliers thraces qui, à la tête de leurs guerriers, sont allées combattre aux côtés de l'armée macédonienne en Asie, n'est jamais revenue.

Il se peut, et cela a été proposé à plusieurs reprises, que les lieux de découverte de ces trésors correspondent au territoire des Triballes, qu'on localise en effet vers l'ouest de la moyenne vallée du Danube[63]. La carte des trésors a même été utilisée pour tenter de préciser le noyau du territoire de ce peuple : A. Fol écrivait ainsi qu'il devait se trouver dans les districts de Mihailovgrad, Vratsa, Pleven, Loveč, 'because most of the treasures have been found there' [64]. Certes, la carte des trésors montre que l'Isker ne joue pas dans leur distribution un rôle de frontière, alors que ce cours d'eau marquait la limite orientale du territoire des Triballes au temps de Thucydide[65], mais ce peuple, qui a manifestement gagné en puissance dans le cours du IVe s, a sans doute dominé des territoires situés à l'est du fleuve. Cela ne permet pas, pour autant, d'attribuer tous ces trésors aux Triballes. Il est en effet impossible de déterminer précisément

---

[60] Duyrat 2011.

[61] Ainsi la période 330-320 est-elle parfois proposée, comme le rappelle M. Vickers (1991, 34). V. Hind (1989, 38-43), ainsi que M. Tatcheva (1986, 27-30), estiment que le trésor de Rogozen a dû être enfoui au moment de l'invasion celte; S.Z. Archibald (1998, 275) suggère dans le même sens que les invasions celtes ont pu être le contexte de l'enfouissement des grands trésors d'orfèvrerie, qu'il s'agisse de Rogozen ou de Panagjurište.

[62] Elles sont soulignées par exemple chez Strab. 7.5.5.

[63] Les Triballes apparaissent comme un peuple puissant de la plaine danubienne, échappant à la domination des Odryses au Ve siècle et devenus menaçants au IVe siècle avant J.-C., comme le montre leur raid sur Abdère en 375 puis leurs conflits avec Philippe II et les Scythes, cf. le texte de Justin cité ci-dessous et un stratagème de Polyen (7.44.1). Sur leur territoire, voir en particulier Strab. 7.5.11-12.

[64] Selon l'opinion de cet auteur en effet, ces vases, cadeaux diplomatiques des Odryses aux Triballes, ont été offerts au Ve ou dans la première moitié du IVe siècle : A. Fol 1989 a, 19-20.

[65] Thuc. 2.96.4. Le fait a déjà été souligné par S.Z. Archibald (1998, 237).

l'étendue de la domination de ce peuple sur une plaine danubienne où étaient également installés, vers l'est, les Gètes, les Scythes et sans doute d'autres tribus sur lesquelles nous ne savons rien. Surtout, nous ne sommes pas parvenus à dater de manière certaine l'enfouissement ou l'abandon de ces trésors. Or dans cette région, la géographie tribale paraît non seulement incertaine mais aussi mouvante, du fait des conflits entre les tribus et avec les Macédoniens, des migrations de certains peuples guerriers[66], et peut-être aussi de la diplomatie macédonienne.

Le pic d'abandon de vases en or et en argent dans la partie occidentale du bassin du Danube pendant la seconde moitié du IVe et le IIIe siècle avant J.-C. doit donc être associé aux troubles qui caractérisent durablement la région pendant cette période. Il reste cependant à expliquer pourquoi ce phénomène semble avoir concerné presque exclusivement cette partie de la Thrace, en admettant que la carte des trésors ne reflète pas le seul hasard des découvertes.

Aucun trésor n'a été découvert à proximité immédiate d'un site identifié comme une agglomération ou une résidence royale. Mais ce type de localisation, qui a été utilisé pour essayer de prouver le caractère rituel de ces enfouissements[67], ne permet-il pas, plutôt, de donner des informations d'ordre social, voire sociopolitique, sur les peuples de cette région? La répartition et la localisation de ces trouvailles semblent en effet témoigner de la coexistence, dans cette partie de la Thrace, d'un certain nombre de dynastes, d'aristocrates cavaliers ou d'autres figures guerrières plus ou moins riches. L'interprétation de ces trésors doit tenir compte des riches ensembles funéraires de 'la vallée des rois', au pied des monts Balkans, et des trésors de monnaies d'or et d'argent des IVe et IIIe siècles avant J.-C, nombreux dans cette Thrace de l'intérieur et que l'on trouve également très loin vers le nord, y compris sur le territoire de la Roumanie actuelle. L'enrichissement, à partir du milieu du IVe siècle, d'une 'aristocratie de *basileis*' et de nombreux guerriers, qui sont rentrés des campagnes macédoniennes avec leur solde, payée en or ou en argent, indique en effet que certains peuples guerriers de Thrace, et particulièrement leurs élites, ont bénéficié de la situation nouvelle créée par l'anéantissement du pouvoir odryse. Le fait que les riches tombes thraces soient situées dans les régions où ont aussi afflué les monnaies d'or et d'argent nous invite à considérer que les rois ou dynastes locaux ont dû être les premiers bénéficiaires des recrutements de guerriers par les rois de Macédoine, puis dans les armées des différents royaumes hellénistiques[68].

Conclusion

Il n'est pas possible de reconstituer tous les circuits empruntés par ces vases, entre le moment de leur fabrication et celui de leur abandon, mais les trésors d'orfèvrerie,

---

[66] Cf. notamment Strab. 7.3.13 et 5.6 au sujet des Gètes.
[67] Gergova 1993.
[68] Cf. notre thèse de doctorat en préparation à l'Université Paris Sorbonne (Paris IV), «S'entendre et combattre. Grecs et Thraces aux époques classique et hellénistique.»

éloignés des terres des Odryses, témoignent de la redistribution des richesses et des pouvoirs qui a suivi la défaite de ces rois, vers le milieu du IVe siècle avant J.-C. Cette redistribution au profit des aristocraties locales a pu prendre différentes formes, mais il n'est pas impossible qu'elle ait été en partie le fait de Philippe II lui-même, après le pillage du trésor royal des Odryses, au cours de ses campagnes dans le nord de la Thrace. Les vases précieux dans les tombes et dans les trésors témoignent en tout cas de l'existence, après les campagnes thraces de Philippe II, d'une aristocratie locale qui s'est visiblement enrichie[69]. La comparaison avec la carte des monnaies en or et en argent - particulièrement celles des monnaies d'or frappées à Abydos et à Lampsaque - rapportées par les guerriers thraces à la suite de leur participation à la campagne d'Alexandre en Asie[70] invite à lier cet enrichissement aux recrutements massifs effectués par les armées macédoniennes. On peut d'ailleurs se demander si une partie des pièces d'orfèvrerie thraces n'est pas directement liée au paiement des chefs qui ont accompagné leurs guerriers aux côtés des armées macédoniennes.

Ces pièces de vaisselle d'or et d'argent, qui ont été pesées, enregistrées, offertes comme cadeaux, peut-être versées comme paiement et conservées sous forme de trésors, ont en effet été utilisées à la manière d'un instrument monétaire, cohabitant longtemps avec la monnaie. Constituant en elles-mêmes une réserve de valeur importante, beaucoup plus que n'importe quelle pièce de monnaie, elles ont été des objets de thésaurisation privilégiés et sans doute un moyen d'échange entre les aristocraties de la région ou avec celles de l'extérieur. L'usage des vases en métal précieux comme objets de thésaurisation et d'échange n'était pas propre à ces sociétés[71], mais l'originalité des pays thraces réside à la fois dans un usage particulier de la monnaie, caractérisé par la frappe de très nombreuses imitations, et dans ce goût prononcé pour la vaisselle précieuse. On trouvera peut-être dans ce dernier élément une explication de la faiblesse du monnayage des rois odryses[72] : soulignons par exemple l'absence de monnaies au nom de Sitalkès, alors que le royaume odryse aurait atteint sous son règne son plus haut niveau de revenus en métaux précieux[73].

Il reste sûrement beaucoup à découvrir sur les usages de la monnaie et des divers objets en métal précieux en Thrace. La vaisselle, dont on peut constater qu'elle a circulé, et qui porte des inscriptions de poids, est facilement identifiable comme

---

[69] L'étude des seuls ensembles contenant de la vaisselle est de ce point de vue limitative : il faut prendre en compte la répartition des tombes dites aristocratiques et la carte de distribution des trésors contenant des armes, des bijoux ou des pièces de harnachements de chevaux en métal précieux, qui renforcent cette affirmation.

[70] Cf. *supra*, n. 58.

[71] Des vases portant des inscriptions pondérales ont d'ailleurs été retrouvés en d'autres lieux. Les auteurs de la publication de la coupe de Miho, P. Bernard et H. Inahaki (2000, 1422), apportent ainsi quelques parallèles : outre la coupe de Miho elle-même, une coupe du trésor de Tarente et, à Vergina, cinq des vingt vases en argent de la tombe dite de Philippe ainsi que l'hydrie funéraire en argent de la tombe dite du Prince ; sur ces objets, cf. Andronikos 1984, 157 *sqq*.

[72] Picard 2007, 467.

[73] Thuc. 2.97; Diod. 12.50; Topalov 1994, 64.

objet d'échange et réserve de valeur ; mais il conviendrait, pour prolonger la réflexion, de prendre également en compte les autres pièces d'orfèvrerie en or et en argent qui ont été thésaurisées, armes et bijoux principalement[74].

Les vases constituent cependant en eux-mêmes une très riche source documentaire, qui doit continuer d'être exploitée pour contribuer à l'histoire de la Thrace antique. Le second pic de thésaurisation de vases en vaisselle précieuse dans la région semble correspondre à la période de guerres romaines : il serait utile de mener, là encore, une étude de ces trésors d'orfèvrerie, parallèlement à celle de la circulation monétaire et en empruntant à la méthodologie numismatique. Nous espérons en tout cas que les progrès attendus dans la datation des vases en métal précieux, la localisation des ateliers de fabrication et, peut-être, la détermination des étalons utilisés offriront à ce type d'études de riches développements.

Aliénor RUFIN SOLAS
Collège de France

Bibliographie

Alexandrescu 1983 = P. Alexandrescu, «Le groupe de trésors thraces du nord des Balkans (I)», *Dacia* 28 (1983) 85-98.

Alexandrescu 1993 = P. Alexandrescu, «L'oiseau unicorne. Introduction à l'iconologie de l'art thrace», *Comptes rendus des séances de l'Académie des Inscriptions et Belles-Lettres, 137e année, N. 3* (1993) 725-747.

Andronikos 1984 = M. Andronikos, *Vergina : The Royal Tombs* (Athènes 1984).

Archibald 1998 = S.Z. Archibald, *The Odrysian Kingdom of Thrace. Orpheus unmasked*, (Oxford 1998).

Babelon 1901 = E. Babelon, *Traité des monnaies grecques et romaines*, I, 1 (Paris 1901).

Berciu 1969 = D. Berciu, «Das thrako-getische Fürstengrab von Agighiol in Rumänien», *BRGK* 50 (1969) 209-265.

Bernard & Inagaki 2000 = P. Bernard, H. Inagaki, «Un torque achéménide avec une inscription grecque au musée Miho (Japon)», *Comptes rendus des séances de l'Académie des Inscriptions et Belles-Lettres, 144e année*, 4 (2000) 1371-1437.

Boardman 1993 = J. Boardman, «The Diffusion of Classical Art in Antiquity», *The A.W. Mellon Lectures in the Fine Arts 42*, Bollingen Series 35 (Princeton 1993).

---

[74] Lorber 2008, 4.

Bouzek 1985 = J. Bouzek, «Macedonian, Thracian and Scythian Art in the IVth century B.C.», Πρακτικά του XII Διεθνούς Συνεδρίου Κλασικής Αρχαιολογίας, vol. I, Athènes 1983 (1985) 53-56.

Bresson 2000 = A. Bresson, *La cité marchande* (Paris 2000).

Byvanck-Quarles van Ufford 1990 = L. Byvanck-Quarles van Ufford, «A propos du trésor de Rogozen», *BABesch* 65 (1990) 51-72.

Cahn 1960 = H.A. Cahn, «Die Gewichte der Golgefässe», dans Simon 1960, 26-29.

Callataÿ 1999 = Fr. de Callataÿ «Guerres et monnayages à l'époque hellénistique», *Dossiers d'Archéologie* 248 (1999) 28-35.

Callataÿ 1999 = Fr. de Callataÿ «Réflexions sur les ateliers d'Asie mineure d'Alexandre le Grand», dans M. Amandry and G. Le Rider (éds.), *Trésors et circulation monétaire en Anatolie antique*, Bibliothèque Nationale de France (Paris 1994) 19-35.

Cooks 1989 = B.F. Cooks (ed.), *The Rogozen Treasure. Papers of the Anglo-Bulgarian Conference, 12 March 1987* (Londres 1989).

Dow 1952 = D. Dow, «Greek Numerals», *American Journal of Archaeology* 56 (1952), 21-23.

Duyrat 2011 = F. Duyrat, «Guerre et thésaurisation en Syrie hellénistique, IVe-Ier s. av. J.-C.» dans Th. Faucher, M.-C. Marcellesi et O. Picard (ed.), *Nomisma - La circulation monétaire dans le monde grec antique*, Actes du colloque international, Athènes, 14-17 avril 2010, *Bulletin de Correspondance Hellénique, Supplément* 53 (2011) 417-431.

Filow 1934 = B.D. Filow, *Die Grabhügelnekropole bei Duvanlij in Südbulgarien* (Sofia 1934).

A. Fol 1989 a = A. Fol, «The royal inscriptions on the silver vessels from Rogozen», dans Cooks 1989, 33-37.

A. Fol 1989 b = A. Fol (ed.), *The Rogozen Treasure* (Sofia 1989).

V. Fol 2006 = V. Fol (dir.), *L'or des Thraces. Trésors de Bulgarie*, Catalogue de l'exposition présentée au Musée Jacquemart-André (Paris 2006).

Frolow 1966 = A. Frolow, «L'argent de parure dans des fresques serbes au Moyen Age», *Revue des études byzantines* 24 (1966) 292-307.

Gaillard & Thuillier 1965 = Y. Gaillard, G. Thuillier, «Sur la thésaurisation», *Revue économique*, 16, 5 (1965) 796-808.

Gergova 1993 = D. Gergova, «Common elements in the ritual behaviour of Thracians and Macedonians», *Archaia Makedonia* V (1993) 471-478.

Gill 1988 = D.W.J. Gill, «Expressions of Wealth : Greek Art and Society», *Antiquity*, 662 (1988) 735-743.

Gill 2008 = D.W.J. Gill, «Inscribed Silver Plate from Tomb II at Vergina : Chronological Implications», *Hesperia* 77, 2 (2008) 335-358.

Hatzopoulos 2002 = M.B. Hatzopoulos, «La Thrace au carrefour de deux mondes», *Eight International Congress of Thracology. Thrace and the Aegean*, vol. 1. (Sofia 2002) 265-272.

Hatzopoulos 1987 = M.B. Hatzopoulos, «Le Pont-Euxin et le monde méditerranéen», *Rapport au IXe Congrès international d'épigraphie grecque et latine*, Terra Antiqua Balcanica II (Sofia 1987) 118-129.

Hind 1989 = J. Hind, «The Inscriptions on the Silver *Phialai* and Jug from Rogozen», dans Cooks 1989, 38-43.

Ivanov 1980 = D. Ivanov, «Le trésor de Borovo», dans A. Vulpe, C. Preda et A. Stoia (éds.), *Actes du IIe Congrès International de Thracologie*, 1976 (Bucarest 1980) 391-404.

Kitov 2005 = G. Kitov, *The Valley of the Thracian Rulers*, Slavena (2005).

Lang 1956 = M. Lang, «Numerical Notation on Greek Vases», *Hesperia* 25 (1956) 1-24.

Le Rider 1992 = G. Le Rider, «The Coinage of Philip and the Pangaion Mines», *Philip of Macedon*, dans M. B. Hatzopoulos, L.D. Loukopoulou (eds.), ΕΚΔΟΤΙΚΗ ΑΘΗΝΩΝ, (Athènes 1992) 48-57.

Le Rider & Callataÿ 2006 = G. Le Rider, Fr. de Callataÿ, *Les Séleucides et les Ptolémées. L'héritage monétaire et financier d'Alexandre le Grand* (Paris 2006).

Lorber 2008 = C.C. Lorber, «Weight Standards of Thracian toreutics and Thraco-Macedonian Coinages», *Revue Belge de Numismatique* 154 (2008) 1-29.

Loukopoulou 2008 = L.D. Loukopoulou, «Les inscriptions des trésors nord-balkaniques», *Thrakika Zetemata I*, ΜΕΛΕΤΗΜΑΤΑ 58 (Athènes 2008) 139-169.

Manov 2006 = M. Manov, «Die Inschriften auf den Silbergefässen und dem Bronzehelm von Seuthes III. aus dem Grabhügel Goljama Kosmatka N°3», *Archaeologia Bulgarica* 10, 3 (2006) 27-34.

Marazov 1998 = I. Marazov (éd.), *Ancient gold : the wealth of the Thracians. Treasures from the Republic of Bulgaria* (New York 1998).

Marazov 1996 = I. Marazov, *The Rogozen Treasure* (Sofia 1996).

Marcellesi 2004 = M.-C. Marcellesi, *Milet des Hécatomnides à la domination romaine. Pratiques monétaires et histoire de la cité du IVe au IIe siècle av. J.-C.*, DAI Milesische Forschungen 3 (Mayence 2004).

Marcellesi 2008 = M.-C. Marcellesi, «Sur l'inventaire d'Amos en Carie : le poids des offrandes en métal dans les inventaires des sanctuaires grecs», *Cahiers du Centre G. Glotz*, 9 (1998) 37-48.

Mihailov 1989 = G. Mihailov, «The inscriptions», dans Fol 1989 b, 46-71.

Mihailov 1988 = G. Mihailov, «Il tresoro di Rogozen: le iscrizioni», *Epigraphica : rivista italiana di epigraphia*, L (1988) 9-40.

Nikolov 1989 = B. Nikolov, «Le trésor thrace de Rogozène, dép. de Vratsa, Bulgarie», *Thraco-Dacia* 10 (1989) 189-196.

Painter 1989 = K. Painter, «Inscriptions on forth century silver from Bulgaria», dans COOKS 1989, 73-81.

Panagopoulou 2007 = K. Panagopoulou, «Between Necessity and Extravagance : Silver as a Commodity in the Hellenistic Period», *ABSA*, 102 (2007) 315-343.

Picard 2007 = O. Picard, «Esquisse d'une histoire des rapports économiques entre Grecs et Thraces», *Thrace in the Graeco-Roman World. Proceedings of the Xth International Congress of Thracology, Komotini - Alexandropouli, 18-23 octobre 2005* (Athènes 2007) 464-473.

Picard 2000 = O. Picard, «Monnayages en Thrace à l'époque achéménide», *Mécanisme et innovations monétaires dans l'Anatolie achéménide, Numismatique et Histoire, Actes de la Table Ronde Internationale d'Istanbul, 22-23 mai 1997* (Istanbul 2000) 239-253.

Price 1991 = M.J. Price, *The Coinage in the Name of Alexander the Great and Philip Arrhidaeus* (Zurich / Londres 1991) 47-50 et 66.

Psôma 2011 = S. Psôma, «La circulation monétaire et la thésaurisation en Thrace au Nord des Rhodopes», dans Th. Faucher, M.-C. Marcellesi et O. Picard (éds.), *Nomisma - La circulation monétaire dans le monde grec antique*, Actes du colloque international, Athènes, 14-17 avril 2010, *Bulletin de Correspondance Hellénique Supplément* 53 (2011) 143-168.

Rufin Solas, à paraître = A. Rufin Solas, «La vallée des rois thraces. Problèmes d'interprétation historique», *Proceedings of the XIth International Congress of Thracology, Istanbul, 8-11 nov. 2010* (à paraître).

Simon 1960 = E. Simon, «Der Goldschatz von Panagjurište - eine Schöpfung der Alexanderzeit. Mit einem Beitrag von H. A. CAHN», *Antike Kunst* III (1960) 3-29.

Stronach & Zournati 2002 = D. Stronach, A. Zournati, «Odrysian and Achaemenid Tribute: Some New Perspectives», *Proceedings of the eight international Congress of Thracology. Thrace and the Aegan, Sofia -Yambol, 25-29 septembre 2000*, vol. I (Sofia 2002) 333-344.

Strong 1966 = D.E. Strong, *Greek and Roman Gold and Silver Plates* (1966).

Tatcheva 1987 = M. Tatcheva, *История на българските земи в древността* (Histoire de la Bulgarie dans l'antiquité), Наука и изкуство (Sofia 1987).

Tatcheva 1986 = M. Tatcheva, «Проблеми и становища по историческата интерпретация на Рогозенското съкровище» (Problèmes et opinions sur l'interprétation historique du trésor de Rogozen), *Исторически Преглед* 12 (1986) 15-30.

Thompson 1984 = M. Thompson, «Paying the mercenaries», dans A. Houghton, S. Hurter, P.E. Mottahedeh, J.A. Scott (eds.) *Festschrift für Leo Mildenberg : Numismatik, Kunstgeschichte, Archäologie* (Wetteren 1984) 241-247.

Thompson, Mørkholm & Kraay 1973 = M. Thompson, O. Mørkholm, C.M. Kraay, *An Inventory of Greek Coin Hoards* (1973).

Tod 1936/37 = M.N. Tod, «The Greek Acrophonic Numerals», Annual of the British School at Athens 37 (1936/37) 236-257.

Tod 1950 = M.N. Tod, «The Alphabetic Numeral System in Attica», *BSA* 82 (1950) 305-312.

Tonkova 2008 = M. Tonkova, «Archaeological evidence for the exploitation of gold ore deposits at the villages of Kolio Marinovo (Sarnena Gora Mountain) and Babyak (Western Rhodopes) in Antiquity», dans R.I. Kostov, B. Gaydarska, M. Gurova (ed.), *Geoarchaeology and Archaeomineralogy. Proceedings of the International Conference*, Sofia, 29-30 Octobre 2008 (Sofia 2008) 266-270.

Tonkova 2005 = M. Tonkova, «Jewellery representations on the jugs-rhytons with women's heads from the Panagyurishte treasure», *Heros Hephaistos. Studia in honorem Liubae Ognenova-Marinova*, Veliko Tarnovo (2005) 262-275.

Tonkova 1999 = M. Tonkova, «L'orfèvrerie en Thrace aux Ve - IVe s. av. J.-C. Gisements d'or et d'argent, ateliers, parures», dans H.H. Koukouli-Hrizantaki, A. Muller et S. Papadopoulos (éds.), *Thasos. Matières premières et technologie de la préhistoire à nos jours. Actes du Colloque International*, Thasos, Limenaria, 1995 (Paris 1999) 185-194.

Tonkova 1994 = M. Tonkova, «Vestiges d'ateliers d'orfèvrerie thraces des Ve-IIIe s. av. J.-C. (sur le territoire de la Bulgarie)», *Helis* III (1994) 175-214.

Touratsoglou, 1998 = Y. Touratsoglou, «Back to the future, Alexander the Great's Silver and gold in the Balkans, the hoard evidence», dans A. Burnett, U. Wartenberg & R. Witschonke (eds.), *Coins of Macedonia and Rome : Essays in Honour of Charles Hersh* (Londres, 1998) 71-101.

Treister 1996 = M.Y. Treister, *The Role of Metals in Ancient Greek history*, E.J. BRILL (1996).

Valeva 2006 = J. Valeva, «Gold and Silver Vessels from Ancient Thrace, Part I», *Bulletin of Miho Museum* 6 (2006) 19-37.

Velkov & Danov 1938 = I. Velkov, H. Danov, «Новооткрити старини» (Antiquités récemment découvertes), *Известия на Археологическия институт* 12 (1938) 433-449.

Verdan 2007 = S. Verdan, «Systèmes numéraux en Grèce ancienne : description et mise en perspective historique», Culture*MATH* (2007), sur le site internet www.math.ens.fr.

Vickers 2002 = M. Vickers, «Pots of silver?», *History Today* (Février 2002).

Vickers 1991 = M. Vickers, «Persian, Thracian and Greek Gold and Silver : Questions of Metrology», dans H. Sancisi-Weerdenburg et A. Kuhrt (eds.), *Achaemenid History VI, Asia Minor and Egypt : Old cultures in a New Empire, Proceedings of the Groningen 1988 Achaemenid History Workshop* (Leiden 1991) 31-39.

Vickers 1990 = M. Vickers, «Golden Greece : Relative Values, Minae, and Temple Inventories», *AJA* 94, 4 (1990) 613-625.

Vickers 1989 = M. Vickers, «Panagyurischte, Dalboki, Loukovit and Rogozen : Questions of Metrology and Status», dans Cooks 1989, 103 *sqq*.

Yordanov 2002 = St. Yordanov, «Le royaume des Odryses au nord de l'Hémus – problèmes d'histoire politique et de la chronologie», *Proceedings of the eight international*

Congress of Thracology. Thrace and the Aegan, Sofia – Yambol, 25-29 septembre 2000, vol. II (Sofia 2002) 555-561.

Youroukova 1982 = Y. Youroukova, «Les invasions macédoniennes en Thrace et les trouvailles monétaires», *Actes du 9e Congrès International de Numismatique* (1982) 215-225.

Youroukova 1997 = Y. Youroukova, «The amphora of the Panagyurishte Treasure and the Coinage in the first half of the fourth Century B.C.», *Archaeologia Bulgarica* 1, 1 (1997) 60-66.

Zournatzi 2000 = A. Zournatzi, «Inscribed Silver Vessels of the Odrysian Kings : Gifts, Tribute, and the Diffusion of the Forms of «Achaemenid» Metalware in Thrace », *AJA* 104, 4 (2000) 683-706.

THE 'VICTORY' COINAGE OF PATRAOS OF PAIONIA[1].

Nicholas V. SEKUNDA

A series of silver tetradrachms struck by the Paionian King Patraos (circa 340-315 BC) show on the obverse (**Fig. 1**) the head of a young unbearded male facing right, usually wearing a laurel wreath, or occasionally wearing a fillet, or bare-headed. On the reverse are the letters ΠΑΤΡΑΙΟΥ and a scene of a horseman to the right in the act of spearing a second warrior on foot to the left. The series of coinage includes a whole host of different combinations of dress and equipment carried by both the cavalryman and the warrior on foot.

Fig. 1 *Example of the obverse side of the 'Victory' coinage of Patraos (Oxford SNG 3354) showing a youthful male head crowned with an elaborate laurel wreath (photo: Ashmolean Museum).*

The publication in which the greatest number of examples of the «Victory» tetradrachms of King Patraos of Paeonia are gathered together is still the auction catalogue containing a very large number of examples of these coins, originally presumably coming from a single hoard located somewhere in the south-central Balkans, probably from Bulgaria[2]. In the following three paragraphs which follow describing the range of dress and equipment carried by both the rider and the figure on foot, the numbers in round brackets refer to the coin numbers in this catalogue under which a particular feature currently being described can be found.

---

[1] I would like to take this opportunity to thank Aliénor Rufin Solas and Elpida Kosmidou for their very useful comments on an earlier draft of this article, which saved me from a number of errors, and Elpida Kosmidou for her help in obtaining bibliographic materials which were unavailable to me in Gdańsk.

[2] (Sotheby & Co. 1969).

The riders wear helmets with generously flowing crests. They either wear a cuirass, sometimes with shoulder-guards and groin-flaps (*pteruges*) or sometimes without, or a loose-fitting, long-sleeved tunic, gathered in at the waist by a belt and hanging in vertical folds[3]. In most cases a pair of trousers be made out being worn by the horseman. They are generally shown with a sort of quiver or javelin-holder slung on the right shoulder, and they thrust underarm at the figure on foot with a spear held in their right hand. Horsecloths, with a chest-band, are generally shown plain or with a border, but in some cases elaborate decoration, consisting of horizontal lines[4] or a dot pattern[5] can be made out. In some cases what is probably a brand-mark can be made out on the flank of the horse. The horse is shown as prancing holding its front feet aloft, and generally shown bearing down on the figure on foot, or his shield.

There is an even greater variety in the dress and equipment used by the figures on foot. Sometimes they are depicted naked, or draped with a cloth around the waist. They sometimes shown wearing a crested helmet[6] or are bare-headed. They are usually shown armed with a shield, but occasionally not. Shields can be plain, presumably small, bronze, rimless *peltai*[7] or plain with a circular raised rim, presumably hoplite shields of the traditional type[8] occasionally decorated with a pattern of radial lines[9]. In the overwhelming majority of cases, however, the figure on foot carries a small bronze shield (*peltē*) decorated with a pattern of curving or circular geometric lines, which are distinctive for the Macedonian shield[10]. There were two sizes of bronze Macedonian shield available[11], and the shields shown on the coins seem to be of the smaller variety (*peltē*), about 66cm in diameter. In the overwhelming majority of cases too, the figure on foot wears a knee-length tunic, with or without trousers. In addition he might wear a *kausia*. The *kausia* was a kind of beret made of felt and was the distinctive form of Macedonian national headdress. The *kausia* was an evocative symbol of Macedonian national feeling. In the first round of conflict in the wars of the Diadochoi, Plutarch (*Vit. Eum.* 6.1) tells us that if the Macedonians only caught sight of Krateros' *kausia* they would go over to his side.

Both figures generally stand on a single, small ground-line, or a series of such lines. Occasionally an additional figurative element is shown. For example the long ground line might be broken at left by helmet of plain conical form[12].

---

[3] 134.
[4] 177.
[5] 172.
[6] 182.
[7] 139.
[8] 177.
[9] 134.
[10] Liampi 1998.
[11] Sekunda 2007, 337-339.
[12] 212.

A Celebratory Coinage

It seems beyond reasonable doubt that this series or silver tetradrachms were struck to commemorate a significant historical event some time during the reign of Patraos, the traditional dates for which are between c. 340 and c. 315 BC. The reign of Patraos came to an end before 310, for in that year, according to Diodorus (20.19.1) Kassandros the ruler of Macedonia goes to the aid of Audoleon, king of the Paionians who was fighting against the Autariatai. The trouble is that the reign of Patraos is almost a complete black to us. Even the dates of his reign are uncertain. On page 10 of the 1969 Sotheby catalogue the following statement is made:

'The significance of the headdress and weapons of the fallen foot soldier-the Macedonian causia, or crested helmet and the Macedonian shield-has not been fully explained, though the meaning would appear to be implicit.'

With these considerations in mind Gaebler[13] was the first to note that the spearman shown being ridden down by the horseman in most cases is shown dressed in Persian trousers, a long-sleeved Persian tunic, and a small Macedonian shield, and associated the coin with the following incident. Ariston was the commander of the Paionian squadron of light cavalry serving with Alexander's army. In 331 before the battle of Gaugamela the crossing of the Tigris was disputed by 1,000 Persian cavalry under the command of Satropates. According to Curtius (4.9.24-5) Alexander ordered Ariston to charge them at full speed. Ariston aimed his spear straight at the throat of Satropates and ran it through, then overtaking him as he fled through the midst of the enemy, he hurled him from his horse, cut off his head with his sword, brought it back, and amid great applause, laid it at the king's feet. Thereupon, according to Plutarch (*Vit. Alex.* 39.2) Ariston said «Among us, oh King, such a present is rewarded with a gold drinking-cup!» «An empty one, I suppose,» replied Alexander with a laugh, «but I promise you one of untempered wine.» From this exchange it is clear that Ariston is a Paionian, and it is probable that he is «a prince of the Paeonian royal house»[14]. This interpretation of the iconography of the coin was developed by Merker[15] and has subsequently met with grudging acceptation, among others by myself[16] for want of a better interpretation of the iconography of the coin.

This interpretation has to be rejected, however, for the simple reason that the opponent of the horseman on the Patraos coins is not a cavalryman, as Satropates was. Even if the coins show Satropates unhorsed, as Merker argued, the argument yet again stumbles, because he is carrying equipment which is only suitable for an infantryman, and a Macedonian infantryman at that. It is true that Darius III made attempts to improve the equipment of the Persian infantry for the battle of Gauga-

---

[13] Gaebler 1935, 202.
[14] Sekunda 1984, 21.
[15] Merker 1965, 44-45.
[16] Sekunda & McBride 1984, 21 : «The identification is, however, still far from certain».

mela. Diodorus (17.53.1) tells us that the swords and spears he had made much longer than previously, because it was thought that Alexander had had the advantage in this respect at the battle of Issus, and Curtius (4.8.3) tells us that to those who had javelins before, shields and swords were added. Both these passages presumably refer to the infantry, but the descriptions fall far short of re-equipping the Persian infantry in Macedonian style. This came later.

The Military Reforms of Alexander

At the beginning of his reign it is probably true to say that Alexander had no concrete ideas as to how his empire could be run after the overthrow of the Achaemenid state. It was only in the later years of his reign that Alexander began to made great efforts to integrate Iranian manpower into the «royal army». This change in attitude can be dated to the late summer or early autumn of 330[17], from which time onwards Alexander became «an admirer of Persian ways» (Diod. 18.48.5). Whether this aside of Diodorus is literally true, or whether Alexander was bowing to the inevitable is unknowable and of little consequence.

One strand in his planning was the creation of the *epigonoi*, or «descendants»[18]. This force comprised Iranian young men, who were to be trained in the use of Macedonian weapons, by which we are to understand the Macedonian pike or *sarisa*, and Macedonian shields. When they were originally recruited they were probably adolescents, the equivalent of Greek *epheboi*, and here it is worthwhile emphasizing that Plutarch (*Vit. Alex.* 47.3) uses the term *paides* «boys» to describe them. This force, comprising a total of 30,000 soldiers in number, arrived in Susa in the last years of Alexander's reign (324-3 BC) following his return from the Indian campaign. The *epigonoi* «were warmly commended by the king after demonstrating their skill and discipline in the use of their weapons» (Diod. 17.102.2), and they «displayed remarkable skill and agility» (Plutarch, *Vit. Alex.* 71.1).

According to Arrian (*Anab.* 7.6.1) the name *epigonoi* was given to this new phalanx by Alexander himself, and this, together with the fact that Diodorus (17.108.3) calls the formation an *antitagma*, shows clearly that it was the intention of Alexander to use this new formation to replace the Macedonian phalanx. This was not lost on the Macedonians themselves, and the arrival of the *epigonoi* in Susa precipitated a mutiny in Alexander's forces[19].

The *Epigonoi*

The epigonoi appear after the death of Alexander in a number of armies commanded by the «Diadochoi». They are noticeable, above all, in the service of Eu-

---

[17] Olbrycht 2010, 355.
[18] Olbrycht 2010, 362-3.
[19] Olbrycht 2008.

menes of Kardia. Eumenes was the only Greek who made it to the highest rank in the armies of the Diadochoi. In the last days of Alexander he was in no way a part of the (mainly Macedonian) traditionalist opposition to Alexander's programme of Iranianization of the military and the administration. In fact, at the end of Alexander's reign he had taken as his wife a certain Barsine, a second daughter of Artabazos (Plut, *Vit. Eum.* 1.3), the sister of that Barsine by which Alexander had a son Herakles. Throughout his career Eumenes suffered from discrimination regarding his Greek, rather than Macedonian origins, and there seems to have been no moral dilemma about his making use of the *epigonoi*, originally conceived by Alexander as a replacement to the Macedonian Phalanx.

The *epigonoi* are presumably being referred to by Diodorus at 18.30.4, where he tells us that Eumenes had 20000 foot soldiers, «men of all races» (*pantodapai tois genesin*) in his army in 321 BC. This is not certain, but it is made all the more probable when we bear in mind that in the army ranged against him, under the command of Krateros and Neoptolemos, the infantry phalanx of 20000 were «chiefly Macedonians». Eumenes, we are told, chiefly placed his hopes of victory in his cavalry, of which he had 5000, as opposed to the enemy's 2000. If these 20000 troops are, indeed, to be identified with the *epigonoi*, of which there were 30000 in 324 BC, then it does not account for all of that force.

The *Epigonoi* in the Second War of the *Diadochoi* (317-316 BC)

Eumenes lost command of the troops formerly under his charge in a complex series of events, and the next we hear of the *epigonoi* is in the forces commanded by Peukestas in the satrapy of Persis in 317 BC. We hear from Diodorus[20] that Peukestas had at his disposal 3000 men of every origin (*pantodapoi*) equipped for service in the Macedonian array (taxis). At the battle of Paraitakene in 317/6 BC Eumenes had under his command «about 5000 men equipped in the Macedonian fashion though they were of all races» (Diod. Sic. 19.27.6) and at the later battle of Gabiene «those of the other troops who were armed in the Macedonian fashion» (Diod. Sic. 19.40.3). These 5,000 would have included Peukestas' men and presumably the balance was drawn from the other satrapal contingents that made up Eumenes' army. At the same time we hear of «more than 8000 troops of mixed origin in Macedonian equipment» in the army of Antigonos (Diod. Sic. 19.29. 3).

Starting from the fourth century onwards, mythical figures of «Trojans» are shown in Persian dress, and hybrid figures of hoplites in Persian dress do occur, but these figures are clothed as Persians and carry Greek weapons, not Macedonian. The figures on the coins of Patraos can be described as a unique source. Nowhere else is a mixture of Persian dress and Macedonian equipment depicted in so convin-

---

[20] Diod. Sic. 19.14.5.

Fig. 2 Version of the reverse of the Patraos coin (Gaebler 1935: pl. xxxvii 17) showing an infantryman bearing a Macedonian peltē and wearing Persian trousers and long-sleeved tunic, with what I consider to be a turban as his headdress. Note the thunderbolt behind the horses' legs (photo: Staatliche Museen zu Berlin, Münzkabinett).

cing detail. Only the Macedonian pike (*sarisa*) is not shown at its true length, presumably for compositional reasons.

It is hard to believe that these coins were struck by pure chance, and it must be a logical conclusion that these coins record some specific event: specifically a military encounter where Paionian cavalry met Iranian infantry equipped in Macedonian style. This military encounter must have taken place in the conflicts that arose following the death of Alexander, who was the first person to create a force of oriental infantry trained in the use of Macedonian weapons, which took place in 323 BC, and the death of Patraos shortly before 310 BC.

The only possible candidate for this historical incident we know of from the historical sources dealing with this period (which are preserved in considerable detail thanks to the survival of Diodorus) is the Asian campaign during the so-called «The Second War of the Diadochoi». It should be stressed that no force of *epigonoi* infantry are known to have been sent to Europe to participate in the Lamian War, although we do hear of 1000 Persian bowmen and slingers being among the forces with which Leonnatos was sent from Asia to the help of Antipatros after his initial defeat (Diod. Sic. 18.16.4). In the «Second War of the Diadochoi» Eumenes commanded a coalition of satrapal forces loyal to Olympias, which was opposed by Antigonos Monophthalmos, who was in command of forces in Asia opposed to Olympias (Kassandros, son of Antipatros commanding the forces in Europe), and more specifically the forces which fought at the battles of Paraiakene fought in late 317 and Gabiene fought in early 316.

The infantryman shown on the coin illustrated here as **Fig.2** is dressed in a Persian tunic, trousers and shoes, and uses Macedonian equipment. Around his head he wears what appears to be a head-band. It is of a markedly different shape from the *kausia* worn by the figures on the other coins, and, though the *kausia* could come in a wide variety of variations, I do not believe that this figure wears the famous national Macedonian headgear. Rather he could be wearing what Strabo (15.3.19) describes as the «muslin rag» that Persian commoners wore around their head. Seemingly only Persian nobles were allowed to wear the Persian «hood» that is usually associated with Achaemenid Persian dress.

The figure of the young cavalryman, captured in action at his moment of triumph riding down an infantryman, although his armour and dress are is not ethnically specific, is surely to be identified as a Paionian. How did a Paionian cavalryman find himself on Asian battlefields during the Second War of the Diadochoi? Among the cavalry units mentioned by Diodorus (19.29.4) as participating on the side of Antigonos in the battle of Paraitakene are 500 mercenaries «of mixed origin» (*pantodapoi*), a thousand Thracian cavalry, and 500 horse from the allies (*symmachoi*), all drawn up on the right wing. They presumably fought at Gabiene too, although they are absent from the account of Diodorus dealing with the latter battle. It is possible that a Paionian unit of cavalry, or a single prominent Paeonian individual, was serving with all three of these units. The unit of mercenaries «of mixed origin» is obviously a composite unit and could have included a sub-unit of Paionian mercenaries. «Thracian» is an all-embracing ethnic that could be extended to include Paionians. But it is surely most probable that a squadron of Paionians sent by Patraos fought among the 500 allied cavalry. There was after all a precedent for this in the despatch of the Paionian squadron commanded by Ariston some 19 years earlier. As has already been mentioned, in 310 Kassandros the ruler of Macedonia goes to the aid of Audoleon, king of the Paionians, and successor to Paionios, who was fighting against the Autariatai[21]. It is possible that Paionios was in alliance with Kassandros seven years earlier, and the Paionian contingent was sent to Antigonos on the strength of this alliance.

The *Argyraspides*

Also present at the two battles were the regiment called the *argyraspides*[22]. The term *argyraspides* («silver shields») first appears as an alternative title for the Macedonian *hypaspistai* at the battle of Gaugamela in Diodorus (17.57.2) and Curtius (4.13.27). This appears to be retrospective, for Justin (12.7.5; cf. Curt. 8.5.4) tells us that before the Indian Campaign Alexander had the men's arms overlaid with silver, and he called the army the *argyraspides* after their silver shields, so the change in regimental title came, in fact, later. The official renaming, therefore, seems to have taken place before the Indian Campaign.

---

[21] Diod. Sic. 20.19.1.
[22] Anson 1981.

After the death of Alexander the *argyraspides* are known to have been commanded by Antigenes and Teutamus (Plut. Vit. Eum. 13.2) and are given the strength of 3000 (Diod. Sic. 18.58.1, 59.3). Antigenes is first mentioned as a commander of the *hypaspistai* after the promotions of Sittacene in 331. In 318 BC the 3000 *argyraspides* first came under the command of Eumenes, on the orders of Polyperchon representing Olympias, who was acting in support of Alexander's infant heir Alexander IV (Diod. Sic. 18.58.1). At the battle of Paraitakene in 317/6 BC Eumenes drew up the Macedonian *argyraspides*, more than 3000 in number, «undefeated troops the fame of whose exploits caused much fear among the enemy» (Diod. Sic. 19.28.1). Eumenes' men were victorious in the phalanx battle because of the valour of the *argyraspides*. «These warriors were already well on in years, but because of the great number of battles they had fought they were outstanding in hardihood and skill, so that no one confronting them was able to withstand their might. Therefore although there were only 3000 of them, they had become the main force of the army» (Diod. Sic. 19.30.5-6). Eumenes drew up the *argyraspides* in the centre of the line at the battle of Gabiene as well (Diod. Sic. 19.40.3). At this battle, fought in 316 BC, it is mentioned (Diod. Sic. 19.41.2; Plut. *Vit. Eum.*) that the youngest of the argyraspides were about 60 years old, most of the others about 70, and some even older; «but all of them were irresistible because of experience and strength, such was the skill and daring acquired through the unbroken series of their battles». So, if most of the argyraspides were aged 70, they would have been born about 387 BC, and so aged 43 when the army crossed over to Asia in 334 BC.

Diodorus (19.43.1) continues in his description of the battle «As for the infantry, the *argyraspides* in close order (συμφράξαντες) fell those drawn up against them, killing some of them in hand to hand fighting and forcing the others to flee. They were not to be checked in their charge an engaging the entire opposing phalanx, showing themselves to be so superior in skill and strength that of their own men they lost not one, but of those who opposed them they slew over 5000 and routed the entire force of infantry, whose numbers were many times their own».

Although victorious on the battlefield, the other units of Eumenes' army were not, and «the Macedonians (*argyraspides*) formed themselves into a square and withdrew safely to the river» where they were joined by Eumenes «about the time for lighting lamps»[23]. During the battle Antigonos had captured the baggage train of the *argyraspides*, and the latter troops were persuaded to surrender Eumenes up to Antigonos, following which Eumenes was put to death. Antigonos also seized Antigenes commander of the *argyraspides*, put him into a pit, and burned him alive[24].

After the battle the most turbulent of the *argyraspides* were assigned to Sibyrtios the satrap of Arachosia «ostensibly that they might be useful in war, but in reality to ensure their destruction; for he had privately directed the satrap to send a few at a time on duties in which they were bound to be killed»[25]. The *argyraspides* eventually ended up in Seleucid service.

---

[23] 19.43.5.
[24] 19.44.2.
[25] 19.48.2.

I believe the *argyraspides* to be shown on other variants of the victory coinage of Patraos of Paionia. On one example shown here as (**Fig. 3**) the Paionian horseman, dressed in different armour to the previous coin, is shown riding down an infantryman dressed in a style which is purely Macedonian, and carrying Macedonian weapons. He does not wear trousers, and he wears a sleeveless tunic falling to the knee, and a *kausia* on his head. The coin could represent any kind of Macedonian infantryman of course, but given the historical context of the series of coins as a whole I believe him to represent an infantryman of the *argyraspides* regiment.

The *Hypaspistai*

Alongside the argyraspides at the battles of Paraitakene and Gabiene the *hypaspistai* are also mentioned. Modern historians are divided as to what Diodorus means by this

Fig. 3 *Version of the reverse of the Patraos coin (Gaebler 1935: pl. xxxvii, 15) showing an infantryman bearing a Macedonian peltē, bare-legged, and wearing a sleeveless tunic and a Macedonian kausia (photo: Staatliche Museen zu Berlin, Münzkabinett).*

term. It has been suggested by Hammond[26] that the Greek should be understood to mean that they are the sons of the *hypaspistai*, but I personally much more favour the suggestion of Bosworth (2002: 82-4) that they are oriental troops.

---

[26] Hammond 1978, 135; 1989, 67.

At Opis in 324 we get the first clear reference to troops called *hypaspistai*[27] whom we can distinguish from the *argyraspides*, who had previously borne the same regimental title. These same Persians, a thousand in number, are called *hypaspistai* by Diodorus[28]. The establishment of a guard of a thousand young Persians is also mentioned by Justin[29]. The establishment of these oriental guards is dated as early as 330 BC in a second passage of Diodorus[30] where he calls them doryphoroi, or «spear-bearers», the semantic equivalent in Greek of the Old Persian *arštibara*[31].

From the fact that Arrian[32] mentions that Alexander created «a taxis of Persian *argyraspides*» we can assume that the Persian *hypaspistai* had silver Macedonian pel-

Fig. 4 *Version of the reverse of the Patraos coin (Oxford SNG 3354) showing an infantryman bearing a Macedonian peltē and wearing a Persian tunic and trousers and a Macedonian kausia (photo: Ashmolean Museum).*

tai too. The strength of the Persian *hypaspistai* is later given as 3000, at the battles of Paraitakene and Gabiene. It seems likely that the expansion in their strength from one to three thousand came before the death of Alexander, who envisioned the formation as a counterpoise to the *argyraspides*. The first thousand might have constituted an elite within the *hypaspistai* as a whole, in which case they would have been, in fact, a re-creation of the elite Achaemenid infantry regiment of 1000 *arštibara*, or «spear-bearers», which were the premiere infantry regiment of the «Immortals».

---

[27] Arr. Anab. 7.8.3.
[28] Diod. Sic. 117.110.1.
[29] Just. Epit. 12.12.
[30] Diod. Sic. 17.77.4.
[31] Sekunda 1988, 70-72.
[32] Arr. Anab. 7.11.3.

Curtius (3.3.15), in a rather garbled passage dealing with the military review which took place at Babylon prior to the battle of Gaugamela, tells us that the «spear-bearers» according to Achaemenid practice, «alone were allowed to wear the royal dress» (*soliti vestem excipere regalem*).

After his change in policy in the late summer or autumn 330 BC[33]: 355-6), Alexander is mentioned as wearing a long-sleeved tunic of sea-purple with a white stripe down the front (Diod. Sic. 17.77.5). The Greek lexicographers Hesychius and Photius (*s.v. sarapis*) both inform us that *sarapis* was the name given in former times to the tunic with its white centre, as worn by the (Persian) kings. According to some authorities he wore this tunic in conjunction with the Persian, or more properly Median[34] royal hood, or *kidaris* (Arr. Anab. 4.7.4), but according to others he wore not the *kidaris*, but the diadem alone, a band of purple cloth variegated in white (Curt. 6.6.4). According to Eratosthenes (Plut. *Mor*. 330A) he wore a combination of Persian and Macedonian dress[35]. According to Athenaeus (12.537A) Ephippus of Olynthos wrote in his work *On the death of Hephaistion and Alexander* (FGrH 126 F 5) that Alexander would wear in his everyday dress a purple cloak and a *chiton* with a white stripe down the middle and a *kausia* with the royal diadem. This would have been at the end of Alexander's reign, and we can reconcile these seemingly irreconcilable references if we postulate that Alexander at first, indeed adopted the Median *kidaris*, but later on replaced it with the Macedonian *kausia*. The accounts of the partial adoption of Persian dress by Alexander given in Plutarch's *Life of Alexander* (45.2) and Justin (12.3.8) are confused.

Therefore, it is reasonable to believe, that after his adoption of Achaemenid practices, Alexander allowed the «spear-bearers» alone to wear the mixed Perso-Macedonian dress that he had adopted. This is suggested by a passage Phylarchus, preserved in Athenaeus 12.539e-f (cf. Ael. *VH* 9.3), describing the military guard surrounding the court of Alexander in the last years of his reign. According to this passage there came first 500 Persian «apple-bearers» who were dressed in sea-purple and quince-yellow, and after them archers to the number of a thousand, some dressed in flame-colour and others in scarlet, many of them also had dark-blue outer garments wrapped around them, at the head of these stood 500 Macedonian *argyraspides*.

In 321 BC Perdikkas, the regent established after Alexander's death, moved against Ptolemy in Egypt. To storm the river Nile he selected the *hypaspistai* and «the bravest of the cavalry» (Diod. Sic. 18.33.6, 34.2). The operation ended disastrously in defeat, and Perdikkas was killed by his own troops. It seems that the Macedonian *argyraspidai* cannot be meant, for, as we have seen previously, they had a reputation for being undefeated in battle. We are left to suppose that Diodorus has in mind the Persian *hypaspistai*. Diodorus nowhere gives the strength of these *hypaspistai* operating in 321 BC. The situation is further complicated by the fact that Diodorus mentions in other pas-

---

[33] Olbrycht 2010, 355-356.
[34] Sekunda 2010.
[35] Coppola 2010, 144.

Fig. 5 Version of the reverse of the Patraos coin (Bibliothèque National, Paris 6.14.1857C) showing an infantryman bearing a Macedonian peltē and wearing Persian trousers and tunic and a probable Macedonian kausia, though the last detail runs off the edge of the coin (photo: Bibliothèque National, Paris).

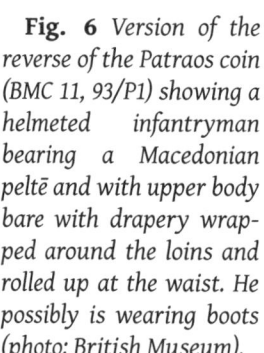

Fig. 6 Version of the reverse of the Patraos coin (BMC 11, 93/P1) showing a helmeted infantryman bearing a Macedonian peltē and with upper body bare with drapery wrapped around the loins and rolled up at the waist. He possibly is wearing boots (photo: British Museum).

sages forces of other *hypaspistai* in the forces commanded by satraps, for example at 18.45.3 he mentions Alketas with his own *hypaspistai* and *paides*.

At the battle in Paraitakene Eumenes stationed the Macedonian *argyraspides*, next to «the men from the *hypaspistai* more than 3000, the whole force being commanded by Antigenes and Teutamos» (Diod. Sic. 19.28.1). At Gabiene Eumenes placed the *hypaspistai* in the line first, and then the *argyraspides* after (Diod. Sic. 19.40.3).

On some variants of the Patraos coins (**Fig. 4**) the figure of the infantryman carries a Macedonian shield and is dressed in mixed dress of Persian trousers and (presumably) long-sleeved tunic, though the long sleeves are difficult to see on the coins, and Macedonian *kausia*. I believe that this figure represents a Persian *hypaspistēs* from the elite *chiliarchia*, who alone were allowed to wear the dress of the king himself. In my belief, the interpretation of this figure is decisive. On no other representation are Persian tunic and trousers and the Macedonian *kausia* found in conjunction. It is possible that the other 2000 *hypaspistai* and the *epigonoi* were permitted to wear the Macedonian *kausia* as well.

Conclusion

The best interpretation of the «Victory» coinage of Patraos of Paionia is that it records a military victory of some sort. The historical sources for the period of the reign of Patraos, conventionally given as c. 336-315 BC, are unusually full for any period of ancient history. Even so, we must within these dates look for an occasion when Paionian horsemen met with infantry units dressed and equipped in Macedonian fashion, equipped in Macedonian fashion and dressed in oriental fashion, and equipped in Macedonian fashion and wearing oriental trousers and Macedonian *kausiai*.

The battles of Paraitakene and Gabiene are the only occasion in which such an encounter could have taken place. The iconography of the coins of Patraos should not be interpreted too literally. It should be sufficient to demonstrate that the various categories of infantry depicted fought on the opposite side, not that the Paionian cavalry were in all parts of the battlefield to actually the various categories of enemy infantry down in turn. The other types of infantrymen shown on the further variants of the coins (eg. **Fig.5**), other than the three categories dealt with in detail here, could have been met with on the same occasion. Diodorus (19.27.6) also mentions a force of 6000 mercenaries (*xenoi*) drawn up by Eumenes on the left flank of his phalanx at the battle of Paraitakene. Alternatively, the other variants in the infantrymen shown on the coins could represent other Paionian victories over other enemies we do not hear about in the historical sources, although this is on balance less likely.

All the variants of the coins, and there are a considerable number of them, could reflect a series of statues or paintings commissioned by Patraos immediately after the battle, which were placed in the royal palace at the Paionian capital Bylazora.

The only problem with this interpretation, it seems, is that we have to fit the very considerable number of variants of these coins in between the last of these battles in 316 BC, and the death of Patraos, which is conventionally put in 315 BC, furthermore, according to Sotheby & Co.[36] 'The coins of Patraos divide readily into the ear-

---

[36] Sotheby & Co 1969,10.

lier issues, with dotted border on the obverse, and the later issues without a border. Many of the later issues are struck on cast flans', but I will leave these problems to the numismatists.

Nicholas V. Sekunda
University of Gdańsk

Bibliography

Anson 1981 = E. M. Anson, «Alexander's Hypaspistsand the Argyraspides», *Historia* 30 (1981)117-120.

Anson 1988 = E. M. Anson, «Hypaspists and Argyraspids after 323» *AHB* 2 (1988) 131-133.

Bosworth 2002 = A. B. Bosworth, *The Legacy of Alexander. Politics, Warfare, and Propaganda under the Successors* (Oxford 2002).

Coppola 2010 = A. Coppola, «Alexander's Court» in Bruno Jacobs, Robert Rolliger (eds.), *Der Achämenidenhof, The Achaemenid Court, Akten des 2. Internationalen Kolloquiums zum Thema «Vorderasien im Spannungsfeld klassischer und altorientaischer Überlieferungen» Landgut Castelen bei Basel, 23.-25. Mai 2007* (Wiesbaden 2010) 139-152.

Gaebler 1935 = H. Gaebler, *Die Antiken Münzen Nord Griechenlands (Makedonia und Paionia)* (Berlin 1935).

Hammond 1978 = N. G. L. Hammond, «Note on Argyraspides (Silver Shields) and Hypaspists (Shield-Bearers)», *Classical Quarterly* ns. 28 (1978) 135.

Hammond 1989 = N. G. L. Hammond, «Casualties and Reinforcements of Citizen Soldiers in Greece and Macedonia» *JHS* 109 (1989), p. 56-68.

Liampi 1998 = K. Liampi, *Der makedonische Schild* (Bonn 1998).

Merker 1965 = I. L. Merker, «The ancient kingdom of Paionia», *Balkan Studies* 6 (1965) 33-54.

Olbrycht 2008 = M. J. Olbrycht, «Curtius Rufus, the Macedonian Mutiny at Opis and Alexander's Iranian Policy in 324 BC» in J. Pigoń (ed.), *The Children of Herodotus* (Newcastle 2008) 231–52.

Olbrycht 2010 = M. J. Olbrycht, «Chapter17 Macedonia and Persia» in J. Roisman and I. Worthington (eds.), *A Companion to Ancient Macedonia* (2010 Blackwell Publishing Ltd.) Chapter 17, 342-369.

Sekunda & McBride 1984 = N. V. Sekunda, A. McBride, *The Army of Alexander the Great*, Osprey Men At Arms Series 148 (London 1984).

Sekunda 1988 = N. V. Sekunda, «Achaemenid Military Terminology», *Archäologische Mitteilungen aus Iran* 21 (1988) 69-77.

Sekunda & Chew = N. V. Sekunda, S. Chew, *The Persian Army 560-330 B.C.*, Osprey Elite Series No. 42 (London 1992).

Sekunda 2007 = N. V. Sekunda, «Military Forces in the Hellenistic World and the Roman Republic (a) Land Forces», in *The Cambridge History of Greek and Roman Warfare*, Vol. I Chapter 8 (Cambridge 2007) 325-57.

Sekunda 2010 = N. V. Sekunda, «22. Changes in Achaemenid Royal Dress» in J. Curtis, St J. Simpson (eds.), *The World of Achaemenid Persia. History, Art and Society in Iran and the Ancient Near East* (London, New York 2010) 255-272.

Sotheby & Co., *Catalogue of the Paeonian Hoard*, London (16 April 1969).

LES SELEUCIDES ET LES BALKANS : LES THRACES DANS L'ARMEE SELEUCIDE[1]

Adrian George DUMITRU

Écrire l'histoire des soldats d'origine thrace qui ont combattu sous les ordres des rois séleucides est une tâche presque impossible, car des péripéties de ces aventuriers il ne nous reste plus que des bribes de récits, éparpillés dans les sources anciennes. A la différence des soldats thraces qui ont choisi l'Egypte, ceux qui ont préféré les enseignes des successeurs de Séleucos Ier n'ont laissé des traces que lorsqu'ils étaient en campagne avec l'armée royale. En effet, si les *papyri* que nous a légués le climat chaud de l'Egypte nous font voir la vie de soldats de toutes nations en temps de paix, à travers leurs actes privés, les militaires des armées séleucides ne se laissent connaître que par les batailles qu'ils ont gagnées ou perdues, et qui ont dû être suffisamment importantes pour que les historiens de l'antiquité les décrivent dans leurs livres -si tant est que ceux-ci nous soient parvenus. Depuis la mise au point de Marcel Launey, dans sa monumentale synthèse sur les armées hellénistiques[2], de nouvelles découvertes épigraphiques ainsi qu'un réexamen des témoignages littéraires invitent toutefois à rouvrir le dossier de la présence des Thraces dans les armées des Séleucides.

L'objet de cet article est de réexaminer de manière systématique les différentes occurrences de celle-ci. Nous présenterons les attestations établies de manière certaine dans un premier temps, puis nous discuterons celles qui ont été supposées.

Polyen 4, 16

Malgré le fait qu'il y a dû avoir une forme quelconque de domination séleucide en Thrace après 281 avant J.-C. (avec la défaite de Lysimaque à Kouroupédion et la conquête de son royaume par Séleucos Ier), ce qui est prouvé par l'existence d'un atelier monétaire séleucide à Lysimacheia[3] (frappant des pièces avec les effigies des rois Antiochos Ier, Antiochos II et Antiochos III, sans oublier l'usurpateur Antiochos Hiérax), nous ignorons tout ce qui est de l'administration royale de ces contrées et, par voie de conséquence, s'il y a eu ou non un recrutement (qu'il soit soutenu ou sporadique) de Thraces dans l'armée royale.

---

[1] La rédaction de cette communication doit beaucoup à la bourse Jacoby offerte par la *Komission für Alte Geschichte de Munich* en juillet-août 2011, qui nous a permis d'élargir notre documentation, mais aussi à la patience et à l'εὔνοια de M. Nicholas V. Sekunda et de Mme Aliénor Rufin Solas, qui est responsable de la correction de bon nombre d'erreurs de notre français. Notre reconnaissance ne saurait oublier l'appui et les suggestions, directes ou indirectes, que nous ont prodigués MM. Olivier Picard et Adrian Robu. Qu'ils en soient tous remerciés, tout en assumant pour notre part la responsabilité des éventuelles erreurs qui pourraient se retrouver ici.
[2] Launey 1949-1950.
[3] Le Rider 1988, 195-207 ; Houghton & Lorber 2002, vol. I, 173 *sqq*., 304 *sqq*., et 367.

La première mention sûre de la présence d'un Séleucide dans la Thrace figure parmi les ruses de guerre de Polyen : «*Antiochus attaquait Cypsèle, ville de Thrace. Il avait avec lui un grand nombre de Thraciens des meilleures maisons, à la tête desquels étaient Tyris et Dromichetès. Il leur donna à tous des colliers d'or et des armes garnies d'argent, et s'avança pour livrer combat. Ceux de Cypsèle, voyant des gens de leur pays et de leur langue si richement parés d'or et d'argent, les estimaient heureux de servir sous Antiochus. Ils mirent bas les armes, et se joignant à lui, d'ennemis qu'ils étaient auparavant, se rendirent ses alliés.*»[4]

Pour ce qui est de la figure historique qui se cache derrière le récit de Polyen, il faudrait se résigner : on ne peut savoir avec certitude s'il s'agit d'Antiochos II ou de son fils, Antiochos Hiérax[5], et on a même contesté la véracité de cette anecdote[6]. La solution la plus probable, cependant, est qu'il s'agit du roi Antiochos II. L'important est que nous voyons à travers cet exemple les mécanismes à l'œuvre pour le recrutement des Thraces dans l'armée royale, qui ne sont, à première vue, pas très différents de la façon dont les Diadoques entendaient se faire la guerre, en persuadant leurs ennemis de se joindre à eux. C'était une sorte de *circulum viciosus* : on cherchait

---

[4] Polyen 4, 16, " Ἀντίοχος ἐπολιόρκει Κύψελα, Θρᾷτταν πόλιν, ἔχων σὺν αὐτῷ Θρᾳκῶν εὐπατρίδας πολλούς, ὧν ἡγοῦντο Τήρης καὶ Δρομιχαίτης. τούτους κοσμήσας στρεπτοῖς χρυσοῖς καὶ ὅπλοις ἀργυροπάστοις προῆλθεν ἐπὶ τὴν μάχην. οἱ δὲ ἀπὸ τῶν Κυψέλων ἰδόντες τοὺς ὁμοφύλους καὶ ὁμογλώσσους πολλῷ χρυσῷ καὶ ἀργύρῳ κεκοσμημένους, μακαρίσαντες αὐτοὺς τῆς μετ' Ἀντιόχου στρατείας, τὰ ὅπλα καταβαλόντες Ἀντιόχῳ προσέθεντο καὶ ἦσαν ἀντὶ πολεμίων σύμμαχοι", traduction Liskenne et Savan 1840.

[5] Antiochos II : Niese 1899, t. II, 137 *sqq.*; Bouché-Leclercq 1913, t. I, 77 *sqq.*; Launey 1949, t. I, 373; Will 1979², t. I, 247 *sqq.* (non sans réserves) et 297 *sqq.* (sans pour autant se décider pour Antiochos Hiérax) ; Youroukova 1982, 120 *sqq.* ; Schettino, 1998, 235 et n. 70; Delev 2003, 113 ; Avram 2003, 1181-1213 ; Grainger 2010, 144 . Cf. Beloch 1925, t. IV 1², 672 n. 4 qui suivait une tradition commencée par Niebuhr et voyait dans l'Antiochos du texte de Polyen la figure d'Antiochos Hiérax. Il faut aussi noter l'opinion singulière de Griffith 1934, 166, qui rattache au texte de Polyen le roi Antiochos III, ce qui est impossible car le roi du texte de Polyen est un Antiochos, fils d'Antiochos, tandis qu'Antiochos III est le fils cadet de Séleucos II.

[6] Avram 2003, 1201 *sqq.* : «Et puis, les alliances avec les roitelets thraces, dont Polyen n'a retenu que les anecdotes, ne cacheraient-elles pas les jalons de la même politique ? Les princes thraces à cuirasses et à armes en or et argent n'étaient sûrement pas Térès et Dromichaitès ; ce n'est que Polyen qui, sans trop se soucier du contexte, aura donné aux alliés d'Antiochos II des noms de Thraces censés être célèbres. N'empêche que la tradition utilisée par Polyen eût fait état de subsides et d'autres privilèges accordés aux princes locaux, afin que ceux-ci se rangent du côté d'Antiochos». A notre avis, le fait que des princes thraces aient pu porter des noms célèbres, comme Térès et Dromichaitès, ne saurait être un argument pour annuler leur existence historique. Comme le remarque Dan Dana, ces noms «incolores et neutres du type Βιθυς, Κοτυς, Σευθης ou Τηρης [...] correspondant aux banaux Ἀπολλώνιος ou Δημήτριος», furent «portés par des dizaines d'individus» (Dana 2011, 94) ; pour les occurrences de ces anthroponymes, jusqu'à l'époque romaine, voir Detschew 1976², 158 *sqq.* (Dromichaitès) et 500-502 (Térès). Ajoutons, en ce qui concerne le «prince Dromichaitès», qu'on n'est qu'à une distance de 50 à 80 ans du règne du vainqueur de Lysimaque qui a inspiré tant de *topoi* aux historiens anciens. Sans aller jusqu'à dire qu'il s'agissait peut-être ici d'un des ses descendants, comme le fait John D. Grainger (2010, 144), on peut accepter que ce nom avait pu gagner beaucoup de succès auprès des Thraces et des Gètes après la *Gesta* de Dromichaitès, le vainqueur de Lysimaque. Pour ce qui est du nom de Térès, il est porté notamment par le fils de Seuthès et de Bérénikè, cité à la l. 8 de la grande inscription de Seuthopolis, cf. G. Mikhailov *IGBulg* III², 1964, 147 *sqq.*, no. 1731 et Elvers 1994, 244 *sqq.* D'ailleurs, certains identifient ce prince au personnage du stratagème de Polyen: Venedikov 1976, 176 *sqq.* ; Delev 2003, 113.

à gagner des batailles pour enrôler dans son armée les soldats de l'ennemi, mais on faisait aussi tout pour attirer à soi les soldats de l'ennemi afin de gagner les batailles[7]. Ainsi, en appliquant une ruse de guerre qui suggérait aux Thraces qui s'opposaient à lui que le roi Antiochos savait récompenser ceux qui combattaient pour lui, le Séleucide mentionné par Polyen put élargir cette armée qui opérait en Thrace, qui ne devait pas être très nombreuse, et qui comprenait beaucoup de soldats recrutés sur le champ. Les possessions séleucides en Thrace se maintinrent pour la moitié d'un siècle, ce qui expliquerait la frappe, presque régulière (quoique peu soutenue –pour un laps de temps de cinquante ans) des tétradrachmes d'argent par l'atelier de Lysimacheia[8]. Le Roi offrait donc son or et son argent, en échange de quoi les Thraces lui offraient leurs bras et leurs talents guerriers. Etait-ce du mercenariat au sens propre du terme ? Il nous est impossible de trancher. Pour certains savants, il s'agit d'un appui militaire entraîné par le jeu des alliances, sans doute consolidées par des donations et des cadeaux[9]. De toute façon, le texte de Polyen nous fait voir que ce que les défenseurs de Kypséla ont vu en premier lieu, c'est l'or et non pas le traité d'alliance[10].

L'origine des Thraces présents à Raphia

Les grandes campagnes des Séleucides de la fin du IIIe et du début du IIe siècle avant J.-C. sont mieux connues, grâce aux récits de Polybe, qui nous fournissent un regard mieux documenté sur la présence des Thraces dans l'armée séleucide. Ainsi, nous savons qu'un corps thrace était présent à Raphia en 217[11], puisqu'on le retrouve dans la description de l'armée séleucide avant la bataille : « *Ensuite venaient deux*

---

[7] Parmi plusieurs exemples qui nous ont été fournis par les Anciens, nous allons nous contenter de trois. Ainsi, en combattant Cratère en 321 (ou en 320 avant J.-C), Eumène de Cardia prit toute les précautions afin que ses soldats ignorent jusqu'à la fin le nom du général ennemi, pour ne pas se laisser séduire par la charisme de celui-ci (Plut., *Vit. Eum.*, 6-7; Diod., 18, 31-32 ; Nepos, *Eum.* 4, 3). A la fin de la bataille, après la mort de Cratère et de Néoptolème, un héraut d'Eumène offrit à la phalange ennemie non pas de se rendre, mais de rejoindre ses rangs, proposition qui fut vite acceptée (Diod., 18, 32, 2). La dernière bataille livrée par Eumène, celle de Gabiène (316 avant J.-C.) fut perdue à cause de la désertion de sa phalange (et notamment des Argyraspides), dont les bagages (et les familles) furent enlevés par Antigone le Borgne (Plut., *Eumen.*, 17, 1, 3 ; Diod., 19, 43, 8-9 ; Polyen, 4, 6, 13 ; Justin., 14, 4, 1). Les négociations menées par les phalangites avec Antigone auront comme résultat le fait qu'Eumène fut capturé et que son armée fut intégrée dans l'armée du vainqueur. Voir aussi, plus récemment, Anson 2004, 107-110 et 187-189. Avant même que la bataille d'Ipsos (301 avant J.-C.) ne fut perdue par Antigone le Borgne, une bonne partie de sa phalange, dépourvue de l'appui de la cavalerie, fut encerclée et passa dans les rangs de l'armée de Séleucos Ier (Plut. *Dem.* 29, 5-6 ; Billows 1997, p. 184 *sqq.*).

[8] En nous basant sur le catalogue le plus récent, celui de Houghton, Lorber 2002, I, 173 *sqq.*, 304 *sqq.*, 367: trois types monétaires sont attribués à Antiochos II (avec 14 variations, signalées par des combinaisons des marques de contrôle), trois autres à Antiochos Hiérax et un dernier à Antiochos III. Pour les monnaies de bronze, voir Youroukova 1982, 115-127 et pl. XVII.

[9] Ainsi, Launey 1949, t. I, p. 373.

[10] Jordanka Yourokova expliquait le stratagème de Polyen en ces termes: «les habitants de Cypsela se sont rendus de bon gré aux troupes d'Antiochos ayant remarqué dans leurs formations des Thraces» (Youroukova 1982, 121).

[11] Bouché-Leclercq 1913, I, 150-153 ; Bevan 1902, I, 317-320 ; Griffith, 1934, 143 *sqq.*; Launey 1949, I, 378 *sqq.* ; Walbank 1957, I, 667 *sqq.* ; Bar-Kochva 1979, 50 *sqq.*, 128-141; Galili 1967-1975, 52-156 ; Grainger 2010, 213 *sqq.*

mille Agrianes et Perses, archers et frondeurs ; avec eux mille Thraces, commandés par Ménédèmos d'Alabanda. [...] à la suite, les soldats légers de Ménédèmos, au nombre de trois mille environ [...]»[12]

Sur la provenance de ce corps, plusieurs opinions s'opposent, que nous pouvons résumer ainsi :

a - ces Thraces étaient des mercenaires et ont été recrutés en Europe[13] ;

b - il s'agissait de descendants des colons militaires établis en Asie Mineure par Alexandre ou par les Séleucides eux-mêmes, à une époque inconnue[14] ;

c - les Thraces sont associés aux Agrianes et aux Perses sous un commandement unique, justement parce qu'il s'agissait d'un corps d'infanterie légère (surtout des archers) recruté parmi les colons militaires de Perse (dont on discutera *infra*)[15].

Malheureusement Polybe ne nous donne aucun indice qui nous permettrait de trancher entre ces hypothèses. La dernière peut paraître séduisante - et confortée par l'idée qu'avant la bataille de Raphia le roi Antiochos III avait fait campagne contre Molon, en Mésopotamie : il a donc pu disposer des troupes de Satrapies Supérieures - mais elle n'a aucun fondement sérieux, comme les deux autres et surtout la première, car on voit mal comment Antiochos III aurait pu faire venir des mercenaires depuis une Thrace toujours contrôlée par son rival Ptolémée IV, ou à travers une Asie Mineure sous l'autorité de l'usurpateur Achaios[16].

La reconquête de la Thrace séleucide – aussi éphémère qu'elle fût – par Antiochos III ne semble pas avoir fait accroître les effectifs des Thraces dans son armée. Ainsi les Thraces font-ils étrangement figure d'absents à la bataille de Magnésie[17]. Pourtant, malgré la mobilisation de toute l'armée royale (qui est allée jusqu'à laisser presque toutes les garnisons sans effectifs, comme en Pamphylie, lors de la campagne de Manlius Vulso), le roi avait laissé des garnisons en Thrace, pour défendre des places fortes comme Ainos et Maronée. L'armée romaine, dans sa marche vers l'Asie Mineure, avait ignoré les garnisons séleucides stationnées en Thrace, qui ne se sont rendues qu'après la défaite de Magnésie, dans les mains du préteur Q. Fabius Labeo, venu pour exiger la capitulation avec trois navires[18].

Quelle était la nature de ces troupes laissées en Thrace par Antiochos III, et pour quelles raisons? On pourrait se demander s'il ne s'agissait pas justement d'unités composées de Thraces ; des recrutements sur place doivent en effet avoir eu lieu, vu que la nouvelle satrapie de la Thrace, avec sa capitale, Lysimacheia, était censée devenir le centre d'une nouvelle vice-royauté, que le roi voulait confier à son fils

---

[12] Pol. 5, 79, 6 , " πρὸς δὲ τούτοις Ἀγριᾶνες καὶ Πέρσαι τοξόται καὶ σφενδονῆται δισχίλιοι. μετὰ δὲ τούτων χίλιοι Θρᾷκες, ὧν ἡγεῖτο Μενέδημος Ἀλαβανδεύς. [...]" et 82, 11" τῆς δ' εὐωνύμου τάξεως ἐπ' αὐτὸ [...] ἑξῆς δὲ τούτοις τοὺς ὑπὸ Μενέδημον εὐζώνους, ὄντας εἰς τρισχιλίους", Paris, Les Belles Lettres, 1977.

[13] Griffith 1934, 143 *sqq*.

[14] Launey 1949, I, 378 *sqq*.

[15] Bar-Kochva 1979, 50 *sqq*.

[16] Nous nous rangeons donc à l'opinion de Walbank 1957, I, 668.

[17] Launey 1949, I, 382.

[18] Tite Live, 37, 33, 1; 60, 7.

Séleucos[19]. Le roi Antiochos a mené trois longues campagnes dans la région, entre 197 et 195[20]. Son monnayage à Lysimacheia n'est pas très important[21], ce qui implique qu'il n'a pas dû avoir un contingent très important avec lui : nous pouvons conjecturer en toute sécurité qu'il a eu tout intérêt à faire grossir les effectifs de son armée avec des Thraces. S'est-il souvenu du stratagème dont un autre Antiochos, probablement son grand-père avait dû se servir jadis? On l'ignore. Ses campagnes dans la Thrace ont certainement eu comme adversaires des tribus thraces et (peut-être) des Celtes, soit de bonnes opportunités pour recruter des mercenaires. Le seul indice dont nous disposons pour déduire que quelques tribus thraces ont pu être amies avec le roi séleucide est donné par la mésaventure du proconsul Manlius Vulso et de son armée, lors du retour de l'Asie Mineure, après les victoires remportées contre les Galates. Chargés de butin, les Romains ont été attaqués par les Thraces qui sont parvenus à leur en enlever une partie. Mais c'est peut-être davantage à cause de l'appât du butin que par amitié avec le Roi Antiochos III que les Thraces ont attaqué les troupes de Manlius Vulso.

Une autre manière de voir les choses serait de considérer que les Thraces n'ont pas voulu de l'amitié et de l'alliance (même si elle était bien rémunérée) du roi Antiochos qu'ils ont combattu. Combler le vide de puissance laissé par la disparition successive de la domination des Celtes, des Lagides et des Antigonides dans la région de la Thrace et des Détroits pourrait avoir été une raison suffisante pour les inviter à s'opposer aux plans d'Antiochos de restaurer l'ancienne domination des Séleucides dans ces contrées.

Si les Thraces sont absents à la bataille de Magnésie, il reste difficile de déterminer s'il y a eu des recrutements des mercenaires pour l'armée séleucide ou si les Thraces se sont farouchement opposés à la pression d'Antiochos III comme, ensuite, au passage de l'armée romaine par leur territoire.

La paix d'Apamée et ses conséquences sur les recrutements de soldats thraces.

La défaite d'Antiochos III à la bataille de Magnésie et le traité de paix d'Apamée-Kibôtos de 188 avant J.-C. ont apporté un changement considérable pour l'armée séleucide, car une des conditions du traité de paix était de renoncer à tout recrutement au-delà du mont Taurus, l'Europe y comprise[22] – Griffith résume assez bien la

---

[19] Pol. 18, 50, 8; Tite Live, 33 40, 6; App., *Syr.* 1; 3; Grainger 1997, 747, *s.v.* Lysimacheia.
[20] Grainger 1996; Grainger 2002, 67-71, 81-3.
[21] Cf. *supra* n.7
[22] Pour se faire une image de la vaste littérature dédiée à la paix d'Apamée (et surtout à sa clause territoriale), voir : Pol. 21, 24; T.L. 38, 38; App., *Syr.* 39 (200-204); Mommsen 1879, 511-545; Viereck 1909, 371-375; Cardinali 1910, 249-251; De Sanctis, IV 1, 206-209; Bouché-Leclercq 1913-1914, 216, 576; Kahrstedt 1923, 93 *sqq.* ; Pais 1926., 534 *sqq.*; Ruge, R.E., II 2, coll. 2169 *sqq.*, s.v. «Tanais»; Holleaux, «La clause territoriale du traité d'Apamée», *REG* (1932), 304-319 = Holleaux 1957, 208-243 ; Magie 1950, 19, 758-764; McShane, 1964, 149-164; McDonald 1967, 1-8; McDonald, Walbank 1969, 30-39; Liebmann-Francfort 1969, 48-64; Walbank. 1979, III, 157-162; Adam 1982, L-LVII; Will 19822, II, 221-238; Paltiel 1979, 30-42 ; Giovanini 1982, 224-236 ; Gruen 1984, 640-643; Le Rider 1992, 267-277 ; Dumitru 1999, 25-34 ; Dimitriev 2003, 39-63.

nouvelle situation : «*By the treaty of Apameia the kings of Syria had been forbidden to recruit mercenaries from the Roman sphere of influence, or even to receive them if they came to them of their own accord. They were thus cut off from all supplies of soldiers from Greece, from the Thracians and Gauls of Europe, from Crete, and from the Greeks or natives of much Asia Minor*»[23].

On peut cependant se tourner vers Polybe pour trouver des informations sur les Thraces, que l'on peut voir en effet à la parade de Daphné, organisée par Antiochos IV en 166 avant J.-C. pour rivaliser avec la célébration de la victoire romaine sur Persée et la Macédoine. L'armée séleucide rentrait chez elle après des longues campagnes en Egypte et se préparait pour une nouvelle expédition militaire, l'anabase d'Antiochos IV vers les satrapies supérieures[24]. Parmi la phalange et la cavalerie royale (auxquelles on avait ajouté le nouveau corps de 5000 soldats équipés à la romaine), le public de Daphné a pu admirer encore comment : «*trois mille Thraces et cinq mille Galates marchaient derrière eux [sc. les Mysiens et les Ciliciens] précédant ainsi vingt mille Macédoniens et cinq mille fantassins armés de boucliers d'airain [...]*»[25]

La première chose que l'on peut observer, c'est que ces Thraces sont des fantassins, comme ceux de Raphia, portant, très probablement, des armes légères. Mais d'où venaient-ils? Etaient-ils des colons militaires thraces provenant de Syrie –voir des soldats armés «à la manière des Thraces»[26] - ou des mercenaires[27]?

Les auteurs modernes, comme Griffith que nous avons cité, hésitent à se prononcer sur la provenance des unités de l'armée séleucide à la parade de Daphné, considérant que les rois séleucides ont vraiment dû observer les conditions du traité d'Apamée. Mais ces scrupules ne semblent pas avoir été partagés par ces derniers. Eliezer Paltiel a ainsi formulé de sérieuses réserves sur la manière dont le traité d'Apamée a dû être observé[28]. Il a souligné le fait que les Séleucides, à l'époque d'Antiochos IV, avaient une flotte qui a dû excéder les limitations d'Apamée et violer la limite de navigation qui devait être le Cap de Sarpédon, car elle a dû manœuvrer sur les côtes de Chypre afin d'y transporter l'armée royale, en 168 avant J.-C.[29]. Qui plus est, il avait reconstitué un corps d'éléphants (ces bêtes étant, elles aussi, interdites par les clauses du traité de 188 avant J.-C.), dont il avait offert une partie aux Romains eux-mêmes, lors de leur campagne contre

---

[23] Griffith 1934, 146 *sqq*.
[24] Pol. 30, 16 = Athen. 5, 194c; 10, 439b; Diod. 31, 16. La littérature dédiée à la parade de Daphné est elle aussi, vaste, on se contentera de quelques titres: Tarn 1938, 193 sq.; Launey 1949, I, 99, 319; Downey 1961, 117 sq.; Morkholm 1966, 97-101; Bunge 1976, 53-71; Gruen 1984, 661-3; Will 19822, t. II, 344-348; Bar Kochva 1989, 30-40; Sekunda 2006, 84-98.
[25] Pol. 30, 25, 5, «ἐπὶ δὲ τούτοις Θρᾷκες τρισχίλιοι καὶ Γαλάται πεντακισχίλιοι. τούτοις ἐπέβαλλον Μακεδόνες δισμύριοι καὶ χαλκάσπιδες πεντακισχίλιοι κτλ», traduction française de J.A.C. Buchon (Paris 1838).
[26] C'est l'opinion de Launey 1949; I, 384, Griffith 1934 *loc. cit supra* n. 13 et Walbank 1979, III, 450.
[27] Cf. Sekunda 1994, 17 *sqq*.
[28] Paltiel 1979, 30-42.
[29] Tite Live, 45, 11 *sqq*.

Persée[30]. Trente-six éléphants ont en outre défilé à la parade de Daphné. Le recrutement de mercenaires dans les îles grecques, quoique défendu par le traité d'Apamée, a également dû continuer, car l'armée de Lysias, qui opérait en Judée contre les rebelles, disposait des telles troupes[31]. En ce qui concerne les mercenaires thraces, il faut rappeler qu'Antiochos IV entretenait de bonnes relations avec Eumène II, le roi de Pergame, qui l'avait aidé à monter sur le trône après l'assassinat de Séleucos IV[32] ; or c'était le royaume de Pergame qui contrôlait alors la région de la Thrace hellespontique, ce qui a pu faciliter l'activité des agents recruteurs des Séleucides.

Exclure l'hypothèse du recrutement des mercenaires thraces pour la seule raison que la paix d'Apamée avait dû l'interdire serait donc négliger tout un chapitre des activités des rois séleucides et appliquer un chablon très étroit sur une réalité qui s'avère bien plus complexe qu'on ne le croyait.

On ne saurait cependant écarter l'hypothèse de la colonisation des Thraces dans diverses régions de l'empire séleucide, et surtout près des places fortifiées qui devaient exiger la présence permanente des soldats royaux. On n'a, il est vrai, aucune preuve péremptoire que cette colonisation a effectivement existé [33], mais on sait que c'était une des pratiques des Séleucides, dont l'exemple le plus connu est donné par la lettre d'Antiochos III au vice-roi de l'Asie Mineure, Zeuxis, pour arranger la colonisation des Juifs en Asie Mineure, qui nous a été transmise par Flavius Josèphe[34].

La dernière mention sûre des Thraces dans l'armée royale séleucide est très proche de la parade de Daphné, pendant la bataille de Marissa (163 avant J.-C.)[35], entre le général séleucide Gorgias et les forces des rebelles juifs. L'auteur du second Livre des Maccabées nous en donne ce récit d'un bel exploit chevaleresque : «*le dénommé Dosithée, cavalier du corps des Toubiens, homme vaillant, se rendît maître de la personne de Gorgias et, l'ayant saisi par*

---

[30] Polyen, 4, 21 nous raconte le stratagème de Persée qui, sans pouvoir disposer de vrais éléphants afin d'habituer ses hommes et ses chevaux à leur présence, «fit faire par des ouvriers des figures de bois, auxquelles on donna la forme et la couleur des éléphants». La ruse était nécessaire car il était « informé que les Romains amenaient des éléphants, les uns venus de Libye, les autres qui étaient des Indes, que leur avait envoyés Antiochus, roi de Syrie». Tite Live, 45, 13, 3 nous dit cependant que le roi Antiochos IV n'avait contribué en rien à la troisième guerre de Macédoine.

[31] *I Mac.* 6, 29, mais aussi chez Jos. *Ant. Jud.* 12, 7, 2.

[32] *OGIS* 248; Pol. 30, 30, 4-7; App. *Syr.* 45; Gruen E.S., 1984, 417 n. 106, 556; Sekunda 2003, 145-149 (avec traduction allemande de l'inscription, mise au jour de la bibliographie et analyse du contexte historique. Pour Nicholas Victor Sekunda, les soldats venus du territoire pergaméen qui ont appuyé l'avènement d'Antiochos IV sont justement les Mysiens de la parade de Daphné).

[33] Réalisant ce que Louis Robert avait jadis suggéré de faire, Dan Dana a réalisé une très importante étude de l'onomastique thrace dans des quelques régions d'Asie Mineure (Lydie, Phrygie, Pisidie et Carie) : Dana 2011, 106 *sqq*. Il s'agit surtout de noms provenant d'inscriptions d'époque impériale et, quoi qu'il est tenant de supposer qu'il s'agit de colons militaires de l'époque séleucide, nous n'en avons aucune preuve ; il pourrait s'agir aussi bien de descendants de Thraces installés comme colons par les Attalides ou établis das la région dans les circonstances dramatiques des guerres mithridatiques. Pline l'Ancien, *NH* 5, 95 mentionne les descendants des Thraces dans les villes du Nord de la Pisidie, mais sans rien dire du moment ni des circonstances de leur arrivée dans la région.

[34] Jos. *Ant. Jud.* 12, 147-152. Pour la littérature secondaire, voir, par exemple Cohen 1978, 5-8.

[35] Bevenot 1931, 231 *sqq*.; Bunge 1971, 246-252; Bar-Kochva 1979, 186, 194 *sqq*.; Bar-Kochva 1989, 69 *sqq*.

la chlamyde, il l'entraînait de force en vue de capturer vivant ce maudit, mais un cavalier thrace se jetant sur Dosithée, lui trancha l'épaule, et Gorgias s'enfuit à Marissa.»[36] Jusqu'à présent on n'a eu affaire qu'à des fantassins – c'est la première mention sûre d'un Thrace à cheval dans l'armée séleucide. Nous ignorons cependant si le cavalier thrace qui sauva la vie de son général était un mercenaire perdu dans une unité composite, formée de gens avec des origines ethniques diverses, ou s'il faisait partie d'une unité de cavalerie formée exclusivement de Thraces[37]. Les plus récents des travaux des modernes penchent pour cette deuxième variante, ce que nous allons discuter dans la dernière partie de cette étude, consacrée à quelques occurrences douteuses de Thraces dans l'armée séleucide.

Dubia

I. Seron et les Thraces de Judée

Dans le premier livre des Maccabées, nous rencontrons un certain Seron (Σήρων ὁ ἄρχων τῆς δυνάμεως Συρίας[38]), vaincu par Judas Maccabée à Beth-Horon en 165 avant J.-C. Or, Bezalel Bar Kochva observait que : «*the name Seron itself appears only once in the Greco-Macedonian onomasticon. If we take into account certain possibilities of error arising from the Hebrew pronunciation and transliteration from the Hebrew original, the name is reminiscent of a number of Thracian names*»[39]. Cela se peut, car des variations de ce nom sont à rencontrer dans le monde thrace, ainsi Σιρουων, Σουρις, Σουρα[40], Σερος, Serrus, Σερεις ou des toponymes comme Σερρειον, Σερριον, Σερρα, Serrium[41].

Le vainqueur de Dosithée appartenait-il à une unité des cavaliers thraces cantonnée en Judée ? C'est une hypothèse assez récente, élaborée par Bezalel Bar Kochva qui donnait comme garnison de cette unité la ville de Iamnia, en s'appuyant sur deux autres passages des livres des Maccabées[42]. Cela ne va pas sans poser problème cependant. Nous connaissons déjà la deuxième référence : c'est l'épisode de Dosithée et du

---

[36] II Macc., 12, 35 : «Δοσίθεος δέ τις τῶν Τουβιήνων, ἔφιππος ἀνὴρ καὶ καρτερός, εἴχετο τοῦ Γοργίου καὶ λαβόμενος τῆς χλαμύδος ἦγεν αὐτὸν εὐρώστως καὶ βουλόμενος τὸν κατάρατον λαβεῖν ζωγρίαν, τῶν ἱππέων τινὸς Θρακῶν ἐπενεχθέντος αὐτῷ καὶ τὸν ὦμον καθελόντος διέφυγεν ὁ Γοργίας εἰς Μαρισα.» tr. fr. sous la direction de l'Ecole Biblique de Jérusalem, Paris, 1998 (il y a des manuscrits qui donnent τῶν τοῦ Βακήνορος pour τῶν Τουβιήνων. Voir l'analyse la plus récente de la lection dans Bar Kochva 1989, 70 n. 3).

[37] Bar-Kochva 1979, 222 n. 84: «the Thracian cavalry probably garrisoned the citadel [sc.- de Iamnia, en Palestine]»; Bar Kochva 1989, 69 *sqq*., 111 *sqq*., 133 *sqq*., 260; Sekunda 1994, 17 *sqq*.

[38] *I Mac.* 3, 13-24; Jos. *Ant. Jud.* 12, 288-292; Grainger 1997, 116.

[39] Bar Kochva 1989, 133.

[40] IGBulg nos. 203, 507, 844, 1690, 2149, 2274, 2291, 2314, 2330, 2337, 2338 : ces inscriptions sont citées par Bar Kochva pour argumenter sa position, Dans un cas, au moins, cependant, il se trompe. L'inscription *IGBR* IV (1966), no. 2314, trouvée à Piperica et conservée au musée de Sofia (no. inv. 5709) donne, à la l. 2, καὶ Σουρα τη γυναικὶ. C'est une pierre funéraire d'époque romaine, et notre Soura a toute vraisemblance d'être une femme d'origine syrienne, très probablement de statut servile, et non un vaillant cavalier thrace.

[41] Detschew 19762, 433.

[42] Bar Kochva 1989, 69 *sqq*., 118 *sqq*., 133 *sqq*; *Mac.* 5, 58-59 et II *Mac.* 12, 35.; cf. Sekunda 1994, 18 I.

cavalier thrace au cours de la bataille de Marissa. Quant à la première, elle ne nous dit rien, sinon que Gorgias voulait défendre la ville d'Iamnia avec ses troupes. C'est donc très peu pour conclure en faveur d'une unité de Thraces stationnée à Iamnia.

Une inscription, peut-être un serment, qui implique un Arés Aulétès (qu'on a lu d'abord Athlètes)[43], s'est vue donner l'interprétation suivante : «*As to the origin of oathtakers, the description of Ares as a flute player (Αὐλητὴς) may suggest that they were Thracian, for that epithet is not found among the many attached to Ares in the Greek and Hellenistic culture, all of which stress his warlike attributes, cruelty, lack of restraint etc. The epithet can be explained however, by the connection between Ares Dionysus in the Thracian culture. Described as a flute player, Dionysus was known in Thrace as a god of war, and Ares, who like Dionysus originated in Thrace, is a nickname for the latter or his stand-in, or even his twin*» avec comme conséquence le fait que le serment «*may be attributed to the garrison in the city citadel at the time of the Revolt*» et «*seems to contain some indication of the Thracian descent of at least some of the soldiers. These Thracians were indigenous, probably equipped as semi-heavies in the Thracian style which was somewhat lighter than the other semi-heavies of the period*»[44].

Comme on peut le voir, cette interprétation s'appuie sur l'argument que le serment était prêté à Ares Aulétès : les soldats qui adoraient ce dieu ne pouvaient être que des Thraces, car cette variante d'épithète cultuel est par ailleurs inconnue dans le monde grec ; si un groupe de Thraces se trouvait dans l'Acra de Jérusalem, c'est qu'une unité de Thraces devait y être détachée. Cependant un examen plus attentif de la pierre a apporté de nouvelles précisions, et une nouvelle lecture de l'inscription a reconsidéré le caractère divin du porteur du nom d'Ares, désormais vu comme un être humain[45].

En fin de comptes, on pourrait considérer Seron comme ayant une origine thrace, et nous savons qu'au moins un soldat (un cavalier) thrace se trouvait dans la Judée à l'époque de la révolte des Maccabées. Il est tout à fait possible d'en conclure qu'il y avait une unité de Thraces – cette fois-ci, des cavaliers. Pour ce qui est des autres conjectures (à savoir, s'il y avait aussi une unité des fantassins, des «*semi-heavies*» ou si ces unités étaient cantonnée à Iamnia ou dans l'Acra de Jérusalem, ou s'il s'agissait des descendants des colons militaires thraces, peut-être des mercenaires à l'origine, ou encore s'il s'agissait des mercenaires qu'on avait fait venir d'Europe), il faudrait adopter la bonne devise des sceptiques et suspendre là notre jugement.

II. Kendebaios

«Sous Antiochos VII Sidétès, un stratège séleucide, dans la lutte contre Simon, porte le nom thrace (?) de Kendebaios»[46].

Cette phrase de Marcel Launey pose (ou perpétue) un faux problème, c'est-à-dire l'origine thrace de Kendebaios. Il est vrai que le radical κενθος, *centhus*, *centus*, κεντιος,

---

[43] *SEG* XXX (1980), 483 sqq. (lemma par H.W. Pleket)= *CIJud* I1, 39 *sqq.*, no. 1 (lemma par Eran Lupu).
[44] Bar Kochva 1989, 119 sq.
[45] E. Lupu, lemma pour *CIJud* I1, 40, no. 1. Voir aussi Ricl 2006, 51-57.
[46] Launey 1949, I, 389, 621; I Mac., 15, 36 Tite Live, *Ant. Jud.* 13, 225. Sur Kendebaios, voir: Grainger 1997, 99; Savalli-Lestrade 1998, 84, no. 85.

centius, κενθις etc., soit comme suffixe, soit comme préfixe, participe à la formation des beaucoup de noms thraces[47], et donc il serait extrêmement tentant de rapprocher le nom du stratège séleucide de l'onomastique thrace. Et pourtant, les savants qui ont commenté les inscriptions de Lycie (comme, e.g., Adolph Wilhelm[48] ou Louis Robert[49]) ont rencontré plusieurs occurrences de diverses variantes de ce nom, telles Κενδηβες, Κενδηβου, Κενηβης, qui étaient très proches de ceux recensés par Sundwall dans son catalogue des noms Lyciens : Κανδηβα, Κενδιβης, Κενδηβις, Κενδηβιος et le toponyme Κανδυβα[50]. Notre Kendebaios a donc toutes les chances d'être un Pisidien ou, mieux encore, un Lycien (ce qui conviendrait très bien pour un stratège royal séleucide de l'époque d'Antiochos Sidétès, qui coïncide avec le moment de la main mise des Romains sur Pergame et les dépendances de ce royaume dans la région des détroits).

Il aurait été trop beau d'avoir un Thrace comme stratège ayant l'importance du rang de Kendebaios : cela reste à attendre, peut-être, des découvertes futures.

III. Une colonie de soldats thraces en Perse

Un stratagème de Polyen nous présente une histoire qui se passe en Perse, à l'époque séleucide mais à une date qui reste à déterminer[51] : «*Seilès ayant dessein de faire mourir trois mille Perses qui voulaient se soulever, feignit que Séleuchus lui avait écrit des lettres menaçantes, mais qu'il voulait se servir de leur secours pour le prévenir. Pour prendre conseil avec eux là-dessus, il leur donna rendez-vous au village de Randa. Ils le crurent, et vinrent l'y trouver. Il y avait tout auprès un lieu creux et marécageux, où Seilès fit mettre en embuscade trois cents cavaliers macédoniens et thraces, et trois mille fantassins armés de toutes pièces, avec ordre, quand ils verraient élever un écu d'airain, de fondre sur ceux qu'ils trouveraient assemblés, et de les mettre à mort. L'écu fut levé, et l'embuscade donnant sur les trois mille Perses, les extermina tous.*»[52]

---

[47] Detschew 1976², 239 *sqq.*; Sturtevant 1926, 235-249.
[48] Wilhelm A., *Griechische Inschrift aus Klaeinasien*, SB Berlin 1932, 858 = Wilhelm 1974, II, 402: „Ich kann nicht umhin, mit diesen Namen den des Kendaivbo~ IG XII 8, 159 zusammenzubringen; C. Fredrich bemerkt, Κενδαιβιον eundem esse atque Kendebaion Antiochi Sidetae ducem editores suspicantur. At nomina at stirpe Kend derivata in Thracia saepius inveniuntur'".
[49] Robert 1938, 280 : «*Cf. le nom pisidien et lycien Κενδηβας, Κενδηβης, Κενδηβιος* (Ad. Wilhelm, Sitzungsber. Ak. Berlin. 1932, 1858, rétablissant Κενδη[β]ας dans un épitaphe d'Arykanda maltraitée par B.Pace)». Notons en passant l'erreur de la référence de Louis Robert, qui passe telle quelle chez Ivana Savalli-Lestrade.
[50] Sundwall 1913, 92, 101.
[51] Gutschmid 1888, 27 *sqq.*; Niese 1899, II, 163; Launey 1949, I, 374; Bar-Kochva 1979, 33 *sqq.*, 50 *sqq.*; Sekunda 1994, 17 *sqq.*; Grainger 1997, 116.
[52] Polyen, 7, 39, «Σείλης τρισχιλίους Περσῶν νεωτερίζοντας κτεῖναι βουλόμενος ἐσκήψατο Σέλευκον αὐτῷ δι' ἐπιστολῆς χαλεπῶς ἀπειλεῖν· αὐτὸς δὲ τῇ τούτων συμμαχίᾳ χρησάμενος ἐθέλειν αὐτὸν προλαβεῖν. ὅπως δ' ἂν βουλὴν ἀγάγοιεν, συνέταξεν αὐτοῖς ἀπαντᾶν ἐς κώμην Ῥάνδα καλουμένην. οἱ μὲν πιστεύσαντες ἧκον, ὁ δὲ, ἦν γὰρ ἕλος βαθὺ καὶ κοῖλον ὑπὸ τὴν κώμην, ἐνταῦθα Μακεδόνων καὶ Θρακῶν ἱππεῖς τριακοσίους, ὁπλίτας τρισχιλίους ἀποκρύψας συνέταξεν, ὅταν ἴδωσι πέλτην χαλκῆν ἀρθεῖσαν, ἐκδραμόντας ἀναιρῆσαι πάντας τοὺς ἠθροισμένους. ἀνεδείχθη μὲν ἡ πέλτη, οἱ δὲ ἐκδραμόντες τοὺς τρισχιλίους Πέρσας κατεφόνευσαν.», traduction Liskenne et Savan, 1840, dont nous avons gardé telle quelle l'orthographe tout particulière des noms comme Seilès et Séleucos.

En partant d'un passage de Diodore[53] qui décrit l'aile gauche de l'armée d'Eumène de Cardia à la bataille de Gabiène (316 avant J.-C.), et où l'on retrouve des Thraces (selon toute apparence, des cavaliers) installés comme colons en Iran à un moment entre le règne d'Alexandre le Grand et 316 avant J.-C., Bezalel Bar Kochva[54] déduit que dans le texte de Polyen il s'agit de soldats provenant d'une colonie militaire de Thraces, en Perse, dont les descendants seraient à retrouver à la bataille de Raphia. Cependant il s'agit de cavaliers thraces, et non d'archers comme ceux de Raphia, et le stratagème de Polyen nous les présente en tant que soldats de l'armée d'un roi Séleucos en service en Perse, et non comme de colons militaires. D'ailleurs, les Thraces de Polyen sont à retrouver quelque part en Perside, dans le voisinage du village de Rhanda, tandis que les *katoikoi* de Diodore sont venus des Satrapies Supérieures, sans doute pas de Perside, mais des régions voisines de la Paropanisade, donc de l'autre côté de l'Iran actuel.

Pour ce qui est de la date de l'incident, il y a trois hypothèses :
a. l'époque de Séleucos Ier [55]
b. le règne de Séleucos II[56], de toute façon, au IIIe siècle[57]
c. le règne de Séleucos IV[58]

Commençons par remarquer qu'il est très difficile de connecter Polyen 7, 39 avec Polyen 7, 40, quoique la plupart des modernes l'aient fait, considérant que la suite de l'histoire de l'embuscade de Seilès devait être la stratagème suivante, celle qui décrit comment « trois mille hommes de ceux qui étaient venus de Perse » se font massacrer par un certain Oborzos[59]; mais on ignore s'il s'agit des ceux qui ont monté l'embuscade décrite par Polyen dans le stratagème précédent. Les deux stratagèmes n'ont en commun que le lieu de l'action (la Perside), ce qui est insuffisant pour conclure qu'il y a une continuité entre les deux. Ce détail est important, car on a tendance à lier l'embuscade de Seilès avec les monnaies frappée en Perside par les *fratadara*, notamment par Vahuberz[60] (notre Oborzos, chez Polyen VII, 40), et ensuite d'en tirer des conclusions, notamment d'ordre chronologique.

Il y a eu une colonie militaire de Thraces dans les Satrapies Supérieures, peut-être même dans la satrapie de la Perside, mais il est très difficile de lier entre eux les trois passages de Diodore et de Polyen, et force est de se résigner à tout ignorer sur le sort des cavaliers thraces que le destin a jeté sur les contrées de l'Asie centrale. Il est cependant très probable que les Séleucides ont essayé de maintenir la *katoikia* thrace implantée jadis par Alexandre.

---

[53] Diod. 19, 27, 5 : ἑξῆς δ' ἦσαν πεντακόσιοι μὲν ἐκ Παροπανισαδῶν, οἱ δὲ τούτοις ἴσοι Θρᾷκες ἐκ τῶν ἄνω κατοικιῶν, « venaient ensuite cinq cent hommes du pays des Paropamisades, ainsi qu'un nombre égal de Thraces, venus des colonies des régions supérieures (...) », traduction Fr. Bizière, 1975.
[54] Bar-Kochva 1979, 50 *sqq.*
[55] Launey 1949, I, 374.
[56] Newell, *ESM*, 160 *sqq.*; Eddy 1961, 75 *sqq.*
[57] Bevan 1902, I, 291.
[58] Will Ed., I, 1979², 280 et 1982, t. II, 350.
[59] Polyen, 7, 40, « τρισχιλίους ἄνδρας τῶν ἐν τῇ Περσίδι κατοίκων », traduction Liskenne et Savan, 1840.
[60] Pour le monnayage de Vahuberz/Oborzos, voir Hill 1922, CLXVII *sqq.*, 197, 1 –3, pl. XXVIII, 10-12 et Sellwood 1983, 299-321 (surtout 301 *sqq.*).

IV. La stèle de Ménas

Une stèle de Nikaia[61] a conservé le récit des exploits et de la mort d'un cavalier bithynien, dans un beau poème funéraire : «(...) *Fantassin, au premier rang, j'ai soutenu le choc de la cavalerie quand nous combattîmes dans la plaine du Kouros ; après avoir abattu un Thrace en armes, puis un Mysien, je tombai valeureusement. Aussi peut-on louer l'agile fils de Bioéris, le Bithynien Ménas, cet officier d'élite* [...] *Mais moi, qui près du courant du Phrygios, combattais pour ma patrie et mes illustres parents, la terre me reçut, glorieux* (...)»[62]

On voit bien que Ménas a pris part à la bataille de Kouroupédion[63], dont la date a fait naître un long débat parmi les savants. La plupart des Modernes avait opté pour une des trois conjectures suivantes: juillet-août 282[64], avril-mai 281[65] et juillet-août 281[66]. L'enjeu était rien moins que tout l'échafaudage de la chronologie hellénistique, vu que la mort de Séleucos Nicator survient sept mois après la bataille de Kouroupédion, selon les dires de Justin[67], et que la mort de ce roi est un repère pour définir l'invasion des Celtes en Europe. Heureusement, la publication d'une tablette cunéiforme[68] a fourni une réponse situant la mort de Séleucos Ier entre le 25 août et le 24 septembre 281, ce qui place la bataille de Kouroupédion en février-mars 281.

Force est toutefois de constater que l'inscription ne nous offre aucun élément de datation, et que la bataille de Kouroupédion dont il est question sur la pierre peut être n'importe quelle autre bataille que nous ignorons et qui a pu avoir lieu dans cette plaine. La suggestion selon laquelle la bataille dont il serait question dans l'inscrip-

---

[61] Mendel 1900, 380 *sqq.* ; Keil 1902, 257-262 ; Bouché-Leclercq A., 1914, II, 533 *sqq.*; Hiller von Gaertringen 1926, no. 91; Pfühl 1932, 2-7 (avec photo); Pfühl 1933, 751-4; Robert 1933, 490 n. 3 (remarquant la similarité de la graphie d'un A à barre brisée avec celle des autres inscriptions contemporaines à la fin du règne de Lysimaque); Launey, 1950, t. II, 370, 434, 438, 448, 791, 806-7, 1211; Peek 1955, no. 1965; Seibert 1983, 166; Sahin 1979- 1987, no. 751 ; Corsten 1985, no. 98; Hammond, Walbank, 1988, 241; Lund 1992, 206, 259; Hannestad 1996, 71 *sqq.*; Carsana 1996, 141, n. D2; Merkelbach, Stauber 2001, 170 *sqq.*; Couilloud-le-Dinahet 2003, 76 ; Dana 2011, 106, n. 49 ; Avram *s.p.*, no. 540.

[62] Cette traduction française est reprise de Launey 1950, II, 807. L'original grec donne : πεζομάχος δ' ἱππεῖας ἐνὶ προμάχοισιν ἔμεινα. / ὁππότε περ Κούρου μαρνάμεθ' ἐμ πεδίωι./[Θ]ρήϊκα δὲ προπάροιθε βαλὼν ἐνὶ τεύχεσιν ἄνδρα / [κ]αὶ Μυσόν, μεγάλας κάτθανον ἀμφ' ἀρετᾶς· / τῶι <τ>ις ἐπαινήσειε θοὸν Βιοήριος υἷα / Βιθυνὸν Μηνᾶν, ἔξοχον ἡγεμόνα. /[...] αὐτὰρ ἐμὲ Φρυγίοιο παρὰ ῥοόν, ἀμφί τε πάτρης, / ἀμφί τε κυδαλίμων μαρνάμενον τοκέων /εὐκλέα δέξατο γαῖα μετὰ προμάχοισι δαμέντα.

[63] Date et localisation: Euseb., *Chron.*, 1, pp. 233-4 (éd. Schoene); App. *Syr.*, 42, 329 (qui; malgré une opinion assez répandue parmi les savants –e.g. Bürchner, R.E., X, s.v. Κόρου πεδίον, col. 1440-, ne nomme pas Kouroupédion en tant que tel, mais se contente de dire que la bataille a eu lieu περὶ Φρυγίαν τὴν ἐφ᾽ Ἑλλησπόντῳ /). Voir aussi Beloch 1904, t: III 2, 384-8, 1927, t. IV 1², 458-61 ; Bouché-Leclercq 1913 – 1914, I – II, 48, °532 *sqq.*; Magie 1950, II, 727, n. 5; Vitucci G., 1953, 17 *sqq.*; Heinen 1972, 20-36 ; Will 1979², I, 100 *sqq.* ; Seibert 1983, 165-7 (avec un très utile status quaestionis); Mehl 1986, 296-298; Lund 1992, 205 *sqq.*, 259; Grainger 1997, 739.

[64] Corradi 1916 = Corradi 1929, 64 *sqq.*
[65] Droysen 1843 (1885), III, 630-633.
[66] Beloch 1904, III 2, 384-8, 1927, t. IV² 2, 107 *sqq.*
[67] Just. 17, 2, 4: «post menses admodum septem».
[68] *BM* 35603 ; Sachs & Wiseman 1954.

tion de Ménas serait celle de Magnésie[69] (donc cent ans plus tard) n'est pas convaincante car on aurait du mal à voir un officier bithynien combattant pour sa patrie à la bataille de Magnésie en 188 avant J.-C. Il est bien connu en effet que le royaume de Bithynie est resté neutre durant la guerre antiochique, malgré la démarche du roi Antiochos III pour persuader Prusias Ier de se joindre à lui à cause surtout – aux dires de Polybe et de Tite Live – d'une belle lettre écrite par Scipion (appuyée par une ambassade de C. Livius Salinator) qui expliquait au roi de Bithynie que Rome n'était point l'ennemie des rois, mais tout au contraire[70]. Cette neutralité s'est d'ailleurs avérée coûteuse, car le traité d'Apamée obligeait Prusias à céder la Phrygie Epictète. A moins qu'on ne fasse de ce texte la seule preuve de la participation du royaume de Bithynie à la guerre antiochique, il vaut donc mieux abandonner cette hypothèse.

Notre Ménas est mort, très probablement, pendant une guerre défensive et il est vrai que, ainsi que la plupart des cités grecques du monde anatolien, la Bithynie avait, elle aussi, tout intérêt à voir brisé une fois pour toutes le pouvoir de Lysimaque, car les relations entre les deux royaumes n'ont point été amicales[71]. Mais on voit mal comment un corps bithynien aurait pu participer à la bataille de Kouroupédion de 281 avant J.-C. aux côtés de Séleucos Ier (comment aurait-il pu autrement tuer un Thrace et un Mysien ? Il a dû, le pense-t-on d'habitude, combattre contre les soldats de Lysimaque). Il faudrait ainsi supposer l'existence d'un traité d'alliance (ou au moins d'une Entente informelle)[72] entre Prusias Ier et Séleucos Ier, afin de justifier la mort de Ménas en défendant sa patrie. Mais, dans ce cas, on comprend mal pourquoi Lysimaque aurait permis à un contingent bithynien de traverser une bonne partie de son royaume asiatique pour se joindre au Séleucide afin d'augmenter l'armée de son rival, lorsqu'il avait tout le temps et tous les moyens de l'en empêcher (si on garde à l'esprit la position géographique de la Bithynie).

Ménas n'était pas un mercenaire, car il combattait «pour sa patrie et ses illustres parents », et donc l'unité d'infanterie légère qu'il commandait a dû participer a une bataille qui aurait pu décider du sort de la Bithynie. Voilà une bonne raison de partager l'avis de Giovanni Vitucci : «non è affato escluso che ivi possa trattarsi di una lotta sostenuta posteriomente dai Bitini contro i Pergamo»[73].

La solution du problème tient donc à deux variables, que seules des découvertes à venir pourraient éclairer :

1. Soit la bataille de Kouroupédion de notre inscription est celle de 281 avant J.-C. (chose suggérée par la paléographie de l'inscription, selon Louis Robert) : dans ce cas, il serait plus naturel de penser que la Bithynie a dû se retrouver dans les rangs

---

[69] Hannestad 1996, 72; Merkelbach & Stauber 2001, 170 ; Couilloud-le-Dinahet 2003, 76.
[70] Pol. 21, 11; Tite Live, 37, 35, 4-15; Hansen 1947, 92 sq.; Vitucci 1953, 54 sqq.; Will 1982², II, 212, 228 (un peu contradictoire, car d'abord il range Prusias Ier de Bithynie «dans le camp anti-séleucide» pour parler ensuite de sa «neutralité») ; Gruen 1984, 86, 151, 225, 239, 550, 638.
[71] Memnon 20, 3 = FHG 3, p. 536; Vitucci 1953, 16 sqq. Le roi de Bithynie, Zipoïtes, l'avait maintes fois emporté contre les stratèges de Lysimaque, et, une fois, contre Lysimaque lui-même.
[72] Cette hypothèse semble être agréée par plusieurs modernes, comme Launey 1950, II, 434, 438- mais il est très peu probable que Ménas fut un mercenaire, voir infra; Vitucci 1953, 18.
[73] Vitucci, op. cit.

des alliés de Lysimaque (car il arrive souvent que les puissances mineures parviennent à trouver un moyen de s'entendre avec leurs voisins plus grands qu'elles ont vaincu sur les champs de batailles. Après plusieurs expéditions, il est probable que Lysimaque ait pu arriver à la conclusion qu'il vaut mieux avoir l'alliance de Prusias que le détruire. Ce serait, d'ailleurs, la répétition du même scénario de l'histoire de Dromichaitès et de Lysimaque). Comme l'armée de Séleucos Ier a pu comprendre dans ses rangs des Thraces (les colons militaires des satrapies supérieures, si jamais cela a été le cas), il n'y a rien qui s'opposerait à ce que Ménas ait fait ses deux victimes parmi les soldats de Séleucos (et non de Lysimaque), et dans ce cas, la stèle de Nikaia dont il est question serait une preuve supplémentaire que les Thraces ont pu être présents dans l'armée séleucide dès le début du IIIe siècle avant J.-C.

2. Soit cette bataille de Kouroupédion n'est pas celle de 281, mais une autre du IIIe siècle, qui impliquait la Bithynie et une puissance étrangère inconnue qui employait des Thraces et des Mysiens ; or, parmi les puissances qui ont menacé le royaume de Bithynie et qui ont pu bénéficier de l'apport militaire des Thraces, les Séleucides sont de bons candidats. On pourrait penser, par exemple, à la défaite du général séleucide Hérmogènes d'Aspendos, en 280 avant J.-C. devant les forces de Zipoitès, le roi de Bithynie[74], sans rien dire d'Antiochos Hiérax ou d'Achaios, vice-rois séleucides à l'origine, devenus ensuite des usurpateurs (d'ailleurs, Achaios a été à un pas d'entrer en conflit avec la Bithynie, lors de la guerre des détroits de 220 avant J.-C., quand il avait promis son appui aux Byzantins, alors en guerre avec Prusias et Rhodes[75]) et qui ont pu se heurter à leur voisin du nord-ouest de l'Anatolie.

Conclusion

Arrivés à la fin de notre démarche, force est de constater qu'on ignore plus qu'on ne connaît du destin des Thraces dans les rangs de l'armée séleucide. On n'a qu'à envier les historiens de l'Egypte lagide qui sont en mesure d'entreprendre des études sociologiques d'une armée qu'ils peuvent envisager aussi bien en temps de guerre qu'en temps de paix. Il reste beaucoup à attendre des futures recherches archéologiques, les seules en état de nous apporter davantage d'informations.[76]

Dans l'état actuel de nos connaissances, fondées sur des informations éparpillées çà et là, qui nous portent partout à travers l'Empire séleucide, de Thrace jusqu'aux Satrapies supérieures de l'Iran et de la Bactriane jusqu'aux villes de Judée, et ne pouvant étudier que l'armée séleucide en temps de guerre, sans rien dire de ce qui se passe dans les garnisons en temps de paix, tout ce que nous pouvons faire est d'examiner avec soin toutes les informations disponibles et de garder que celles vraiment sûres.

---

[74] Memn. 15 = *FHG* III, 534 sq.; Bengtson 1952, III, 200; Vitucci 1953, 20; Will 1979², I, 142.
[75] Pol. 4, 47, 8, 47-52; Vitucci 1953, 41; Will 1982², II, 46 *sqq.*
[76] Il ne faudrait pas négliger l'apport des études onomastiques, comme celle de Dana 2011, 106 *sqq.* qui s'attaque au problème de l'installation de colons thraces en Asie mineure par les Séleucides, auquel nous n'avons pas touché ici car notre objet était d'identifier les occurrences de ces Thraces ayant fait effectivement partie de l'armée séleucide.

Ainsi, conjecturer sur l'armement et l'équipement des unités thraces dans l'armée séleucide est une entreprise risquée, car on a vu qu'on peut facilement commencer la recherche d'une unité des cavaliers pour aboutir à une unité d'archers. Avec ce qu'on connaît déjà, tout ce que nous pouvons dire est que les Séleucides ont employé des Thraces dans les troupes à cheval ainsi que dans les détachements de l'infanterie. L'armée royale séleucide rassemblée en vue d'une campagne ne semble pas avoir compté des cavaliers Thraces, mais seulement des fantassins (très probablement, des fantassins légers). Les unités séleucides détachées dans le provinces, faisant le service de contrôle et de répression des éventuelles révoltes, ont compris aussi des unités de cavalerie thraces (c'est le cas de ces Thraces que Polyen nous montre en Perside et de ceux qu'on peut deviner en Judée, à travers les livres des Maccabées).

Le peu de choses qu'on puisse dire sur la méthode de recrutement nous les montre surtout attirés par des beaux objets en métal précieux (comme ceux qui ont essayé de défendre Kypséla) – ce qui pourrait nous expliquer l'importance réduite de la frappe de monnaie dans l'atelier de Lysimacheia. Mais il ne faudrait pas pour autant exagérer l'importance du stratagème d'Antiochos II – Polyen l'a gardée parmi les ruses à recommander justement parce que c'était une situation qui n'arrivait pas trop souvent dans la guerre. L'étude des trésors (des objets en métaux précieux ainsi que des monnaies) est la seule en mesure de nous promettre des bons résultats afin de pouvoir mieux éclairer les problèmes posés par le mercenariat thrace à l'époque hellénistique, et dans l'Orient[77]. Ainsi que les inscriptions nouvelles de l'Asie Mineure, de la Syrie, de la Palestine et de l'Iran, qui se font toujours attendre. Mais pas pour longtemps, on l'espère.

Adrian George DUMITRU
Université Paris-Sorbonne (Paris IV)

Abréviations

ESM = E.T. Newell, *The Coinage of the Eastern Seleucid Mints, from Seleucus I to Antiochus III*, Numismatic Studies 1 (New York 1938).

FGH = *Fragmenta Historicum Graecorum*, ed. Müller C. & Th. ed (Paris 1849-1885).

Bibliographie

Adam 1982 = R. Adam, Tite Live. *Histoire Romaine. Introduction* (Paris, Belles Lettres, 1982).

Anson 2004 = E.M. Anson, *Eumenes of Cardia, A Greek among Macedonians* (Boston & Leiden 2004).

---

[77] Cf. l'étude d'Aliénor Rufin Solas, dans le présent volume.

Avram 2003 = A. Avram, «Antiochos II Théos, Ptolémée II Philadephe et la Mer Noire», *CRAI* 97 (2003) 1181-1213.

Avram s.p., = A. Avram, *Prosopographia Ponti Euxini Externa*, sous presse.

Bar-Kochva 1979 = B. Bar-Kochva, *The Seleucid Army. Organization and tactics in the great campaigns* (Cambridge 1979).

Bar-Kochva 1989 = B. Bar-Kochva, *Judas Maccabaeus* (Cambridge 1989).

Beloch 1904-1925-1927 = K.J. Beloch, *Griechische Geschichte* (Strasbourg, t. III 1-2, 1904, Berlin-Leipzig, t. IV 12 1925, t. IV 12 1927).

Bengtson 1952 = H. Bengtson, *Die Strategie in die hellenistischen Zeit. Ein Beitrag zum antiken Staatsrecht* (München, t. III, 1952).

Bevan 1902 = E. Bevan, *The House of Seleucus* (Londres 1902).

Bevenot 1931 = H. Bevenot, *Die Beiden Makkabäerbücher* (Bonn 1931).

Billows 1997 = R.A. Billows, *Antigonos the One-Eyed and the Creation of a Hellenistic Kingdom* (Berkeley 1997).

Bouché-Leclercq 1913-1914 = A. Bouché-Leclercq, *Histoire des Séleucides* (Paris, tt. I – II, 1913 – 1914).

Bunge 1971 = J.G. Bunge, *Untersuchungen zum zweiten Makkabäerbuch. Quellenkritische, literarische, chronologische und historische Untersuchungen zum zweiten Makkabäerbuch als Quelle syrisch-palästinensischer Geschichte im 2. Jh. v. Chr.* (Bonn 1971).

Bunge 1976 = J.G. Bunge, «Die Feiern Antiochos' IV in Daphne im Herbst 166», *Chiron* 6 (1976) 53-71.

Cardinali 1910 = G. Cardinali, «Ancora i confini nella pace di Antioco», *Klio* 10 (1910) 249-251.

Carsana 1996 = C. Carsana, *Le Dirigenze citadine nello stato seleucidico* (Como 1996).

Cohen 1978 = G.M. Cohen, *The Seleucid Colonies. Studies in Founding; Administration and Organization* (Wiesbaden 1978).

Corradi 1929 = G. Corradi, *Studi ellenistici* (Turin 1929).

Corradi 1916 = G. Corradi, «La fine del regno di Seleuco Nicatore», *RFIC* 44 (1916) 297-318, 409-423 = Corradi 1929, 64 *sqq.*

Corsten 1985 = Th. Corsten, *Die Inschriften von Kios, IK 29* (Bonn 1985).

Couilloud-le-Dinahet 2003 = M.-Th. Couilloud-le-Dinahet, «Les rituels funéraires en Asie Mineure et Syrie à l'époque hellénistique (jusqu'au milieu du Ier siècle av. J.-C.)», dans F. Prost (éd.), *L'Orient méditerannéen de la mort d'Alexandre aux campagnes de Pompée. Cités et royaumes à l'époque hellénistique. Actes du colloque international de la SOPHAU, Rennes, 4-6 avril 2003* (Rennes, 2003) 65-95.

Dana 2011 = D. Dana, «Les Thraces dans les armées hellénistiques : essai d'"histoire par les noms"», dans J.-C. Couvenhes, S. Crouzet, S. Péré-Noguès (éds.), *Pratiques et identités culturelles des armées hellénistiques du monde méditerranéen*, Ausonius, Scripta Antiqua (Bordeaux 2011) 87-115.

Delev 2003 = P. Delev, «From Corupedion towards Pydna: Thrace in the Third Century», *Thracia* 15 (2003) 107-120.

De Sanctis 1913 = G. De Sanctis, *Storia dei Romani*, IV, 1 (Florence 1913).

Dimitriev 2003 = S. Dimitriev, «Livy's Evidence for the Apamean Settlement (188 B.C) », *AJAH* 21 (2003) 39-63.

Downey 1961 = G. Downey, *A History of Antioch in Syria from Seleucus to the Arab Conquest* (Princeton 1961).

Droysen 1843 (1885) = J.G. Droysen, *Geschichte des hellenismus*, Gotha III (1843), (éd. fr. Paris 1885).

Dumitru 1999 = A. Dumitru, «Considérations sur la politique romaine envers l'Orient hellénistique. La paix d'Apamée», *Erasmus* 9-10 (1999) 25-34.

Eddy 1961 = S.K. Eddy, *The King is Dead. Studies in Near Eastern Resistance to Hellenism 334-31 B.C.* (Lincoln, Nebraska 1961).

Elvers 1994 = K.-L. Elvers, «Der Eid der Berenike und ihrer Söhne», *Chiron* 24 (1994) 241-266.

Detschew 1976 = D. Detschew, *Die Thrakischen Sprachreste* (Vienne 1976^2).

Galili 1967-1975 = E. Galili, «Raphia 217 B.C.E. Revisited», *Scripta Classica Israelica*, 3 (1967-1975) 52-156.

Giovanini 1982 = A. Giovanini, «La clause territoriale de la paix d'Apamée», *Athenaeum* 60 (1982) 224-236.

Grainger 1990 = J.D. Grainger, *Seleukos Nikator. Constructing a Hellenistic Kingdom* (Londres & New York 1990).

Grainger 1996 = J.D. Grainger, «Antiochus III in Thrace», *Historia* 45 (1996) 336-340.

Grainger 1997 = J.D. Grainger, *A Seleukid Prosopography and Gazetteer* (Leiden – New York – Köln 1997).

Grainger 2002 = J.D. Grainger, *The Roman War of Antiochos the Great* (Leiden & Boston, 2002).

Grainger 2010 = J.D. Grainger, *The Syrian Wars* (Leiden & Boston, 2010).

Griffith 1934 = G.T, Griffith *The Mercenaries of the Hellenistic World* (Cambridge 1934).

Gruen 1984 = E.S. Gruen, *The Hellenistic World and the Coming of Rome* (Berkeley 1984).

Gutschmid 1888 = A. von Gutschmid, *Geschichte Irans und seiner Nachbarländer von Alexander der Grosse bis zum Untergang der Arsaciden* (Berlin 1888).

Habicht 1995 = Chr. Habicht, *Athen. Die Geschichte der Stadt in hellenistischer Zeit* (Munich 1995).

Hammond & Walbank 1988 = N.G.L. Hammond, F.W. Walbank, *A History of Macedonia* (Oxford, t.III, 1988).

Hannestad 1996 = L. Hannestad, «'This contributes in no small way to one's Reputation'. The Bithynian Kings and Greek Culture» dans Bilde P. & alii (eds.), *Aspects of Hellenistic Kingship* (Aarhus 1996) 67-99.

Hansen 1947 = E.V. Hansen, *The Attalids of Pergamon* (Ithaca N.Y., 1947).

Heinen 1972 = H. Heinen, *Untersuchungen zur hellenistischen geschichte des 3. Jh. zur Geschichte der Zeit des Ptolemaios Keraunos und zum Chremonideischen Krieg* (Stuttgart, 1972).

Hill 1922 = G.F. Hill, *A Catalogue of the Greek Coins in the British Museum: Arabia, Mesopotamia and Persia* (Londres 1922).

Hiller von Gaertringen 1926 = F. Hiller von Gaertringen, *Historische griechische Epigramme* (Bonn 1926).

Holleaux 1957 = M. Holleaux, *Etudes d'épigraphie et d'histoire Grecque* (Paris, t. V, 1957).

Houghton & Lorber 2002 = A. Houghton, C. Lorber, Seleucid Coins. *A Comprehensive Catalogue*, New York & Lancaster, Part I, Vol. 1-2 : *Seleucus I through Antiochus III*, 2002.

Kahrstedt 1923 = U. Kahrstedt, «Zwei Urkunden aus Polybios. I Die Westgrenze des Seleukidischenreiches seit 188», *Nachrichten von der Königlichen Gesellschaft der Wissenschaften zu Göttingen* (1923) 93-98.

Keil 1902 = B. Keil, «Κορου πεδιον», Rev. Philol., 26 (1902) 257-262.

Launey 1949-1950 = M. Launey, *Recherches sur les armées hellénistiques* (Paris, t. I-II, 1949-1950).

Le Rider 1988 = G. Le Rider, «L'atelier séleucide de Lysimachie», QT 17 (1988) 195-207.

Le Rider 1992 = G. Le Rider, «Les clauses financières des traités de 189 et 188» BCH 1992, 267-277.

Liebmann-Francfort 1969 = Th. Liebmann-Francfort, *La frontière orientale dans la politique extérieure de la république romaine* (Bruxelles 1969).

Lund 1992 = H.S. Lund, Lysimachus. *A study in early hellenistic kingship* (Londres & New York 1992).

Magie 1950 = D.D. Magie, *Roman Rule in Asia Minor* (Princeton 1950, tt. I-II).

McDonald 1967 = A.H. McDonald, «The Treaty of Apamea (188 B.C.)», JRS 57 (1967) 1-8.

McDonald & Walbank 1969 = A.H. McDonald, F.W. Walbank, «The Treaty of Apamea: The Naval Clauses», JRS 59 (1969) 30-39.

McShane 1964 = R.B. McShane, *The Foreign Policy of the Attalids of Pergamum* (Urbana 1964).

Mehl 1986 = A. Mehl, *Seleukos Nikator und sein Reich* (Louvain 1986).

Mendel 1900 = G. Mendel, «Inscriptions de Bithynie», BCH 24 (1900) 361-423.

Merkelbach & Stauber 2001 = Rh. Merkelbach, J. Stauber, *Steinepigramme aus dem griechischen Osten. Bd. II. Die NordKüste Kleinasiens. Marmarameer und Pontos* (München 2001).

Mommsen 1879 = Th. Mommsen, *Der Friede mit Antiochus und die Kriegzüge des Cn. Manlius Vulso*, Römische Forschungen, II (Berlin 1879) 511-545.

Morkholm 1966 = O. Morkholm, *Antiochus IV of Syria* (Copenhague 1966).

Niese 1893-1899-1903 = B. Niese, *Geschichte der griechischen und makedonischen Staaten seit der Schlacht bei Chaeroneea* (Gotha, tt. I-III, 1893-1899-1903).

Pais 1926 = E. Pais, *Histoire Romaine. I. Des Origines à l'achèvement de la conquête (133 av. J.-C.)* (Paris 1926).

Paltiel 1979 = E. Paltiel, «The Treaty of Apamea and the Later Seleucids», *Antichton* 13 (1979) 30-42.

Peek 1955 = W. Peek, *Griechische Versinschriften* (Berlin 1955).

Pfuhl 1932 = E. Pfuhl, «Zwei Kriegerabmäler», *A.A.* (1932) 2-7.

Pfuhl 1933 = E. Pfuhl, «Zum Grabstein des Bithyners Menas», *A. A.* (1933) 751-4.

Ricl 2006 = M. Ricl, «A confession inscription from Jerusalem», *Studia Classica Israelica*, 25 (2006) 51-57.

Robert 1933 = L. Robert, «Notes d'épigraphie hellénistique», *BCH* 57 (1933) 485-491.

Robert 1938 = L. Robert, *Etudes épigraphiques et philologiques*, Paris 1938.

Rosivach 2000 = V. Rosivach, «The Thracians of the IG II2 1956», *Klio* 82 (2000) 379-381.

Sachs & Wiseman 1954 = A.J. Sachs, D.J. Wiseman, «A Babylonian King List of the Hellenistic Period», *Iraq* 16 (1954) 202-301.

Sahin 1979-1987= S. Sahin, *Katalog der antiken Inschriften des Museums von Iznik*, tt. I- II, IK 9-10 (Bonn 1979-1987).

Savalli-Lestrade 1998 = I. Savalli-Lestrade, *Les Philoi Royaux dans l'Asie hellénistique* Genève, 1998).

Schettino 1998 = M.T. Schettino, *Introduzione a Polieno* (Florence 1998).

Seibert 1983 = J. Seibert, *Das Zeitalter der Diadochen* (Darmstadt, 1983).

Sekunda 1994 = N. Sekunda, *Seleucid and Ptolemaic reformed armies 168-145 B.C. Volume I. The Seleucid Army under Antiochus IV Epiphanes* (Stockport 1994).

Sekunda 2003 = N. Sekunda, «OGIS 248 und die Söldnerregimente des Heeres Antiochos IV Epiphanes», Collectanea Classica Torunensia 14 (2003) 145-149.

Sekunda 2006 = N. Sekunda, *Hellenistic Infantry Reform in the 160's B.C.* (Gdansk 2006).

Sellwood 1983 = D. Sellwood, *Minor States in Southern Iran*, dans Yarshater E. (éd.), Cambridge History of Iran, t. III 1 (Cambridge 1983).

Strobel 1996 = K. Strobel, *Die Galater : Geschichte und Eigenart der Keltischen Staatenbildung auf den Boden des hellenistischen Kleinasien* (Berlin, I, 1996).

Sturtevant 1926 = E.H. Sturtevant, «Centaurs and Macedonian Kings», *CPh* 21 (1926) 235-249.

Sundwall 1913 = J. Sundwall, *Die einheimischen Namen der Lykier nebst einem Verzeichnisse kleinasiatischer Namenstämme* (Leipzig 1913).

Tarn 1938 = W.W. Tarn, *The Greeks in Bactria and India* (Cambridge 1938).

Venedikov 1976 = I. Venedikov, «Les migrations en Thrace», *Pulpudeva*, 2 (1976), 162-180.

Viereck 1909 = P. Viereck, «Die Festsetzung der Grenze im Frieden des Antiochus», *Klio* IX (1909) 371-375.

Vitucci 1953 = G. Vitucci, *Il Regno di Bitinia* (Rome 1953).

Youroukova 1982 = J. Youroukova, «La présence des monnaies de bronze des premiers séleucides en Thrace. Leur importance historique», dans Scheers S. (éd.), *Studia Paulo Naster Oblata. I. Numismatica Antiqua*, Orientalia Lovaniensia Analecta 12 (Louvain, 1982) 115-127.

Walbank 1957-1967-1979 = F.W. Walbank, *A Historical Commentary on Polybius* (Oxford, t. I-III, 1957-1967-1979).

Wilhelm 1974 = A. Wilhelm, *Akademieschriften zur griechischen Inschriftenkunde (1895-1951)* (Leipzig, t. II, 1974).

Will 1979-1982 = Ed. Will, *Histoire politique du monde hellénistique* 2 (Nancy, t. I-II, 1979-1982).

THE BURNING OF THE TEMPLE AT DELPHI, THE ROMAN GOVERNOR L. SCIPIO AND THE ROUT OF THE SCORDISCI

Peter DELEV

The Roman province of Macedonia inherited from the Macedonian kingdom of the Antigonids its vulnerability to invasions from its Thracian, Illyrian and Celtic neighbours in the north. Foremost among the main perpetrators were the Scordisci, a belligerent Gaulish tribal group which was established in the early third century BC on the right bank of the Danube and along the lower courses of its righthand tributaries, the Drava, the Sava and the Morava[1]. For some two centuries the Scordisci remained a major military power until, following a raid in Greece in which Delphi was sacked and the temple of Apollo burnt, they were crushed by a Roman general, L. Scipio. The date and circumstances of these last events remain controversial; the present paper attempts a re-examination of some of the pertaining problems.

First encounters with the Romans

In the late 140s, only a few years after the establishment of the province of Macedonia, the Romans suffered a major defeat at the hands of the Scordisci[2]. A few years later, the praetor M. Cosconius, governor of Macedonia in 135-134 BC, fought successfully with them, presumably after renewed incursions[3]. There are no records for the next 15 years or so, until the death of Sextus Pompeius, a *propraetor* of Macedonia in his second or third year of office at the time; he was killed in battle with the Scordisci in either 120 or 119 BC. His *quaestor* Titus Annius prevented with great effort a joint invasion of the province by the Scordisci and the Maedi under their prince Tipas and was honoured for this feat in a decree issued by the city of Lete near Thessaloniki in July 119 (day 20, month Panemos, year 29)[4].

In 114 B.C. Macedonia was placed in the care of a consul, C. Porcius Cato, presumably because of increased difficulties with the Scordisci and other barbarian neighbours. He sustained a large defeat at their hands, losing his whole army in

---

[1] On the Scordisci cf. Fluss 1921; Garašanin 1963; Alföldy 1964; Todorović 1974; Papazoglou 1978, 271-389.
[2] *Epit. Oxyr.* 54: „in Scordiscis cladis accepta". Brennan 2000, 227-228 dates the event to 141 BC.
[3] Liv. *Epit.* 56. Cf. Broughton 1951, 491; Sarikakis 1971, 44-45; Brennan 2000, 228.
[4] Dittenberger *Syll*³ 700. Cf. Cuntz 1918; Papazoglou 1978, 291, n. 62; Kallet-Marx 1995, 38; Brennan 2000, 521-522. The date of the inscription is by the Macedonian provincial era; the current attribution of its start to 148 and not 146 BC (cf. Tod 1919) places Panemos of year 29 in the summer of 119 (some authors however still use Dittenberger's date, 117 BC: cf. Gerov 1961, 171; Yordanov 1978, 22; Danov 1979, 105). The defeat of Pompeius occurred according to the Lete inscription «near Argos» (εἰς τοὺς κατὰ Ἄργος τόπους); this could not possibly be identified with Argos Orestikon at the border with Epirus, as suggested by Brennan (2000, 521). The battle most probably took place near the homonymous town in the Axios valley, presumably located near the village of Vodovrati, north-west of Stobi (Papazoglou 1978, 292, n. 63; 1988, 311-312).

battle[5]. The next three governors of Macedonia were also consuls; two of them received triumphs for important victories over the Scordisci, first C. Caecilius Metellus Caprarius (cos. 113) and then Marcus Minucius Rufus who stayed in the province for five years between 110 and 106; the victories of Minucius, one over the Scordisci and another over the Bessi and other Thracians, are noted in honorific decrees from Delphi and Europos[6]. A few years later, probably in 100 BC, a praetorian governor of Macedonia, T. Didius, also won a triumph, presumably for another major victory over the northern barbarians[7].

Julius Obsequens mentions under the year 655 a.u.c. (97 BC) renewed Roman actions against the Maedi and Dardanians, no doubt in retaliation for their continuing inroads on the territory of Macedonia[8]. Some authors would connect these events with (Manlius?) Vulso, probably another governor of Macedonia in this period, who according to Annius Florus had „penetrated the Rhodope and Haemus"[9]. The passage of Florus, however, is just a list of undated Roman campaigns in Thrace, in which Vulso is placed after Minucius (Rufus) and before (C. Scribonius) Curio, Appius (Claudius Pulcher) and (M. Terentius Varro) Lucullus; this is not enough to connect him with the equally uninformative passage of Obsequens on the Roman victory over the Maedi and Dardanians in 97 BC[10].

The praetorship of C. Sentius Saturninus (93-87 BC)

The Roman victories between 114 and 97 BC evidently did not have any long lasting effect; the continuing efforts to restrain the barbarians bear witness to their partial and inconclusive character. During the long stay of the *propraetor* C. Sentius Saturninus in Macedonia between 93 and 87 BC, the northern frontier of the province remained extremely unstable[11]. Julius Obsequens mentions a serious incursion by the Maedi in Macedonia in 92 BC; according to his laconic note they cruelly ravaged the whole province[12]. The *periochae* of Livius mention new Thracian incursions in Macedonia twice in the years of the Social War.[13] A new factor was added to the already critical situation in the region with the anti-Roman propaganda of Mithridathes Eupator, who won to his cause many of

---

[5] *Per.* 63; Flor. 1.39.4: *totus interceptus exercitus*; Ruf. Fest. *Brev.* 9.1. Cf. Brennan 2000, 522.
[6] Broughton 1951, 543; Brennan 2000, 522-523.
[7] Broughton 1951, 577; Brennan 2000, 523-525.
[8] Jul. Obs. 108 (97 BC): *Celtiberi, Medi, Dardani subacti.*
[9] Flor. 1.39: *Volso Rhodopen Haemumque penetravit.* Cf. Gerov 1961, 171; Yordanov 1978, 23; Tacheva 1997, 66.
[10] Appius Claudius Pulcher was governor in Macedonia before C. Scribonius Curio (Appius in 78-76, Curio in 75-73 BC), so the list of Florus is not chronologically sustainable. The large interval (almost 30 years!) between the governorships of Minucius Rufus and Appius Claudius leaves a wide margin for the dating of the expedition of Vulso. Moreover, Florus places his actions in the Rhodope and Haemus mountains, which does not match the anonymous victories over the Maedi and Dardanians mentioned by Obsequens.
[11] Brennan 2000, 525.
[12] Iul. Obs. 113 (660 a.u.c.): *Medorum in Macedonia gens provinciam cruente vastavit.* Cf. Gerov 1961, 171.
[13] *Per.* 74, 76: *praeterea incursiones Thracum in Macedonia<m> populationesque continet.*

the Thracians[14]. A fragment of Cassius Dio mentions out of context an incursion of the Thracians, instigated by Mithridates, reaching as far as Epirus and the sanctuary at Dodona, where they sacked the temple of Zeus[15]. Paulus Orosius adds more details presumably about this same invasion; in his version a Thracian king, Sothimus, invaded Macedonia with a large army and reached Greece, untill he was finally repelled by the *praetor* C. Sentius (Saturninus) and returned to his own kingdom[16]. It has been suggested that Sothimus was the king of the Maedi, but this remains purely conjectural[17]. The passage of Orosius is in chronological context and the Thracian invasion that he speaks of can be dated with some certainty to 88 BC. It is probably to these same events that Cicero refers in his invective against Lucius Calpurnius Piso Caesoninus; he mentions «a general revolt of the barbarians» during the office of the praetor C. Sentius, when the province was saved by the Dentheletae, who remained loyal to Rome[18].

The years of the First Mithridatic War

In 87 BC, Sentius Saturninus was still in office in Macedonia, and evidently had his hands full of other problems, for it was one of his legates, Bruttius Sura, who fought successfully in Greece against the Mithridatic admirals Metrophanes and Archelaus in late 88 and early 87. It must have been at about the same time that Mithridates sent a large land army to invade Macedonia through Thrace and eventually move on into Greece to combine forces with Archelaus. This army was lead by the king's son Ariarathes (or Arcathias) and the general Taxiles, and its advance might have been the main problem for the Macedonian *propraetor*[19]. With the arrival of the army of Sulla in Greece later in 87, the *quaestor* L. Lucullus who lead his advance force ordered Sura back to his superior in Macedonia. The dismissal of Sura might have been linked to the imminent danger from the Pontic land army. However,

---

[14] App. *Mith.* 57; Dio Cass. 31, fr. 101.2. The Odrysians however remained true to their Roman allegiance, cp. Diod. 37.5a (king Kotys). In the battles of Chaeronaea and Orchomenos in 86 some Odrysian cavalry fought on the side of Sulla; it was sent by the successor of Kotys, Sadalas, and was commanded by an Odrysian aristocrat, Amadokos the son of Teres (Holleaux 1919). There is a huge litterature on Mithridates Eupator and the Mithridatic wars; cf. e. g. Meyer 1878; Niese 1887; Reinach 1890; Rostovtzeff 1932; Geyer 1932; Castagna 1938; Guggan 1959; Bengtson 1975, 251-278; Молев 1976; Glew 1977; McGing 1986; Hind 1992; Antonelli 1992; Ballesteros Pastor 1996; Strobel 1996; Callataÿ 1997; Mastrocinque 1999 (1-2). On the Thracians and Mithridates cf. Gaggero 1978.

[15] Dio Cass. 31, fr. 101.2: ὅτι οἱ Θρᾷκες ἀναπεισθέντες ὑπὸ τοῦ Μιθριδάτου τήν τε Ἤπειρον καὶ τἆλλα τὰ μέχρι τῆς Δωδώνης κατέδραμον, ὥστε καὶ τὸ τοῦ Διὸς ἱερὸν συλῆσαι. Cf. Danov 1979, 112, n. 337.

[16] Oros. 5.18.30: *Isdem temporibus rex Sothimus cum magnis Thracum auxiliis Graeciam ingressus cunctos Macedoniae fines depopulatus est tandemque a C. Sentio praetor superatus redire in regnum coactus est.*

[17] Detschew 1957, 465; Gerov 1961, 172; Yordanov 1978, 24; Walbank 1981, 16; Tatcheva 1997, 67.

[18] Cic. *in Pis.* 84: *Denseletis, quae natio semper oboediens huic imperio etiam in illa omnium barbarorum defectione Macedoniam C. Sentio praetore tutata est.* It remains unclear how the Dentheletae contributed to the success of C. Sentius Saturninus. It could have been a treacherous attack on the territory of their neighbours while these were away raiding Macedonia.

[19] McGing 1986, 124 and note 161 opts for the possibility of an even earlier date, eventually in 88. However, according to Memnon 22.12, Amphipolis was taken by Taxiles only in 87, and this preceded the fall of Macedonia to Mithridates.

Macedonia fell after limited resistance[20]; the Roman forces there[21], with or without Sura, were no match for the huge army of Ariarathes. Appian mentions that the latter took the time to appoint satraps over the conquered territories. He seems to have spent the winter of 87 BC in Macedonia, and his delay to move more rapidly south to unite his forces with Archelaus would have made possible the double success of Sulla in taking both Piraeus and Athens early in 86 BC[22].

The march of the army of Ariarathes to the south started probably only in the spring of 86; Sulla dispatched a part of his army under the legate Hortensius to Thessaly in an attempt to prevent or delay it. Ariarathes died unexpectedly in Thessaly[23]. The bulk of his army under Taxilles, however, effectively reinforced Archelaus, who had retained his maritime supremacy even after being forced to evacuate Piraeus. Archelaus was able to offer two large-scale land battles to Sulla later in the same year near Chaeronaea and Orchomenos in Boeotia, losing both to the Romans. This was the turning point of the First Mithridatic war.

The Pontic dominance over Macedonia was of short duration. At an unspecified time during the same year (86 BC), a new Roman army appeared on the scene. Sent by the Marian government in Rome, this army was led by the suffect consul L. Valerius Flaccus, who was elected to office after the unexpected death of Marius in January. Valerius had at his disposal only two newly mobilized legions. He suffered losses from a tempest and the fleet of Archelaus during the crossing from Brundisium, while an advance force sent to make contact with Sulla, now outlawed in Rome, defected to the Sullan camp[24]. Plutarch places a northward move of Sulla's army to Thessaly, presumably to meet the incoming army of Valerius, between the battles of Chaeronea and Orchomenus; then Sulla retreated at the news of the arrival of the new Pontic army led by Dorylaus in Boeotia[25]. This might have been the occasion for the mentioned desertion, but the exact timing of events in this period remains impossible to define. The whole army of Valerius Flaccus was of uncertain allegiance and might have followed this example if given a chance. So the consul wisely decided to go straight to Asia along the Via Egnatia, evading any further contacts with Sulla. While the Marian army was crossing through Macedonia, the legate Fimbria who led the cavalry before the main corps gave his men free hand to ravage the country as enemy land. The locals complained to the consul, and he demanded a return of the stolen goods. The order rendered him unpopular amongst his own soldiers and prepared the subsequent coup in which he lost his life, while

---

[20] App. *Mith.* 35, 41; Plut. *Sulla* 11; Memnon 32; Licinianus, p. 27 f.

[21] Sentius Saturninus had under his command two legions.

[22] App. *Mith.* 35. It has been suggested that Ariarathes must have believed that the purpose of his mission was to create a kingdom for himself in Thrace and wasted valuable time endeavouring to organize the conquered territory. (Reinach 1890, 160-161, 166-167; Rostovtzeff 1932, 248).

[23] The young prince might have been murdered on the orders of his father for failing to act more expeditiously.

[24] App. *Mith.* 51.

[25] Plut. *Sulla* 20.

Fimbria assumed the command[26]. These events happened when the army was already crossing from Thrace into Asia. The sources give no further details on the situation in Macedonia.

The *periochae* of books 81 and 82 of Livy mention new Thracian incursions in Macedonia. The main story of the first book was Sulla's siege of Athens and Piraeus in late 87 and early 86 BC, while the second focused on the two battles in Boeotia in the summer of 86, the passing of the Marian army through Macedonia and Thrace and the death of the consul Valerius Flaccus. It remains, however, impossible to place these Thracian attacks in the chronological sequence of the fast changing events in Macedonia before, during or after its short-lived occupation by the Mithridatic forces.

Sulla, who wintered in Thessaly, moved to the north presumably early in 85 BC. While still in Thessaly, he was delayed for some time in Larissa by the illness of Archelaus, who had become the main mediator in the peace talks with Mithridates. Then he moved on to Macedonia and, while awaiting there the answer of Mithridates to his conditions for an honourable capitulation, he undertook a retributory operation against some of the restless barbaric tribes. The *periocha* of Livy's book 83 mentions a succession of battles, in which Sulla defeated the Thracians[27]. Appian lists the Eneti, the Dardanians and the Sinti as his adversaries, adding that by ravaging their lands Sulla not only kept his army in good shape, but also enriched his soldiers[28]. Eutropius gives another list: the Dardanians, the Scordisci, the Dalmatians (= Dentheletae?) and the Moesians (= Maedi?)[29]. Plutarch makes the Maedi Sulla's main military objective in his biography; after invading their country and laying it waste, he retreated back to Eastern Macedonia to meet Archelaus upon his return from the talks with Mithridates in Philippi[30]. The last detail – the mention of Philippi – gives some support to Plutarch's version, for the city is well placed to serve as a base for military operations in the middle Strymon valley[31]. Granius Licinianus also points to Maedica as the main objective of Sulla's Thracian operation, adding that the Dardanians and Dentheletae, who had also been invading Macedonia, surrendered without fight. He adds another interesting detail: during the meeting of Sulla and Mithridates in Dardanos on the Hellespont, the Sullan legate Hortensius led a further campaign against the Maedi and Dardanians, whom he routed[32].

---

[26] Diod. fr. 38.8; Cass. Dio. 31, fr. 104.2; App. *Mith*. 51.

[27] T. Liv. perioch. 83: *Sylla compluribus proeliis Thracas cecidit*.

[28] App. *Mith*. 55.

[29] Eutrop. brev. 5.7.1: *Interim eo tempore Sylla etiam Dardanos, Scordiscos, Dalmatas [Denseletas?] et Moesos [Maedos?] partim vicit, alios in fidem accepit*.

[30] Plut. *Sulla* 23: ἐπὶ τούτοις ἐκπέμψας ἐκεῖνον αὐτὸς εἰς τὴν Μαιδικὴν ἐνέβαλε, καὶ τὰ πολλὰ διαπορθήσας πάλιν ἀνέστρεψεν εἰς Μακεδονίαν, καὶ τὸν Ἀρχέλαον ἐδέξατο περὶ Φιλίππους ἀγγέλλοντα καλῶς ἔχειν πάντα.

[31] Gerov 1961, 172.

[32] Gran. Licinian. 35.78-81: *Is ipse Mithridates cum Sulla <ap>u<d> Dardanum <c>o<m>positis, gratia <P. R.> reconciliata, Ariobardianen ut servum respuit, reliqua classe in Pontum proficiscitur. Ac dum de condicionibus disceptatur, M<a>edos et Dardanos, qui socios vexabant, Hortensius <l>e<gatus> fugaverat. ipse Sulla ex<er>citum in M<a>edi<c>am ind<u>xerat, priusquam in A<siam> a<d> conloquium transiret. quo Dardanos e<t> Denseletas caesis hos<tibus>, qui Macedoniam ve<xa>bant, in deditionem recepit*.

The sack of Delphi

One of the most impressive events in the long series of barbarian incursions and Roman counter-campaigns was the sack and incineration of the sanctuary of Apollo at Delphi by the Maedi, Scordisci and Dardanians. The date of this memorable event, however, remains doubtful[33]. It must have made a lasting impression on the contemporaries, for it is repeatedly mentioned in the preserved historical tradition. Plutarch makes a passing note in the biography of Numa Pompilius, ascribing the sacrilege to the Maedi. His text contains the chronological indication that it happened «during the Mithridatic war and the civil war of the Romans», thus pointing to the period between 88 and 82 BC[34].

The Illyrian book of Appian offers more details. According to Appian, the Scordisci, the Maedi and the Dardanians had jointly invaded «Macedonia and Greece». They plundered many sanctuaries, including the one at Delphi, but they also lost many men in the action. In a retaliatory campaign, a Roman army under the command of a certain Lucius Scipio invaded the lands of the perpetrators, who were abandoned by all the neighbouring tribes because of the sacrilege. Scipio destroyed the greater part of the Scordisci, while those remaining «fled to the Danube and settled on the islands in that river». However, he made peace with the Maedi and Dardanians and accepted from them as a bribe a part of the gold robbed from the temple. «One Italic writer» – adds Appian – «says that this was the chief cause of the numerous civil wars of the Romans after Lucius Scipio's time till the establishment of the monarchy». The text of Appian contains a chronological clue: according to him, the sack of Delphi occurred 32 years after the first encounter between Romans and Celts, who had been fighting intermittently ever since that time[35].

This last assertion has brought to life various attempts at a chronological reconstruction. Some authors have counted the 32 years from some important event in the late second century, which could have been taken as «the first encounter between Romans and Celts», such as the invasion of the Cimbri in 113 BC, the defeat of C. Porcius Cato by the Scordisci in Macedonia in 114, or the invasion of the Maedi and Scordisci in 119 mentioned in the Lete inscription. Alternatively, after a slight emendation of the number (302 instead of 32 years), others have counted from the sack and burning of Rome by the Celts in the early fourth century (dated to 390 or to 387/6 BC). These calculations have produced a number of different dates in the interval between 88 and 81 BC[36].

---

[33] Perdrizet 1896, 493-494; Reinach 1910, 313-322; Dobiáš 1929, 47-67; Papazoglou 1978, 179, 315-327.

[34] Plut. *Numa* 9.6: ἐν Δελφοῖς δὲ τοῦ ναοῦ καταπρησθέντος ὑπὸ Μήδων, περὶ δὲ τὰ Μιθριδατικὰ καὶ τὸν ἐμφύλιον Ῥωμαίων πόλεμον ἅμα τῷ βωμῷ τὸ πῦρ ἠφανίσθη, οὔ φασι δεῖν ἀπὸ ἑτέρου πυρὸς ἐναύεσθαι, καινὸν δὲ ποιεῖν καὶ νέον, ἀνάπτοντας ἀπὸ τοῦ ἡλίου φλόγα καθαρὰν καὶ ἀμίαντον. Despite the transcription of the name (Μήδων) it is clear that Plutarch means the Thracian Maedi, which is corroborated by the other sources.

[35] App. *Ill.* 12-14 (1.5): Ῥωμαῖοι δ' ἔχοντες ἤδη δεύτερον καὶ τριακοσ<ιος>τὸν ἔτος ἀπὸ τῆς πρώτης ἐς Κελτοὺς πείρας.

[36] For a review of different opinions cf. Papazoglou 1978, 315-323.

A third piece of information on the incineration of the temple at Delphi also bears on the chronological problem: in the chronicle of Eusebius of Caesarea, the sacrilege is ascribed to «Thracians» and dated in the first year of the 174th Olympiade together with the burning of the Capitol in Rome[37]. The first year of the 174th Olympiade was the year 84 BC, while the Capitol was incinerated in 83 BC[38]. Many authors have accordingly opted for dates around 84 or 83 BC for the sack and burning of the Delphic temple[39]. Additional support for this view is drawn from the fact that Sulla confiscated the treasures of the main Greek sanctuaries, including Delphi, in the winter of 87/86 BC[40]. This is well attested, and the sources would have mentioned a recent major barbarian raid devastating Delphi. Diodorus even reminds on this occasion the sack of Delphi by the Phocians in the fourth century. So the Sullan campaign against Athens and Piraeus is taken as a *terminus post quem* for the Thracian invasion of Delphi.

The praetorship of L. Scipio

Another opinion on this chronological problem has been gradually gaining ground; it is centered on the figure of the Roman general who first punished the perpetrators in Appian's version, Lucius Scipio. It has been suggested for a long time that he should be identified with the consul of 83 BC, L. Cornelius Scipio Asiaticus (or Asiagenes), who played an important part in the civil war and ended his life, proscribed by Sulla, as an exile in Massalia. He was the great grandson of Lucius Cornelius Scipio Asiaticus, cos. 190, the brother of the famous Scipio Africanus and victor over Antiochus III early in the second century, hence the title Asiaticus (or Asiagenus) which was transmitted in the family. The future cos. 83 was *triumvir monetalis* probably in 106 BC, and *pontifex* since 88 BC; his consulship, however, excludes the possibility of his presence on the Balkans in 83 or even late in 84 BC. Friedrich Münzer suggested in the *Realencyclopaedie der Klasichen Altertumswissenschaft*, summing up 19th c. German scholarship, that Scipio Asiagenus might have been *praetor* in Macedonia in 88 BC, referring to that date the story of Appian[41]. This however contradicts the explicit indications that the long governorship of C. Sentius Saturninus lasted into 87 BC and probably ended only with the advance of the Pontic army of Arcathias. Georges Daux and Ernst Badian have both added to the elucidation of the chronological problems around the sack and burning of Delphi and the presumed Macedonian promagistracy of Scipio Asiagenus [42]. Following these developments, Robert Broughton suggested in the second volume of «The Ma-

---

[37] Euseb. 2.133 (Schoene): *Ol. CLXXIV.1. Templum tertio apud Delphos a Thracibus incensum, & Romae Capitolium.*
[38] On the date of the incineration of the Capitol cf. Tac. *hist.* 3.72: in the consulship of Lucius Scipio and Gaius Norbanus.
[39] Gerov 1961, 173 with note 2; Papazoglou 1978, 322-323 with note 144; Walbank 1981, 16.
[40] Plut. *Sulla* 12; Diod. fr. 38.7; Paus. 9.7.4.
[41] F. Münzer, RE 4.1 (Stuttgart, 1900), 1484, s. v. Cornelius (No 338).
[42] Daux 1936, 392-397; Badian 1958, 6-7; 1964, 81-82.

gistrates of the Roman Republic» an eventual praetorship of Scipio Asiaticus in 86 and his prorogation as governor of Macedonia as certain in 85 and probable in 84 BC; he still however placed the raid on Delphi «in late 85 or early 84»[43]. T. Corey Brennan in «The Praetorship in the Roman Republic» has recently added further considerations. According to Brennan, Scipio was probably in the *provincia* of Macedonia in late 86, and certainly by 85. He suggests also that it would have been Scipio who recovered Macedonia for the Romans, and ascribes to him the conquest of Philipi, which, according to Granius Licinianus (35.70), brought about the retreat of the remaining Pontic garrisons from Abdera and other cities. He further surmises that Scipio would have left when Sulla marched north in 85 and that he must have returned to Italy in 84 at the latest in order to stand for consul for the next year.

Brennan's book contains another pertinent suggestion, drawn from a casual remark of Cicero, namely that between 83 and 81 BC Macedonia was governed by *legates without imperium*. He hesitates between a choice of either L. Hortensius or Servius Sulpicius Galba, two known legates of Sulla who conspicuously miss from the accounts of the civil war in Italy[44].

Brennan's surmises deserve some further consideration. Is it feasible to suggest, as he has done, that L. Cornelius Scipio Asiagenus could have been the liberator of Macedonia from the temporary Pontic occupation of 87-86 BC, moving presumably in advance of the Marian army of Flaccus and Fimbria in 86 BC? In my opinion, no. The explicit story of Fimbria's cavalry treating Macedonia as enemy territory contradicts such an assumption. Theoretically, Scipio could have advanced together with the army of Flaccus to occupy his post of provincial governor. However, it seems more appropriate to suggest that he was sent only *after* the passing of the consular army to stabilize the situation in the province, probably later in 86, and evidently with an army of his own with which he undertook his campaign against the Scordisci. He could well have been one of the praetors of that year.

On the other hand, it seems difficult to sustain a long stay of Scipio in Macedonia. Probably in early summer of 85 the northern advance of Sulla with the bulk of his army would have made the position of a Marian governor untenable. It is therefore no wonder that Sulla, evidently assuming the care of the province, campaigned against its northern neighbours, the Maedi and Dardanians, in the summer of 85, while he was waiting for the issue of the preliminary talks with Mithridates. Where was Scipio at that time? He could have retreated to the western reaches of his province, nearer the Adriatic coast, or he could have crossed over to Italy for good, where we find him a year later as a consular candidate. In any case, it is very unlikely that he could have reassumed his authority over Macedonia thereafter. Sulla would not have given up on such a strategically important area while preparing for the final showdown in Italy. It seems pertinent to recall here the action of Sulla's legate Hortensius in Macedonia at the time of the Dardanos talks. Hortensius might

---

[43] Broughton 1952, 54, 58, 61; 1960, 20; 1986, 71.
[44] Brennan 2000, 527-528.

very well have been the first of those *legates without imperium*, who seem to have run the province not only between 83 and 81, as Brennan suggested, but probably all the way down from 85 BC when Sulla first assumed power over it.

Another reason to maintain this proposition comes to mind. As already noted above, Appian suggested that after severely punishing the Scordisci for their participation in the raid on Delphi, Scipio pardoned the other perpetrators, the Maedi and Dardanians, having received a bribe from them. The real reason, however, could have been other than avarice. The northward march of Sulla in 85 could have left no time to the provincial governor to finish his campaign and would have forced him to withdraw in haste, making an improvised settlement with the two still unpunished tribes. The fact that Sulla and his legate Hortensius went on to fight exactly against the Maedi and Dardanians, as if to finish the unfinished job of Scipio, fits perfectly into this scenario; they would not have felt obliged by whatever settlement the Marian governor had reached with these tribes.

Implications

What are the implications of dating the governorship of Scipio Asiagenus to between late in 86 and the first half of 85 for the disputed chronology of the raid on Delphi? The raid could have occurred during Scipio's stay in the province and provoked his fast retaliation. But if Scipio had enough troops to later punish the invaders, would he not have been able to stop their march through Macedonia and southward into Central Greece in the first place? Thus, it seems more pertinent to suggest that the raid occurred before the arrival of Scipio, which could have been the Roman response to this new threat. The Delphic raid could accordingly be dated to the presumed interval after the passing of the army of Flaccus through Macedonia and before the arrival of the new governor Scipio there, sometimes in the second half of 86 BC. It may also have happened somewhat earlier, after the bulk of the Pontic army had left Macedonia in spring 86 to fight Sulla and before the arrival of the Marian army there, so roughly around the time of the battle at Chaeronea. Both suggestions place the sack and burning of Delphi by the Scordisci, Maedi and Dardanians either earlier or later in the same year, i.e. 86 BC.

The campaign of L. Cornelius Scipio Asiagenus against the Scordisci would then have taken place either late in 86 or, more likely, early in 85 BC. As mentioned at the beginning of this paper, the Romans had already had a long series of conflicts with this warrior Celtic tribe in the late second and early first century BC. Despite the fact that several triumphs had been given to provincial governors who fought successfully against them, Scipio seems to have been the first to ferociously attack the Scordisci in their own territory and to inflict a defeat from which they never fully recovered. The text of Appian unfortunately gives only a few details about this campaign: it mentions that the Scordisci received no help from their neighbours, that Scipio utterly destroyed the majority of them, and that those who escaped «fled to the Danube and settled on the islands in that river». However, there are no sizeable islands in that part of the Danube. It could be suggested that Scipio evicted the Scordisci from the southern bank of the Danube and the Sava, and that Appian's «islands» are in fact the lands enclosed between the Danube and the Sava and Drava, to which they were thus displaced.

Both the expedition of Scipio against the Scordisci and the campaigns of Sulla and Hortensius against the Maedi and Dardanians invite a different apprehension when they are viewed as a part of the major conflict of the age, the war between Rome and Mithridates of Pontus. Regardless of its exact timing, the Delphic invasian of the Maedi, Scordisci and Dardanians could have been instigated by Mithridatic agents as a distraction or disruption in the rear of Sulla in Greece. In any case, such an action in a time of war would have been perceived by the Romans as hostile and would automatically have placed the three tribes in the enemy list. Hence the severity of the Roman reprisals, which put an end to the whole affair and which resemble in magnitude and implacability the punishments inflicted on other Mithridatic allies.

Peter Delev
University St. Kliment Ohridski, Sofia

Bibliography

Alföldy 1964 = G. Alföldy, «Des territoires occupés par les Scordisques», *AAntHung* 12/1-2 (1964) 107-127.

Antonelli 1992 = G. Antonelli, *Mitridate, il nemico mortale di Roma* (Roma 1992).

Badian 1958 = E. Badian, «Notes on Provincial Governors from the Social War down to Sulla's Victory», *Proceedings of the African Classical Associations* (1958) 1-18.

Badian 1964 = E. Badian, *Studies in Greek and Roman History* (Oxford 1964).

Ballesteros Pastor 1996 = L. Ballesteros Pastor, *Mitrídates Eupátor, rey del Ponto* (Granada 1996).

Bengtson 1975 = H. Bengtson, *Herrschergestalten des Hellenismus* (München 1975).

Brennan 2000 = T.C. Brennan, *The Praetorship in the Roman Republic*, Oxford University Press (Oxford 2000).

Broughton 1951 = T.R.S. Broughton, *The Magistrates of the Roman Republic. Vol. 1, 509 B.C. - 100 B.C.*, American Philological Association (New York 1951) (= Philological Monographs 15/1).

Broughton 1952 = T.R.S. Broughton, *The Magistrates of the Roman Republic. Vol. 2, 99 B.C. – 31 B.C.*, American Philological Association (New York 1952) (= Philological Monographs 15/2).

Broughton 1960 = T.R.S. Broughton, *Supplement to the Magistrates of the Roman Republic*, American Philological Association (New York 1960) (= Philological Monographs 15/3).

Broughton 1986 = T.R.S. Broughton, *The Magistrates of the Roman Republic. Vol. 3, Supplement*, Scholars Press (Atlanta 1986).

Callataÿ 1997 = Fr. De Callataÿ, *L'histoire des guerres mithridatiques vue par les monnaies* (Louvain-la-Neuve 1997).

Castagna 1938 = M. Castagna, *Mitridate VI Eupatore re del Ponto* (Portici 1938).

Cuntz 1918 = O. Cuntz, «Zum Ehrendekret von Lete in Makedonien für M. Annius», *Hermes* 53 (1918) 102-104.

Danov 1979 = Chr. Danov, «Die Thraker auf dem Ostbalkan von der hellenistischen Zeit bis zur Gründung Konstantinopels», *ANRW* 2.7.1 (1979) 21-185.

Daux 1936 = G. Daux, *Delphes aux IIe et Ier siècles, depuis l'abaissement de l'Étolie jusqu'à la paix romaine (191-31 avant J.-C.)* (Paris 1936).

Detschew 1957 = D. Detschew, *Die thrakischen Sprachreste* (Wien 1957, 1976^2).

Dittenberger *Syll* = W. Dittenberger, *Sylloge Inscriptionum Graecarum* 1-4 (Lipsiae, 1915-1924^3).

Dobiáš 1929 = J. Dobiáš, *Studie k Appianově knize illyrské* (Praha 1929).

Fluss 1921 = M. Fluss, «Skordisci», *RE* 2A (1921) 831-835.

Gaggero 1978 = E.S. Gaggero, «Relations politiques et militaires de Mithridate VI Eupator avec les populations et les cités de Thrace et avec les colonies grecques de la Mer Noire occidentale», *Pulpudeva* 2 (1978) 294-305.

Garašanin 1963 = M. Garašanin, «Contributions à l'archéologie et l'histoire des Scordisques», *Mélanges P. Bosch-Gimpera* (Mexico 1963) 173-180.

Gerov 1961 = B. Gerov, «Проучвания върху западнотракийските земи през римско време [част 1]», *Годишник на Софийския университет, Филологически факултет* [Annuaire de l'Université de Sofia, Faculté Philologique] 54/3 (1961 [1959/1960]) 153-407.

Geyer 1932 . F. Geyer, «Mithridates (No 12)», *RE* 15 (1932) 2163-2205.

McGing 1986 = B.G. McGing, *The Foreign Policy of Mithridates VI Eupator, King oj f Pontus*, Brill (Leiden 1986).

Glew 1977 = D. Glew, «Mithridates Eupator and Rome: A Study of the Background of the First Mithridatic War», *Athenaeum* 55 (1977) 380-405.

Guggan 1959 = A. Guggan, *King of Pontus: The Life of Mithradates Eupator* (New York 1959).

Hind 1992 = J. Hind, «Mithridates», *CAH* 92 (1992) 129-164.

Holleaux 1919 = M. Holleaux, «Décret de Cheronée relatif à la première guerre de Mithridates», *REG* 32 (1919) 320-337.

Mastrocinque 1999 = A. Mastrocinque, *Le guerre di Mitridate* (Milano 1999).

Mastrocinque 1999a = A. Mastrocinque, *Studi sulle guerre Mitridatiche* (Stuttgart 1999).

Kallet-Marx 1995 = R.M. Kallet-Marx, *Hegemony to Empire. The Development of the Roman Imperium in the East from 148 to 62 B.C.* (Berkeley 1995).

Meyer 1878 = E. Meyer, *Geschichte des Konigreichs Pontos* (Berlin 1878).

Molev 1976 = E.A. Molev, *Митридат Евпатор. Создание черноморской державы* (Saratov 1976).

Niese 1887 = B. Niese, «Die Erwerbung der Küsten des Pontos durch Mithridates VI (Straboniana 6)», *RhM* 42 (1887) 559-574.

Papazoglou 1978 = F. Papazoglou, *The Central Balkan Tribes in Pre-Roman Times. Triballi, Autariatae, Dardanians, Scordisci and Moesians* (Amsterdam 1978).

Papazoglou 1988 = F. Papazoglou, *Les villes de Macédoine à l'époque romaine* (Paris 1988) (= *BCH* suppl. 16).

Perdrizet 1896 = P. Perdrizet, «Inscriptions de Delphes. V. Le Proconsul M. Minucius Rufus, vainqueur des Gaulois Scordistes et des Thraces», *BCH* 20 (1896) 481-496.

Reinach 1890 = T. Reinach, *Mithridate Eupator, roi de Pont* (Paris 1890).

Reinach 1910 = A.-J. Reinach, «Delphes et les Bastarnes», *BCH* 30 (1910) 249-330.

Rostovtzeff 1932 = M.I. Rostovtzeff, «Pontus and its neighbours: the first Mithridatic War», *CAH* 9 (1932) 211-238.

Sarikakis 1971 = Th. Chr. Sarikakis, Ρωμαίοι άρχοντες της επαρχίας Μακεδονίας, Μέρος Α'. Από της ιδρύσεως της επαρχίας μέχρι των χρόνων του Αυγούστου (148-27π. Χ.) (Thessaloniki 1971).

Strobel 1996 = K. Strobel, «Mithridates VI. Eupator von Pontos: der letzte grosse Monarch der hellenistischen Welt und sein Scheitern an der römischen Macht», *Ktema* 21 (1996) 55-94.

Tatcheva 1997 = M. Tatcheva, *История на българските земи в древността през елинистическата и римската епоха* (Sofia 1997²).

Tod 1919 = M.N. Tod, «The Macedonian Era», *ABSA* 23 (1918/1919) 206-217.

Todorović 1974 = J. Todorović, *Skordisi: istorija i kultura*, Institut za izučavanje istorije Vojvodine (Beograd 1974).

Walbank 1981 = F.W. Walbank, «Prelude to Spartacus: The Romans in Southern Thrace, 150-70 B.C.», in *Spartacus. Symposium rebus Spartaci gestis dedicatum 2050 a.* (Sofia 1981) 14-27.

Yordanov 1978 = K. Yordanov, «Медике, Македония и Рим», *Thracia Antiqua* 4 (Sofia 1978) 17-33.

THRACE UNDER ROMAN SWAY (146 BC – AD 46) BETWEEN WARFARE AND DIPLOMACY

Maria-Gabriella PARISSAKI

After the suppression of Andriscus' revolt and the conversion of Macedonia into a province of the Roman Empire in 146 BC, Rome had no choice but to bear the burden of all the human and financial resources that were necessary in order to protect its new province from the incursions of barbarian tribes dwelling in the north. In fact, the protection of Macedonia from its northern neighbours was a constant and major prerequisite of Macedonian policy since at least the reign of Philip II. Ancient sources explicitly state that the famous expedition of Alexander the Great against the Triballoi was a necessary step to be taken before the launching of the great campaign into Asia[1]; and the founding of cities along the great Hebrus plain —mainly Philippopolis, but also Cabyle and Beroe— as well as in the regions of Maedica and Parorbelia also played an important part in this effort of Macedonian kings to effectively control the Thracian hinterland and its land communications[2].

Despite the upheavals that the conflicts between the Hellenistic kingdoms and the creation of the Celtic kingdom of Tylis produced in Thrace during the third century BC, Macedonian policy toward Thrace was revived during the last Antigonids and especially during the reign of Philip V and his heir Perseus. Modern historians have not failed to remark that the first campaign of Philip V into Thrace occurred in 211 BC, that is just one year after the abolition of the kingdom of Tylis, and have many times pointed out that this chronological proximity should not be taken as a coincidence but as a sign of the importance Macedonian kings still gave to the effective control of the Thracian hinterland[3]. Moreover, and notwithstanding the fact that the Roman stranglehold became all the more pressing as the Macedonian kingdom approached its demise, no modern historian has doubted the basically successful character of the last Antigonids' policy towards that direction. In two articles published in *Pulpudeva* of 1983 and in the *Third International Congress of Thracology* one year later, Miltiades Hatzopoulos described the stages of the Antigonid

---

[1] See Arr. *Anab.* 1.1.4. From the extensive bibliography on the expedition of Alexander against the Triballoi, see the detailed analysis of Papazoglou 1978, 25-40 and, more recently, Boteva 2002, 27-31, with further references. For Polybius' statement (9.35.2-4) that Macedonia operated as a πρόφραγμα (barrier) for the protection not only of herself but of all of Greece from the plundering expeditions of barbarians dwelling in the north, see e.g. Hatzopoulos 1980, 80, n. 4.

[2] For the founding of cities in the Thracian interior, see Popov 2002. For the region of Parorbelia, see Papazoglou 1988, 346-350 and for the valley along the middle course of the Strymon, *op. cit.* 366-376. For Maedica, see Gerov 1961, 159-214.

[3] For the kingdom of Tylis, see recently *In Search of Celtic Tylis in Thrace (III c. BC). Proceedings of the interdisciplinary colloquium arranged by the National Archaeological Institute and Museum at Sofia and the Welsh Derpartment, Aberystwyth University held at the National Archaeological Institute and Museum, Sofia 8 may 2010*, ed. Lyudmil F. Vagalinski (Sofia 2010). For the chronological proximity between the abolition of the kingdom and the first expedition of Philip V into Thrace, as well as a concise narration of the expeditions of Philip V in Thrace, see Hatzopoulos 1980, 82-84.

expansion to the east and outlined the basic strategic principles behind their policy: the creation of two concentric perimetres of security («deux périmètres concentriques de sécurité») along the eastern and northern borders of the kingdom, of which the first included the territory of Thracian tribes that were incorporated to Macedonia and the second the territory of allied tribes[4]. Despite its schematic and for that reason somehow simplified description, this pattern effectively describes the essence of Macedonian policy during these last decades of its life. Moreover, modern scholars outlined the importance of the diplomatic means put forward in order to foster the results of military activities : dynastic marriages, gifts and payments, all means were used in order to effectively implement Macedonian policy in Thrace[5].

The most expedient way to assess the effectiveness of the last Antigonids' policy in Thrace is an even cursory look at the number of predatory incursions of Thracian and other northern tribes into Macedonia that occurred after her incorporation into the Roman Empire in 146 BC. The literary, epigraphic and numismatic evidence all combined together prove, beyond a shadow of a doubt, that from 146 BC and for almost a century the repulse of these attacks formed the main and most important activity of the Roman governors of Macedonia[6]; sometimes —as revealed by the famous inscription of Lete (*Syll*[3] 700)— success was achieved only at a considerable cost. The history of these incursions has been many times narrated and commented on; from all the relevant bibliography, I would like to mention a recent and very important contribution of Prof. O. Picard in the *Comptes Rendus de l'Académie des Inscriptions et Belles Lettres* of 2008, where he focused on the impact these incursions had on the monetary activity of the whole region; his very useful table at the end of the article containing Thracian incursions into Macedonia from 146 BC to the expedition of L. Calpurnius Piso in 55 BC covers five pages[7]! Notwithstanding the interest these incursions obviously have for the history of the region, in this paper I will try to draw attention on a different though quite closely related subject; that of the diplomatic means put forward by Rome during the two centuries spanning from the provincialisation of Macedonia in 146 BC to the provincialisation of Thrace in AD 46, in an effort to better appreciate the way by which the Romans achieved a *modus vivendi* with the Thracian tribes by gradually adjusting the policy of the last Antigonids into their own political concepts.

---

[4] More specifically, Hatzopoulos 1980, 86 defines the first zone as an «unité administrative politico-militaire sous le contrôle direct des représentants du pouvoir royal» and the second (*op. cit.* p. 85) as a zone of «contrôle indirect par le biais d'alliances inégales avec des dynastes clients». See also 1984, 140-141.

[5] See Hatzopoulos 1980 ; see also Rufin Solas (forthcoming).

[6] See Papazoglou 1979, 311: «la protection de la province des incursions déprédatrices des peuplades limitrophes qui ne cessaient de violer ses frontières fut, dans la période présullanienne du moins, la principale préoccupation des gouverneurs de la Macédoine».

[7] See Picard 2008, 489-493.

Romans in Thrace from 146 BC to the middle of the first century BC

The first region of Thrace to attract Roman interest was the zone along the north Aegean coast east of the Nestus, where the via Egnatia was built just a few years after the conversion of neighbouring Macedonia into a province of the Roman Empire; taking into account the interests of Roman foreign policy in the middle of the second century BC, this was a zone of major strategic importance, since it offered the most immediate land connection between Europe and Asia Minor, where Rome —and Roman traders— had vital interests since the very beginning of that century. As explicitly stated by Diodorus and Titus Livius, the three Greek colonies along this zone —that is Abdera, Maronea and Aenus— where declared *civitates liberae*, but the other possessions of the last Antigonids east of the Nestus river where incorporated in the first Macedonian μερίς; Diodorus qualifies these possessions as ἐρύματα, while Titus Livius uses the terms *oppida, vici et castella*[8]. This zone extended initially to the east till the Hebrus' estuary but it also incorporated the region of the Thracian Chersonese and the Caenice after Titus Didius' campaign in 100 BC, as revealed by the now famous *Lex de Provinciis Praetoriis*, previously known as the *Lex de Piratis Persequentis*. Unfortunately, the extent of this zone towards the north is difficult to assess, due to the vague terminology used by the ancient sources mentioned above; still, both testimonies permit the assumption that no significant modifications were made to the previous period of Antigonid control[9]. Furthermore, the wish of the Romans to maintain a second protective zone along the borders of the Thracian lands incorporated into the first Macedonian μερίς —thus duplicating the policy of their Macedonian predecessors— is suggested by the easiness with which they immediately forgave the king of the Odrysians Kotys, despite his loyal support to Perseus till the very end[10]. This same effort of Rome to maintain a protective zone along the eastern borders of the first Macedonian μερίς may be behind its alliance to the Cainoi, the Thracian tribe living immediately east of the Hebrus river and north of the Chersonese. According to ancient sources, a Thracian king named Diegylis —the tribal affinity of who is not explicitly stated but who many modern

---

[8] See Livy 45.29.5-7 (*Deinde in quattuor regiones dividi Macedoniam: unam fore et primam partem quod agri inter Strymonem et Nessum sit amnem; accessurum huic parti trans Nessum ad orientem versum, qua Perseus tenuisset, vicos, castella, oppida, praeter Aenum et Maroneam et Abdera*) and Diod. Sic. 31.8.8 (Τὴν δὲ χώραν ὅλην διεῖλον (sc. οἱ Ῥωμαῖοι) εἰς τέσσαρα μέρη, ὧν πρῶτον τὸ μεταξὺ Νέστου ποταμοῦ καὶ Στρυμόνος καὶ τὰ πρὸς ἀνατολὴν τοῦ Νέστου ἐρύματα πλὴν τὰ πρὸς Ἄβδηραν καὶ Μαρώνειαν καὶ Αἶνον πόλεις).

[9] The history of this zone and of its gradual expansion towards the east has been exposed with great detail by Loukopoulou 1987; see also Hammond & Walbank 1988, appendix 6 : Some Holdings of Perseus in Thrace, 611-612. For the *Lex de Provinciis Praetoriis, see Roman Statutes* (ed. M.H. Crawford), London 1996, vol. I, 231-270.

[10] For the attitude of Rome towards Kotys, see Polyb., 30.17, Livy 45.42.6-12 and the famous inscription from Teos *Syll*³, 656 (=*IThrAeg* E5 with relevant bibliography).

historians consider as Caenic— played an important part in promoting Roman policy in the region during the disputes between the kings Prusias II of Bithynia and Attalus II of Pergamon in the middle of the second century BC[11]. During this same period no information is available for the Thracian tribes living in the interior of the Rhodope mountains; but Sapaioi, if not actually incorporated into the lands of the first μερίς, certainly remained loyal allies of the Romans. So, judging by the available evidence on Thrace but also from a general tendency in Roman foreign policy to initially maintain the *status quo* during the annexation of new territories, we could surmise in a general way and at least initially that the wish of Rome regarding its Thracian policy was to maintain the situation inherited by the last Antigonids.

However and despite this initial wish, changes were soon to occur; and these were largely due to the Romans themselves, since their continuing expansion towards the East was bound to provoke opposition and disruptions in the *status quo*. The first serious shake occurred of course with the Mithridatic danger, which in one way or another affected all regions of Thrace[12]. The magnitude of the upheaval the Mithridatic wars produced in Thrace obliged Romans to realise on the one hand the inadequacy of the protective zone under these new, wider realities and on the other hand the strategic importance of a second zone along the Istrus river; Lucullus campaign there in 72 BC is the telling realisation of the importance of this zone[13]. Still, and despite Rome's final success in the field, the situation in Thrace during the first half of the first century BC was probably quite different from the one the Romans wished to have had; despite the handling of the predatory attacks of northern tribes, despite Roman expeditions in the interior of Thrace and the gradual incorporation of new territories into the province of Macedonia, the detailed description of Appian of the movements of the Roman armies before the battle at Philippoi in 42 BC is a further proof of the flimsy control Romans had on territory that nominally belonged to them[14]. That this zone was still considered theirs, though, is proved by a passage in the *Bellum Civilis* (3.4), where Caesar enumerates the forces of Pompeius; five hundred men were sent to him by *Kotys ex Thracia*, under the command of his son Sadalas, while two hundred more were sent *ex Macedonia*, under the command of Rhaskuporis, who bears no title but is described as a man of marked valour (*excellenti virtute*). So, in 48 BC the territory of this Sapaean chieftain was differentiated from Thrace and considered part of Macedonia.

---

[11] See Loukopoulou 1987, 66-72 *passim*.

[12] For Thracian cities and tribes during the Mithridatic wars, see generally Gaggero 1976 and Avram & Bounegru 2006; for the Greek colonies of the north Aegean coast, see *IThrAeg*, 166 and 327 with further bibliography. For further bibliography, seel also Delev in this same volume.

[13] For a brief description of this campaing, see Danov 1979, 115-116.

[14] For the manoeuvres of the Roman troops along the north Aegean coast before the battle of Philippoi, see App., Ῥωμαϊκῶν Ἐμφυλίων 4.11.87-113 and 4.13.105 (and also below, n. 20), Dio Cass., Ῥωμαϊκά 47.35 and Plut., *Brut*. 38; cf. the comment of Cicero in *De provinciis consularibus* 2.4 that *via illa nostra militaris, quae per Macedoniam est usque ad Hellespontum militaris, non solum excursionibus barbarorum sit infecta, sed etiam castris Thraeciis distincta ac notata*.

Romans and the client-kingdom of Thrace

Under this perspective, it is interesting to note that somewhere around the middle of the first century BC —that is *grosso modo* in the years following the upheaval created by the Mithridatic wars and the even more serious disruption of the civil wars— Rome emerges with a new interlocutor in Thracian affairs, the never heard-of before client-kingdom of Thrace. Many facets pertaining to the history of this kingdom from the middle of the first century BC to the provincialisation of Thrace in AD 46 still remain unknown and are subject of debate among modern scholars. Since the end of the nineteenth century AD onwards, research has mainly focused on the effort to reconstruct the genealogy of the ruling family, a reconstruction seriously complicated by the fact that all male members share only two names, Kotys and Rhoemetalkes[15]. But lack of adequate information is also responsible for our gaps on other equally important issues, and one of them is the process of emergence and the beginnings of this client-kingdom, to which we shall focus here.

Since Dessau's fundamental studies on the genealogy of the Sapaean kings, it is generally believed that this new kingdom emerged with the unification of two dynastic branches, namely that of the Sapaioi with that of the Astai, by way of a marriage[16]. This marriage is never explicitly mentioned in our sources, but Dessau's proposal is still considered by modern historians as the best possible explanation. If it actually occurred, no one can overlook its political significance; but in modern historiography this marriage is often described as a common phenomenon of intermarriage among Thracian dynastic families —which it certainly was— and, consequently, as an initiative emanating by the Thracian families themselves[17]. But if we focus on the great political significance that the creation and solidification of this client-kingdom played in the control of Thracian affairs till AD 46, we should at least wonder about the role Rome may have played in this alliance. In fact, according to our view, the creation of this new situation in Thrace should not be considered a result of inner Thracian activity that Rome followed passively but a result of Rome's active effort to control Thracian affairs by adapting Thracian realities to principles familiar to its society and policy; and three particular aspects of the client-kingdom of Thrace will be stressed here in order to support this view:

(a) The importance of the Sapaean branch, which from the very beginning emerges as the key element of the client-kingdom despite the fact that —according to Dessau's reconstruction mentioned above— it contributed the female and not the

---

[15] The use in modern studies of two systems of enumeration for the representatives of the ruling family —one continuous for the Astaean and Sapaean house used by Karhstedt in the relevant articles in the *RE* and one differentiating between the two, used by Mihailov in *IGBulg*— has further complicated the problem; for a concise prosopography of the representatives of the Astaean and Sapaean family, see Sullivan 1979 and also Tatcheva 1985 and 1995.

[16] See Dessau 1913, 699, Bowersock 1965, 152 *sqq.* and Sullivan 1979, 193-194.

[17] See e.g. Jones 1971, 9 : «Cotys paved the way to the unification of Thrace by arranging a matrimonial alliance with the other most powerful royal family of Thrace».

male side of the alliance with the Astai. The relatively frequent mention of Sapaioi in ancient Greek and Latin sources from the sixth century BC to the second century AD permits us to locate their homeland in a more or less accurate way in the vicinity of Abdera and Maronea stretching towards the north into the Rhodopes. The identification of the Sapaean mountain (Σαπαίων ὄρος) mentioned by Appian in 42 BC with the Lekane mountain and of the Sapaean pass (τὰ Σαπαίων στενά) with a pass at the south or south-west of this mountain —near Acontisma or, more probably, at the pass of Aghios Silas north/north-west of the modern town of Kavala— demonstrates that their location during the first century BC was still the same as in earlier times[18]. And it is this location that brings forward a most important element in our effort to understand the emergence of the client-kingdom of Thrace: the land of the Sapaioi —or at least a substantial part of it— probably belonged to the territories incorporated into Macedonia by the last Antigonids and were a part of the first Macedonian μερίς since the very beginning[19]. Moreover and even before the fall of the Macedonian kingdom, the Sapaioi were constant allies of the Romans and no change of attitude towards them appears in ancient sources. On the contrary, and as already stated above, the Sapaioi were particularly helpful to Roman armies in their march towards Philippoi in 42 BC. In a very telling way, Appian narrates how the two Sapaean brothers Rhaskos and Rhaskuporis took up arms for different sides, Rhaskos for Antony and Rhaskuporis for Cassius (Ῥωμαϊκῶν Ἐμφυλίων 4.11.87) and how both received high praise by the Romans for their services (op.cit. 4.13.104)[20].

(b) A second indication of the decisive role Romans may have played in the creation of this kingdom of Thrace is offered by the immediate control the Sapaioi seem to have exercised on the coastal zone east of the Nestus river and north of the Greek cities of Abdera and Maronea from the middle of the first century BC onwards, as revealed by the description of Appian mentioned above, but mostly by a series of inscriptions mentioning the Sapaean dynasts[21]. This control, which certainly reflects a drastic change compared to the settlement of Thracian affairs of 146 BC, is usually interpreted in modern historiography as an acknowledgement from the part of Rome of its inefficiency in controlling Thracian affairs. But it should be remembered that in many cases Rome showed no hesitation in abandoning conquered

---

[18] See mainly Ῥωμαϊκῶν ἐμφυλίων 4.13.103. For a thorough analysis regarding the identification of this pass, see Parissaki 2000-2003, with all the relevant references and previous bibliography.
[19] See above, p. 98.
[20] See above, n. 14 and also Sullivan 1979, 195-196.
[21] These are basically (from west to east) : (a) one inscription from a quarry named Tzari in the area of Nea Karvali, that is ten kilometres east of Kavala, see Bakalakis 1935, 302-310, fig. 1-2 (=Οἶνος Ἰσμαρικός 19-27); (b) the inscription IThrAeg E83 of unknown exact origin, but from a place lying west of Abdera ; (c) probably IThrAeg E207 from Maronea ; (d) and one more from Perinthos, see Sayar 1998, no 5. For the historical conclusions to be drawn from the presence of these inscriptions within or close to the territory of Greek cities, see Loukopoulou 1987, 88—91 and more precisely p. 91 where the author concludes that these inscriptions *"make it sufficiently clear in our opinion that during the last decades of the pre-Christian era and the early decades of the first century A.D. the Thracian coasts of the Aegean and the Propontis fell under the sovereign rule or the suzerainty of the Thracian kings and, in consequence, were outside the limits of direct Roman rule and beyond the bounds of provincial administration"*.

territory to the control of local dynasts, if this was considered more expedient to her policy and it is to this «abandonment» that lays the very *raison d'être* of many client kingdoms in the East. From the many examples one could mention, suffice it here to remember the history of the province of Cilicia, first created in 102 BC to include a region stretching along the southern coast of Asia Minor, lessened to include only *Cilicia Campestris* during Antony and Augustus —when wide domains were granted to local kings— and then augmented again under Vespasian in AD 72, when these local dynasties were finally suppressed[22].

(c) One last point should be stressed in order to get a better grasp of the Roman factor in the emergence of this new kingdom of Thrace. The initial unification of the two Thracian tribes of the Astoi and Sapaioi led to a gradual and loose —and for that reason very difficult to define geographically— political unification of Thrace that lasted all along the last century of its «independent» history[23]. Of how unstable and precarious this unification was, the very history of this kingdom is the telling proof; but notwithstanding its character, this political unification of Thrace would not have lasted without the constant support of the Romans. In the most important crises that the Thracian kings had to face during this last century, the intervention of Rome seems to have been immediate and effective; this is explicitly mentioned in the sources for AD 21, when Rhoemetalkes II was besieged in Philippopolis by the joint forces of the Coelaletae, Odrysae and Dii (Tac. *Ann.* 3-38-39) and again a few years later during the revolt of the Bessoi (Tac. *Ann.* 4. 46-51)[24].

If we accept that Rome was the *éminence grise* behind the formation of this new kingdom of Thrace, then one more question should be addressed: was this initiative finally successful? As underlined above, the history of the client-kingdom of Thrace seems to have been one of constant instability and, consequently, a source of recurrent concern for Rome. Dynastic rivalries among the ruling family were fierce and in two cases they finally led to the subdivision of the kingdom. But when considering the final goal behind this Sapaean-Astaean alliance —that is the effective control of the Thracian tribes and the protection of the Roman province of Macedonia from their incursions— then this policy should certainly be considered much more effective than the one pursued during the first period. From the middle of the first century BC to AD 46 AD the mobilisation of the Roman army due to the incapacity of the client-kingdom to effectively control Thracian tribes seems to have been necessitated only in a few occasions, basically during the two revolts mentioned above; and more important still, it seems that during this same period the province of Macedonia was not seriously threatened by Thracian incursions. Moreover, it should be remembered that inner-dynastic quarrels might not have been unpleasant or burdensome to Rome, since they actually contributed in keeping the Thracian dynast at charge under Ro-

---

[22] For the quite complicated administrative history of the region, see the concise summary of Sartre 1991, 258-260.
[23] For the gradual character of this unification, see also Sullivan 1979, 188, n. 2.
[24] For a brief description of the events of these years, see Jones 1971, 8-10 and Danov 1979, 127-145.

man check. If Luttwak's remark in his book entitled «The Grand Strategy of the Roman Empire» that the success of a client-kingdom may be assessed by its lifespan be accepted as correct, then it should be remembered that the client-kingdom of Thrace with its history of almost a century should be counted among the most long-lived ones and, consequently, among the most successful.

To sum up, from 146 BC to AD 46 two periods may be discerned as far as the handling of Thracian affairs by the Romans is concerned. During the first one —spanning from the provincialisation of Macedonia in 146 BC and the first direct involvement of Romans in the region to approximately the second quarter of the first century BC— Roman policy in Thrace may be interpreted as an effort to duplicate Antigonid expertise; but this effort seems to have been a failure, either because of Roman unawareness of local conditions or because of changing realities, or maybe because of both. After the disruption provoked by the Mithridatic threat and the civil wars of Rome, a second period can be clearly discerned spanning from about the middle of the first century BC till the provincialisation of Thrace in AD 46. During this last century of Thracian «independence» Romans shifted subtly to a scheme that both suited Thracian realities and their own political and social concepts, namely the traditional pattern of patron-client relationship (*clientela*). If focusing on diplomacy in a volume dedicated to military activities may be excusable, it is precisely because knowledge of the strategic aims lying behind military activities is a prerequisite for their better understanding. For in Thrace of the second century BC to the first century AD, just as in many other cases where Rome decided to avoid direct annexation, military activities seem to have been either a means of creating the necessary ground for alliances or a means to remedy their failure.

Maria-Gabriella Parissaki
Institute of Historical Research,
Research Centre for Greek and Roman Antiquity (KERA, Athens)

Bibliography

Avram & Bounegru 2006 = A. Avram and O. Bounegru, «Mithridates VI. Eupator und die griechischen Städte an der Westküste des Pontos Euxeinos», in S. Conrad, R. Einicke, A.E. Furtwängler, H. Löhr, A. Slawisch (eds), *Pontos Euxeinos. Beiträge zur Archäologie und Geshchichte des antiken Schwarzmeer- und Balkanraumes*, Schriften des Zentrums für Archäologie und Kulturgeschichte des Schwarzmeerraumes 10 (Langenweißbach 2006) 397-413.

Bakalakis 1935 = G. Bakalakis, «Θρακικὰ Εὐχαριστήρια εἰς τὸν Δία», *Thrakika* 6 (1935) 302-318 = *Οἶνος Ἰσμαρικός. Τιμητικὸς τόμος γιὰ τὸν καθηγητὴ Γ. Μπακαλάκη* (Thessalonike 1990) 19-35.

Boteva 2002 = Dilyana Boteva, «An Attempt at identifying Alexander's Route towards the Danube in 335 BC», *Jubilaeus V. Сборник в чест на проф. М. Тачева* (Sofia 2002) 27-31.

Bowersock 1965 = G. Bowersock, *Augustus and the Greek World* (Oxford 1965).

Crawford 1996 = M.H. Crawford (ed.), *Roman Statutes* (London 1996).

Danov 1979 = Chr.M. Danov, «Die Thraker auf dem Ostbalkan von der hellenistischen Zeit biz zur Gründung Konstantinopels» *ANRW* 7.1 (Berlin-New York 1979) 21-185.

Dessau 1913 = H. Dessau, «Miscellanea Epigraphica I et II» *EphemEpigr* 9 (1913) 691-706.

Gaggero 1976 = E.S. Gaggero, «Relations politiques et militaires de Mithridate VI Eupator avec les populations et les cités de la Thrace et avec les colonies grecques de la mer Noire occidentale» *Pulpudeva* 2 (1976) 294-305.

Gerov 1961 = B. Gerov, «Проучвания върху западно тракийските земи през римско време (Untersuchungen über die Westthrakischen Länder in römischen Zeit)» *AUS* 54.3 (1959/1960) 154-407 = *Beiträge zur Geschichte der römischen Provinzen Moesien und Thrakien. Gesammelte Aufsätze* (Amsterdam 1998) 1-252 (bulgarian, with german summary).

Hammond & Walbank 1988 = N.G.L. Hammond and F.W. Walbank, *A History of Macedonia, vol. III, 336-167 BC* (Oxford 1988).

Hatzopoulos 1984 = M.B. Hatzopoulos,, «Les politarques de Philippopolis. Un élément méconnu pour la datation d'une magistrature macédonienne», *Dritter Internationaler Thrakologischer Kongress, Wien 1980* (Sofia 1984) vol. II, 137-149.

Hatzopoulos 1980 = M.B. Hatzopoulos, «La politique Thrace des derniers Antigonides», *Pulpudeva* 4 (1980) [Sofia 1983] 80-87.

IThrAeg = L. D. Loukopoulou, M.-G. Parissaki, S. Psôma, A. Zournatzi, Ἐπιγραφές τῆς Θράκης τοῦ Αἰγαίου: μεταξύ τῶν ποταμῶν Νέστου καί Ἕβρου, Νομοί Ξάνθης, Ῥοδόπης καί Ἕβρου (Inscriptions of Aegean Thrace) (Athens 2005).

Jones 1971 = A.H.M. Jones, *The Cities of the Eastern Roman Provinces* (Oxford 1971[2]).

Loukopoulou 1987 = L.D. Loukopoulou, «*Provinciae Macedoniae Finis Orientalis*. The Establishment of the Eastern Frontier», in M.B. Hatzopoulos and L.D. Loukopoulou, *Two Studies in Ancient Macedonian Topography* (ΜΕΛΕΤΗΜΑΤΑ 3; Athens 1987) 61-110.

Papazoglou 1978 = F. Papazoglou, *The Central Balkan Tribes in pre-Roman Times. Triballi, Autariatae, Dardanians, Scordisci and Moesians* (Amsterdam 1978).

Papazoglou 1979 = F. Papazoglou, «Quelques aspects de l'histoire de la province de Macédoine» *ANRW* 7.1 (Berlin-New York 1979) 302-369.

Parissaki 2000-2003 = M.-G. Parissaki, «Les défilés des Corpiles et des Sapéens. Réexamen d'un problème topographique» *Ἥρος* 14-16 (2000-2003) 345-362 (in greek, with french summary)

Picard 2008 = O. Picard, «Les tétradrachmes à types thasiens et les guerres thraces au début du Ier siècle avant notre ère» *CRAI* (2008) 465-493.

Popov 2002 = Chr. Popov, *Урбанизация във вътрешните райони на Тракия и Илирия през VI - I век преди Христа* (*Urbanisierung in den inneren Gebieten Thrakiens und Illyriens im. 6.-1. Jhd. V. Chr.*) (Sofia 2002).

Rufin Solas (forthcoming) = A. Rufin Solas, «War and *Philia*. The last Antigonids and the warrior peoples of Thrace (196-168 BC)», communication présentée à l'occasion de la *Classical Association Annual Conference*, 7-10 avril 2010, Cardiff (forthcoming).

Sartre 1991 = M. Sartre, *L'Orient Romain. Provinces et sociétés provinciales en Méditerranée orientale d'Auguste aux Sévères (31 avant J.-C.-235 après J.-C.)*, (Paris 1991).

Sayar 1998 = M.H. Sayar, *Perinthos-Herakleia (Marmara Ereglisi) und Umgebung. Geschichte, Testimonien, griechische-lateinische Inschriften* (Vienna 1998).

Sullivan 1979 = R.D. Sullivan, «Thrace in the Eastern Dynastic Network» *ANRW* 7.1 (Berlin-New York 1979) 186-211.

Tatcheva 1985 = M. Tatcheva, «On the genealogy of the last kings of Thracia (100 BC-45 AD)» *Studia in honorem Chr. M. Danov. Terra Antiqua Balcanica II* (Sofia 1985) 412-417.

Tatcheva 1995 = M. Tatcheva, «The last Thracian independent dynasty of the Rhascuporids», *Studia in honorem Georgi Mihailov* (Sofia 1995) 459-467.

Walbank 1985 = Fr.W. Walbank, «*Via illa nostra militaris*: some thoughts on the Via Egnatia», *Selected Papers. Studies in Greek and Roman History and Historiography* (Cambridge 1985) 193-209.

GUERRE ET CIRCULATION MONÉTAIRE: LE CAS DES DRACHMES DE DYRRACHION

Albana META

A partir du dernier quart du IIe siècle avant J.-C., et pendant près de 70 ans, le nord de la péninsule balkanique connaît une période d'intense circulation de monnaies de types très divers. Outre les drachmes de Dyrrachion, qui font l'objet de cet article, les tétradrachmes de Thasos et de Maronée[1], les stéphanéphores d'Athènes (principalement dans le territoire de la Macédoine)[2], les drachmes d'Apollonia d'Illyrie[3], ainsi que les monnaies de la province romaine de Macédoine Première[4] puis les deniers romains (essentiellement à partir de l'an 60 avant J.-C.)[5] ont circulé dans la région balkanique. Ces différents types, souvent accompagnés dans les trésors de nombreuses imitations locales, y ont été intensivement thésaurisés, formant une masse monétaire remarquable.

On constate trois zones principales de concentration de trésors contenant des drachmes de Dyrrachion. La première se trouve tout au nord de la péninsule, dans le territoire géto-dace, et plus précisément dans l'actuelle Transylvanie et, dans l'arc carpatique ; elle s'étend jusqu'en Hongrie et à l'est de la Transylvanie, sur le territoire de l'actuelle Moldavie[6]. La deuxième zone concerne l'ancien territoire des Scordisques, tout le long des vallées des fleuves Drave et Save et suivant le cours du Danube jusqu'aux confins des peuples thraces. La troisième zone de concentration se situe quant à elle dans la basse vallée du Danube : elle s'étend sur une partie du territoire thrace et dans le Banat et la Valachie jusqu'aux vallées des fleuves Arges et Ialomita[7]. (Fig. 1)

On distingue bien un autre groupe de trouvailles, constitué de monnaies provenant de la vallée de la Neretva, qui s'étend en partie sur le territoire des Ardiéens[8]. Une observation attentive nous apprend cependant que dans la plupart des cas il s'agit de trouvailles isolées, les monnaies étant moins nombreuses dans cette région. De fait, la thésaurisation y a été moins intensive et concernait des émissions qui circulaient ailleurs dans les Balkans, simultanément aux autres. Une dernière région nous intéresse : la Pannonie ; I. Mirnik a rassemblé quelques unes des trouvailles provenant de Croatie, publiant même la liste des monétaires qui figurent sur les drachmes[9]. (Fig. 2)

---

[1] Picard, à paraître à l'été 2011.
[2] Voir Callataÿ 1991-92, 11-20.
[3] Gjongecaj - Picard 2005, 140.
[4] Voir Prokopov 1994.
[5] Voir Crawford 1985, 229-233.
[6] Poenaru Bordea 1983, 224-225 ; Mihailescu – Birliba 1980, 29.
[7] Gjongecaj & Picard, 2005, 140.
[8] Sašel Kos 2005, 224.
[9] Mirnik 1996, 526-529.

Fig. 1 *Carte des trésors de drachmes de Dyrrachion découverts dans la région balkanique*

Il est important ici de préciser les limites chronologiques de ce phénomène particulier de circulation monétaire. La datation des monnaies de Thasos et de Maronée[10], celles de leurs imitations «barbares» et des monnaies alexandrines et de Macédoine Première ainsi que, surtout, les études sur la pénétration du denier républicain romain dans la région balkanique[11] ont fourni des indices fondamentaux sur la question et ont permis d'établir l'an 120 avant J.-C. comme date du début de l'intensification de la circulation monétaire dans les Balkans[12]. A partir de cette date les Scordisques, les Thraces, les Daces, les Gètes, les Illyriens, les Macédoniens et bien évidemment les Romains sont les acteurs principaux dans cette arène de conflits que constitue alors la région balkanique.

Une première tentative de datation de l'enfouissement des trésors balkaniques de drachmes de Dyrrachion a été réalisée par N. Conovici. Celui-ci a identifié un pre-

---

[10] Picard 2008a, 471-481; voir aussi Callataÿ 1991, 213-226.
[11] Crawford 1985, 229-233.
[12] Gjongecaj & Picard, 2005, 139-154.

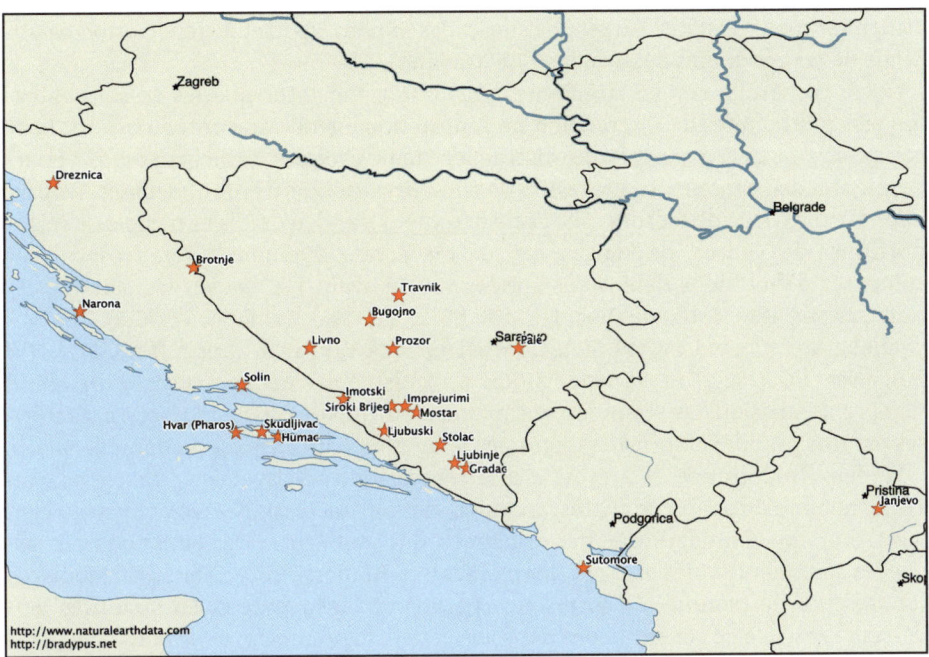

Fig. 2 *Carte des trouvailles isolées de la vallée de Neretva et de la Pannonie*

mier groupe dans le dernier quart du IIe siècle avant J.-C., un deuxième dans les années 100-85 et un autre dans la période 85-50, avec un enfouissement massif dans les années 70-60[13]. Cependant, nous avons constaté que les limites chronologiques ne sont pas si nettes pour la période 120-85. Les trésors datés par Conovici dans les années 120-100 (trésors de Dieci I et II) comprennent un nombre trop élevé d'émissions pour qu'elles aient été frappées en seulement vingt ans. De la même façon, il nous semble très difficile de classer les émissions en périodes très brèves. Nous avons constaté que pendant une première période les trésors ne sont composés que de monnayages grecs et ce n'est qu'ultérieurement qu'on constate la présence du denier romain. La chronologie des tétradrachmes de Thasos et les études sur l'introduction du denier dans la région nous fournissent bien une limite chronologique sur les deux périodes. La circulation massive des premiers s'arrête dans les années 80-75 avant J.-C[14]. Ce moment signe un changement dans la structure des trésors, qui contiennent toujours moins de monnaies thasiennes et qui, à la fin des années 60, sont dominés par le denier romain. Dans leur travail sur la circulation des drachmes d'Apollonia et de Dyrrachion dans les Balkans, O. Picard et Sh. Gjongecaj

---

[13] Conovici 1983-1985, 87-88.
[14] Picard 2011a.

avaient proposé de dater l'arrêt de celle-ci des années 80-70 et la pénétration balkanique de ces monnaies des années 120-70 avant J.-C[15].

Notre recherche sur les drachmes nous a fait constater que les trésors balkaniques de drachmes de Dyrrachion ne sont ni homogènes, ni contemporains. Leur composition nous a permis de distinguer deux groupes principaux qui appartiennent à deux moments successifs de thésaurisation et d'enfouissement. Le premier est constitué de trésors mixtes de drachmes des deux cités et parfois de tétradrachmes de Thasos, de Maronée et de Macédoine Première[16]. Ces trésors sont composés d'émissions datées des années 120-70 avant J.-C. Parmi les plus importants, citons les trésors de Dieci I, II, III[17] (*IGCH* 594-595), Zaklopaca[18] (*IGCH* 579), Michailovgrad[19] (*CH*, vol. IV, 62), Sieu-Odorhei (*CH*, vol. VIII, 493), Rupci[20] (*IGCH* 572), NW Bulgarie[21] (*IGCH* 612) et Panade[22] (*IGCH* 620). Ils sont tous composés d'un grand nombre d'émissions, certaines ayant même été frappées avant 120, sont caractérisés par une grande quantité de monnaies mais aussi par l'absence du denier romain.

Le deuxième groupe de trésors a une composition relativement homogène : un grand nombre de deniers romains, accompagnés de drachmes de Dyrrachion, ou bien des trésors ne contenant que des drachmes, qui sont toutes des émissions sur lesquelles sont mentionnés au droit les monétaires Silanos, Philôn, Xénon ou Méniskos (la présence de monnaies d'autres types étant peu fréquente et en quantités modestes). L'absence de ces émissions dans les trésors du premier groupe nous a incité à les considérer comme un groupe à part, qui constitue à notre avis la dernière phase des drachmes de Dyrrachion. La quantité des trésors ainsi que des monnaies est remarquable. Quant à la chronologie des trésors, il est bien évident que ceux-ci sont enfouis après l'introduction du denier dans la région, la pénétration massive de ce celui-ci étant datée des environs de l'an 60 avant J.-C. M. Crawford a souligné que des pièces plus anciennes ont été prélevées de la masse monétaire circulant en Italie dans les années 80-60. D'après lui, la date de la frappe du denier le plus récent ne saurait constituer une limite chronologique pour l'enfouissement du trésor qui le contient : «*it would clearly be extremely hazardous to argue that the hoards were deposited immediately after the date of the latest coin in them*»[23]. Cette argumentation nous semble préférable et nous resterons fidèles à la datation de Crawford sur la pénétration massive des deniers romains dans les Balkans vers les années 60 avant J.-C. En conséquence, nous admettrons que la plupart de ces trésors mixtes de drachmes et deniers romains ont été enfouis après les années 60. Les trésors du tableau ont un point en commun : ils sont tous composés d'émissions de Méniskos, Xénôn, Philôn et en grand partie aussi de

---

[15] Picard – Gjongecaj 2000, 157-158.
[16] Picard 2011c.
[17] Săşianu 1980, 109-120.
[18] Petrović 1932, 40-65.
[19] Youroukova 1977, 69.
[20] Gerasimov 1963, 261.
[21] Gerasimov 1955, 607.
[22] Brudiu 1971, 173-176 ; Mitrea 1971b, 177-207.
[23] Crawford 1985, 232.

Silanos. Nous avons constaté que dans les trésors où l'on observe la présence de plusieurs autres émissions, le rapport numérique entre celles-ci et les émissions de Méniskos, Xénôn et Philôn est en faveur des dernières. Cela est renforcé par l'existence d'autres trésors composés principalement de ces émissions. Ainsi le trésor de Tileagd n'est-il composé que de drachmes d'Apollonia et de Dyrrachion, ces dernières toutes émissions de Xénôn et Méniskos[24]. Celui de Budoi-Marghita n'est composé que d'émissions de Silanos, Xénôn et Méniskos[25], tandis que celui de Panade représente l'un des plus grands trésors de drachmes de Dyrrachion, avec 273 exemplaires. Constatons que les émissions de la phase précédente, comme Ktètos, Eynoys, Euktèmôn, Philôtas, Philèmôn etc., ne sont représentées que par une ou deux monnaies. Sur le total des monnaies, 253 sont des émissions de Philôn, Xénôn, Méniskos[26]. Une composition similaire est à constater dans les trésors de Grozeşti, Voivodeni, Bessarabie et Viişoara. Le premier comporte 180 drachmes de Dyrrachion dont 167 sont des émissions des monétaires en question[27]. Dans le trésor de Voivodeni, ces dernières constituent environ 60% du total. Celui de Bessarabie contient 334 drachmes de Dyrrachion et 52 d'Apollonia. Des premières, 297 sont émissions des quatre monétaires de la dernière phase[28]. Le trésor de Viişoara fournit la preuve la plus évidente de la massivité de ces émissions. Il contient 12 monnaies émises par Silanos, 82 par Philôn, 145 par Xénôn ainsi que 543 par Méniskos. Ce nombre est très élevé par rapport aux 18 exemplaires provenant de la phase précédente[29].

La composition des trésors mixtes de deniers et de drachmes suggère que les émissions de ces dernières ont été en utilisation longtemps après qu'ils ont pénétré la région balkanique. Le trésor de Dolj[30] (*IGCH* 673) qui comprend des drachmes et des deniers romains, le plus récent datant de l'an 37 avant J.-C., le prouve. L'état d'usure des monnaies montre également une utilisation sur une durée considérable[31]. Il est curieux de noter aussi que les trésors de ce groupe ne comprennent que rarement, ou pas du tout, d'émissions de la dernière phase des drachmes d'Apollonia, dont la circulation balkanique s'arrête apparemment vers les années 80-70[32]. Nous découvrons donc que, curieusement, les drachmes de Dyrrachion continuent à circuler en même temps que les deniers romains dans les Balkans et que leur circulation ne s'arrête pas en même temps que celle des drachmes d'Apollonia. Même s'il est difficile de savoir précisément jusqu'à quand ces monnaies avaient une valeur sur le marché, les trésors montrent qu'elles ont circulé au moins jusqu'aux années 40 avant J.-C.

---

[24] Mitrea 1960, 465-466.
[25] Luchian 1971, 364.
[26] Brudiu, 1971, 182-183.
[27] Mitrea, 1971a, 26.
[28] Popilian 1974, 55-56.
[29] Mitrea 1958, 77-78.
[30] Conovici 1985, 59-74.
[31] Les monnaies sont en général très usées: nous n'avons que rarement observé des pièces bien conservées.
[32] Gjongecaj & Picard 2005, 140-153.

Quant aux motifs pour lesquels les drachmes ont circulé dans les Balkans, ils ont longtemps été cherchés dans le commerce et le développement économique des peuples balkaniques[33]. Nous voudrions opposer à cela quelques arguments. Premièrement, les trouvailles monétaires au nord des Balkans ne sont pas équivalentes à celles de l'autre partie de la péninsule: la concentration de trésors de drachmes est plus forte, et le contenu plus diversifié au nord que dans le reste de la région. Que ce soit à Dyrrachion ou à Apollonia, on ne constate pas de changement dans la circulation monétaire. Dans cette partie de la péninsule il n'y a ni concentration élevée de trésors, ni circulation massive d'autres types monétaires. Deuxièmement, il n'existe de grand flux de produits provenant du nord des Balkans ni à Dyrrachion et Apollonia, ni dans l'Illyrie Méridionale. Cela n'exclut pas l'existence d'échanges commerciaux entre les peuples illyriens, thraces, gètes et daces, mais cela ne peut suffire à expliquer la circulation massive de drachmes en Dacie et en Thrace. L'argument commercial ne permet pas non plus d'expliquer pourquoi on ne constate cette grande monétarisation des échanges que pour une période limitée, qui, d'ailleurs, ne constitue pas une période de développements économiques régionaux remarquables. Il resterait aussi à expliquer le grand nombre d'imitations de ces monnaies. Enfin, M. Crawford avait finement noté l'absence des petites dénominations dans les trésors, fait qui contredit l'hypothèse du commerce et d'une économie de marché[34].

Une explication alternative à ce phénomène d'intense circulation monétaire dans les Balkans nous est fournie par Crawford. Il explique la pénétration massive des deniers romains dans la péninsule par le commerce des esclaves : après la victoire du Cn. Pompeius contre les pirates en 67, la région constituait désormais une source alternative d'esclaves pour Rome[35]. La thèse de Crawford, même si elle offre une explication pour la pénétration du denier romain, est cependant insuffisante pour expliquer pourquoi une si grande quantité de drachmes de Dyrrachion de la dernière phase ont circulé parallèlement aux deniers romains.

Si la grande masse monétaire circulant dans la région n'est une conséquence ni de l'économie monétarisée, ni du commerce, quelle qu›aient été sa nature et ses produits, il faut alors en chercher les raisons ailleurs. L'événement auquel les numismates pensent naturellement chaque fois qu'il y a un changement dans la masse monnayée ou dans la circulation monétaire est la guerre[36]. La phrase qui caractérise le mieux la relation entre argent et guerre est celle de Cicéron, «l'argent est le nerf de la guerre»[37]. A partir de l'an 120 jusqu'aux années 80 avant J.-C., les peuples de la région sont les acteurs principaux des conflits guerriers avec la nouvelle province romaine de Macédoine. Il semble en effet que la majorité des conflits régionaux ont deux acteurs principaux, les peuples balkaniques et Rome. A partir de l'an 119 avant J.-C., les Scordisques

---

[33] Mihailescu & Birliba 1980, 30 ; Chitescu, 1980, 128 ; Ceka 1965, 36-37.
[34] Crawford 1985, 229.
[35] *Ibid*, 233.
[36] Howgego 1990, 8; voir aussi Callataÿ 1999, 28-35.
[37] Cicéron *Phil.*, V, 5.

et les autres peuples balkaniques devenus leurs alliés ont attaqué l'armée des gouverneurs romains de la Macédoine sans répit, obligeant Rome à envoyer régulièrement des armées consulaires. A l'est, l'autre grand ennemi de Rome était le roi Mithridate VI Eupator qui, après avoir conclu des alliances avec les cités du Pont, en élargissant les domaines de son royaume, a entrepris des invasions en territoires thrace et macédonien en 87-86 avant J.-C. Ces conflits furent suivis par ceux conduits par Burebista qui, après être devenu le roi des Gètes et des Daces, a traversé l'Ister et a entrepris des pillages en Thrace jusqu'en Macédoine et en Illyrie, et anéantit peu après les Boii et les Taurisci[38]. Son grand empire était certainement un problème pour Rome.

Il faut souligner qu'il existe une concordance entre les lieux de trouvailles des trésors et les territoires engagés dans la guerre. Nos trésors se trouvent dans le territoire des Scordisques, des Thraces, des Daces et des Gètes. Les trouvailles indiquent que la pénétration des drachmes dans la région balkanique s'est faite par la vallée du fleuve Morava, qui débouchait dans le Danube à Viminacium[39]. De Lissus, dans l'arrière-pays de Dyrrachion, le passage vers la Morava était garanti par une route passant dans le territoire de la Dardanie, connue pendant la période romaine comme la Via Lissus–Naisus[40]. De Viminacium, on avait accès au cours du Danube, d'où l'on remontait jusqu'au cours moyen du Mureș pour arriver en Transylvanie[41].

Il reste à expliquer pourquoi utiliser les drachmes de Dyrrachion et d'Apollonia dans des territoires qui sont relativement loin des deux cités. Il est nécessaire de rappeler ici que la région située au nord des Balkans était importatrice de monnaies étrangères. Les peuples locaux frappaient monnaie de façon irrégulière et, souvent, n'avaient pas de monnaie propre. Ainsi, des types étrangers étaient importés[42] et se substituaient aux types frappés localement. Cela nous aide à comprendre que ces peuples n'avaient pas de préjugés quant à l'utilisation et la circulation massive de monnaies étrangères. Doit-on admettre alors que ce sont les peuples balkaniques qui ont préféré l'importation des drachmes de Dyrrachion et d'Apollonia pour leurs besoins de financement ses conflits militaires? Ou sont-ce plutôt les Romains qui sont à l'origine de la distribution de ces milliers de drachmes dans la région ? Il est important à ce point de notre exposé de faire quelques constatations sur les relations entre Rome, Dyrrachion et Apollonia. Les dommages causés aux ports des deux cités par la piraterie illyrienne[43], leur soumission dans le cadre du protectorat romain à la fin du IIIe siècle avant J.-C.[44], ainsi que la présence d'hommes d'affaires et de négociants à Dyrrachion et Apollonia[45], ont beaucoup affecté leur politique envers Rome. Les deux cités ont suivi, à partir de la fin du IIIe siècle et jusqu'à la fin

---

[38] Sašel kos 2005, 500.
[39] Mitrea 1958, 185.
[40] Voir Hoxha & Perzhita 2003, 26, 128.
[41] Poenaru Bordea & Stoica 1975, 30 ; Ceka, 1966, 222-223.
[42] Gjongecaj & Picard 2005, 146 – 147.
[43] Polybe II, 8, 1-3.
[44] Ferrary 1978, 733.
[45] *Ibid.*, 782-783 ; cf., dans le présent volume, la contribution de S. Shpuza *Ibid.*, 782-783 ; cf., dans le présent volume, la contribution de S. Shpuza.

des guerres civiles à Rome, une politique favorable à Rome, en étant ses alliées. Leur position géographique, surtout en ce qui concerne Dyrrachion, fait qu'elles sont très importantes dans la communication entre les deux rives de la mer Adriatique. Se trouvant en face de la côte italique, toutes deux ont joué un rôle fondamental dans les routes commerciales qui connectaient l'Italie avec les Balkans[46]. Ce rôle grandit, surtout après le milieu du IIe siècle, avec la construction de la *Via Egnatia*, faisant de Dyrrachion l'un des points de départ de la route qui liait Rome avec l'Orient[47]. Etant les ports les plus proches de Rome dans les Balkans, Dyrrachion et Apollonia ont fourni une base pour le débarquement des troupes militaires pendant les guerres de Macédoine[48] et pendant les conflits suivants, et ceci jusqu'à la fin des guerres civiles. Un trésor composé de 1874 monnaies républicaines romaines, des deniers et quelques quinaires, tous datés entre 179 et 45 avant J.-C., ainsi que d'un hémidrachme de Dyrrachion a été trouvé à Apollonia en 1974[49]. Il est intéressant que l'on puisse, dans un même trésor, trouver trace des mouvements de l'armée romaine d'une rive à l'autre de l'Adriatique. Cela nous aide également à mieux comprendre l'importance, pour Rome, de la cité à l'est de l'Adriatique.

Nous pensons que les passages répétés des armées romaines dans le territoire des deux cités a été fondamental pour la distribution des drachmes dans les Balkans. Nous ne doutons pas qu'entre les deux cités et les territoires au nord de la région il y a eu des contacts, même avant la présence romaine dans la péninsule. Il n'y a pas non plus de doute sur le fait que les drachmes étaient connues par ces peuples avant même la pénétration romaine. Mais ce sont les conflits militaires continus qui ont rendu possible le mouvement massif et intense du monnayage. Toutefois, il nous semble évident que cette circulation n'est pas liée qu'aux passages de l'armée. La quantité considérable de drachmes circulant dans les Balkans montre clairement qu'il y a eu la volonté, de la part de Rome, de les utiliser dans la région. Nous pensons que Rome a utilisé les drachmes de Dyrrachion pour financer ses campagnes militaires dans les Balkans. Ce ne serait pas le premier monnayage grec mis à la disposition des Romains ou frappé par eux[50] pour leurs besoins dans la région. La preuve la plus claire de notre affirmation est fournie pas les drachmes de la dernière phase. L'étude minutieuse de ces émissions a mis en évidence des particularités que nous n'avons pas constatées pour les phases précédentes. Le grand nombre de monnaies frappées pendant une brève période de temps, leur circulation très intensive dans un territoire précis, le style médiocre de ces pièces, la mauvaise gravure et les fautes dans la gravure des noms, la quantité élevée des monnaies hors flan ainsi que la présence considérable d'imitations de ces émissions nous ont amenée à les considérer comme des émissions de guerre.

---

[46] Bandelli 2001, 217, 220-221.
[47] Deniaux 2007, 76.
[48] Gjongecaj & Picard 2005, 145.
[49] Gjongecaj 1981, 105-152.
[50] Voir Callataÿ 1996, 114; Callataÿ 1998, 117 ; Prokopov & Callataÿ 1998, 235 ; Picard 2011b, 84-90.

En l'état de nos connaissances sur la cité, il est impossible d'établir comment les événements se sont déroulés, ni dans quelle mesure la présence continue des Romains dans la cité a pu affecter l'activité de l'atelier monétaire à Dyrrachion. Nous n'avons pas non plus de sources écrites qui peuvent nous renseigner sur les détails de «l'amitié» entre la cité et les Romains. Mais le fait que ces dernières émissions de drachmes ont circulé parallèlement aux deniers romains n'est pas fortuit. La coïncidence des lieux de trouvailles des deux monnayages ainsi que leur présence jumelée dans les trésors le prouve. Après l'étude des trésors albanais et balkaniques, nous avons constaté que ces émissions ont été frappées pendant une brève période de temps et qu'après avoir été introduites dans la circulation régionale, elles ont continué à y être échangées jusqu'aux années 40 du Ier siècle avant J.-C. et même quelques années après. Certes, nous ne sommes pas en train de proposer que l'atelier monétaire de Dyrrachion a été occupé par les Romains. Nous constatons simplement que le début des conflits balkaniques et la présence militaire romaine ont fait que la cité frappe des drachmes en grandes quantités pour les besoins de Rome. Nous ne trouvons aucun autre besoin de nature économique ou quoi que ce soit d'autre qui puisse justifier la frappe de milliers de monnaies par la cité pendant presque soixante-dix ans. Soulignons aussi que Dyrrachion n'était pas qu'une cité «amie» de Rome, ni un simple pont de passage pour l'armée romaine. Quelques inscriptions grecques du Ier siècle avant J.-C. à Dyrrachion témoignent de la présence d'une catégorie particulière de noms latins qui sont différents de ceux des colonisateurs. L'analyse de ceux-ci fait conclure à une présence romaine importante dans la cité avant l'arrivée des colonisateurs dans les années 30 du Ier siècle avant J.-C.[51]

Un des facteurs qui ont influencé directement la distribution des drachmes de Dyrrachion et d'Apollonia dans les Balkans est le besoin de payer la solde de l'armée[52]. Il est crucial à cet égard de souligner que la région s'est caractérisée par l'emploi d'hommes dans les différentes armées comme mercenaires[53]. Il s'agit en effet de peuples guerriers, qui vendent leurs services militaires à plusieurs dynastes et chefs, selon les besoins du moment. Il suffit de relever à quel point les divers peuples se sont engagés aux côtés de l'un ou l'autre des acteurs de la guerre pendant les conflits[54]. A la participation dans les conflits militaires des peuples gètes, daces et thraces nous ajouterons aussi celle des Illyriens[55]. Les trouvailles monétaires dans le territoire des Dalmates, des Liburnes, des Ardiéens et des Pannoniens nous apprennent qu'ils ne furent pas exclus des événements militaires de l'époque. Les Illyriens sont en outre évoqués par les auteurs anciens pour avoir vendu leurs services comme mercenaires: au IIIe siècle avant J.-C., ils sont mentionnés, parmi d'autres

---

[51] Wilkes 2002, 386.
[52] Kraay 1984, 3-18 ; cf. Saimir Shpuza, *loc. cit. supra*, n. 45.
[53] Gjongecaj & Picard 2005, 148.
[54] Picard 2008b, 181.
[55] On fait référence ici surtout aux tribus illyriennes du Nord, dans le voisinage des Thraces et des Daces, la situation étant différente dans l'Illyrie méridionale pendant cette période.

peuples, comme faisant partie des troupes mercenaires du *koinon* achaien[56]; en 231, la Macédoine «loua» leurs services pour protéger l'Acarnanie contre les attaques des Etoliens[57] ; dans deux autres exemples, nous trouvons les Parthiniens engagés comme cavaliers dans l'armée romaine pendant la guerre contre le roi illyrien Genthios[58] ainsi que dans l'armée de Brutus, dans la bataille de Philippes[59]. Cela nous donne donc toutes les raisons de croire que des hommes des différentes tribus illyriennes ont été engagés comme mercenaires au service de Rome ou d'autres peuples régionaux durant les conflits du IIe et du Ier siècle. Etant donné que les drachmes représentaient une monnaie acceptée et connue dans la région, le paiement des troupes était probablement fait avec cette monnaie.

Ensuite, dès qu'un ou plusieurs types monétaires s'introduisent dans une région, il y a d'autres facteurs qui peuvent rendre possible leur distribution dans un vaste territoire. Tout d'abord, en marge des troupes militaires, suivait un grand nombre de marchands et d'hommes d'affaires dont l'objectif était de commercer dans les diverses régions traversées. Plusieurs exemples dans le monde grec montrent bien que l'armée était souvent suivie d'une caravane de marchands qui exerçaient leurs activités[60]. Etant donné que les ports d'Apollonia et de Dyrrachion étaient les portes d'entrée des Romains dans les Balkans, on peut en déduire que ces marchands pouvaient utiliser les drachmes des deux cités pour leurs activités. A cela il faut ajouter que le produit des pillages faits par les combattants[61] des deux camps était vendu sur les marchés, ce qui occasionnait un mouvement de l'argent.

Rappelons aussi que l'armée, pendant les campagnes, avait besoin d'être nourrie, ce qui faisait d'elle une consommatrice de biens dont l'achat nécessitait la monnaie. Tout cela faisait circuler le numéraire, et il n'est donc pas étonnant de trouver des drachmes de Dyrrachion et d'Apollonia sur le territoire des guerres. Cela expliquerait d'ailleurs pourquoi les lieux de trouvailles ne se situent pas près des grandes routes de commerce mais à l'intérieur des terres. Il est certain que c'est le grand mouvement des troupes, le paiement des mercenaires, les raids, les batailles, la vente du butin, l'activité du commerce et le besoin de nourrir des troupes qui ont engendré la circulation d'un grand nombre de types monétaires dans une région qui produisait peu ou pas du tout de monnaie propre. Nous voudrions ajouter à ce cadre un dernier élément : le versement de cadeaux ou de tributs aux chefs des tribus pour des services rendus. Les sources anciennes nous renseignent bien sur cette activité[62] et il n'est pas à exclure qu'une partie de ces versements aient pu s'effectuer en argent monnayé, ce qui expliquerait une partie des trésors.

---

[56] Grandjean 2000, 318.
[57] Ferrary 1978, 733.
[58] Tite Live 44.30. 13.
[59] Appien *Bell. civ.* 4. 88. 373.
[60] Couvenhes 2006, 418-419.
[61] *Ibid.*, p. 419.
[62] Cicéron *Pisonem*, 35, 85 ; Pline *N. H.*, 7, 26 (27), 98.

En conclusion, nous pensons que la circulation des drachmes de Dyrrachion dans la région balkanique a été le résultat des conflits militaires qui ont concerné la région pendant le dernier quart du IIe siècle jusqu'aux années 40 du Ier s. avant J.-C. C'est Rome qui, pour les besoins de financement de ses campagnes militaires, utilisa un grand nombre de monnaies de Dyrrachion alors que le denier n'était pas encore une monnaie importante dans la circulation locale balkanique et même, apparemment, quand le denier commença à pénétrer massivement dans la région.

Albana META
Institut archéologique de Tirana

Bibliographie

Bandelli 2001 = G. Bandelli, «Dallo spartiaticque appenninico all'altra sponda : Roma et l'Adriatico fra il iv e il ii secolo a.c.», *L'archeologia dell' Adriatico* (2001) 210-225.

Brudiu 1971 = L. Brudiu, «Tezaurul de drahme din Dyrrhachìum de la Pănade (Transilvania), conditiile de descoperire», *Apulum* IX (1971) 173-186.

Ceka 1965 = H. Ceka, *Probleme të numizmatikës Ilire, me një katalog të monetave të pabotueme apo të rralla të Ilirisë së jugut*, Universiteti Shtetëror i Tiranës (Tirana 1965) 19-42.

Ceka 1966 = H. Ceka, *Studia Albanica*, III, 1, Akademia e Shkencave të Shqipërisë (Tirana 1966) 213-223.

Chirilă 1968 = E. Chirilă, «Tezaurul de monede Dyrrhachiene de la Voivodeni», *Apulum* VII/I (1968) 123-144.

Chitescu 1980 = M. Chitescu, «Les monnaies géto-dace du type romain républicain et impérial», dans *Dialogues d'Histoire Ancienne*, vol. 6 (1980) 123-138.

Conovici 1985 = N. Conovici, «Date noi despre un tezaur de monede antice descoperit în judeûl Dolj», *Thraco-Dacica* 6 (1985) 59-74.

Conovici 1983-1985 = N. Conovici, «Aspecte ale circulatei drahmelor din Dyrrhachìum si Apollonia în peninsula Balcanica si în Dacia», *Buletinul Societății Numismatice Române*, 131-133 (1983-1985) 69-88.

Couvenhes 2006 = J.-Chr. Couvenhes, «La place de l'armée dans l'économie hellénistique : quelques considérations sur la condition matérielle et financière du soldat et son usage dans les marchés», dans *Approches de l'économie hellénistique*, Entretiens d'archéologie et d'histoire 7, 6-7 mai 2004 (Saint-Bertrand-de-Comminges 2006) 397-495.

Crawford 1985 = M. Crawford, «*Coinage and money under the Roman Republic. Italy and the Mediterranean economy*» (Berkeley and Los Angeles 1985) 219-235.

Callataÿ 1991 = Fr. de Callataÿ, «Un tétradrachme de Mithridate surfrappé à Maronée», *Quaderni ticinesi di numismatica e antichità classiche*, vol. XX (1991) 213-226.

Callataÿ 1991-1992 = Fr. de Callataÿ, «Athenian New Style Tetradrachms in Macedonian Hoards», *American Journal of Numismatics* 3-4 (1991-1992) 11-20.

Callataÿ 1996 = Fr. de Callataÿ, «Les monnaies au nom d'Aesillas», dans T. Hackens and G. Moucharte (éds), *Italiam Fato Profugi, Numismatic Studies Dedicated to Vladimir and Elvira Eliza Clain-Stefanelli* (Louvain-La-Neuve 1996) 113-151.

Callataÿ 1998 = Fr. de Callataÿ, «The Coins in the Name of Sura», dans A. Burnett, U. Wartenberg and R. Witschonke (eds), *Coins of Macedonia and Rome : Essays in honour of Charles Hersh* (London 1998) 113-117.

Callataÿ 1999 = Fr. de Callataÿ, «Guerres et monnayages à l'époque hellénistique», *Dossiers d'Archéologie* 248, «Numismatique grecque, romaine et celte» (1999) 28-35.

Callataÿ 2009 = Fr. de Callataÿ, «Armies poorly paid in coins (the Anabasis of the ten-thousands) and coins for soldiers poorly transformed by the markets (the hellenistic thasian type tetradrachms) in ancient Greece», *From mints to markets : the mechanisms of coin transformation in ancient times*, Revue Belge de Numismatique et de Sigillographie 155 (2009) 51-70.

Deniaux 2007 = E. Deniaux, «Recherches sur le port de Dyrrachium à l'époque romaine : fabri tignuarii et saccarii», *Epire, Illyrie, Macédoine, Mélanges offerts à P. Cabanes* (Clermont-Ferrand 2007) 71-79.

Ferrary 1978 = J.-L. Ferrary, *Rome, les Balkans, la Grèce et l'Orient au IIe siècle av. J.-C.* (Paris 1978) 730-790.

Gerasimov 1955 = Th. Gerasimov, «Колективни монетни находки през 1951, 1952, 1953, 1954 (Trésors monétaires découverts en Bulgarie en 1951, 1952, 1953 et 1954)», *ИАИ (Bulletin de l'Institut Archéologique Bulgare)* 20 (1955) 602-611.

Gerasimov 1963 = Th. Gerasimov «съкровища от монети, намерени в българия през 1960 и 1961 г. (Trésors monétaires découverts en Bulgarie en 1960 et 1961)», *ИАИ (Bulletin de l'Institut Archéologique Bulgare)*, 26 (1963) 257-270.

Gjongecaj 1981 = S. Gjongecaj, «Një thesar monedhash antike nga Apollonia», *Iliria* 2 (1981) 105-153.

Gjongecaj & Picard 2005 = S. Gjongecaj, O. Picard, «Drachmes d'Apollonia et de Dyrrachion dans les Balkans», *Studia Albanica*, vol. 38, 1 (2005) 139-154.

Grandjean 2000 = C. Grandjean, «Guerre et monnaie en Grèce ancienne : le cas du koinon achaien», dans *Guerre et économie dans les sociétés antiques*, Entretiens d'archéologie et d'histoire 5 (Saint-Bertrand-de-Comminges 2000) 315-336.

Howgego 1990 = Chr.J. Howgego, «Why did ancient states strike coins?», *The Numismatic Chronicle*, vol. 150 (1990) 1-25.

Hoxha & Perzhita 2003 = G. Hoxha, L. Perzhita, *Fortifikime të shekujve IV-VI në Dardaninë Perëndimore* (Tirana 2003).

Kraay 1984 = C.M. Kraay, «Greek coinage and war», dans *Ancient coins of the Graeco-Roman world : The Nickle Numismatic Papers*, ed. Waldemar Heckel and Richard Sullivan (Waterloo, Ontario 1984) 3-18.

Luchian 1971 = O. Luchian, «Tezaurul monetar de drahme din Apollonia şi Dyrrachium de la Budoi – Marghita», *Studii şi Cercetări de Numismatică* V (1971) 362-371.

Mihailescu-Birliba 1980 = V. Mihailescu-Birliba, *La monnaie romaine chez les Daces orientaux*, Editura Academiei Republicii Socialiste România (Bucharest 1980) 1-40.

Mirnik 1996 = I. Mirnik, «A contribution to the study of the circulation of the drachms of Apollonia and Dyrrhachium in Southern Pannonian Plain», *Annotazioni Numismatiche* 24 (1996) 526-529.

Mitrea 1958 = B. Mitrea, «Monedele oraselor Dyrrhachìum şi Apollonia în Moldova (Tesaurul de la Viişoara, r. Tg. Ocna)», *Studii şi Cercetari de Numismatica* II (1958) 27-93.

Mitrea 1960 = B. Mitrea, «Cu privire la monedele din Apollonia şi Dyrrhachium găsite la Tileagd», *Studii şi Cercetări de Numizmatică* III (1980) 465-466.

Mitrea 1971a = B. Mitrea, «Alte drahme din Dyrrhachium descoperite în Moldova şi drumul lor de pătrundere la est de Carpaţi.» Tezaurul de la Grozeşti (Jud. Bacău), *Studii şi Cercetari de Numismatica* V (1971) 21-38.

Mitrea 1971b = B. Mitrea «Note, comentarii si catalogul drahmelor din Dyrrhachìum descoperite in tezaurul de la Pănade», *Apulum* IX (1971) 177-207.

Petrovič 1932 = J. Petrovič, «Grcko blago iz sela Zaklopace kraj Beograda», *Starinar* 7 (1932) 40-65.

Picard 2008a = O. Picard, «Les tétradrachmes à types thasiens et les guerres thraces», *Comptes rendus de l'Académie des Inscriptions et des Belles-Lettres* (2008) 471-481.

Picard 2008b = O. Picard, «Thasische Tetradrachmen und die Balkankriege im ersten Jahrhundert v. Chr.», in Fr. Burrer, H. Müller (Hrsg.), *Kriegskosten und Kriegsfinanzierung* (Darmstadt 2008) 175-192.

Picard 2011a = O. Picard, «Types monétaires et trésors : le cas de Thasos», dans Fr. de Callataÿ éd., *Quantifying Monetary Supplies in Greco-roman Times*, Pragmateiai 19 (Bari 2011).

Picard 2011b = O. Picard, «La circulation monétaire dans le monde grec : le cas de Thasos», in Th. Faucher, M.-Chr., O. Picard éd., *Nomisma. La circulation monétaire dans l'antiquité, BCH Suppl* 53, 77-107.

Picard 2011c = O. Picard, «La monnaie dans les contacts entre les peuples des Balkans, (Ve – Ie s. av. J.-C.)», *Association internationale d'études du Sud-Est Européen, Xe congrès*, Paris 24-26 septembre 2009 (Paris 2011).

Picard & Gjongecaj 2000 = O. Picard, S. Gjongecaj, «Les drachmes d'Apollonia à la vache allaitante», *Revue Numismatique* 155 (2000) 137-160.

Poenaru Bordea 1983 = G. Poenaru Bordea, «Circulation des monnaies d'Apollonia et de Dyrrachion en Dacie préromaine et dans la région du Bas-Danube», in *L'Adriatico tra Mediterraneo e penisola balkanica nell'antichità, Lecce-Matera, 21-27 octobre 1973* (Tarente 1983) 221-237.

Poenaru Bordea & Stoica 1973 = G. Poenaru Bordea, O. Stoica, «Câteva descoperiri monetare din Oltenia preromană», *Buletinul Monumentelor istorice*, Bucarest, 42, 1 (1973) 25-30.

Popilian (1974) = G. Popilian, «Monedele oraşelor Dyrrhachium şi Apollonia in Oltenia», *Historica* III (1974) 43-65.

Price (1985) = M.J. Price, *Coin Hoards, Volume VII, Greek Hoards*, The Royal Numismatic Society (Londres 1985).

Prokopov 1994 = I. Prokopov, *The Tetradrachms of the First Macedonian Region* (Sofia 1994).

Prokopov & Callataÿ 1998 = I. Prokopov, Fr. de Callataÿ «A late hellenistic hoard from South-West Bulgaria (Area of Gotse Deltchev)», *Numismatic Chronicle*, 158 (1998) 228-236.

Sašel kos 2005 = M. Sašel Kos, *Appian and Illyricum, Narodni muzej Slovenije* (Ljubljana 2005).

Săşianu 1980 = A. Săşianu, *Ancient Coinage in Western and North-Western Romania*, Muzeul arii Crisurilor (Oradea 1980) 109-120.

Thompson, Mørkholm & Craay 1973 = M. Thompson, O. Mørkholm, colin m. Craay, (eds.), *An Inventory of Greek Coin Hoards*, American Numismatic Society (New York 1973)

Wartenberg, Price & McGregor 1994 = U. Wartenberg, M.J. Price, and K.A. McGregor, *Coin hoards, Volume VIII : Greek hoards*, The Royal Numismatic Society (Londres 1994).

Youroukova 1977 = Y. Youroukova, «Монетните находки, открити в България през 1971 и 1972 г. (Monnaies trouvées en Bulgarie en 1971 et 1972)», *Arheologija* 1 (1977) 69.

Zoltan 1980 = S. Zoltan, «Tezaurul Monetar de le Hilib, Jud. Covasna», *Cercetari Numizmatice* 3 (1980) 3-10.

ILLYRIENS ET ROMAINS.
DU CONFLIT À L'INTÉGRATION

Saimir SHPUZA

La proximité de l'Italie avec l'Illyrie a rendu possible des contacts étroits et une bonne connaissance du territoire illyrien par les auteurs romains. L'Adriatique semble avoir eu un statut particulier dans les relations entre les deux littoraux[1]. En effet, ce sont les relations fréquentes en Adriatique qui ont créé les conditions du développement de la piraterie sur une longue période chez les Illyriens, phénomène qui serait d'ailleurs l'une des principales raisons de l'intervention romaine.

Ces limites chronologiques nous sont imposées par les riches événements politiques et militaires qui la caractérisent. L'année 229 marque le début des guerres contre les Illyriens; en 168, la dynastie des rois illyriens disparaît, et la création de la province de Macédoine en 148 intègre définitivement ces territoires au contrôle de Rome. Pendant ces trois siècles, ce territoire devient même le théâtre de plusieurs événements où se joue le sort de Rome. Les guerres civiles entre César et Pompée se déroulent notamment dans cette région. En outre, l'Illyrie se transforme en tête de pont de l'expansion romaine dans les Balkans.

C'est au cours de cette période que l'on peut distinguer les différents mécanismes qui ont mené à l'intégration des Illyriens dans l'Empire. Le processus d'intégration des Illyriens dans l'Empire a connu, au cours de cette période, plusieurs phases et différents acteurs comme les guerres illyro-romaines, la création d'un protectorat romain en Illyrie, l'organisation administrative romaine, le changement des statuts des villes illyriennes dans le cadre de l'Empire romain et l'installation des hommes d'affaires italiques.

Les guerres illyro-romaines

Le cadre historique des guerres illyro-romaines a déjà fait l'objet de plusieurs études[2] et il constitue la partie la mieux documentée et la mieux connue de l'histoire des Illyriens[3]. Il nous semble cependant important de porter un nouveau regard sur ces guerres, puisqu'il s'agit du premier pas vers l'intégration de ces régions dans l'Empire romain. Leur déroulement et leurs effets aident à mieux comprendre

---

[1] Pour certains, elle représente un obstacle de voyage et une mer toujours à craindre, voir Bertrand 1987, 263-270. Pour d'autres, elle est le pont qui a réuni les deux rives italienne et illyrienne. Voir Deniaux 2005, 7-14.

[2] Ugolini 1929, 373-376; Mustilli 1942, 3-17 ; Holleaux 1952, 76-114 ; Holleaux 1969, 173-205 ; Islami 1972, 31-78 ; Islami 1974, 5-44; Ceka, Ceka 1969, 133-143 Ceka 1969, 347-351; Wilkes 1969, 13-29 ; Ferrary 1978, 729-752 ; Gruen 1984, 359-399 ; Cabanes 1983, 187-204.

[3] Polybe, *Histoires*, 2-19 (traduction P. Pédech 1970); Dion Cassius, *Histoire Romaine*, 47, 3 et 51, 1 (traduction M.-L. Freyburger-Galliand 2002) ; Appien, *Histoire Romaine*, VII - VIII (traduction D. Gaillard 1998) ; Pline, *Histoire Naturelle*, XXXIV (traduction H. Le Bonniec 1953); Tite-Live, *Histoire Romaine*, XXII – XLV (traduction P. Jal 1979).

le comportement initial des Romains en Illyrie. C'est durant cette période que les Illyriens entrent directement en contact avec Rome et deviennent les acteurs principaux d'événements qui se déroulent en Méditerranée et dans les Balkans. Ces guerres constituent donc bien la meilleure introduction au processus de l'intégration de l'Illyrie dans l'Empire romain.

Agron, le roi des Illyriens, commence à jouer pendant la deuxième moitié du IIIe siècle avant notre ère un rôle très important dans les affaires militaires des Balkans[4]. L'accroissement de la puissance illyrienne est lié aux difficultés que traversent la Macédoine et l'Épire à cette époque. Après la mort du roi Agron, son épouse Teuta s'empare du pouvoir. Pendant son règne, la piraterie illyrienne devient une des menaces les plus dangereuses de la Méditerranée[5]. La première ville à souffrir du danger illyrien est Phoinikè. Polybe raconte que des Italiens se trouvaient dans cette ville, peut-être pour faire du commerce, au moment de l'attaque des Illyriens[6]. Après Phoinikè, Teuta entreprend de placer sous son contrôle les colonies grecques de la côte adriatique, Issa, Apollonia et Dyrrachion. Issa est la première à être attaquée. Ces actions accréditent l'idée que les Illyriens sont en train de se transformer en un État impérialiste susceptible de mettre en danger tous les autres peuples balkaniques.

Tous ces événements, la montée en puissance du royaume illyrien, la volonté de Teuta de contrôler les colonies grecques ainsi que la piraterie illyrienne qui ruine les propriétaires italiens poussent les Romains à entrer en guerre. Ils traversent la mer en 229 avant notre ère et lancent leur première campagne militaire de l'autre côté de l'Adriatique. Cette expédition prélude à d'autres interventions qui aboutissent à la domination romaine sur les Illyriens, les Grecs, les Macédoniens et d'autres peuples balkaniques. Une grande armée, composée de 20 000 soldats, de 2000 cavaliers et de 200 navires se rassemble à Brundisium[7]. Les consuls eux-mêmes prennent la tête de l'armée. Les dimensions de l'intervention romaine expliquent son succès immédiat. Corcyre se soumet aux Romains et Démétrios de Pharos hérite d'un royaume illyrien diminué. En revanche, après la victoire romaine sur la reine illyrienne Teuta, Polybe et Appien nous informent que les deux colonies grecques faisaient désormais partie d'un protectorat romain[8]. Leurs ports deviennent des points stratégiques pour l'armée romaine[9]. C'est sur la base de ce protectorat que 300 Apolloniates combattirent du côté romain dans la bataille de Cynoscéphales. Il

---

[4] Polybe, *Histoires* II, 2, 4 : «*Le roi des Illyriens, Agron, qui était le fils de Pleuratos, possédait sur terre et sur mer une puissance militaire plus considérable qu'aucun de ceux qui avaient régné avant lui sur les Illyriens*».

[5] Voir l'analyse du phénomène et des sources faite par Šašel Kos 2002, p. 137-155.

[6] Polybe, *Histoires*, II, 8, 1-2 : «*Les Illyriens, même aux temps antérieurs, inquiétaient continuellement les navigateurs venus d'Italie, et, pendant qu'ils assiégeaient Phoinikè, des détachements encore plus nombreux de leur flotte s'en prirent à quantité de marchands, dont ils dépouillèrent les uns, massacrèrent les autres et emmenèrent en captivité une bonne partie qu'ils avaient faits prisonniers*».

[7] Polybe, *Histoires*, II, 11, 1, 7.

[8] Polybe, *Histoires*, II, 9-12 ; Appien, *Illyr.*, VII: «*Les Romains ont répondu que Corcyre, Pharos, Issa, Epidamne et parmi les Illyriens, les Atintanes étaient désormais sujets des Romains*».

[9] Par exemple *L. Cornelius Scipio*, en 190 avant notre ère, débarque à Apollonia pour aller combattre en Thessalie.

semble que Rome ait établi des relations individuelles avec chaque cité ou tribu illyrienne ; Apollonia, Dyrrachion, Issa ainsi que les tribus des Parthiniens et des Atintanes. Ainsi, l'établissement du protectorat romain semble se constituer de petites structures souveraines qui obéissent à Rome, mais en réalité il s'agit seulement d'un devoir moral envers elle, sans qu'ils perdent pour autant leur liberté[10].

Dix ans après la première guerre, les Romains se rendent compte que Démétrios de Pharos œuvre en fait contre leurs intérêts. A première vue, il ne semble pas que ce dernier ait menacé les alliés de Rome, mais il est probablement à l'origine de la renaissance de la piraterie en Adriatique puisque l'on constate l'attaque de navires romains par des pirates basés en Istrie. Selon Dion Cassius cependant, en 222 avant notre ère, Démétrios de Pharos est parvenu à réunir les deux parties du royaume illyrien divisé en 228[11]. Selon Appien, il aurait réussi à détacher les Atintanes du protectorat romain[12]. Ainsi les Romains interviennent-ils de nouveau en Illyrie en 219[13].

Les Romains attaquent Dimale, la meilleure forteresse aux mains de Démétrios, et s'en emparent après sept jours de siège. Après la chute de Dimale toutes les autres cités s'offrent aux Romains[14]. Même Dimale se range désormais parmi les *amici* de Rome[15]. Toutefois, toutes ces actions militaires n'aboutissent pas à une installation romaine en Illyrie. Rome a seulement manifesté sa force et assuré la paix en Adriatique. Les problèmes en Illyrie n'étaient en effet pas très importants comparés au péril carthaginois. Cependant, même si Rome retire ses troupes de l'Illyrie, l'existence du protectorat montre qu'elle avait commencé à jouer le rôle d'arbitre dans les affaires en Illyrie. Elle a choisi de traiter les tribus vaincues en *amici*, présentant aux Illyriens l'image d'une alliée, ce qui conforte l'idée du pragmatisme plutôt que de l'impérialisme romain.

Skerdilaïdes, frère d'Agron, semble alors avoir pris la tête de la dynastie illyrienne, après la fuite de Démétrios de Pharos en Macédoine et la mort de Pines, fils d'Agron. Il reste fidèle aux Romains jusqu'à sa mort et utilise l'alliance avec les Romains comme contrepoids à la puissance croissante du roi Philippe V de Macédoine. Son fils, Pleuratos, qui arrive probablement au pouvoir vers 200 avant notre ère, conserve la politique paternelle d'alliance avec Rome. Le territoire sous son contrôle s'étend du fleuve Genusus (l'actuel Shkumbin) jusqu'au lac Lychnides (actuel lac d'Ochrid)[16]. Ainsi, à la fin de la période hellénistique, le royaume illyrien représente-t-il une force modeste mais stable.

---

[10] Voir sur ce sujet Cabanes 1976, p. 220-222.
[11] Dion Cassius, *Histoire Romaine*, 53.
[12] Appien, *Histoire Romaine*, VIII.
[13] Polybe résume quant à lui toutes les actions de Démétrios qui ont entraîné la seconde guerre d'Illyrie: Polybe, *Histoires*, III, 16, 3-4 : «*Il s'était mis à ravager et à dévaster les cités d'Illyrie soumises aux Romains; il avait d'autre part, contrairement aux traités, navigué au-delà de Lissos avec cinquante navires et ravagé de nombreuses îles des Cyclades. Les Romains, voyant cela et considérant la prospérité du royaume de Macédoine, songèrent d'abord à se garantir à l'est de l'Italie, avec la certitude qu'ils auraient le temps de corriger la sottise des Illyriens d'une part, de réprimander, de châtier l'ingratitude et la témérité de Démétrios d'autre part*».
[14] Polybe, *Histoires*, III, 16, 3-4.
[15] Polybe, *Histoires*, VII 9.13.
[16] Polybe, *Histoires*, XVIII.47.12.

A la mort de Pleuratos en 181 avant notre ère lui succède son fils, Genthius. Sans s'exposer beaucoup aux yeux des Romains, Genthius a élargi son contrôle sur les tribus vivant plus au nord et à l'ouest. Son pouvoir militaire repose sur des navires de guerre (*lembi*). Politiquement, sur la base de l'*amicitia*, il est un allié de Rome, mais ses actions montrent qu'il ne semble pas avoir d'obligations vis-à-vis du Sénat romain. Probablement, l'*amicitia* présuppose davantage la notion de respect réciproque qu'une hégémonie. Il est possible que les deux parties le perçoivent de la même manière. Rome ne semble pas avoir d'intérêts spécifiques dans le territoire contrôlé par Genthius et sa politique montre une continuité qui consiste surtout à garder le contrôle des événements avec un minimum d'implication.

Genthius semble avoir longtemps hésité entre l'appui des Romains et celui des Macédoniens. Le roi Persée de Macédoine parvient finalement à le convaincre d'entrer en guerre contre Rome, en lui promettant que le conflit n'aura pas de conséquence financière pour lui, puisque la Macédoine fournirait l'argent nécessaire. Cette alliance entraîne *de facto* la fin de l'*amicitia* avec Rome. Le Sénat romain décide alors d'envoyer L. Anicius Gallus qui, après avoir battu la flotte illyrienne, accule Genthius dans sa capitale à Scodra. La ville est prise en 30 jours. Après la guerre, le roi et sa famille sont pris en otage et emmenés en Italie[17].

La brève période qui voit l'effondrement du royaume illyrien témoigne encore une fois que Rome ne s'est jamais vraiment intéressée aux territoires illyriens mais qu'elle intervient en réaction aux menées des Illyriens. Cette politique était aussi conditionnée par l'absence d'infrastructures. Premièrement l'infrastructure interne de l'Etat romain et son organisation hiérarchique ne permettaient pas encore le contrôle effectif d'un espace outre-mer. Deuxièmement, les infrastructures physiques manquaient, comme les voies de communication et les installations militaires. Ainsi la politique romaine en Illyrie reste-t-elle pragmatique jusqu'à la fin des hostilités. Il faut ensuite attendre 80 ans pour que Rome établisse un contrôle administratif direct sur ces territoires.

L'organisation administrative romaine en Illyrie

Après 168 avant notre ère, quand l'invasion romaine mit fin au royaume illyrien de Genthius, jusqu'en 148, Rome n'exerçait pas de contrôle direct sur le territoire illyrien. On apprend par Tite-Live[18] qu'Anicius, le général romain qui avait battu Genthius, réunit tous les *princeps* illyriens de la région pour leur transmettre les décisions de Rome. Selon le Sénat, la majorité de la population était libérée de tout tribut parce qu'elle avait abandonné le roi illyrien pendant la guerre. En revanche, les habitants de Scodra, les Dassarètes et les Selepitani étaient obligés de payer la moitié du tribut qu'ils versaient à leur roi. Ensuite, on prévit de diviser le royaume illyrien en trois parts : la région de Scodra, qui était aussi la capitale, celle des La-

---

[17] Tite-Live, *Histoire Romaine*, XLIIII, 30.6 – XLIIII, 32.
[18] Tite-Live, *Histoire Romaine*, XLV, 26.

béates et une troisième région où se trouvaient les Rhizonitae, les Olcinitae et d'autres populations. Cette politique avait pour but la rupture des liaisons politiques précédentes entre les tribus illyriennes, et le développement de relations exclusives entre Rome et chaque tribu ou cité. Ainsi, Rome suivit dans ces régions le même comportement adopté pour la conquête de l'Italie, montrant son tact et sa prudence dans les rapports internationaux.

La création de la province de Macédoine en 148 avant notre ère marque un moment important dans la politique étrangère de Rome[19]. Cette période est caractérisée par une plus grande détermination de la part du Sénat et de l'élite romaine pour la gestion des territoires conquis. Mais il faut noter que pendant cette période la notion de province ne désignait pas encore autre chose qu'une zone contrôlée par un magistrat[20].

En 59 avant notre ère, l'Illyricum, dont la côte dalmate et illyrienne faisait partie, était sous le contrôle de César. À la suite de son meurtre, le Sénat confie le commandement de l'Illyricum, de la Macédoine et de l'Achaïe à Brutus. Quatre ans après, la Paix de Brindisi accorde l'Illyricum à Octave et la Macédoine à Antoine.

Pendant l'époque romaine, le territoire de cette province n'a jamais été très stable et il a connu des limites toujours variables. Il se peut que ce manque de stabilité soit le résultat de l'insécurité provoquée par les autres tribus illyriennes dans le sud de la Dalmatie. La révolte des Désidiates et des Breuques dirigés par les deux Bato contre les Romains avait mis en danger l'autorité de Rome dans la région et la survie des colonies de l'Adriatique[21]. Tibère lui-même aurait dirigé les opérations pour vaincre les Illyriens. Ainsi ces régions ne sont-elles pas tout à fait pacifiées avant le règne d'Auguste, lequel arrive à repousser les frontières de l'Empire jusqu'au Danube. La province dalmate s'étendant de l'Istrie orientale jusqu'aux alentours de Lissus, à l'embouchure du Drin, a en effet été créée par Auguste après la conquête totale de ces régions.

Le territoire de la province de Macédoine ressemble à un rectangle qui s'étendrait de l'Adriatique jusqu'à la mer Egée. Lissus au nord et Patras au sud constituaient les limites de la bordure maritime de cette province. Ensuite, à l'intérieur, c'est-à-dire vers l'est, la province s'étend jusqu'à Stobi et vers le sud elle avance à Pydna en joignant aussi l'Épire et la Thessalie[22].

Un siècle plus tard, en 27 avant notre ère, les régions de la Grèce centrale sont séparées de la province de Macédoine pour former la nouvelle province d'Achaïe. Par le nom d'Achaïe, les Romains désignaient la Grèce conquise après la victoire sur la Ligue Achéenne et la destruction de Corinthe. Jusqu'à ce moment, l'Épire faisait

---

[19] Sur l'histoire de la province voir Papazoglou 1979, p. 303-369.
[20] Crawford 1990, p. 105.
[21] Sur ces révoltes voir Anamali 1987, p. 5-23.
[22] Pline, *Histoire Naturelle*, III, 145. Quant à Pline, il la décrit ainsi : «*Immédiatement après Lissos commence la Macédoine, où sont les ethné des Parthins, puis derrière eux, ceux des Dassarètes, les monts Candaviens à 78 miles de Dyrrachium ; et, en suivant la cote Denda, cité romaine, Épidamne dont le nom sinistre a été changé en celui de Dyrrachium par les Romains*».

également partie de la province de Macédoine; quand l'Achaïe s'en sépare, en 27 avant notre ère, elle s'intègre à cette nouvelle province. De 15 à 44 de notre ère, ce qui reste de la Macédoine devient une province impériale, avant de retrouver son statut sénatorial sous le règne de Tibère. Le gouverneur de la province était normalement un préteur ou un propréteur[23]. C'est sous Trajan, en 108, que l'Épire constitue une province impériale à part, à laquelle sont rattachées les îles ioniennes de Corcyre et de Zakynthos. Cette province s'étend des monts Acrocérauniens jusqu'en Acarnanie.

La particularité de la période pré augustéenne est la mauvaise gestion des provinces par des gouverneurs corrompus ou incompétents. Le cas le plus connu est celui de Calpurnius Pison, proconsul de Macédoine pendant les années 57-55 avant notre ère. Le récit de ses abus nous est parvenu à travers les paroles de Cicéron, qui s'adressait au Sénat[24]. En revanche, Polybe nous apprend que les provinces de Macédoine et d'Achaïe se lamentaient parce que les Romains ne s'occupaient pas des Illyriens situés sur les côtes de l'Adriatique[25].

Les municipes

Un autre aspect de l'organisation administrative romaine en Illyrie et qui à joué un rôle important dans l'intégration des Illyriens dans l'Empire est la création des *municipia*. Le principe de la politique romaine consistait dans la diffusion de la vie municipale dans les territoires conquis. Les municipes étaient le plus souvent des centres urbanisés de taille modeste, avec une population sûrement pas très nombreuse, dans la majorité des cas. Selon Aulu-Gelle, les municipes sont des villes où les citoyens romains conservent leurs lois et leurs propres droits et qui ne bénéficient des droits et des devoirs du peuple romain qu'à titre honorifique[26]. Il existait un certain nombre de critères pour accéder au rang municipal: l'existence d'un centre de citoyens romains suffisamment dense, l'exploitation fiscale des communautés locales par des administrateurs romanisés et le recrutement des soldats parmi la population locale.

En Illyrie et en Chaonie, on connaît trois *oppida civium romanorum*, à Lissus, Scodra et Bouthrotos. Apparemment, ces trois fondations correspondent à la période pendant laquelle César commandait ces régions. Mais il est probable que le titre de *conventus civium romanorum* accordé par César à ces villes fût le résultat d'une présence antérieure de citoyens romains, peut-être dès la destruction du royaume de

---

[23] Sur l'organisation administrative de ces provinces voir Rougé 1987, p. 255 ; Bucci 1998, p. 50-95 ; Cabanes 1998, p. 305-306.

[24] Cicéron, *Discours, Contre Pison*, 40 (traduction P. Grimal, 1966), : «*Dyrrachium et Apollonia ravagés, Ambracie pillée, les Parthinii et les Byllinii sans illusions, l'Épire complètement en ruines, la Macédoine aux mains des barbares, beaucoup de gens ont abandonné leurs maisons et leurs terres, tous sont venu témoigner que tu les as dévastés et traités comme des ennemis*» [...] «*les tributs et les impôts de Dyrrachium sont tournés au profit seul du Pison*».

[25] Polybe, *Histoires*, XXXII, 13,5.

[26] Aulu-Gelle, *Les nuits Attiques*, (traduction. Y. Julien, 1998) XVI, 13, 6.

Genthius. D'une manière générale, pendant cette période, il n'y a eu aucune politique ou acte autoritaire pour romaniser la population. Les Illyriens ont continué à mener leur vie comme avant.

Les petites agglomérations rurales étaient incluses, également, dans le réseau administratif et hiérarchique romain. Elles sont soit des *vici*, soit des *pagi*, une organisation qui structurait la population dans le système administratif et fiscal de Rome. Les seuls exemples documentés de *vici* sont Scampis, que nous connaissons par la trouvaille de la stèle funéraire du *quaestor* Q. Mussius[27], et Asparagium Dyrrachinorum, mentionné par César mais pas encore identifié[28]. Il est probable que l'un des deux sites à proximité de Dyrrachion, Rrogozhina ou Bashtova, corresponde à Asparagium.

La fondation des colonies

La fondation des colonies romaines sur le territoire de l'Illyrie du sud et de l'Épire est un projet commencé par César et continué plus tard par Auguste[29]. Cette période est marquée par des événements très importants pour l'État romain: les guerres civiles, le Triumvirat et la naissance de l'Empire. La fondation de ces colonies stimulera plusieurs transformations de nature politique, économique, territoriale et aussi sociale. Toutes ces colonies s'établirent dans les endroits les plus stratégiques de ce territoire et elles devinrent des centres de liaison entre Rome et l'Illyrie, la Grèce, la Macédoine et l'Asie Mineure. Leur position géographique importante et l'aide continue apportée par Rome ont rendu la vie de ces villes plus commode par rapport à celle des autres cités. Les villes où les Romains fondent leurs colonies sont Bouthrotos, Dyrrachion, Byllis et Scodra. Elles sont toutes situées près des routes principales, pourvues d'un port et riches en terres fertiles. Elles disposaient de tous les éléments nécessaires à Rome pour une expansion militaire et économique. Par conséquent, nous considérons que la fondation de cette chaîne de colonies faisait partie d'un programme bien établi par Rome et qui ne devait rien au hasard. Cette nouvelle politique de Rome avait pour but non seulement l'établissement des vétérans sur des terres promises, mais aussi la concentration du pouvoir provincial dans ces villes chargées de stimuler le développement régional. Leur importance administrative et les connections avec Rome rendaient possible un meilleur contrôle du territoire et des habitants.

Les villes qui deviennent des colonies romaines jouent déjà un rôle régional important et avaient établi des relations amicales avec Rome depuis la première guerre illyro-romaine; certaines étaient déjà des bases principales pour l'armée romaine, comme Dyrrachion et Apollonia, ou bien étaient peuplées depuis des années par les hommes d'affaires d'origine italique, comme Bouthrotos.

---

[27] *CIL* III, 609.
[28] César, *Bellum civile*, 41.1.
[29] Sur la colonisation romaine en Illyrie voir Shpuza 2006, p. 126-130.

De manière générale les Romains et les Italiens venus en Illyrie et en Épire y ont trouvé un environnement favorable. Leur fusion avec les populations locales a généré une évolution urbaine renouvelée et a introduit une vie cosmopolite ouverte aux nouvelles conditions de l'Empire.

Les hommes d'affaires italiques. L'apport des inscriptions bilingues

Rome, dès le début de sa présence en Illyrie, a favorisé l'installation dans la région des *mercatores* italiens qui travaillaient sous son contrôle. Ils formaient la classe sociale la plus active et étaient prompts à établir des liens entre les Romains et les Illyriens. Leur présence, bien connue en Épire, a aussi été notée en Illyrie[30]. Leur activité économique en Epire semble avoir été principalement dirigée vers l'élevage et l'agriculture, tandis que les Italiens établis à Lissus, Apollonia et Dyrrachion s'occupaient plutôt du commerce du vin et de l'huile. Toutefois, il est à supposer que les profits financiers de ce commerce les ont conduits vers l'achat de propriétés foncières et vers la production agricole. De plus, une grande partie d'entre eux étaient des *negotiatores*, attirés de plus en plus par l'existence de la *Via Egnatia*.

Leur présence a rendu possible une longue coexistence entre Illyriens, Grecs et Romains[31]. Cette situation est aussi manifestée dans certaines inscriptions bilingues, qui sont une expression de biculturalisme. Toutefois, les inscriptions bilingues sont très rares par rapport aux inscriptions employant le grec ou le latin de manière exclusive. En Albanie, on a retrouvé seulement quatre inscriptions bilingues : deux épitaphes, une évergésie et une dédicace aux Dioscures. Cette dernière est la seule trouvée en territoire rural, les trois autres provenant de villes.

Les deux épitaphes ont été trouvées à Dyrrachion et appartiennent à une même famille, celle des *Maximi*[32]. Cette famille faisait probablement partie de la communauté italienne établie dans la ville avant la fondation de la colonie romaine. Une des inscriptions bilingues mentionne une *Maxima Pomenteinos* et un *Gaios Pomenteinos*[33]. Il s'agit probablement d'une famille italienne établie sur la côte est de l'Adriatique pendant la période républicaine. Même si l'inscription est bilingue, son contexte semble local. Le formulaire funéraire, très simple, emploie le grec et mentionne seulement la défunte, omettant le *commemorator*, à l'inverse de la tradition épigraphique romaine.

---

[30] César, *Bellum civile*, III 9, 2; Pline, *Histoire Naturelle*, III, 145.
[31] Sur les premiers noms italiens présents en Illyrie voir Cabanes 1996, p. 89-104.
[32] Les inscriptions ont été trouvées dans l'actuelle Durrës lors de travaux de construction. Malheureusement, on ignore leur contexte archéologique, mais il s'agit probablement d'une nécropole d'époque républicaine (la datation des de cette période repose sur leur étude paléographique et iconographique).
[33] Ma[xima] [Po]mentinos/ Ma[xima]a Aninia/ Maxima Pomentein(os)/ Gaios Pomentein(os). Ce nom apparaît également sur une autre inscription du corpus des inscriptions de Dyrrachion (n° 297). Selon Cabanes, le nom serait originaire de la cité volsque de Pometia.

L'existence du bilinguisme à Dyrrachion avant la fondation de la colonie romaine constitue un phénomène essentiel dans la compréhension des relations sociales organisant cette ville. Le fait que les Italiens installés à Dyrrachion choisissent, dans leurs manifestations publiques, de recourir aux deux langues est une preuve de leur volonté de s'intégrer au milieu indigène et témoigne en même temps de liens culturels étroits avec leur patrie. Ces inscriptions bilingues manifestent la symbiose culturelle qui s'est opérée à Dyrrachion. Dans ce contexte, le fait que les inscriptions bilingues appartiennent à la sphère privée montre la profondeur du processus d'acculturation dans cette ville.

Ainsi, l'emploi du grec par les Romains pour s'adresser aux indigènes n'est pas seulement un geste de bonne volonté, c'est un effort de séduction à l'attention des autochtones pour faciliter un rapprochement entre communautés. On voit alors que les Romains apprennent le grec pour des raisons complètement différentes de celles des locaux, lesquels recourent au latin pour s'intégrer à la société romaine.

Il est intéressant de noter que dans les autres villes d'Épire, le phénomène du bilinguisme semble inconnu même s'il existait une forte communauté de Romains qui a sans doute été hellénisée au point d'employer le grec sur ses inscriptions. Cela s'explique aussi sans doute par le fait que l'écriture n'a jamais été beaucoup utilisée dans les régions épirotes, sauf à Bouthrotos au IIe siècle avant notre ère. Dans les autres villes, comme Phoinikè ou Antigoneia, les inscriptions sont fort rares.

L'apparition du latin dans les inscriptions bilingues suggère que cette langue avait commencé à devenir d'un usage courant. Ce phénomène coïncide avec l'installation de l'administration romaine et de ses structures militaires et économiques. De manière plus générale, le bilinguisme a joué un rôle majeur dans la transformation du pouvoir romain en le rendant plus accessible aux populations locales. Il a en effet constitué le prélude à l'introduction de l'écriture latine en Illyrie, illustrée par les inscriptions relatives aux travaux publics et au culte impérial.

Conclusions

En conclusion, on peut affirmer que les trois derniers siècles avant notre ère ont jeté les bases de la culture provinciale illyrienne qui s'épanouit ensuite pendant l'époque impériale. Pour une longue période, entre les trois guerres, les Illyriens sont demeurés sous le protectorat romain, qui présupposait une autonomie et un respect réciproque. Ceci constitue d'ailleurs la principale action politique qui intégra Rome dans les affaires Balkaniques.

L'instauration de relations amicales et la conquête graduelle des territoires ont favorisé l'installation d'Italiens qui avaient pour but l'exploitation économique de ces régions. Cette période coïncide aussi avec l'organisation provinciale que Rome mit en place, un nouveau cadre juridique qui a fait disparaître les formes d'organisation traditionnelles des Illyriens.

Pendant le Ier siècle avant notre ère, les guerres civiles impliquèrent largement ces territoires et on relève l'organisation des municipes pour l'intégration des Italiens.

Finalement, le processus de colonisation a joué le rôle principal dans le processus d'intégration territoriale, économique et sociale de ces populations dans l'Empire romain : celui-ci est en effet plus apparent dans les régions où la présence des Romains s'avère considérable. Leur installation fut donc un facteur déterminant dans la diffusion de la civilisation romaine.

Saimir SHPUZA
Institut archéologique de Tirana

Bibliographie

Anamali 1987 = S. Anamali, Kryengritja ilire e viteve 6-9 të e. sonë, *Iliria* 1 (1987) 5-23.

Bertrand 1987 = J.-M. Bertrand, *Continent et outre-mer, l'espace vécu des Romains*, dans P. Cabanes (éd.), *L'Illyrie Méridionale et l'Epire dans l'Antiquité*, actes du colloque international, Clermont-Ferrand 22-25 octobre 1984 (Paris 1987) 263-270.

Bucci 1998 = O. Bucci, *Le provincie orientali dell'Impero Romano. Una introduzione storico-giuridica* (Rome 1998).

Cabanes 1976 = P. Cabanes, *L'Epire de la mort de Pyrrhos à la conquête romaine, 272-167 av. J.-C.*, Annales littéraires de l'Université de Besançon, 186, Centre de Recherche d'Histoire Ancienne, vol. 19 (Paris 1976).

Cabanes 1983 = P. Cabanes, *Notes sur l'intervention romaine sur la rive orientale de la mer Adriatique 229-228 avant J.-C.*, dans Association internationale d'études du Sud-Est européen, *L'Adriatico tra Mediterraneo e penisola balcanica nell'antichità* (Tarente 1983) 187-204.

Cabanes 1996 = P. Cabanes, *Les noms latins dans les inscriptions grecques d'Épidamne-Dyrrachion, d'Apollonia et de Bouthrotos*, dans A. RIZAKIS (éd.), *Roman Onomastics in the Greek East. Social and Political Aspects*, Proceedings of the International Colloquium on Roman Onomastics (Athènes, 7-9 Septembre 1993), Meletimata 21 (1996) 89-104.

Cabanes 1998 = P. Cabanes, *Le monde grec européen et la Cyrénaïque*, dans C. Lepelley (éd.), *Rome et l'intégration de l'empire, 44 av. J.-C. - 260 ap. J.-C. Tome 2, Approches régionales du Haut Empire romain*, (Paris 1998).

H. Ceka & N. Ceka 1969 = H. Ceka, N. Ceka, *Mbi zhvillimin e shtetit tek ilirët*, Studime Historike, 2 (1969) 133-143.

Ceka 1969 = N. Ceka, *Vendi dhe roli i parthinëve në Ilirinë e jugut në shek III-I p.e.re*, dans *Konferenca II e Studimeve Albanologjike* (Tirana 1969) 347-351.

Crawford 1990 = M. Crawford, *Origini e sviluppo del sistema provinciale romano*, dans *Storia di Roma, L'impero Mediterraneo. La repubblica imperiale I* (Turin 1990).

Deniaux 2005 = E. Deniaux, *Introduction. Le Canal d'Otrante et la Méditerranée antique et médiévale*, dans E. Deniaux (éd.), *Le Canal d'Otrante et la Méditerranée antique et Médiévale*, colloque organisé à l'Université de Paris X – Nanterre, 20-21 novembre 2000 (Bari 2005) 7-14.

Ferrary 1978 = J.-L. Ferrary, *Rome, les Balkans, la Grèce et l'Orient au deuxième siècle av. J.-C.*, dans Cl. Nicolet (éd.), *Rome et la conquête du monde Méditerranéen 2. Genèse d'un Empire*, Nouvelle Clio (Paris 1978) 729-752.

Gruen 1984 = E. Gruen, *The Hellenistic world and the Coming of Rome* (Berkeley 1984).

Holleaux 1952 = M. Holleaux, *Les Romains en Illyrie*, dans *Etudes d'épigraphie et d'histoire grecques. Rome, la Macédoine et l'Orient Grecque*, tome IV (Paris 1952) 76-114.

Holleaux 1969 = M. Holleaux, *Rome, la Grèce et les monarchies hellénistiques au IIIe siècle avant J.-C. (275-205)* (Paris 1969).

Islami 1972 = S. Islami, *Shteti ilir, vendi dhe roli i tij në botën mesdhetare*, Studime Historike 3 (1972) 31-78.

Islami 1974 = S. Islami, *Shteti ilir në luftrat kundër Romës*, Iliria III (1974) 5-44.
Mustilli 1942 = D. Mustilli, *Roma e la sponda Illirica*, dans *Roma e il Mediterraneo II*, Reale Istituto di studi Romani, XXI (1942) 3-17.

Papazoglu 1979 = F. Papazoglu, *Quelques aspects de l'histoire de la province de Macédoine*, Aufstieg und Niedergang der römischen Welt, 7.1 (1979) 303-369.

Rougé 1987 = J. Rougé, *La place de l'Illyrie Méridionale et de l'Epire dans le système des communications de l'Empire Romain*, dans P. Cabanes (éd.), *L'Illyrie méridionale et l'Epire dans l'antiquité*, actes du colloque international, Clermont-Ferrand, 22-25 octobre 1984, (Clermont-Ferrand 1987).

Šašel Kos 2002 = M. Sasel Kos, *From Agron to Genthius : Large Scale Piracy in the Adriatic*, dans *I Greci in Adriatico*, 1, Hesperia 15 (2002) 137-155.

Shpuza 2006 = S. Shpuza, *The Roman Colonies of South Illyria: a review*, dans L. Bejko, R. Hodges (éds.), *New directions in Albanian archaeology*, International Centre for Albanian Archaeology, Monograph Series No. 1 (Tirana 2006) 126-130.

Ugolini 1929 = L.-M. Ugolini, *Penetrazione romana nell'antica Albania*, dans *Atti del congresso nazionale di studi romani*, vol. I (Rome 1929) 373-376.

Wilkes 1969 = J.J. Wilkes, *Dalmatia* (Londres 1969).

THE IMPACT OF ROMAN IMPERIALISM ON THE FORMATION OF GROUP IDENTITIES IN SOME INDIGENOUS SOCIETIES FROM THE EASTERN ADRIATIC HINTERLAND[1]

Danijel DZINO

The region which was to become the Roman province of Dalmatia was comprised of different Iron Age indigenous communities before the Roman conquest in the later first century BC and early first century AD. In the past they were perceived, described and labelled by outsiders with different identity-tags. The best known of these labels is without doubt, 'Illyrians', developed in Archaic and Classical Greece, and extended on wide territory between the Adriatic and Danube in the context of the early Roman imperial (re)construction of conquered spaces in continental Europe. The label was reinvented in the early modern era,[2] and perpetuated in political contexts of the 19th and 20th centuries as a multifaceted body of knowledge frequently used to justify different, and sometimes conflicting, political claims on the ancient past. More recent scholarship has perceived these groups as different ethnicities, classified roughly into supra-ethnic categories such as Illyrians, Pannonii/Pannonians, and northern Adriatic peoples (Iapodes, Liburni, Histri). This classification of indigenous populations used a methodology based on combined evidence from archaeology (Iron Age archaeological cultures), written sources and anthroponymy (onomastics)[3]. Such a methodology has significant shortfalls, most significant being the impact of the approaches based on cultural history and the attempts to relate pre-conquest and post-conquest (Roman provincial) groups and merge them into a continuous historical narrative[4].

However, if traps of anachronistic blending of pre-conquest and conquest societies are avoided and the written and material sources are analysed as different narratives of the past, the picture of this region in the mid-first millennium BC changes quite substantially. We can see a plurality of small communities, which constructed their identities selectively, combining cultural influences from the Mediterranean world and Central Europe (Hallstatt culture) with the existing local traditions. Mediterranean influences usually came reinterpreted through other regional cultures, such as

---

[1] This paper is part of an ongoing Discovery project DP1095356 *Ancient and Medieval Identity-shifts and the Construction of Identities in Post-Yugoslav Space*, sponsored by the Australian Research Council. I am in much debt to the book editors, and to Martina Blečić Kavur (University of Rijeka) for their positive criticism and useful suggestions for improving this paper.

[2] Frequently cited claim of Wilkes 1992, 4-5 that modern reinventions of Illyrian identity started only with 19th century Illyrian movement in Croatia overlooks a long local tradition of «Illyrian ideologem», which was developed as identity-template by intellectual elites of Dalmatian cities in 15th and 16th century, Blažević 2007.

[3] For «Illyrians» in antiquity and methodology of research recently Šašel Kos 2005a, 219-244, and for perceptions of «Illyrians» in different modern contexts see: Dzino 2008a, 44-45; 2011, 198-199; Xohaj 2005; Šašel Kos 2007, and in wider regional context Vranić 2011, 662-671.

[4] See for example Novaković 2011, 347, 382; Dzino 2009; 2011; Vranić 2011, 659-662.

the Situla art in the Eastern Alps, and the Glasinac and Mati cultural complex in the central Balkan Peninsula. These Iron Age communities were exposed to a significant «culture shock», in *ca.* 400 BC. The Syracusan and Parian colonisation of the central Adriatic islands Vis and Hvar significantly increased interactions between the region and the Mediterranean world, coinciding with the simultaneous spread of La Tène influences from central Europe into the Pannonian plains and the valley of the river Sava. Very soon after that, southern parts of the region entered the zone of competing powers of the Hellenistic era as contact points between Macedonian and Roman zones of political influence. After the establishment of Rome as the dominant political power in the Mediterranean in *ca.* mid-second century BC, the Romans exercised their political influence indirectly in this region, using the help of their political allies and military campaigns of limited range. The change in the nature of Roman imperialism in the first century BC resulted in the peaceful incorporation of their allies in the region, the military conquest of the groups which opposed Rome and the gradual establishment of an imperial provincial framework. Roman imperialism first constructed Illyricum, which was later transformed into new imperial artefacts – the provincial societies of Pannonia and Dalmatia[5].

This paper will focus on identity-transformation and social changes within indigenous groups known from the sources as the Delmatae, Iapodes and southern communities of those known as the Pannonii (the Mezaei and Daesitiates)[6]. These are all distinct groups, but have been chosen for analysis due to several important things they have in common. They all shared similar social structures until *ca.* 400 BC, constructing their identities through local and regional negotiations of global cultural templates coming from the Mediterranean and Central Europe. Warrior attributes appear to be significant in all three groups, whether as a part of the cultural and/or social male identity-construct, or as a part of everyday needs to protect the local community. It is interesting to note that thus far, neither «princely tombs»[7], nor tumuli burials have been found in the regions connected with these groups, although these were part of the funeral practices of neighbouring communities and an important part of their social and communal identity-construction templates. They are also all absent from the earliest layer of written sources on this region – the Greek-language ethnographic and geographic tradition developing from the sixth to the late fourth centuries BC (e.g. Hecataeus, Herodotus, Theopompus, Ephorus, pseudo-Aristotle, the periplus of pseudo-Scylax, etc.), and appear for the first time in written sources only in the second century BC onwards[8]. It is unlikely that these groups were compact politi-

---

[5] See Dzino 2012 («culture shock»); Šašel Kos 2005a, 249 ff.; 2011; Dzino 2010 (the conquest).

[6] See in comparative perspective, the research of proto-historic groups from the region of central Balkan peninsula, which is adjacent to the region under consideration, Papazoglu 1978.

[7] Elaborate funerary assemblages from early Iron Ages, usually including luxurious objects from archaic Greek workshops placed – see Babić 2002 in English, and Vasić 2004; 2007 on «princely graves» of Glasinac and Mati cultures in central Balkan peninsula (cf. Map 1).

[8] On fifth century BC Greek ethnographic perceptions see the recent Matijašić 2011. Earlier significant works on the earliest Greek perceptions of the eastern Adriatic are, amongst others: Katičić 1995; Kozličić 1990, 35-186.

cal blocks continually opposed to the Romans, but rather, individual clans and communities were pursuing their own interests in different circumstances. Nevertheless, the sources are quite conclusive that the majority of these communities engaged in intense political conflicts with Rome. The fact that these conflicts occurred over several generations embedded warfare within identity-construction narratives as the shared experience of these groups[9]. The conflicts occurred sporadically from *ca.* 150 BC, gaining intensity in the late first century BC and early first century AD. These conflicts appear most intense during the campaigns of Octavian (35-33 BC) and the *bellum Pannonicum* conducted by Tiberius (12-9 BC), but also the bloody *bellum Batonianum* (AD 6-9) which seriously challenged early Roman rule over this region. These conflicts occurred in different historical and political contexts, as it is difficult to establish that Rome had «grand plans» for the conquest of the region. Roman expansion was, as elsewhere, driven by fear, greed and glory, not geo-strategic pursuits, or economic imperialism[10].

The Delmatae

The Delmatae first appear in the written sources «in the late 180s BC.», when they apparently seceded from the Illyrian kingdom during the early years of its last king Genthius. They engaged in conflicts with the Roman Republic in 156-155 BC, 119-118 BC, 78-76 BC and later in a series of conflicts starting from 50 BC, to be conquered finally by Octavian in 33 BC[11]. Roman rule was challenged a few more times, the most serious and last challenge being their participation in the bellum Batonianum, where, at is seems, most of the Delmataean communities joined together with the Pannonian communities[12]. Not much is known about this group, apart from the evidence in the written sources. It seems that the earliest political centre of the Delmatae was in Duvanjsko *polje*, the plains around modern Tomislavgrad, where the Romans destroyed the chief settlement of Dalmion/Delmion in 155 BC[13]. However, the political power of this group extended towards the coast and the right bank of the river Neretva. They probably subjugated the culturally akin but different coastal communities, known from earlier sources as the Hylloi and Nestoi and maybe even the Manioi and Boullinoi, some times in the first century BC[14].

---

[9] Dzino 2009, 35-39.
[10] Rich 1993; Eckstein 2006, cf. most recently Mattingly 2011, 15-22, and for case-study of motives for Roman expansion in Illyricum see Dzino 2010.
[11] The first mention is Polyb. 32.9.3-4, and also a first epigraphic mention of one Babos Delmata (Βάβος Δελμάτα) in the inscription from Astakos in Akarnania dated to the second century BC (IG 9² 1, 434; SEG 1.213; 19.411). On the Roman conflicts with the Delmatae see in English Šašel Kos 2005a, 292-313, 442-450; Dzino 2010, 62-69, 112-114.
[12] They are not mentioned by name in the sources for *bellum Batonianum*, but it is very difficult to believe that at least a majority of these communities did not participate in this conflict, see Dzino 2010, 144.
[13] Its location is disputed. The most plausible location seems to be the hill-fort Lib above Borčani, which dominates the plains, see Šašel Kos 2005a, 303-306 with literature.
[14] Mentioned in Ps-Scylax 22-24; Ps-Scymnus, 404-412 (citing also Eratosthenes and Timaeus, FrGrHist 566 F77); Apol. Rhod. 4.522-551, 1214-1215 and some later sources. Whether they existed as such in the

Scholars connect this group with what archaeologists define as the Central Dalmatian (or Gorica) Iron Age archaeological culture, which covers a much wider region between the rivers of Krka and Neretva, including the Central Adriatic islands and the hinterland. The material culture of these communities was strongly influenced by the North Adriatic in the earliest centuries of the Iron Age. However, around the turn of the millennium, influences from the east and south increased. These were coming especially from the Glasinac-Mati world, which acted as a gateway in cultural exchange, accepting, processing and spreading influences from Archaic Greece. These influences were used selectively; some regional identity-templates such as the sporadic use of Illyrian helmets (earlier known as Graeco-Illyrian) as important social symbol were adopted,[15] but no princely burials are recorded. In the later Iron Age, Mediterranean influences on material remains of this culture are best visible on the coast, while the hinterland, where the sources locate the political core of the Delmatean communities, was more restrictive towards Mediterranean influences, with some limited influence from the La Tène world such as fibulae, and weapons[16].

Although this question cannot be decisively answered with the present corpus of evidence, it seems that the Delmatae were a recent social formation, not much older than its first mention in written sources,[17] in essence being at first a political alliance of culturally similar clans, rather than a distinct ethnic group. The Delmatae are absent from the earliest written sources, which report the ethnographic situation from the mid-fourth century BC and earlier – Hecataeus, Theopompus, Ephorus, pseudo-Aristotle, the periploi of pseudo-Scylax, and pseudo-Scymnus, etc. This fact justifies pushing the date of the foundation of this political alliance to the late fourth/early third century BC, or even later. The earliest political core of the alliance develops in the karst regions in particular plains known as *polje*, which are occasional flat-floored fertile depressions between the karst-mountains (Livanjsko, Duvanjsko, Sinjsko, Imotsko and Glamočko *polje*) in region encompassing parts of western Herzegovina, south-western Bosnia and Dalmatian Zagora. The particular geography and ecology of those inwards-looking plains surrounded by infertile and stony mountains was an important factor in the formation of regional identities within these plains. The sense of regional identity was certainly strengthened and deepened with the existence of joint sacral spaces such as the hill-fort Mandina gradina in Duvanjsko *polje* near Tomislavgrad[18]. Lack of iron ore deposits in the region ascribed to the Central Dalmatian archaeological culture is contrasted with

---

first century BC, we do not know, but scholars agree that the Delmatae expanded their political control over the coast between the very late second century BC and the 40s BC, Čače 1994/95, 118-120; Zaninović 2007, 97-101; Šašel Kos 2005a, 293; cf. Dzino 2010, 40, 93.

[15] On significance of Illyrian helmets and their finds see Blečić 2007; Blečić Kavur and Pravidur 2012.

[16] Unfortunately, the material evidence is dispersed and there are not many synthetic works - the most important works are Batović 2004 and Čović 1987, 442-480, see in English Wilkes 1992, 189-192. For Mediterranean influences on the coastal communities after ca. 400 BC see Kirigin et al. 2005; Kirigin 2010.

[17] Supra n. 11.

[18] On Mandina Gradina see Benac 1985, 16-20, 198, 205; Čović 1987, 474.

the military strength of the Delmatae. It indicates that the alliance had significant political influence or a friendly relationship and/or alliance with the indigenous elites located further inland which were controlling substantial iron ore deposits. This in particular relates to communities belonging to the Central Bosnian, or Donja Dolina-Sanski Most archaeological cultures (cultural complex), which were exporting iron, whether in ingots or as finished products[19].

What we know from written evidence might indicate that this group attempted to gain control over the points associated with trade routes which were established for exchange with the Mediterranean world, especially after the Romans divided the Illyrian kingdom in the southern Adriatic 167 BC. The disappearance of the powerful Illyrian kingdom, in the southern Adriatic gave an opportunity for other social formations to claim power and control over the trade routes. The Delmatae conflicted with the Roman allies, such as the Daorsi, an indigenous community which controlled exchanges with the hinterland via the harbor Desilo in Hutovo Blato. They also threatened interests of the Issaean Greeks in the bay of Kašteli, near Salona, future capital of Roman Dalmatia. Finally, conflict arose over control of the community in Promona, described as Liburnian by the sources, and situated near the important harbour in Scardona and communication-routes on the river Krka[20]. These conflicts caused Roman interventions on behalf of their allies the Daorsi, Issaeans and Liburnian communities. However, before Octavian's expedition, Roman interventions did not result in what can be perceived as territorial conquest, or placement of Roman garrisons in the region.

The Iapodes

Similar to the Delmatae, the Iapodes do not appear in the earliest layer of information from this region. The earliest written reference concerning the Iapodes is associated with the failed campaign of the consul Gaius Cassius Longinus towards Macedonia in 171 BC and the official Roman apology to the groups which were attacked without authorisation by the returning army[21]. The Iapodes were defeated by the Romans in 129 BC, but Roman control and direct involvement must have been short-lived.[22] It is assumed that one or two more conflicts might have occurred in the first half of the first century BC, until their final defeat by Octavian in 35 BC. However, this group was also noted as the allies of Rome by Cicero in the early 50s BC, so we cannot view the relationship of all of these communities with Rome as continually hostile[23].

---

[19] Čović 1987, 480.
[20] For sources and their interpretation see Šašel Kos 2005a, 292-313, 442-450; Dzino 2010, 62-69, 112-114, see also Zaninović 2007, 15-42. Recently excavated harbor in Desilo-Hutovo Blato is connected with indigenous community from Ošanići settlement near Stolac, usually identified as the Daorsi from written sources, Vasilj and Forić 2008. On Promona as conflict-zone between the Liburnian communities and the group known as the Delmatae, see Čače 1993, 2-14.
[21] Livy, 43.1.4-12; 43.5.1-10.
[22] App. *Illyr.* 10.
[23] Cic. *Balb.* 32. On Roman conflicts with the Iapodes see Šašel Kos 2005a, 321-329, 422-437; Olujić 2007, 73-102; Dzino 2010, 69-74, 85.

The Iapodes are located by the sources in the region recognised by archaeologists as belonging to a distinct Iron Age Iapodean culture. The communities belonging to the Iapodean culture show the existence of strong regional traditions - in some regions these traditions are formed within *poljes* in the *karst*, similar to the Delmatae, but also in the river valleys, such as the valleys of Gacka and Una. Some shared social-cultural-religious markers within the group can be assumed through continuing bi-ritualism in the funeral tradition as well as distinctive gender markers such as metal female head-covers used in the funerals in the late Hallstatt period.[24] These communities held an important place in the amber trade, together with Liburnian communities, starting in ca. 800 BC, increasing their importance in early Iron Age wider networks of exchanges and interactions[25]. Figural representations from Iapodean cinerary urns, the earliest of which should probably be dated to the fifth and fourth century BC, show the connections with, and influences of, Situla art from the south-eastern Alpine communities, which processed and reworked Etruscan influences[26]. Material culture also shows that communities in this region in the later Iron Age were simultaneously negotiating Mediterranean and La Tène influences in specific ways. Such developments led some ancient sources to imagine them within the lines of a literary construct: «the mixture of Illyrians and Celts»[27].

Similar to the Delmatae, the appearance of the Iapodes in written sources coincides with the arrival of their region in the zone of Roman imperialism – they are absent from the earliest layer of ethnographic information about the northern Adriatic. It is difficult to surmise when the Iapodes appear as a more or less formed trans-regional identity (either externally or internally perceived), especially taking into account the ethnonymes «Iapodes/Iapydes/Iapudes», possibly used to describe different groups in the North Adriatic region, such as the Iapudes mentioned on the Iguvine tablets in Umbria[28]. The reason for their conflicts with Rome is not known, but might have been related to the increasing importance of a trade route from Aquileia through Tergeste, Nauportus (Vrhnika), the valleys of Ljubljanica and Sava towards the Pannonian plains, mentioned by Strabo[29]. Scholars are in disagreement whether there were one or two distinct alliances in the first century BC, as the sources separately mention Transalpine and Cisalpine Iapodes with political centres in Metulum and Aruvium (near modern Ogulin and Otočac)[30]. The existence of

---

[24] Location by written sources: Šašel Kos 2005a, 424-426; Olujić 2007, 118-134, archaeological culture: Drechsler Bižić 1987; Wilkes 1992, 57-58; Raunig 2004; Balen Letunić 2006; Olujić 2007, 51-62, 144-194.

[25] Palavestra 1993, 275-286; Blečić 2009a; 2009b.

[26] Vasić 1967; Wilkes 1992, 198-200; Raunig 2004, 230-233; Balen-Letunić 2007, 386, 390.

[27] Strabo, 4.6.10; 7.5.2, 4. On material sources see Olujić 2007, 177-194, and on Strabo's literary strategies: Dzino 2008b.

[28] *Iguvinae* 1b 17, 6b 54, 58-59, 7a 12, 47-48; Devoto 1940, 64, 96, 275; Poultney 1959, 165, 275. Different Iapodes: Vedaldi Iasbez 1994, 267; Olujić 2007, 67-69, cf. Čače 1987/88, 79-80.

[29] Strabo 4.6.10; 7.5.2, see Šašel Kos 2002b; 2005, 424-426; Dzino 2010, 70-71 with bibliography.

[30] Olujić 2007, 87, 95-96, 219 argues that there was one, while the idea of two related but distinct alliances is supported by Čače 1979, 67; Šašel Kos 2005a, 422-437; Dzino 2008b, 376-377; 2010, 41, 109.

strong regional cultural traditions[31] and the absence of a dominant political and/or economic centre suggest internal rivalry and political heterogeneity within this cultural group. So, it would not be surprising to find significant fluency in social organisation, and the frequent appearance and disappearance of political alliances in this region.

The Pannonii

The Pannonii is an unfortunate identity-label applied by written sources to various indigenous communities from future southern Pannonia and northern Dalmatia, such as the Segestani (Segesticani), Breuci, Mezaei, Daesitiates, Ditiones, etc. The Pannonii are mentioned for the first time in the second century BC in the written sources[32]. As a common label it was applied to different communities between the Sava and Drava and south of Sava in modern-day northern and central Bosnia, in relation to their conflicts with the Romans in the second and first centuries BC and the *bellum Batonianum* from AD 6-9. The original perception of the indigenous Pannonii in Hellenistic ethnography was formed through the outside recognition of existing cultural similarities within the wider region, rather than being a self-perception shared by those Iron Age groups. This outside perception, which is partly preserved in very similar ways in Appian and in Strabo, imposes a certain order and logic for external observers. It projects a single ethnographic stereotype onto political and kin-based groups, which participated in maintaining a joint wider cultural *habitus*. However, this cultural *habitus* of the Pannonii was visibly fragmented by a complex set of horizontal and vertical social networks established between the groups, which were defined through different mechanisms of inter-group negotiations, appearing as either social inclusions or exclusions[33].

The communities perceived as the Pannonii in the written sources were not part of the same Iron Age archaeological culture as the previously discussed two. The communities discussed here are considered to be part of the Donja Dolina-Sanski Most and Central Bosnian cultures (cultural complex), both located south of the river Sava – Donja Dolina-Sanski Most in western Bosnia and Krajina and Central Bosnian in the lower valley of Bosna, the valley of Lašva and the wider area of central Bosnia. Unfortunately, both of these groups are insufficiently known, due to limited and insufficient excavation records. More knowledge is available on Donja Dolina-Sanski Most, which played an important role in early Iron Age exchange routes as a link between Glasinac, the south-eastern Alps and northern Adriatic, as important producers of iron, thanks to abundant regional deposits[34]. The Central Bosnian culture is less known, but shows continuous development of a few important sites,

---

[31] Balen Letunić 1995/96, 27-28; 1999/2000, 31-32; Olujić 2007, 180-185.
[32] Polyb., frg. 64, cf. Wallbank 1979, 748. Graeco-Roman perception of the Pannonian communities is best preserved in Strabo, 7.5.3, 7.5.10 and App. *Illyr.* 22.
[33] Dzino and Domić Kunić 2012, 95-100, see also Šašel Kos 2005a, 375-80, 83-84; 2005b.
[34] Marić 1964; Čović 1987, 232-288; Gavranović 2011.

such as Debelo Brdo-Sarajevo and Pod near Bugojno. Recent finds in Čolaci near Donji Vakuf promise to provide more insight into the significance of these communities in the production and exchange of iron in the Iron Ages.[35]

These cultures shared a similar cultural habitus, but there were also visible differences with Pannonian communities north of the Sava. Again, there is no evidence that either of these cultures had «princely tombs», although Donja Dolina maintained close links with the neighbouring Kaptol finds near Požega, where «princely tombs» are discovered. Pannonian communities north of the Sava rapidly transformed ca. 400 BC and the area between the Drava and Sava becomes strongly impacted by La Tène culture. The change south of the Sava is proportional with the proximity to this river – strongest in Donja Dolina, less strong in Sanski Most, and even less visible in Central Bosnian communities, although it would be wrong to say that there were no La Tene influences there, or that they were minimal. These communities were much more eclectic in combining La Tène with existing traditions and Mediterranean influences coming from the south, as we can see in the example of Kamenjača cemetery in the valley of the river Bosna.[36]

The communities known as the Daesitiates and Mezaei are not mentioned by name before the indigenous uprising in the *bellum Batonianum*, and as a matter of fact, there is no written record of any community living in this area before the first century BC[37]. It is possible that the Romans entered into conflict with the Daesitiates as early as Octavian's campaign. Appian, in his *Illyrian wars*, mentions the group of Daisioi, who apparently gave strong resistance to Octavian, and who are considered by most authorities to be the Daesitiates, or some of these communities from central Bosnia[38]. The fact that these groups participated in the uprising against Roman power makes clear that they willingly or unwillingly earlier accepted Roman power and certain obligations such as the provision of auxiliaries and the payment of tribute. The most likely period for this was during earlier Roman operations in the wider region, known as *bellum Pannonicum*, which were directed mostly against the group of the Breuci, across the Sava[39].

Heterarchical societies

These indigenous groups did not exist in isolation from the wider world. They belonged and should be seen in wider contexts. The most recent research on Iron Age communities in temperate Europe sees it as a world of complex social networks and political decentralisation, devoid of significant urban structures and social hierarchy. Power was negotiated between different social groups unified through networks of

---

[35] Čović 1987, 481-530, Wilkes 1992, 51-54, see Pravidur forthcoming and Pravidur-Vuković 2011 for Čolaci.
[36] See Dzino 2009; 2012. Kamenjača cemetery: Paškvalin 2008.
[37] Dio, 55.29.2; 55.32.4; Strabo, 7.5.3; Vell. Pat. 2.115.4 – all related to the *bellum Batonianum*.
[38] Daisioi and the Daesitiates: App. *Illyr*. 17; Šašel Kos 2005a, 458-459; Dzino 2010, 113-114.
[39] Domić Kunić 2006; Dzino 2010, 129-136, cf. also Wilkes 1969, 62-65.

kinship, adoptive kinship and clientship, into specific social structures referred to by some authors as «heterarchical societies». The elites were not entrenched by law or birth, but dominated by members of the community who exercised power through personal influence, acceptance of community and display of wealth – also known as «Big-men» in anthropological jargon, after influential study of Sahlins.[40] Iron Age Europe shared common cultural templates such as religious, agricultural, warfare and technological practices, or aesthetic traditions. These common templates were reassessed with the appearance and spread of the La Tène cultural complex from *ca.* 450 BC, which (re)established new cultural «language» amongst these communities, shifted inter-regional networks of power and exchange, still maintaining highly localised identities. These society-structures started to change more significantly only in contact with the Mediterranean world, either through Greek colonial encounters, or Roman expansion[41].

In the last centuries BC, pre-conquest societies of future Roman Dalmatia became strongly influenced by both Mediterranean and La Tène cultural and social models. Indigenous elites started to adopt Hellenistic and later, Roman cultural templates, in order to legitimise and strengthen domination within their communities. They did it through centralising power in new political alliances and attempting to control exchange-routes controlled by other communities. The existence of these political alliances convinced our sources to see them as «ethnic» identities – as they did elsewhere in contacts with similar communities[42]. The influence of La Tène culture is more difficult to describe and assess south of the Sava valley. However, it is possible to assume it in more general matters such as weapon technology or warfare practices, strong collective identities on a local level, the values of warrior-ship and the presence of the ideological affiliation of social groups through use fibulae of the La Tène scheme. It is also possible to speculate (more evidence is certainly required), about the appearance of bands of horsemen (*comitatus*) used by the 'Big-men' to exert their will, and challenge the earlier established balance of negotiated power within different segments of society[43].

The three groups briefly discussed broadly follow similar patterns of social development in the Iron Ages, while maintaining their different cultural traditions. In essence, these all can be described as heterarchic societies. They did not develop social stratification, or a significant degree of competition between different regional «Big-men» before *ca.* 400 BC, as occurred in the neighbouring Glasinac and Mati cultural complex or eastern Hallstatt communities present in southern Pannonia through so-called Martijanec-Kaptol and affiliated Budinjak and Colapian cultural

---

[40] Sahlins 1963.
[41] There is significant corpus of recent works on the topic. See for example Collis 1994; Hill 1995; Woolf 1997; Dietler 1997; 1999; James 1999, 86-96; Moore 2007; Haselgrove and Moore 2007; Thurston 2009; 2010; Blečić Kavur, Kavur 2010.
[42] Wells 1999, 33, 57. Cf. Nash 1978; Slofstra 2002; Roymans 2004; Oltean 2007, 41-53; Papworth 2008; Whittaker 2009.
[43] See speculations on this idea in Dzino 2012.

groups. Some of these communities were privileged by geographic position, which enabled them to participate more effectively in wider early Iron Age exchange networks, such as the Iapodean communities or those of Donja Dolina, while Delmatean and Central Bosnian communities probably played a secondary role in these wider exchange networks[44]. It seems that kinship connections played important role in establishment and maintenance of these exchange networks, but also in forging political ties between different communities[45]. The acquirement and redistribution of Mediterranean imports was used by influential individuals and clans to justify and strengthen their claims on power, thus starting more intense competition amongst indigenous communities. This firstly occurs on the Adriatic coast and can be observed through the development of social stratification in the material record. Material evidence from Liburnia and the Central Dalmatian coast shows that from *ca.* 400 BC there was increasing social stratification and new strategies for the display of wealth and social status. These changes were probably increased by the Greek settlement of the central Adriatic islands: Vis, Hvar and Korčula, and in Liburnian case, with the existing connections with Italy. A similar social transformation can be noted in the southern Adriatic, which was interacting even further with the Greek world through the Corinthian colonies of Apollonia and Epidamnus/Dyrrachium on modern-day Albanian coast. All these, initially Greek, communities interacted with their indigenous surroundings forming in a few generations specific culture, which maintained outside shell of Greekness, but was in the essence result of intense negotiation between the Greek and indigenous cultures[46].

Material evidence from indigenous burial assemblages in the southern Adriatic, the coast and hinterland between the rivers Neretva and Drilo, after *ca.* 500 BC shows connections between social status and recently developed military hierarchies, and probably even a change in warfare strategies[47]. Written evidence related to the Illyrian kingdom in the southern Adriatic shows in broad strokes how the building of these political institutions was made: local communities were organised in a political alliance dominated by the strongest 'Big-men', perceived as the «king» by written sources, and this balance of power shifted on occasions to different groups, or rather their leaders[48]. Only very late in the third century, the «kings» of the Illyrian kingdom tried to establish hereditary ruling dynasties and use Helle-

---

[44] New discoveries in this underexplored region can certainly change this view - on present state of evidence from early Iron Ages Central Bosnian culture see Gavranović 2011.

[45] Teržan 1995: 99-100 implies role of females given in marriage in forging links between the coastal communities and the hinterland in the early Iron Age. Cf. the example of the Hallstatt-era female cremation in tumulus with the Iapodean artifacts in Libna, eastern Slovenia, in cemetery which is ascribed to the Dolenjska cultural group, Preložnik 2007.

[46] Liburnia: Batović 1974; Central Dalmatia: Kirigin et al. 2005; Southern Adriatic: Ceka 1985b; Cabanes 1988, 207-233; Wilkes 1992, 156-180. Greek colonial encounters in the Eastern Adriatic coast are continually reassessed, see for example the papers from Cambi et al. 2002; Cabanes 2008, and recent literature in Dzino 2012. See also recent suggestions about the Macedonian influences in Blečić Kavur and Kavur 2010; Blečić Kavur and Miličević-Capek 2011.

[47] Blečić Kavur and Miličević-Capek 2011, for military strategies see Marijan 2000, 83 and Periša 2003, 95.

[48] Carlier 1987, cf. Šašel Kos 2002a, 110-114.

nistic templates to justify their claims to power, but were continuously challenged and obstructed by local «Big-men», called the «dynasts» by Polybius[49].

This process of inter-communal competition spreads to the clans in the hinterland, where new regional and political identities were beginning to be forged after *ca.* 400 BC. The best evidence for these changes is the appearance of strong political groups, such as the Delmatae or Iapodes, in third and second century BC sources, and the simultaneous disappearance or transformation of earlier groups, known (or perceived) from ethnographic discourse of the earlier period. The main drive for beginning of this social restructuring was probably either the desire to increase the exchanges, or resist cultural change, or even both. For example, material evidence from the core of the Delmataean region in the Dalmatian Zagora and *karst* plains in the immediate hinterland shows that those communities did not import Hellenistic pottery-vessels for wine, and probably even resisted wine-consumption habits, unlike coastal communities which show an abundant display of wine-drinking vessels such as *kantharoi*[50]. The evidence for these groups, which seem to be newly formed, such as the Delmatae or Iapodes, shows that they made a strong effort to take control over the existing exchange networks with the Mediterranean world, the valleys of Neretva and Krka and the emporium of Salona (Delmatae) or the Aquileia-Pannonia trade network[51].

Roman interaction with the eastern Adriatic frontier-zone

This wider region of the western part of the Balkan Peninsula becomes an important place in the conflict between Rome and Macedonian kingdom in the later third century BC – especially the Adriatic coast and the islands. The initial establishment of indirect Roman political influence in the third and second centuries BC necessitated the creation of networks of friendly indigenous leaders and groups. Roman Republican relationship with the wider region of the eastern Adriatic and its hinterland presents a complex political, cultural and economic interaction, which can no longer be reduced to a simplistic notion of a gradual conquest of this space. Important obstacle for such a view is growing awareness that Roman perception, visualization and representation of space substantially differed from ours. The usual mode of spatial perception, then, was 'linear' view of space, as is well known from many of the Hellenistic periploi and Roman itine-

---

[49] Polyb, 5.4.3 *polidunastai*. See primary sources and their analysis in: Cabanes 1988, 255-334; Šašel Kos 2005a, 249-290; Dzino 2010, 44-60. The material record of late third/early second century from southern Adriatic is nicely seen in Velje Ledine cemetery near Gostilj: Basler 1972.

[50] Kirigin *et al.* 2005, 8, 11. Resistance to wine-drinking practices as part of identity-construction narrative is argued in Dzino 2006.

[51] Above n. 16 for the Delmatae, and n. 23 for the Iapodes. In addition should be mentioned the recent idea that the lower Neretva became an important wine-producing region for the Issaean and late republican Italian investment, in the late second and early first centuries BC, Lindhagen 2009.

raries. This agrees with the belief established in more recent scholarship that the Romans themselves in this period did not strive to dominate and conquer space, but rather to dominate other nations and groups[52]. Such an approach results in a frontier-zone being established around a Roman polity, composed of allies and clients. At the same time this functioned as a protective buffer zone, as well as areas of interaction with communities outside this border zone. The frontier-zone played a linking role as a contact-zone between indigenous communities and the Roman polity, allowing contacts and conflicts, but also economic and cultural exchanges. These exchanges resulted in the emergence of specific hybrid frontier societies and cultures with overarching differences to both indigenous and Roman-Mediterranean cultural forms[53].

The area of the eastern Adriatic and its hinterland in the third century BC was formed as a frontier-zone between Macedonia and northern Italy, which in the beginning mainly related to the coast and islands. Its position fits well into what Dyson has for a long time called «republican borders» on the western borders of Rome: the area of interaction that connects, rather than separates, the Roman provincial administration and indigenous polities, through a complex web of diplomacy and personal contacts[54]. Roman strategy to interact with the frontier-zones usually was based on indirect control, by establishing alliances with local communities and clans/families, and their military protection against other local communities. Military interventions in most of the second and first half of the first century BC were sporadic and limited to specific objectives, which either expanded the frontier-zone, as in the Southern Alps, or protected indigenous allies when they were exposed to danger from rival polities, as was case in the central and southern Adriatic[55].

Rome preferred to indirectly control this frontier-zone area, which is reflected not only in her unwillingness to establish a provincial policy framework, but also in the absence of a symbolic representation of the Roman presence in the region. Permanent military garrisons and fortresses on the eastern coast of the Adriatic Sea did not exist before Octavian's campaign, and the provincial structure began to be established only with Caesar's pro-consular *imperium*, granted to him by the Vatinian law passed in 59 BC. The convents of Roman citizens on the Adriatic coast were not artificially constructed points to project Roman control over the area, or usurp the space of indigenous communities as elsewhere. They occurred as organic parts of the frontier-society in existing indigenous settlements such as Iader or originally multi-ethnic trading emporia and settlements such as Salona, Narona, or Lissus. Only the establishment of Roman colonies on the Adriatic coast sometimes

---

[52] Nicolet 1991, 57-74; C.R. Whittaker 1994, 10-30; 2004, 63-87; Brodersen 1995; 2004; Elton 1996; Sipilä 2009, 22-30; Dzino 2010, 18-20

[53] Braund 1984, 91-96; Dyson 1985; C.R. Whittaker 1994: 98-131; Elton 1996; Mattern 1999: 109-114, cf. on cultural contacts Malkin 2002; 2004; Ulf 2009.

[54] Dyson 1985.

[55] See Dzino 2005; 2010, 44-79. The Roman interactions with this region in this period are best explored most recently in Bandelli 2004; Čače 1991; 1993; Šašel Kos 2004; 2005a, 291-334, etc.

between mid-40s BC and the early Augustan age transforms them into ideological regional offices of Rome, reflecting imperial ideological discourse and emulating Romanness in the province[56].

Indigenous communities from future Dalmatia appear in the historical records as a very heterogeneous set of communities in constant social and political transformation. Exposed to the influences of the La Tène world from the north and west and the Greek-Hellenistic world from the south-east, they seek to recast global cultural patterns and adapt them to existing local cultural habitat, to that set of practices which they might perceive as their «traditions». Although the processes of social transformation must have started earlier, the Roman political interaction with the region accelerated the formation and restructuring of indigenous political alliances, in which the former clan and family interests began to clash with the interests of the larger regional political alliances, such as the centralization of political power and establishment of hereditary power. Within indigenous communities, the formation of a frontier-zone and its dynamics favored the development of more complex political identities such as Delmatae, Iapodes or Pannonian communities. Our sources distinguished these new political formations as «barbaric *ethne*», fitting them into pre-existing stereotyped notions of the «barbarian» as the communities that exist perpetually in a timeless vacuum, without capability for social change. Thus, we might even dare to say that Rome, through its direct political interaction, indirectly created indigenous «ethnicities».

The establishment of these political formations most certainly occurred through the politicization of similar or common cultural habitats. They might have started as indigenous reactions to the process of acculturation and intensified contacts with the Mediterranean world; however, the process of expansion of the Roman political power exaggerated the intensity and speed of these transitions in indigenous societies. Comparative examples can be seen in pre-Columbian empires in America, or in the interaction of indigenous communities and the European colonial powers in the Americas and Africa. The colonial and/or imperial powers needed indigenous leaders to establish or maintain their dominance, while the indigenous elites needed complex governance structures to establish, justify and strengthen their supremacy and authority[57]. The frontier-zone is not sufficiently politically stable. Indigenous communities were looking primarily after their own interests and frequently changed their positions, negotiating between two basic choices: to be the friend of Rome or her enemy[58]. Nevertheless, the existence of a frontier-zone as a zone of political negotiation compelled these communities to

---

[56] The dating of Roman republican *conventi* and the earliest colonies in the region remains controversial, see Dzino 2010, 88-90, 120-121 listing earlier opinions.

[57] Ferguson and Whitehead 1992 (European colonial encounter); Smith and Montiel 2001 (pre-Columbian Mexico), and Covey 2003 (establishment of the Inca Empire).

[58] Great example is provided in written sources by Demetrios of Pharos, who switched his position from the Roman ally to the Roman enemy in late third century BC. His origines (whether indigenous, Greek or mixed) are not so important here, see Coppola 1993; Zaninović 1998; Šašel Kos 2005a, 262-279.

build basic political structures that would be able to communicate with the Romans and be involved in the Roman way of conducting politics.

Roman interaction with this area created a complex network of alliances with indigenous communities, rewarding those who supported Rome and punishing those who opposed it. Indigenous communities were actively involved in these interactions. They negotiated their own position within the Roman political conglomerate, often combining the resistance with its bargaining position as potential ally against other indigenous communities. In recognizing this process of interaction with the border zone, the indigenous community sets as an equal participants in this respect, as active participants in an interaction balanced between resistance to Roman imperialism, and support for Roman intervention and peaceful inclusion in the Roman political conglomerate.

Conclusion

The most important suggestion offered in this paper is that those indigenous identities, known from the written sources as the Delmatae, Iapodes, and Pannonian groups, are more recent social formations. They did not develop gradually their ethnicity through the Iron Ages, but were formed as local reactions to outside influences, which changed quantitatively and qualitatively after *ca.* 400 BC. Intensified cultural exchanges between the Mediterranean and Central Europe, and later, the influence of Roman imperialism, triggered social change amongst indigenous clans and upset the balance of power between the heterarchic groups that held it before. As a consequence of these influences, new ways of social organisation, competition and power-negotiation developed within the societal groups. Communities from the coast started to develop more elaborate social stratification, while groups from the hinterland, analysed here, built political and military alliances, through internal competition between the clans and regions. Such a competition resulted in a new society dominated by groups of elite warriors and their leaders, preventing, or at least making more difficult, the establishment of hereditary elites and more centralised political entities before the Roman conquest started in the later first century BC.

Danijel Dzino
Macquarie University, Sydney

The impact of Roman imperialism on the formation of group identities in some indigenous societies 159

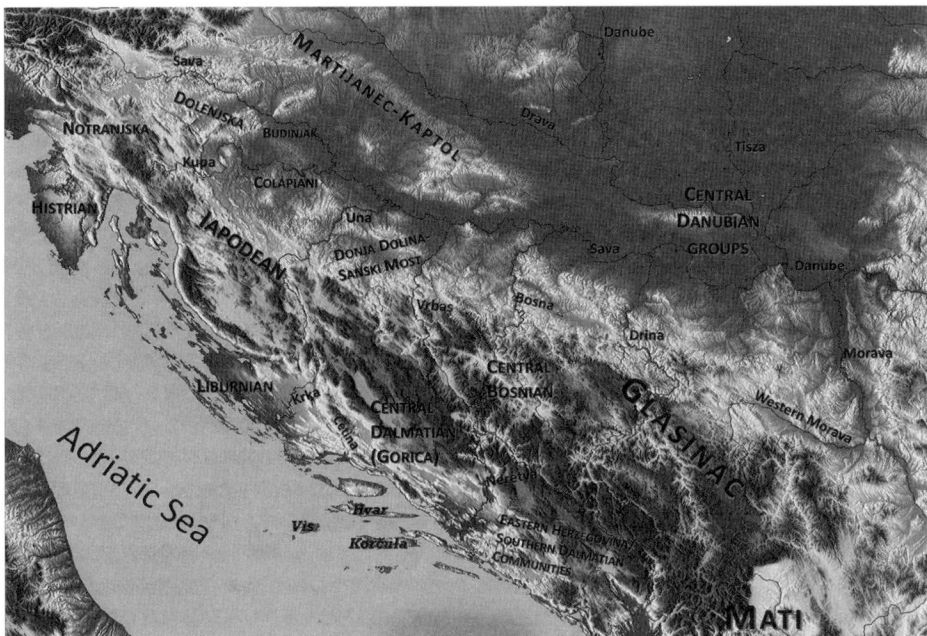

Map 1: *Early Iron Age archaeological cultures in the region, major rivers and islands mentioned in the paper*

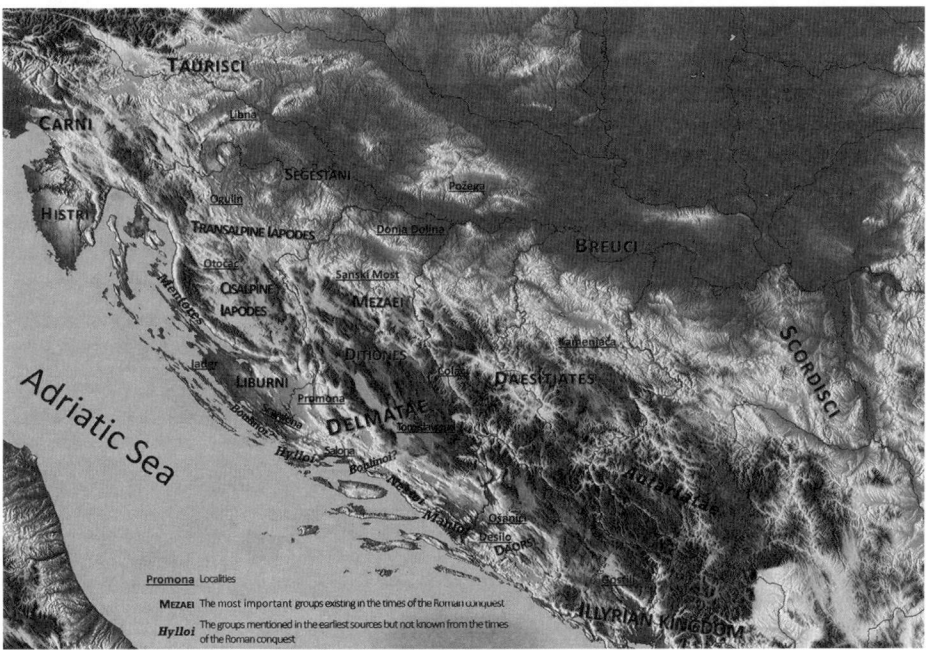

Map 2: *Major indigenous groups recorded in the sources and the locations mentioned in the paper*

Bibliography

Babić 2002 = S. Babić, «'Princely Graves' of the Central Balkans – A Critical History of Research», *JEurArch* 5.1 (2002) 70-88.

Balen Letunić 2007 = D. Balen Letunić, «A new representation of a Iapodian warrior from the Gracac area», in Blečić et al. 2007, 381-390.

Balen Letunić 2006 = D. Balen Letunić, *Japodi. Arheološka svjedočanstva o japodskoj kulturi u posljednjem pretpovijesnom tisućljeću* (Ogulin 2006).

Balen Letunić 1999/00 = D. Balen Letunić, «Japodske nekropole s ogulinskog područja», *Vjesnik Arheološkog muzeja u Zagrebu* 32-33 (1999-2000) 23-62.

Balen Letunić 1995/96 = D. Balen Letunić, «Figuralno ukrašene trapezoidne pojasne kopče tipa Prozor», *Vjesnik Arheološkog muzeja u Zagrebu* 28-29 (1995-1996) 23-38.

Bandelli 2004 = G. Bandelli, «Momenti e forme nella politica illirica della repubblica romana (229-49 a.C.)», in Urso 2004, 95-139.

Basler 1972 = Đ. Basler, «The necropolis of Vele Ledine at Gostilj (Lower Zeta)», *Wissenschaftliche Mitteilungen des Bosnisch-Herzegowinischen Landesmuseums: Heft A – Archäologie* 2 (1972) 5-125.

Batović 2004 = Š. Batović, «Dalmatska kultura željeznog doba» in Š. Batović, *U osvit povijesti (od starijega kamenog doba do Liburna) – Opera Selecta* 2 (Zadar 2004, originally published 1986) 15-78.

Batović 1974 = Š. Batović, «Ostava iz Jagodnje Gornje u okviru zadnje faze liburnske kulture», *Diadora* 7 (1974) 159-245.

Benac 1987 = A. Benac, (ed.), *Praistorija Jugoslovenskih Zemalja Vol. 5: Željezno doba* (Sarajevo 1987).

Benac 1985 = A. Benac, Utvrđena ilirska naselja I: delmatske gradine na Duvanjskom polju, Buškom blatu, Livanjskom i Glamočkom polju (Sarajevo 1985).

Blažević 2007 = Z. Blažević, *Ilirizam prije ilirizma* (Zagreb 2007).

Blečić 2009a = M. Blečić Kavur, «Japodske podlaktične narukvice: Simbolika ženskog principa u optjecanju ideja i djela jadranske kulturne *koine*», *Vjesnik Arheološkog muzeja u Zagrebu* 42 (2009) 231-258.

Blečić 2009b = M. Blečić Kavur, «The significance of Amber in the Kvarner region», in A. Palavestra, C.W. Beck and J.M. Todd, (eds.), *Amber in Archaeology: Proceedings of the Fifth International Conference on Amber in Archaeology, Belgrade 2006* (Belgrade 2009) 142-155.

Blečić 2007 = M. Blečić, «Status, symbols, sacrifices, offerings. The diverse meanings of Illyrian helmets», *Vjesnik Arheološkog muzeja u Zagrebu* 40 (2007) 73-116.

Blečić Kavur and Kavur 2010 = M. Blečić Kavur and B. Kavur, «Grob 22 iz beogradske nekropole Karaburma: Retrospektiva i perspektiva», *Starinar* 60 (2010) 57-84.

Blečić Kavur and Miličević-Capek 2011 = M. Blečić Kavur and I. Miličević-Capek, «On the horizon of warrior's graves from 5th century BC on the territory of the eastern Adriatic coast and its hinterland: the case of the new discovery from Vranjevo Selo near Neum», *Prilozi Instituta za Arheologiju u Zagrebu* 28 (2011) 31-94.

Blečić Kavur and Pravidur 2012 = M. Blečić Kavur and A. Pravidur, «Illyrian helmets from Bosnia and Herzegovina», *Glasnik Zemaljskog Muzeja u Sarajevu* 53 (2012) 35-136.

Blečić et al. 2007 = M. Blečić, M. Črešnar, B. Hänsel, A. Hellmuth, E. Kaiser and C. Metzner-Nebelsick, (eds.), *Scripta praehistorica in honorem Biba Teržan*. Situla 44 (Ljubljana 2007).

Braund 1984 = D. Braund, *Rome and the Friendly king: the character of the client kingship* (New York 1984).

Brodersen 2004 = K. Brodersen, «Mapping (In) the Ancient World», *JRS* 94 (2004) 183-190.

Brodersen 1995 = K. Brodersen, *Terra Incognita. Studien zur römischen Raumerfassung.* Spudasmata 59 (Zürich/New York 1995).

Cabanes 2008 = P. Cabanes, «Greek Colonisation in the Adriatic», in G. Tsetskhladze, (ed.), *Greek colonisation: an account of Greek colonies and other settlements overseas*, Vol. 2, Mnemosyne Suppl. 193. (Leiden/Boston 2008) 155-186.

Cabanes 1988 = P. Cabanes *Les Illyriens de Bardylis à Genthios: IVe-IIe siècles avant J.-C.* (Paris 1988).

Cambi et al. 2002 = N. Cambi, S. Čače, and B. Kirigin, (eds.), *Greek Influence along the East Adriatic Coast: Proceedings of the International Conference held in Split from September 24th to 26th 1998* (Split 2002).

Carlier 1987 = P. Carlier, «Rois illyriens et 'roi des Illyriens'», in P. Cabanes, (ed.), *L'Illyrie méridionale et l'Épire dans l'Antiquité: Actes du Colloque international de Clermont-Ferrand* (Clermont-Ferrand 1987) 39-45.

Ceka 1985 = N. Ceka «Aperçu sur le développement de la vie urbaine chez les Illyriens du Sud», *Iliria* 15.2 (1985) 137-162.

Collis 1994 = J. Collis, «Reconstructing Iron Age society», in K. Kristiansen and J. Jensen, (eds.), *Europe in the First Millennium BC* (Sheffield 1994) 31-39.

Coppola 1993 = A. Coppola, *Demetrio di Faro. Problemi e recherche di storia antica 15* (Rome 1993).

Covey 2003 = R.A. Covey, «A processual study of Inka state formation», *Journal of Anthropological Archaeology* 22 (2003) 333-357.

Čače 1994/95 = S. Čače, «*Dalmatica Straboniana*», *Diadora* 16-17 (1994-1995) 101-133.

Čače 1993 = S. Čače, «Prilozi povijesti Liburnije u 1. stoljeću prije Krista», *Radovi Zavoda za povijesne znanosti Hrvatske akademije znanosti i umjetnosti u Zadru* 35 (1993) 1-35.

Čače 1991 = S. Čače, «Rim, Liburnija i istočni Jadran u drugom stoljeću pr. n. e.», *Diadora* 13 (1991) 55-76.

Čače 1987/88 = S. Čače, «Položaj rijeke Telavija i pitanje japodskog primorja», *Radovi Filozofskog Fakulteta u Zadru* 27/14 (1987-1988) 65-92.

Čače 1979 = S. Čače, «Prilozi proučavanju političkog uređenja naroda sjeverozapadnog Ilirika», *Radovi Filozofskog Fakulteta u Zadru* 18/8 (1979) 43-152.

Čović 1987 = B. Čović, «Donja Dolina – Sanski Most »; « Srednjodalmatinska grupa »; « Srednjobosanska grupa» in Benac 1987, 232-288, 442-528.

Devoto 1940 = G. Devoto, *Tabulae Iguvinae*, 2nd ed. (Rome 1940).

Dietler 1999 = M. Dietler, «Rituals of commensality and the politics of state formation in the 'princely' societies of Early Iron Age Europe», in P. Ruby, (ed.), *Les princes de la Protohistoire et l'émergence de l'état, Cahiers du Centre Jean Bérard, Institut Français de Naples* (Naples 1999) 135-152.

Dietler 1997 = M. Dietler, «The Iron Age in Mediterranean France: Colonial encounters, entanglements, and transformations», *Journal of World Prehistory* 11 (1997) 269-358.

Domić Kunić 2006 = A. Domić Kunić, «Bellum Pannonicum (12.-11. pr. Kr.). Posljednja faza osvajanja južne Panonije», *Vjesnik Arheološkog muzeja u Zagrebu* 39 (2006) 59-164.

Drechler Bižić 1987 = R. Drechler Bižić, «Japodska grupa», in Benac 1987, 391-441.

Dyson 1985 = S.L. Dyson, *The Creation of the Roman Frontier* (Princeton NJ 1985).

Dzino and Domić Kunić 2012 = D. Dzino, A. Domić Kunić, «Pannonians: Identity-perceptions from the late Iron Age to later antiquity», in B. Migotti, (ed.), *Archaeology of Roman Southern Pannonia. The state of research and selected problems in the Croatian part of the Roman province of Pannonia*, British Archaeological Reports—International Series 2393 (Oxford 2012) 93-115.

Dzino 2012 = D. Dzino, «Contesting identities of pre-Roman Illyricum», *Ancient West & East* 11 (2012), in print.

Dzino 2011 = D. Dzino, «Indigene zajednice zapadnog i središnjeg Balkanskog poluotoka i 21. stoljeće: metodološki problemi», *Godišnjak Centra za balkanološka ispitivanja* 40/38 (2011) 197-206.

Dzino 2010 = D. Dzino, *Illyricum and Roman Politics 229 BC - AD 68* (Cambridge 2010).

Dzino 2009 = D. Dzino, «'Dezidijati': Identitetski konstrukt između antičkih i suvremenih percepcija», *Godišnjak Centra za balkanološka ispitivanja* 38/36 (2009) 75-95.

Dzino 2008a = D. Dzino, «Deconstructing 'Illyrians': Zeitgeist, changing perceptions and the identity of peoples from ancient Illyricum», *Croatian Studies Review* 5 (2008) 43-55.

Dzino 2008b = D. Dzino, «*The people who are Illyrians and Celts:* Strabo and the identities of the 'barbarians' from Illyricum», *Arheološki vestnik* 59 (2008) 371-380.

Dzino 2006 = D. Dzino, «Delmati, vino i formiranje etničkog identiteta u predrimskom Iliriku», *Vjesnik za arheologiju i povijest dalmatinsku* 99 (2006) 71-80.

Dzino 2005 = D. Dzino, «Late Republican Illyrian Policy of Rome 167-60 BC: the Bifocal Approach», in C. Deroux, (ed.), *Studies in Latin Literature and Roman History* 12. Collection Latomus 287 (Bruxelles 2005) 48-73.

Eckstein 2006 = A.M. Eckstein, *Mediterranean Anarchy, Interstate War, and the Rise of Rome* (Berkeley/Los Angeles/London 2006).

Elton 1996 = H. Elton, *Frontiers of the Roman Empire* (London 1996)

Ferguson and Whitehead 1992 = R.B. Ferguson and N.L. Whitehead, (eds.), *War in the Tribal Zone: Expanding States and Indigenous Warfare* (Santa Fe NM 1992).

Gavranović 2011 = M. Gavranović, *Die Spätbronze- und Früheisenzeit in Bosnien. Universitätsforschungen zur prähistorischen Archäologie* 195 (Bonn 2011)

Haselgrove and Moore 2007 = C. Haselgrove and T. Moore, «New narratives of the later Iron Age», in C. Haselgrove and T. Moore, (eds.), *The Later Iron Age in Britain and Beyond* (Oxford 2007) 1-15.

Hill 1995 = J.D. Hill, «How should we understand Iron Age societies and hillforts? A contextual study from southern Britain», in J.D. Hill and C.G. Cumberpatch, (eds.), *Different Iron Ages: Studies on the Iron Age in Temperate Europe* (Oxford 1995) 45-66.

James 1999 = S. James, *Atlantic Celts: Ancient People or Modern Invention?* (London 1999).

Katičić 1995 = R. Katičić, *Illyricum Mythologicum* (selected works) (Zagreb 1995).

Kirigin 2010 = B. Kirigin, «Gradina Sutilija povrh Trogira i nalazi rane keramike tipa Alto-Adriatico», in J. Dukić, A. Milošević and Ž. Rapanić, (eds.), *Scripta Branimero Gabričević dicata* (Trilj 2010) 23-55.

Kirigin et al. 2005 = B. Kirigin, T. Katunarić and L. Šešelj, «Amfore i fina keramika (od 4. do 1. st. pr. Kr.) iz srednje Dalmacije: preliminarni ekonomski i socijalni pokazatelji», *Vjesnik za arheologiju i povijest dalmatinsku* 98 (2005) 7-21.

Kozličić 1990 = M. Kozličić, *Historijska geografija istočnog Jadrana u starom vijeku* (Split 1990).

Lindhagen 2009 = A. Lindhagen, «The transport amphoras Lamboglia 2 and Dressel 6A revisited», *JRA* 22 (2009) 83-108.

Malkin 2004 = I. Malkin, «Postcolonial concepts and Ancient Greek Colonization», *Modern Language Quarterly* 65 (2004) 341-364.

Malkin 2002 = I. Malkin, «A Colonial Middle Ground: Greek, Etruscan and Local Elites in the Bay of Naples», in C.L. Lyons and J.K. Papadopulos, (eds.), *The Archaeology of Colonialism* (Los Angeles 2002) 151-181.

Marić 1964 = Z. Marić, «Donja Dolina», *Glasnik Zemaljskog muzeja u Sarajevu* 19 (1964) 5-128.

Marijan 2000 = B. Marijan, «Željezno doba na južnojadranskom području (istočna Hercegovina, južna Dalmacija)», *Vjesnik za arheologiju i historiju dalmatinsku* 93 (2000) 7-221.

Matijašić 2011 = I. Matijašić, «'Shrieking like Illyrians'. Historical geography and the Greek perspective of the Illyrian world in the 5th century BC», *Arheološki vestnik* 62 (2011) 289-316.

Mattern 1999 = S.P. Mattern, *Rome and the Enemy. Imperial Strategy in the Principate.* (Berkeley/Los Angeles 1999).

Mattingly 2011 = D.J. Mattingly, *Imperialism, Power and Identity: Experiencing the Roman Empire* (Princeton/Oxford 2011).

Moore 2007 = T. Moore, «Perceiving communities: exchange, landscapes and social networks in the later Iron Age of western Britain», *OJA* 26.1 (2007) 79-102.

Nash 1978 = D. Nash, «Territory and state formation in central Gaul», in D. Green, C. Haselgrove, and M. Spriggs, (eds.), *Social Organization and Settlement*, vol. 2. British Archaeological Reports Suppl. 47/2 (Oxford 1978) 455-475.

Nicolet 1991 = C. Nicolet, Space, *Geography and Politics in the Early Roman Empire. Jerome Lectures* 19 (Ann Arbor MI 1991).

Novaković 2011 = P. Novaković, «Archaeology in the New Countries of Southeastern Europe: A Historical Perspective», in L.R. Rozny, (ed.), *Comparative Archaeologies: A Sociological View of the Science of the Past* (New York/Dordrecht/Heidelberg/London 2011) 339-362.

Oltean 2007 = I. A. Oltean, *Dacia: Landscape, Colonisation and Romanisation* (London/New York 2007).

Olujić 2007 = B. Olujić, *Japodi. Pristup* (Zagreb 2007).

Palavestra 1993 = A. Palavestra, *Praistorijski ćilibar na centralnom i zapadnom Balkanu* (Belgrade 1993).

Papazoglou 1978 = F. Papazoglou, *The Central Balkan Tribes in Pre-Roman times: Triballi, Autariatae, Dardanians, Scordisci and Moesians* (Amsterdam 1978).

Papworth 2008 = M. Papworth, *Deconstructing the Durotriges: A Definition of Iron Age commnities within the Dorset Environs.* British Archaeological Reports – British series 462 (Oxford 2008).

Paškvalin 2008 = V. Paškvalin, «Kamenjača, Breza kod Sarajeva – mlađeželjeznodobna i rimska nekropola», *Godišnjak Centra za balkanološka ispitivanja* 37/35 (2008) 101-179.

Periša 2003 = D. Periša, «Review of Marijan 2000, (Željezno doba na južnojadranskom području (istočna Hercegovina, južna Dalmacija), Split 2001 (prikaz)», *Obavijesti Hrvatskog arheološkog društva* 35.2 (2003) 90-103.

Poultney 1959 = J.W. Poultney, *The Bronze Tables of Iguvium*. APA Philological Monographs 18 (Baltimore MD 1959).

Pravidur forthcoming = A. Pravidur, «New Research in Early Hallstatt hillforts of Central Bosnia – Excavations in Donji Vakuf» *Internationale Archäologie - Arbeitsgemeinschaft, Symposium, Tagung, Kongress*. Hengist-Studien 3 (Rahden).

Pravidur and Vuković 2011 = A. Pravidur and M. Vuković, «Prilog poznavanju metalurških središta željeznodobnih naselja srednje Bosne u svijetlu novih istraživanja- primjer autohtone i primarne metalurgije željeza u naselju», *Histria Antiqua* 20 (2011) 156-167.

Preložnik 2007 = A. Preložnik, «Japodska princesa z Libne?», in Blečić *et al.* 2007, 505-517.

Raunig 2004 = B. Raunig, *Umjetnost i religija prethistorijskih Japoda* (Sarajevo 2004).

Rich 1993 = J. Rich, «Fear, greed and glory: the causes of Roman war-making in the middle Republic», in J. Rich and G. Shipley, (eds.), *War and Society in the Roman World* (London/New York 1993) 38-69.

Roymans 2004 = N. Roymans, *Ethnic Identity and Imperial Power: The Batavians in the Early Roman Empire*. Amsterdam Archaeological Studies 10 (Amsterdam 2004).

Sahlins 1963 = M.D. Sahlins, «Poor man, rich man, big-man, chief: political types in Melanesia and Polynesia», *Comparative Studies in Society and History* 5.3 (1963) 283-303.

Sipilä 2009 = J. Sipilä, *The Reorganisation of Provincial Territories in Light of the Imperial Decision-Making Process: Later Romnan Arabia and Tres Palastinae as case studies*. Commentationes Humanarum Litterarum 126 (Helsinki 2009).

Slofstra 2002 = J. Slofstra, «Batavians and Romans on the lower Rhine. The Romanisation of the frontier», *Archaeological Dialogues* 9 (2002) 16-38.

Smith and Montiel 2001 = M.E. Smith and L. Montiel, «The archaeological study of empires and imperialism in pre-Hispanic central Mexico», *Journal of Anthropological Archaeology* 20 (2001) 245-284.

Šašel Kos 2011 = M. Šašel Kos, «The Roman conquest of Dalmatia and Pannonia under Augustus - some of the latest research results», in G. Moosbauer and R. Wiegels, (eds.), *Fines imperii-imperium sine fine?: römische Okkupations- und Grenzpolitik im frühen Principat: Beiträge zum Kongress «Fines imperii-imperium sine fine?» Osnabrück vom 14. bis 18. september 2009*. Osnabrücker Forschungen zu Altertum und Antike-Rezeption 14 (Rahden 2011) 107-117.

Šašel Kos 2007 = M. Šašel Kos, «Ethnic manipulations with ancient Veneti and Illyrians», *Portolano Adriatico: Rivista di storia e cultura balcanica* 3/3 (2007) 11-18.

Šašel Kos 2005a = M. Šašel Kos, *Appian and Illyricum*. Situla 43 (Ljubljana 2005).

Šašel Kos 2005b = M. Šašel Kos, «The Pannonians in Appian's Illyrike», in M. Šegvić and I. Mirnik, (eds.), *Illyrica Antiqua. Ob honorem Duje Rendić-Miočević* (Zagreb 2005) 433-439.

Šašel Kos 2004 = M. Šašel Kos, «The Roman conquest of Dalmatia in the light of Appian's *Illyrike*», in Urso 2004, 141-166.

Šašel Kos 2002a = M. Šašel Kos, «Pyrrhus and Illyrian kingdom(s?)», in Cambi *et al.* 2002, 101-120.

Šašel Kos 2002b = «The Noarus river in Strabo's Geography», *Tyche* 17 (2002) 145-154.

Teržan 1995 = B. Teržan, «Handel und soziale Oberschuchten im früheisenzeitlichen Südosteuropa», in B. Hänsel (ed.), *Handel, Tausch und Vekehr im bronze- und früheisenzeitlichen Südosteuropa*. Südosteuropa-Schriften 17/Prähistorische Archäologie in Südosteuropa 11 (Munich/Berlin 1995) 81-150.

Thurston 2010 = T.L. Thurston «Bitter Arrows and Generous Gifts: What Was a 'King' In the European Iron Age?» in T.D. Price and G.M. Feinman, (eds.), *Pathways to Power New Perspectives on the Emergence of Social Inequality* (New York 2010) 193-254.

Thurston 2009 = T.L. Thurston, «Unity and Diversity in the European Iron Age: Out of the Mists, Some Clarity?», *Journal of Archaeological Research* 17 (2009) 347-423.

Ulf 2009 = C. Ulf, «Rethinking Cultural Contacts», *Ancient West & East* 8 (2009) 81-132.

Urso 2004 = G. Urso (ed.), *Dall'Adriatico al Danubio. L'Illirico nell'età greca e romana*. I convegni della fondazione Niccolò Canussio 3 (Pisa 2004).

Vasić 1967 = R. Vasić, «The date of the Iapod urns», *Archaeologia Iugoslavica* 8 (1967) 47-57.

Vasić 2004 = R. Vasić, «Beleške o Glasincu – Autarijati», *Balcanica* 35 (2004) 35-49.

Vasić 2007 = R. Vasić, «Kneginje Centralnog Balkana», in Blečić et al. 2007, 557-562.

Vasilj and Forić 2008 = S. Vasilj and M. Forić, «The secrets of the Illyrian warriors' harbor», *Skyllis* 9.2 (2008) 36-43.

Vedaldi Iasbez 1994 = V. Vedaldi Iasbez, *La Venetia orientale e l'Histria. Le fonti letterarie greche e latine fino alla caduta dell'Impero Romano d'Occidente* (Rome 1994).

Vranić 2011 = I. Vranić, «'Ranoantička naselja' i gvozdeno doba centralnog Balkana: pitanja etničkog identiteta», *Etnoantropološki problemi* 6.3 (2011) 659-678.

Wallbank 1979 = F.W. Wallbank, *Historical Commentary on Polybius* Vol. 3 (Oxford 1979).

Wells 1999 = P.S. Wells, *The Barbarians Speak: How the Conquered Peoples Shaped Roman Europe* (Princeton 1999).

C. R. Whittaker 2004 = C.R: Whittaker, *Rome and its Frontiers: The Dynamics of Empire* (London/New York 2004).

C. R. Whittaker 1994 = C.R. Whittaker, *Frontiers of the Roman Empire* (Baltimore/London 1994).

D. Whittaker 2009 = D. Whittaker, «Ethnic discourses on the frontiers of Roman Africa», in T. Derks and N. Roymans, (eds.), *Ethnic Constructs in Antiquity: The Role of Power and Tradition* Amsterdam Archaeological Studies 13 (Amsterdam 2009) 189-206.

Wilkes 1969 = J.J. Wilkes, *Dalmatia* (London 1969).

Wilkes 1992 = J.J. Wilkes, *Illyrians* (Oxford/Cambridge 1992).

Woolf 1997 = G. Woolf, «Beyond Romans and natives», *World Archaeology* 28.3 (1997) 339-350.

Xoxaj 2005 = E. Xoxaj, «Mythen und Erinnerungen der albanischen Nation. Illyrer, Nationsbildung und nationale Identität», *Tyche* 20 (2005) 47-76.

Zaninović 1998 = M. Zaninović, «Država Demetrija Hvaranina i Šibensko područje», in B. Čečuk, (ed.), *Područje Šibenske županije od pretpovijesti do srednjega vijeka*. Hrvatsko arheološko društvo19 (Zagreb 1998) 89-96.

Zaninović 2007 = M. Zaninović, *Ilirsko pleme Delmati* (Šibenik 2007, orignaly published 1966 and 1967).

TACITUS AND THRACE.
BALKAN AUXILIARIES FROM AN HISTORIAN'S PERSPECTIVE

Katherine LOW

In recent years there has been much interest in ancient authors' representations of «barbarians» and how this may reflect back on Greece or Rome. Within Tacitean studies the *Agricola* and the *Germania*, and what the portrayal there of the Britons and Germans may say about the Romans of the late first and early second centuries, have received particular attention[1]. Several prominent non-Roman figures in the *Annals* have also been considered. For example, the suggestive parallels between Germanicus and Arminius, as well as Tiberius and Maroboduus, king of the Marcomanni, have been explored[2]. Later in the text, correspondences with Parthia and Armenia emerge as Nero's principate becomes more tyrannical[3], and in Book 14 Boudicca joins Calgacus and Caractacus, amongst others, as a foreign critic of Roman imperialism.

However, other episodes in the *Annals* that depict Roman relations with non-Romans have received relatively less attention, and are often dismissed as, for example, «welcome relief from political history» or «interludes in Tacitus» narrative of Roman internal affairs'[4]. In this paper, Tacitus' presentation of Thrace and the Thracians will not be treated as historical evidence *per se* but as a key aspect of his Roman narrative. These episodes are discrete, almost fragmentary, with no reference to the previous revolt of 11 BC or the subsequent conversion of Thrace from a client-kingdom into a province in AD 46: it is not clear if Tacitus covered this event, because the relevant section of the *Annals* does not survive. The three passages, spanning Books 2-4 of the *Annals* – and so cutting across the conventional divide between Books 1-3 and 4-6 – that depict Rome and Thrace's relations between 19 and 26 AD will be examined. Other ancient accounts include none of this material.

In sum, in Book 2 Tiberius outwits the client-king Rhaskuporis, who has sought to enlarge his territory by attacking and then murdering his fellow ruler (*A*.2.64.2-67); in Book 3 a burgeoning Thracian revolt is easily quashed, shortly before a larger-scale rebellion in Gaul (*A*. 3.38.3-39); and in Book 4 a more serious revolt occurs, which the Romans suppress with legionary troops and Thracian auxiliaries (*A*. 4.46-51). Concurrently, in the Roman sphere, the popular Germanicus dies, as does Tiberius' son Drusus, and discontent with the emperor slowly grows. At the beginning of Book 4 the praetorian prefect, Tiberius' confidant Sejanus, is formally introduced and the harm he will do is foreshadowed. By the end of the book Rome seems a very grim place indeed.

---

[1] See e.g. O'Gorman, 1993 and Lavan, 2011.
[2] Pelling 1993, 79-81.
[3] Gilmartin 1973.
[4] Quotations from Goodyear 1981, 348 and Ginsburg 1981, 85.

Admittedly the Thracian sequence finishes with the Romans triumphant; what happens has little effect on affairs in Rome, and no more is heard of Thrace in what survives of the *Annals*. These passages do not alter very much in the world of the text and may indeed seem trivial when juxtaposed with the darkening of Tiberius' principate and the rise of Sejanus. However, it will be suggested that the manner in which Tacitus portrays the Thracians and their interaction with Rome adds an extra dimension to the Roman narrative. The representation of the Thracians and the effect that being Roman subjects has on them form a coherent negative sequence that parallels the situation in Rome.

First, some necessary background. Apparently Thracian auxiliaries served in Roman armies during the republican period, well before the events that Tacitus describes and the conversion of Thrace into a province in 46 AD[5]. By Tacitus' own time, at the beginning of the second century, there were a large number of Thracian units amongst Roman forces[6]. However, despite this sign of apparent integration, and Thrace's internal reorganisation under Trajan at the time that Tacitus was writing, unlike in other western provinces there seems to be little evidence for what has come to be called «Romanisation» in Thrace. A Thraco-Hellenistic culture endured. Of course, there is no way of telling to what extent Tacitus was aware of this and, more importantly, how he incorporated any such knowledge within his work. Emulation of his predecessors, ethnographic stereotypes and a desire to provide an additional angle on the Roman narrative may have been greater influences on the text. However, the following argument does not depend on Tacitus' knowledge of Thrace, although the evidence for this fits what will be said quite well. In the *Annals* Thracians are shown fighting for Rome, but the three episodes in which they figure constitute a narrative of anti-Roman resistance[7].

A. 2.64.2-67

In the first Thracian episode Tacitus describes how Augustus had settled Thrace, assigning part to the last king Rhoemetalkes' son, Kotys, and part to the old king's brother, Rhaskuporis. When Rhaskuporis started encroaching on Kotys' territory and Tiberius sent a message telling the two rulers to desist, Rhaskuporis enticed Kotys to a summit and, after a banquet, imprisoned him. Tiberius invited Rhaskuporis to Rome to explain himself, but the king then had Kotys killed. A Roman envoy, Pomponius Flaccus, was then sent to induce Rhaskuporis to come to Rome. Accusations were laid against him in the senate by Kotys' wife and his punishment was to be kept in custody far from Thrace. The kingdom was divided anew between

---

[5] Saddington 1982, 86.
[6] For more detail see Kraft 1951, 39-40, Jarrett 1969 and Saddington 1982.
[7] All translations in this paper are the author's own. In the interests of consistency with the rest of this volume the Thracian names in Tacitus' text, «Rhescuporis», «Cotys» and «Rhoemetalces», have been replaced with «Rhaskuporis», «Kotys» and «Rhoemetalkes».

Rhaskuporis' son and Kotys' children. Rhaskuporis died in Alexandria – either trying to escape, or on a trumped-up charge, adds Tacitus.

This is the longest of the three Thracian episodes and is not clearly linked to the rest of *Annals* 2. The book focuses on Germanicus and the popular favour he enjoys in contrast with Tiberius, although the latter is not yet the figure of hatred that he will become. There is still some hope for the principate. After being recalled from Germany, Germanicus is sent east and embarks on a kind of touristic voyage, visiting Athens, Troy and Alexandria, until his mysterious death in Antioch (*A.* 2.53-61, 69-72). The reason he is dispatched to the region is the reported political trouble there and at *A.* 2.1-5 Tacitus explains the background to this. The Parthians had deposed their king Vonones. He had been originally sent to Rome by his father Phraates, learnt, so Tacitus says, soft Roman ways, and on returning as king to Parthia was rejected. Vonones flees to Armenia, periodically a point of contention between Rome and Parthia, and Tacitus then gives a brief history of Armenian relations with Rome (*A.* 2.3-4). Mark Antony had offered friendship to an earlier king before treacherously killing him, and other interventions in Armenia followed. Now, when Vonones' presence there threatens to spark war between Rome and Parthia, he is placed in protective Roman custody. At *A.* 2.68, directly after the first Thracian episode, Tacitus reports his death while trying to escape.

A model of Roman treachery when dealing with foreign kings is accordingly established within the text. In addition, the Parthian reaction to Vonones establishes that Roman influence can be detrimental to foreigners, a reversal of the famous Roman stereotype that contact with the east corrupts[8]. Now, the fate of the Thracian king Rhaskuporis, described in a handful of chapters amid Germanicus' travels, may appear as a mere extension of this pattern: Tacitus begins the episode by reporting that Tiberius took him on *astu* («with cunning», *A.* 2.64.2). Rhaskuporis is hardly a likeable figure, but nevertheless he is ultimately another foreign king deceived by Rome. Ending up in Roman hands, he attempts to escape his guards and dies suspiciously, *fugam temptans an ficto crimine* («trying to escape or because of a false charge», *A.* 2.67.1).

However, the intervening narrative is rather more complex. First, although the Romans act treacherously towards Rhaskuporis when they induce him to come to Rome to face justice for his crimes, this is after he has captured Kotys – his own nephew – in a similar way, imprisoning him after a banquet. His behaviour retrospectively illuminates Rome's actions towards foreigners like the Armenian king mentioned above: it means that the Romans are no better than treacherous non-Romans like him. But the parallels between Rome and Thrace go further than that, and are signalled from the beginning of the episode. Augustus' death is the catalyst for Rhaskuporis' aggression towards Kotys. Tacitus reports this in terms that verbally recall the beginning of the Pannonian legionaries' mutiny in Book 1, which also began directly after Augustus died:

---

[8] See e.g. Pol. 31.25.2-7.

...audita mutatione principis immittere latronum globos, exscindere castra, causas bello (A. 2.64.3).

«...when he heard of the change of emperor he sent in bands of brigands and destroyed strongholds – the causes of war».

...Pannonicas legiones seditio incessit, nullis novis causis, nisi quod mutatus princeps.... (A. 1.16.1).

«Mutiny seized the Pannonian legions: there were no novel causes, except the change of emperor...»

The mutinous Roman soldiers are implicitly equated with a troublesome foreign king: once again, the Romans are no better than their barbarian counterparts. But the focus is narrower still. Before hostilities commence between the two Thracian kings, they act *subdola concordia*, with beguiling harmony. Now, the adjective *subdolus* is used five times elsewhere in *Annals* 1-6, and on four occasions it describes an emperor's behaviour, especially that of Tiberius. So Rhaskuporis and Kotys are portrayed with Roman imperial overtones[9].

The two Thracian kings arguably mirror Tiberius and Germanicus, relations who here in the *Annals* similarly maintain an uneasy co-existence. McCulloch has argued that both pairs fit the «treacherous uncle/noble nephew» model[10]. This pattern is found elsewhere in the text, and beyond, not least in Sallust's *Bellum Iugurthinum*, although there the supposedly «noble nephew» Jugurtha eventually becomes rather less noble, partly because of negative Roman influence[11]. Tacitus' Thracian episode actually recalls Sallust's narrative in several ways, notably in the original division of the kingdom between the last king's relatives and, specifically, in the way in which both Jugurtha and Rhaskuporis justify their actions to Rome:

scripsit ad Tiberium structas sibi insidias, praeventum insidiatorem (A. 2.65.4).

«[Rhaskuporis] wrote to Tiberius, saying that plots had been laid against him, and that the plotter had been forestalled».

Adherbalem dolis vitae suae insidiatum... (Sallust, BJ 22.4).

«[Jugurtha said that] Adherbal had treacherously plotted against his life».

However, for the moment Tacitus' focus is on Tiberius and Rhaskuporis. As McCulloch notes[12], Rhaskuporis entices Kotys into his power with a *dolus*, a trick, just as Tiberius is said to wish to expose Germanicus to one when he sends him to the east. Like the Thracian, Tiberius deceives not only foreigners, but his own family:

---

[9] Tiberius' pronouncements about the new form of consular elections are said to have been *speciosa verbis, re inania aut subdola* (A. 1.81.4). His behaviour is described as *occultum ac subdolum fingendis virtutibus, donec Germanicus ac Drusus superfuere* (A. 6.51.3).
See also A. 1.10.3 (Augustus' «critical» obituary), and A. 6.20 (Caligula). The final use of *subdolus* is at A. 3.7.1, of the behaviour of Gnaeus Piso – who is not an emperor, but has strong links to the principate (see O'Gorman 2006, 288-92).
[10] McCulloch, 1984, 91-101.
[11] See Kraus 1999.
[12] McCulloch 1984, 93, 97-8.

Tiberius was glad to hear reports of trouble in the east, *ut ea specie Germanicum... novis... provinciis impositum dolo simul et casibus obiectaret* («so that on that pretext he might give Germanicus responsibility for new provinces and throw him in the way of both treachery and misfortune», A. 2.5.1).

...postquam dolum intellexerat, sacra regni, eiusdem familiae deos et hospitales mensas obtestantem (A. 2.65.3).

«After he understood [Rhaskuporis'] treachery, [Kotys was] appealing to the sanctity of kingship, the gods of their shared family, and the fact that he had been a guest at dinner».

Moreover, Rhaskuporis invites his nephew to the banquet *ficta modestia* («with feigned deference», A. 2.65.2). Both the concept of *modestia* and the adjective *fictus*, most memorably in the context of dissimulation, are closely linked to Tiberius by Tacitus[13]. So Tiberius and Rhaskuporis are indeed an equal match, seeking to trick each other. The Thracian king writes to Rome with a false explanation of his actions (A. 2.65.4) but later Tiberius, using another Roman as an intermediary, gets him to Rome on false pretences (A. 2.67.1).

The ultimate outcome of this episode, with the king betrayed and killed like other client rulers, makes it clear that the equivalence between Tiberius and Rhaskuporis is only temporary. All the same, in these few chapters some striking parallels are drawn between Rhaskuporis and his deceitful actions, and the Roman principate, Tiberius especially. What are the implications of this for Rome? First, Rhaskuporis' echoing of Roman behaviour towards the Armenian and Parthian kings may supply the reader with further reasons to condemn it: Rome cannot even manage a monopoly on such actions. Moreover, there is potential irony in how correspondences are drawn between the supposedly republican-minded Tiberius and the autocrat Rhaskuporis. The tyrannical atmosphere that has settled on Tiberius' court by the end of his reign, when parallels with Parthia can also be felt, may be signposted too. But such points, while enhancing the narrative's texture, do not seem decisive.

Tacitus does not suggest that Rhaskuporis acts thus towards Kotys because, as a client king, he has literally learnt to do so from Rome. This is unlike his analogue Jugurtha. The corrupting influence of mercenary, dishonest Romans, which Jugurtha first encounters when serving under Scipio in Spain, is a key factor in Sallust's portrayal of the deterioration of his character[14]. But the fact that Rhaskuporis' situation echoes that of Jugurtha, and the model in Book 2 of Roman deceit towards foreign kings mentioned above, permit extrapolation. Rhaskuporis' mirroring of

---

[13] *modestia* is associated with Tiberius early on, when he claims it for himself in the ambiguous speech that seems to lead to his accession: *ille varie disserebat de magnitudine imperii, sua modestia* (A. 1.11.1). Meanwhile, when at A. 4.38.4 he forbids the establishment of a cult of himself and Livia, this is attributed by some to his *modestiam* (though by no means all the onlookers cited are so generous), and after her death he is said to reduce the honours voted to her *quasi per modestiam*. Regarding *ficta* and Tiberius in Books 1 and 2, n.b. *trepida civitas incusare Tiberium quod...cunctatione ficta ludificetur* (A. 1.46.1) and *quamquam [Germanicus] fingi ea seque per invidiam parto iam decori abstrahi intellegeret* (A. 2.26.5).

[14] See e.g. Dench, 2005, 89-90, and n. 11 above.

Tiberius seems to suggest that contact with Rome is a negative influence on Thrace, although here this is illustrated in a symbolic manner. For the moment, however, there is nothing that implies that Rome is negatively affected by this.

A. 3.38.3-39

When Tacitus returns to Thrace in the middle of Book 3, Germanicus is dead but Tiberius' son Drusus is still alive and the emperor still commands guarded respect, even though injustice and incipient tyranny are emerging at Rome. The dubious prosecution of a leading Macedonian for complicity with Rhaskuporis (A. 3.38.2) recalls the previous episode and leads into this second one, in which Tacitus describes how the Thracians were angry at their Roman-imposed rulers. Three tribes prepared for war, although their leaders' disorganisation and inability to co-operate prevented a major conflict. However, a large group besieged Philippopolis, and inside it king Rhoemetalkes, Rhaskuporis' son. The Roman commander Publius Vellaeus came to the rescue, defeating the belligerent tribes and raising the siege. The Roman forces easily prevailed.

In passing, Tacitus reminds his readers that the Romans had partitioned the region between Rhoemetalkes, Rhaskuporis' son, and the young children of Kotys: this of course recalls Augustus' original division of the kingdom (A. 3.38.3; cf. 2.64.2) . It looks as if the events of Book 2 will be replayed, but this does not happen. However, Tacitus reports that there was strong anti-Roman feeling and resentment of imperial rule in Thrace at this time. Previously unmentioned tribes, whose typically barbarian qualities are emphasised, target the Roman-sponsored rulers:

...neque minus Rhoemetalcen quam Trebellenum incusans popularium iniurias inultas sinere. Coelaletae Odrusaeque et Dii, validae nationes, arma cepere, ducibus diversis et paribus inter se per ignobilitatem (A. 3.38.3-4).

«[The Thracians were] accusing Rhoemetalkes just as much as Trebellenus [the Roman regent for Kotys' children] of letting injustices against the common people go unpunished. The Coelaletae, Odrusae and Dii, mighty tribes, took up arms. Their leaders were at odds with each other, though all of equally low birth».

These independent Thracians besiege Rhoemetalkes in Philippopolis.[15] However, Roman forces are sent in, and the rebels are brutally overcome in textbook fashion:

neque aciem aut proelium dici decuerit, in quo semermi ac palantes trucidati sunt sine nostro sanguine (A. 3.39.2).

«It would not be fitting to call a fight or battle that in which half-armed men, wandering around, were slaughtered without loss to the Roman troops».

In this episode, there is no sense of similarity between Rome and Thrace, unlike before. The notion of negative Roman influence does not feature, although it will again shortly. But in Book 2 Rhaskuporis' defiance of Rome seemed a personal, self-

---

[15] The rejection of the Roman-reared Vonones by his Parthian subjects at A. 2.2-3 may be recalled.

aggrandising move. The abortive revolt in Book 3, with anger directed at symbols of Roman intervention in Thrace, is a movement against Rome itself, and the *iniuriae* («injustices») inflicted by her representatives. In addition to their own experiences, it is as if the rebels have been reading of the Roman deception of foreigners in Annals 2.

Now, here the Romans easily quash the threat. The situation back in Rome in Book 3 may also be noted: the senate is still functioning with some independence. Although Tiberius intervenes on several occasions he does so ably, as an effective leader[16]; Sejanus' rise has not yet properly begun. Only at the very end of Book 3 will the symbolic obituary of Junia, Cassius' wife and Brutus' sister, mark a kind of belated passing of the republic (A. 3.76). So all seems fairly well, from a Roman angle: there is success abroad and relative calm at home. However, this unsuccessful Thracian revolt is immediately followed in the narrative by a rather more serious rebellion in Gaul (A. 3.40-7). Romanised Gallic leaders complain of Roman misrule and attempt to seize back their freedom:

...per conciliabula et coetus seditiosa disserebant de continuatio tributorum, gravitate faenoris, saevitia ac superbia praesidentium...egregium resumendae libertati tempus (3.40.3).

«In meetings and gatherings they spoke seditiously of the continual demands for tribute, the weight of interest, and the cruelty and pride of those who ruled them... it was an excellent time to regain their liberty».

Tacitus alleges that many Romans rejoiced (A. 3.44), preferring the prospect of a proper war to Tiberius' bloodthirsty accusations, although in the text the worst phase of judicial murders has not yet begun. The Gallic criticism of Rome amplifies the general impression given by the Thracians that Roman rule is harmful to its subjects. In addition, negative imperialism is here closely linked to misrule in Rome itself, via the complaints about Tiberius. The case for this is strengthened by the fact that the Gallic revolt foreshadows the Batavian revolt in Book 4 of Tacitus' *Histories* that crowns the civil wars, the ultimate state of internal disorder[17].

A. 4.46-51

The final Thracian episode in the surviving *Annals* occurs halfway through Book 4. Here, Tacitus notes that another insurrection was building up in Thrace. The Thracians were unwilling to submit to military levies and serve under Roman leaders, and did not want to be split up and stationed far from their homes. They sent envoys to Rome, and declared that if «slavery» was inflicted on them they would not be afraid to defend their liberty to the death. They prepared for a siege, sending their non-combatants to a fortified stronghold. The Roman commanders in the area called on Rhoemetalkes for reinforcements, but his auxiliaries' camp was stormed by the rebellious Thracians, who castigated them as *perfugae et proditores* («turncoats

---

[16] Most notably at A. 3.53-4.
[17] With the Gallic leaders' inflammatory tactics compare the Batavian Julius Civilis' covert garnering of support for his revolt at H. 4.14 and 17.

and traitors», A. 4.48.3) for their treachery to Thrace. However, the Roman leader then laid siege to the main stronghold, where the rebels had retreated. One group surrendered to the Romans, another commited suicide en masse, and a third planned a nocturnal break-out. A battle ensued, and although the Roman troops were victorious, in the darkness conditions were such that it was not always clear who were the besiegers and who were the besieged.

At this point in the narrative Rome is still enjoying military success – the north African rebel Tacfarinas has finally been defeated (A. 4.25), although only after long drawn-out fighting, but the domestic atmosphere is darkening. *Annals* 4 begins by surveying the empire, implying that Tiberius has ruled fairly well this far: now, the second and worse half of his reign is starting (A. 4.4.2-7.1). Sejanus' power begins to grow (n.b. A. 4.1), Germanicus' remaining family come under assault, and the emperor prepares for his withdrawal from Rome to Capri. The ominous murder of an avaricious Roman official in Spain, a depressing doublet of an episode in Sallust's *Bellum Catilinae* (A. 4.45), precedes this second revolt in Thrace. In Book 3 the rebellious Thracians' grievances were briefly summarised (A. 3.38.3); here they are given in more detail:

causa motus super hominum ingenium, quod pati dilectus et validissimum quemque militiae nostrae dare aspernabantur, ne regibus quidem parere nisi ex libidine soliti, aut, si mitterent auxilia, suos ductores praeficere nec nisi adversum accolas belligerare...misere legatos amicitiam obsequiumque memoraturos, et mansura haec, si nullo novo onere temptarentur; sin ut victis servitium indiceretur, esse sibi ferrum et iuventutem et promptum libertati aut ad mortem animum (A. 4.46.2).

'The reason for the disturbance, in addition to the people's temperament, was that they disdained to endure levies and to give up to Roman service all their strongest men, when they were accustomed to obey not even their kings unless they felt like it or, if they did send auxiliary troops, to put their own leaders in charge and only to fight their neighbours...they sent ambassadors to recall their friendship and obedience, and to say that these would continue if they were not incited by any new burden, but if they were prescribed slavery, like a conquered people, they had swords and warriors and a spirit ready for freedom or unto death'.

The idea that that Roman rule is detrimental to those in its sway is thus reiterated, and reinforced. But the Thracians' complaints, like the Gauls' at A. 3.40.3, have a further dimension. Their promise to fight for *libertas* contrasts with the decline of liberty in Tiberius' Rome: as early as the end of Book 1 his principate was said to harbour merely an *imago libertatis* (A. 1.81.4). Moreover, their unwillingness to obey even their own kings is telling. While the expulsion of Tarquinius Superbus was of course a key moment in early Roman history, in the opening chapter of the *Annals* the kings of Rome begin a progression through different forms of autocracy over time that is completed by the principate founded by Augustus[18]. Once again, it appears that a corollary

---

[18] n.b. *urbem Romam a principio reges habuere...Lepidi atque Antonii arma in Augustum cessere* (A.1.1.1). See also Liebeschuetz 1966 and Lavan 2011 on *libertas* in Tacitus in general, and the ironic relevance of foreign *libertas* for Rome.

to the tyrannical rule of others is the deterioration of freedom and good government in Rome. This is reinforced by how, like the complaints of the Gallic rebels, the Thracians' words foreshadow the inflammatory rhetoric of Julius Civilis, instigator of the Batavian revolt[19]. Resentment of how the Romans rule Thrace looks towards the Julio-Claudian principate's implosion in the civil wars of 69-70.

The Romans again react belligerently. Legionary troops are swelled by auxiliaries under Rhoemetalkes, the Roman-sponsored king who at A. 3.38.4 was besieged by insurgent tribes before being rescued. This time, after the retreat of the rebels to a fortified outcrop and various inconclusive skirmishes, the Roman commander moves camp, leaving the Thracian auxiliaries behind with permission to plunder. Becoming decadent and careless, as barbarians in classical literature often do, they fall victim to an attack from the rebel Thracians, who slaughter them, castigating them for their treachery and lack of patriotism:

versi in luxum et raptis opulenti omittere statione<s> lascivia epularum, aut somno et vino procumbere... perfugae et proditores ferre arma ad suum patriaeque servitium incusabantur (A. 4.48.1-3).

«Turning to self-indulgence and rich from what they had plundered, they neglected their guard-posts for fine dining, or reclined in a drunken sleep... they were censured as turncoats and traitors who bore arms in the service of their own and their country's slavery».

The sequence is complete: the personal wickedness of Rhaskuporis has given way to the anti-Roman protests of both groups of Thracian rebels and then to the clear inferiority of those Thracians with Roman links. The effect of contact with Rome is devastatingly illustrated.

This conclusion is arguably not radical, although it offers an important perspective on how *Tacitus presents imperialism*. The criticisms that he makes such figures as Civilis, Calgacus and Boudicca articulate – as well as the Gallic and Thracian rebels – are supplemented by subtle illustration of how Roman rule affects others, in more abstract and then in concrete terms. But how does it affect Rome? Two points remain.

After the slaughter of Rome's allies, actions against the rebels are intensified. Eventually they are besieged in their stronghold, lacking food and water. Eventually those who have not surrendered or committed suicide decide to stage a break-out. This happens at night, echoing the flight from Plataea in Thucydides' Book 3[20], and the Thracians do not disgrace themselves. Because of the dark and difficult conditions, the Romans become confused about who is who:

suorum atque hostium ignoratio et montis anfractu repercussae velut a tergo voces adeo cuncta miscuerant, ut quaedam munimenta Romani quasi perrupta omiserint (A. 4.51.2).

«The inability to distinguish their men and the enemy, and voices that seemed to come from behind them, echoing off the curved side of the mountain, had confused

---

[19] See n. 17 above.
[20] See McCulloch, 1984, 54-5.

everything to such as extent that the Romans abandoned some fortifications, thinking that they had been overrun».

This temporary blurring of identities does not impede the eventual Roman victory, nor is it a trope unique to Tacitus (see e.g. Thuc. 7.44). But in Book 2, when the Romans were still faring well at home and abroad, Rhaskuporis acted like one of them. Now, briefly, Romans have begun to look like Thracians. Again, perhaps the wars which occurred after Nero's death and pitted Roman against Roman are also faintly foreshadowed.

This brief erosion of Roman individuality abroad, along with a sense of the harshness of Roman rule, is matched with deep domestic trouble. The events in Thrace are followed by a return to Rome, where there is trouble, *commota principis domo* ('the imperial house being in turmoil, A. 4.51.2). Tiberius leaves the city for good, and then an amphitheatre at Fidenae collapses (A. 4.62), causing countless deaths. Tacitus describes this in terms that echo the sack of a city[21]: once more it is as if the Romans can no longer distinguish friends and enemies. Those with links to Germanicus are mercilessly hounded, including the knight Titius Sabinus, whose horrible entrapment by so-called friends shows that the Roman tendency to deceive and betray notable foreigners has come closer to home[22]. Then a small revolt amongst the German Frisians leads to an ignominious defeat for Rome (A. 4.72-3), in contrast with the success in Thrace. Tiberius suppresses the news, to avoid having to continue the war, while the senate are too preoccupied by the domestic situation to care.

None of this is causally related to what has happened in Thrace, of course. Not telling the Thracian story would not have changed Tacitus' narrative of affairs in Rome. After the second revolt Thrace's part in the *Annals* seems to be over, although as noted Thrace became a full province in 46. The resistance Tacitus describes was, in a sense, futile. That may be one reason why he is the only source for these rebellions. But the deepening trouble back in Rome in Book 4 can be seen as a corollary to the final stage in the development of Roman relations with Thrace that has been traced in this paper.

It has been shown that Tacitus' presentation of the Thracians is not merely an optional extra, or an interlude in the historical text, but adds an extra dimension to Rome's – and Tiberius' – trajectory in *Annals* 1-6. Tacitus constructs an increasingly negative perspective on Roman imperialism. Those who are subject to it not only resent it but seem to change for the worse through it. But this deterioration is also a way of matching, from an unexpected angle, the descent of Tiberius' principate towards its nadir. It would be rash to suggest that Tacitus thinks that imperialism led to Rome's decline under Tiberius – that Sallustian notion was doubtless in his mind but such an easy explanation is too simple for the *Annals*, and both processes had in any case begun much earlier. But

---

[21] See Woodman, 1998, 138-41.
[22] *tectum inter et laquearia tres senatores haud minus turpi latebra quam destestanda fraude sese abstrudunt, foraminibus et rimis aurem admovent* (A. 4.68.1).

for the historian, what happens in Thrace – or Gaul or Parthia or Armenia, for that matter – is never without significance in Rome. All apparent «evidence» in his work for events abroad must be read with his Roman perspective in mind.

Katherine Low
University of Oxford

Bibliography

Dench 2005 = E. Dench, *Romulus' Asylum*, Oxford University Press (Oxford 2005).

Gilmartin 1973 = K. Gilmartin, «Corbulo's campaigns in the East», *Historia* 22 (1973) 583-626.

Jarrett 1969 = M.G. Jarrett, *Thracian units in the Roman army*, «Israel Exploration Journal» 19 (1969) 215-24.

Kraft 1951 = K. Kraft, *Zur Rekrutierung der Alen und Kohorten an Rhein und Donau*, Francke (Berne 1951).

Kraus 1999 = C.S. Kraus, «Jugurthine disorder», 217-247 in ead., (ed.), *The Limits of Historiography: Genre and Narrative in Ancient Historical Texts* Leiden, Mnemosyne Supplement 191 (Brill 1999).

Lavan 2011 = M. Lavan, *Slavishness in Britain and Rome in Tacitus' Agricola*, «Classical Quarterly' 61 (2011) 294-305.

Liebeschuetz 1966 = W. Liebeschuetz, *The theme of liberty in the Agricola of Tacitus*, «Classical Quarterly» 16 (1966) 126-39.

McCulloch 1984 = H.Y. McCulloch, *Narrative Cause in the Annals of Tacitus*, Hain (Königstein 1984).

O'Gorman 1993 = E. O'Gorman, *No place like Rome: identity and difference in the Germania of Tacitus*, «Ramus» 22 (1993) 135-54.

O'Gorman 2006 = E. O'Gorman, *Alternative Empires: Tacitus' virtual history of the Pisonian principate*, «Arethusa» 39 (2006) 281-301.

Pelling 1993 = C.B.R. Pelling, *Tacitus and Germanicus*, 59-85 in LUCE, T.J. and WOODMAN, A.J., (eds), *Tacitus and the Tacitean Tradition*, Princeton University Press (Princeton 1993).

Saddington 1982 = D.B. Saddington, *The Development of the Roman Auxiliary Forces from Caesar to Vespasian*, University of Zimbabwe Press (Harare 1982).

Woodman 1998 = A.J. Woodman, *History and alternative history*, 104-41 in ibid., (ed.) *Tacitus Reviewed*, Oxford University Press (Oxford 1998).

THE VETERANS AND THEIR DESCENDENTS IN THE ELITE OF PHILIPPOPOLIS, THRACE

Ivo TOPALILOV

The local government was of great importance to the Roman Empire and as such it was strictly controlled by the Roman governors; only trustworthy persons were allowed to participate. These persons, albeit with limited authority, were allowed to maintain the order in their own cities by assisting the collection of taxes, acting as ambassadors before the emperor etc[1]. It is not surprising, therefore, to find among these people the local elite the majority of whom was Romanised. A comprehensive study by L. Mroszewicz has shown that some Roman veterans, although only 5.8%, also participated in public life[2]. Thrace was not an exception. We would like here to establish the extent of the impact of the veterans upon the local society and governing institutions, which is better seen in their service as civic magistrates in Roman Egypt and Syria[3]. According to B. Gerov, the veterans in Thrace had an impact on the provincial society without being involved in the local government. These men were settled in key areas in order to bring these areas under firm Roman control[4]. This idea has gained wide acceptance by scholars[5].

The thesis of B. Gerov seems to exclude the participation of veterans into the local administration. In some cases, however, the author himself arrived to the conclusion, that the veterans or/and their descendents participated in the public life of Philippopolis[6].

A study by V. Kadeev and A. Martemyanov also deals with the participation of veterans in the public life in Thrace. They followed the conclusions of L. Mroszewicz that the veterans were not able to hold the office of civic magistrate because of their limited financial means. The only exceptions were those veterans in possession of villas and estates, which enabled them to increase their income in order to take up the offices of civic magistrate or councilors[7].

Il. Boyanov puts forward another point of view in his study on the veterans in Lower Moesia and Thrace. According to him, following again L. Mroszewicz's conclusion, only a few veterans, i.e. the former centurions and higher ranks, were members of the local aristocracy and no more than 10% participated in the public life because of their wealth. He believes that the remaining veterans were in fact attached to the city because of their local land property and had to finance the

---

[1] See Barton 2001, 202-203.
[2] Mroszewicz 1989, 71 ff.
[3] For these variants – see Haynes 2001, 80-82.
[4] Gerov 1980, 40 ff.
[5] For example, Haynes 2001, 79.
[6] Gerov 1980, 51, n. 117 lists various civic offices, which are known from inscriptions to have been held by the Flavii.
[7] Kadeev, Martemyanov 1996, 82-84.

construction of public buildings or make other donations in order to fit into the local society[8]. I have not been able to find a similar example of such relationship between cities and veterans with local estates in the Roman Empire.

I consider the lack of distinction between the societies in Lower Moesia and those in Thrace by Boyanov, Kadeev and Martemyanov as deeply flawed. It should be remembered that the society in Thrace was different from that of the Danubian or Rhine provinces. It is not just the matter of Romanisation, which played a major role when deciding who should govern. The contrast between these two types of society is clearly visible in Thrace, where, for example, the practice of mentioning both the civic and the military *cursus honorum* of the deceased in their funeral epitaphs was not in use. To the best of my knowledge, there is no inscription from Thrace that mentions the civic and the military status of the deceased at the same time. This is probably the reason why B. Gerov suggested that common veterans were not part of the local elite; there is no explicit evidence for this to date. The family of Virdii, who held high military ranks and were involved in the public life of Philippopolis, was a different case since they were cavalry officers[9]. The problem with the identification of veterans in civic offices remains because of specifics of the Thracian society and the Romanisation of Thrace. The importance of the Roman citizens in Thrace is clearly established, since Thrace was a province with *peregrinae*. As B. Gerov pointed out, the Roman citizenship until the reign of Trajan was awarded to part of the Thracian aristocracy, while common Thracians could claim it after their auxiliary service in the Roman army ended[10]. Not much changed for the Thracians after Trajan and we find veterans, Roman citizens and their descendents in close communities[11]. This is to show that the Roman citizenship was a clear mark of respectability in Thrace and its cities. A case in point is a small marble statue, which was erected by the βουλευτής καὶ γερουσιαστής Αὐρ(ήλιος) Ἀσκληπιόδοτος and underlined his affiliation with Αἴλ(ιος) Ἰουλιανός[12]. We have no clue who Αἴλ(ιος) Ἰουλιανός actually was in Philippopolis, but he seems to be a man of importance. However, it is certain that Αἴλ(ιος) Ἰουλιανός was indeed a veteran and his name was typical for Romans in the army. Therefore, we are dealing here with a descendent of a veteran, who held a civic office in Philippopolis. This case shows a way to study the participation of veterans and their descendents into the society and administration of Philippopolis through onomastics. The results of such a study are discussed in the following paragraphs[13].

---

[8] Boyanov 2008, 265-267.
[9] For *Virdii*, see Sharankov 2005, 62-69.
[10] Gerov 1961, 107-116.
[11] The Roman citizens were buried in specific areas within the eastern necropolis of Philippopolis (see Topalilov 2002, 64); On the close community of descendants of veterans in Philippopolis see the examples of the praetorians in Topalilov 2011, 257-268.
[12] See the inscription in Tsontchev 1941, 30, n.12, tab.12, fig. 43; *IGBulg* III, 1, 1150+ 1151; *IGBulg* V, 5463; Sharankov 1999, 84-85.
[13] See Topalilov 2011a, 536–581.

As most peregrine cities in the eastern provinces, Philippopolis had the typical civic offices of cities of this kind. I discuss here only the most important of these offices, such as the office of πρῶτος ἄρχων, the city council consisting of *bouleutai*, and the «Sacred Gerousia».

The veterans and the office of πρῶτος ἄρχων

Table 1 shows all the known to date πρῶτοι ἄρχοντες (first archontes) from Philippopolis and its territory. It should be mentioned that apart from one exception the examples are dated after the *constitutio Antoniniana* was executed and do not allow a study of the first and second centuries AD. A study of the onomastics has shown that the πρῶτοι ἄρχοντες were Roman citizens. Cases in point are Τ(ίτος) Φλ(άβιος) Πρεισκιανός, who was ἀπὸ προγόνων θρακάρχης, ἀρχιερεὺς καὶ πρῶτος ἄρχων,[14] as well as Μ(ᾶρκος) Αὐρήλιος Εὐστόχιος Κέλερ Ἀσκληπιάδου, who was promoted to θρακάρχης[15]. This shows that we have so far no evidence for any veterans in this office.

Nº	Name	Municipal status	Location	Date	Inscription
1.	---δωρος Βειθυος	α΄ {πρώτου} ἄ[ρχοντος]	Philippopolis	186	IGBulg. III, 1 881
2.	Τ(ίτος) Φλ(άβιος) Πρεισκιανός	[ἀπὸ] προγόνων θρακάρχης καὶ ἀρχιερεὺς καὶ πρῶτος ἄρχων	Philippopolis	222-235	IGBulg. V, 5408 Gerasimova 2003, 197-199
3.	Αὐρ(ήλιος) Ἀπολλωνίδης Ἀπολλοδώρου (sic)	πρωταρχοῦντος	Philippopolis, Cillae, Hissar	235-238	IGBulg. III, 1, 1476 IGBulg. III, 1, 1515 = IGBulg. V, 5548 IGBulg. III, 1, 1476 Sharankov 2006, 234-236
4.	Μ(ᾶρκος) Αὐρήλιος Εὐστόχιος Κέλερ Ἀσκληπιάδου	πρῶτος ἄρχων θρακάρχης,	Boljartzi, Philippopolis terr.	249-250	IGBulg. III, 1449 = IGBulg. V, 5531,2
5.	Πύρρος	πρωταρχοῦντος	Philippopolis	267-268	IGBulg. V, 5409

Table 1. The First *Archontes* from Philippopolis

---

[14] Gerasimova 2003, 197-199; *IGBulg* V, 5408
[15] Gerasimova 2003, 200-201; *IGBulg* III, 1, 1449

The veterans, their descendents and the bouleutai

The results of the onomastics study are given in table 2. The picture seems to be slightly different from that of the first *archontas*, since three out of seven persons are connected with Roman veterans. These are [— — — — Γέ]μελλος Γεμέλλου[16], [Αἴλιος (?)] Κέλσο[ς — —][17] and Αὐρ(ήλιος) Ἀσκληπιόδοτος, whose father was Αἴλ(ιος) Ἰουλιανός. Given the date of these inscriptions prior to *Constitutio Antoniana* and the features of the Romanisation in Thrace, which I discuss later, I am inclined to identify as such bouleutai the veterans, or more likely their descendents, as is the case with two out of the three examples below[18].

Nº	Name	Position	Location	Date	Inscription
1.	[— — — — Γέ-]μελλος Γεμέλλου	βουλευτής	Batkun	II c.	Tsontchev 1941, 21, 2 *IGBulg*. III, 1, 1123
2.	Σεβαστιαν[ὸς] Μουκατραλεος	βουλευτής	Batkun	II c.	Tsontchev 1941, 37, n.1, tab. 22 *IGBulg*. III, 1, 1133
3.	Βειθυνικό[ς]	βουλευτής	Batkun	II c.	Tsontchev 1941, 28, n. 2 *IGBulg*. III, 1, 1143
4.	[Αἴλιος (?)] Κέλσο[ς — —]	ΒΟΥΛ[— — — —]	Hissar	II – III c.	*IGBulg*. III, 1, 1478; *IGBulg*. V, 5536
5.	Αὐρ(ήλιος) Ἀσκληπιόδοτος Αἰλ(ίου) Ἰουλιανοῦ	βουλευτὴς καὶ γερουσιαστής	Batkun	Late II – f. half III c.	Tsontchev 1941, 30, n. 12, tab. 12, fig. 43 *IGBulg*. III, 1, 1150+ 1151 *IGBulg*. V, 5463 Sharankov 1999, 84-85

---

[16] Γέ]μελλος was the Greek variant of the Roman name Gemellus and belonged to a group of Roman cognomina, which were inspired by features of the body, physical appearance etc. As such, it was particularly popular in the Roman army and was adopted by veterans, legionaries, praetorians and in some rare cases by civilians. The name was particularly popular in the provinces Numidia and Africa proconsularis, where it was mainly adopted by soldiers (see the numerous inscriptions cited in *CIL* VIII). Bearing in mind the type of Romanisation of these provinces as well as the specifics of the Romanisation in Thrace, it is more likely that Γέ]μελλος Γεμέλλου was the son of a Roman veterans named Gemellus. However, it does not mean that the son was a veteran.

[17] The cognomen Κέλσος occurs in a number of Thracian cities, especially Philippopolis and Augusta Traiana. It is noteworthy that Roman soldiers were drawn from these regions. The Romanised name of Kelsos, who was apparently not an aristocrat with Roman citizenship or had a Roman name under the *Flavii*, put him in the group of Roman citizens in Thrace with privileges gained upon completion of their military service. The rudeness of the inscription as well as the Thracian name which followed the Roman one argue for his Thracian origin. In fact, this example is among the rare examples in Thrace, where the veterans did not settle in Philippopolis, but in its surrounding territory. It may be even assumed that Kelsos was among these veterans with estates.

[18] See Topalilov 2011a, 547-554.

| 6. | Αὐρ(ήλιος) Ἑρμίας Καλίστου (sic) | βουλευτής | Batkun | F. half. III c. | Tsontchev 1941, 48, n. 13, Tab. 39, fig. 154 |
| 7. | Μουκιανὸς Δοληους | βουλευτής | Cillae | 241-244 | IGBulg. III, 1, 1517 |

Table 2. The known *bouleutai* from Philippopolis and its territory

The veterans and their descendents in the 'Sacred Gerousia'

Having in mind the main responsibilities of the gerousiasts and the institution of gerousia itself, it is not surprising to find that only one out of six gerousiasts known to date was a descendent of veterans: the aforementioned Αὐρ(ήλιος) Ἀσκληπιόδοτος, son of Αἴλ(ιος) Ἰουλιανός (Table 3). There is doubt for another one (.)...ος Πομπέϊος Σατορνεῖνος, who can probably be indentified with Q(uintus) Pompei(us) Saturninus. The latter is known through a seal from the surroundings of the city[19], where his villa allegedly was. However, he was a freedman or the descendant of a freedman[20]. The rest of the gerousiasts belong to the local Romanised elite or were rich freedmen.

N°	Name	Municipal status	Date	Inscription
1.	Αὐρ(ήλιος) Σώστρατος Δοληους	γερουσιαστής Φιλιπποπόλεως	II-III c.	Sharankov 2004b, 201-203, fig. 5, 6, 8a, 8b, 8c
2.	Τιβ(έριος) Κλαύδιος Πασίνους Μουκιανοῦ	ἔκδικος ἡ ἱερὰ γερουσία	II-III c.	IGBulg. III, 1, 885
3.	Ἑρέννιος Ἡρακλιανός	γερουσιαστής Φιλιπποπολείτης	II-III c.	IGBulg. III, 1, 992
4.	(.)...ος Πομπέϊος Σατορνεῖνος	γερουσιαστής Φιλιπποπόλεως	End II – first half III c.	IGBulg. III, 1, 995
5.	Ἐπιγένης Μουκιανοῦ	Φιλιπποπο[λίτης γ] γερουσιαστής	Second half II- first half III c.	IGBulg. V, 5439
6.	Αὐρ(ήλιος) Ἀσκληπιόδοτος Αἰλ(ίου) Ἰουλιανοῦ	βουλευτὴς καὶ γερουσιαστής	End II – first half III c.	IGBulg. V, 5463 Sharankov 1999, 84-85

Table 3. The known *gerousiastes* from Philippopolis and its territory

---

[19] The seal is published in Karadimitorva, Ilieva 2003, 211; 217; 221; the authors believe he was a veteran.
[20] See the discussion in Topalilov 2011a, 556-557.

How can these observations be interpreted?

As was the case with the rest of the studied provinces, the overwhelming majority of the veterans played a significant role in the town council. Out of seven members of the town council known to date, two were veterans and one was the son of a veteran. It is true that the known *bouleutai* are not many and thus the group cannot support a meaningful statistical analysis. However, these inscriptions are in fact of various kinds, including personal *ex-voto* set up in a sanctuary, which I believe was shared by the main groups within this community such as Greeks, Thracians with Greek or Thracian names, and veterans of Thracian or foreign origin. The small number of such examples do not allow to propose that 42.85 % of the town council consisted of veterans or their descendents as seen on Table 2. However, it indicates that the actual percentage must have been higher than the 5.8% proposed by L. Mroszewicz and at least closer to the 20% advanced in the study of Kadeev and Martemyanov[21]. If so, this rough estimation raises the question about the ability of veterans to meet the financial demands of this civic office. Most scholars agree that the veterans did not participate in public life because of the high financial means[22]. The cases from Philippopolis put this view into question. The higher percentage of known *bouleutai*, the massive sarcophagi, which were similar to those of the rich people from Philippopolis[23], the villas[24], the estates and the grave goods from the family graves of the owners of these villas[25] clearly indicate that the veterans were in fact a solid and wealthy group within the society of Philippopolis and as such they should not have any trouble meeting the financial demands of the office under consideration. As M. Tacheva pointed out, most citizens of Philippopolis were middle class and the financial needs of offices could not have been high. Yet, Philippopolis was the biggest city in Thrace. This means that similar financial needs in other Thracian towns were even smaller and therefore easily met by veterans.

The cases of the veterans- *bouleutai* from Philippopolis raise another question

It is widely accepted that the legionary veterans were most influential on the local administration. In his detailed study on the impact of the auxiliary recruitment on provincial society, I. Haynes arrived to the conclusion that «the former auxilia-

---

[21] Kadeev, Martemyanov 1994, 83.
[22] See Mroszewicz 1989, 67; Bojanov 2008, 269.
[23] See the sarcophagi published by Tsontchev 1960, 345.
[24] On the Roman villas in Thrace see Dinchev 1997.
[25] For example, see the grave goods from the family necropolis of a villa near Pastucha (part of modern Peruschtitza, Plovdiv region), which was used from the beginning of II c. till IV c.- Venedikov 1960, 69ff, 74; Gerov 1980, 112-113, n. 409.

ries hardly appeared at all». He continued that «Indeed, there is no known example of any auxiliary *miles* or *eques*, as distinct from an officer, becoming a town decurion anywhere in the north-western provinces or in Dacia».[26] The examples are few and possible explanations vary[27], but what is more important is that auxiliary veterans in the local government did not go beyond the decurion office[28] or the office of the *bouleutai* in the eastern provinces. The epigraphic evidence from Philippopolis shows that the auxiliary veterans were more involved in local institutions than they were in other provinces. Thus, [— — — — Γέ]μελλος Γεμέλλου and [Αἴλιος (?)] Κέλσο[ς — —] were typical for auxiliary soldiers[29], while Αἴλ(ιος) Ἰουλιανός might also have been a veteran from the Horse Guard of the Emperor where *peregrinae* were recruited and he might have received his Roman name when entering the army[30]. In fact, there hardly was a clearly legionary veteran among the civic office holders from the army, while many such veterans and officers are known from Philippopolis and its area[31]. We can only speculate why, but it may well be connected with the distinction of the benefits that legionary and auxiliary soldiers received upon discharge[32]. It also seems that even if the payment of different troops in the Roman army varied[33], money was not the main factor. Money as well as the prestige of serving in the auxiliary units must have been so high that Roman citizens also served in these units after AD 170[34]. As mentioned above, the civic offices in Thrace because of their relatively low expenses were open to auxiliary veterans. The only explanation I find plausible concerns the privileges of the legionary veterans. The matter is further discussed below.

In rare occasions, the veterans held the office of priesthood. A good example is the case of Πό(πλιος) Ἀδριάν(ιος) Σαλλούστι[ος], who was ἀρχιερεὺς δι' ὅπλω[ν][35]. The inscription does not only note the priestly post of the veteran, but also his wealth given his donation and organisation of the *ludi gladiatori* in Philippopolis.

It was not only the civic offices, in which the veterans were involved. For example, we know of the curator of the Cendrisian tribe in Philippopolis: Αὐρ(ήλιος) Ἀπολλωνίδης, son of Aelius Valens[36]. The name of his father, Valens, was certainly a military one and among the widely spread military cognomina.

---

[26] Haynes 2001, 76.
[27] Haynes 2001, 76-78.
[28] Haynes 2001, 78-79.
[29] On the names of the auxiliary soldiers and veterans see Alföldy 1966, 48ff.; Mócsy 1986, 443 ff.; Mann 2002, 227-232.
[30] On the names of the Roman eq. sing. Aug. see Speidel 1965, 2-3; Mócsy 1986, 438 ff.
[31] A list of all known veterans from Philippopolis and its area is given in table 1 in Topalilov 2011a, 539-541.
[32] See the case in Egypt: Haynes 2001, 77-8.
[33] See the discussion in Speidel 1992, 87-106, Alston 1994, 113.
[34] Le Bohec 1994, 98.
[35] *IGBulg* V, 5407.
[36] Sharankov 2005, 62.

These examples show the range of offices accessible to the veterans within the city. The inscriptions, however, also reveal the participation of the veterans in the public life of the province itself. Such an office was that of the Θρακάρχης, who was at the head of the provincial assembly of the Thracians in Philippopolis. Thus, we are aware of [Αἴ(?)]λ(ιος) Κότυος from an inscription from Serdica[37], whose Hadrianic Romanisation is undisputable[38]. The name shows that his Romanisation occurred after the completion of his military service.

It seems that the municipal and the provincial offices were open to veterans in Philippopolis and Thrace respectively. The epigraphic evidence reveals that the highest achievable civic post was that of the city councilor, which in fact was similar to cases in other provinces. However, the cases from Philippopolis show that most veterans among the *bouleutai* were in fact auxiliary veterans, which greatly contrasts the situation elsewhere. This needs explanation.

I see three main reasons for this. The first reason concerns the financial needs of the office of βουλευτής in Philippopolis, which should not be high since, as we already noted, the citizens of Philippopolis were middle class. The second reason may lay with the specifics of the Thracian society and particularly Philippopolis, where the Roman citizens were highly respected regardless of their rank or position. The Romanisation of the society in Philippopolis should also be noted here, especially before the middle of the second century AD, during which period a common Thracian could obtain the Roman citizenship only through the army. There could be a third explanation. As mentioned above, it is very likely that the legionary and auxiliary veterans received different benefits upon discharge. The available material points to the fact that the legionary veterans did not hold any of the municipal offices in Philippopolis. I believe this means that the privileges they received were high enough for them to be recognized, honored and influential on the society of Philippopolis. Alternatively, it could reflect the desire by some of the auxiliary veterans to participate in the public life of the city. Similar may have been the case of the provincial office of Θρακάρχης, whose responsibilities were however higher.

The desire of the auxiliary veterans and their descendents to play a certain role in the public life of the province as well as of Philippopolis is clearly seen in the cases of Αὐρ(ήλιος) Ἀσκληπιόδοτος, son of Αἴλ(ιος) Ἰουλιανός as well as Πό(πλιος) Ἀδριάν(ιος) Σαλλούστι[ος], who was ἀρχιερεὺς δι' ὅπλω[ν]. Both offices required high financial means, which the Thracian Romanised aristocracy of the province had as opposed to most common veterans. The case explicitly shows that the benefits received by the veterans upon discharge were high enough not only to obtain a prestigious office in Philippopolis and Thrace, but also to secure future wealth. We

---

[37] See the inscription in *IGBulg.*, IV, 1972.
[38] See Topalilov 2011a, 562.

can also point that many land estates were established by veterans and consequently prospered as the grave goods in the family necropolis show. Such are the cases of the land estate near Perushtitza (Stara Pastucha), where fourteen chariots were found in the family grave[39]. The military diploma of the auxiliary veteran Meticus Solae f. Bessus[40] dated in August, 14, 99 AD could name the owner of this estate and possibly villa. Similar examples are numerous in Thrace[41].

It is worth mentioning that the participation of veterans and their descendents in such highly paid offices was rather occasional and therefore not available to any of them.

The question of why the legionary soldiers were not deeply involved in the public life of Philippopolis remains open. It seems to me that B. Gerov's view that these veterans had an impact on the provincial society without being involved in the local government is closer to the truth, since their prestige was acknowledged in the province and Philippopolis and there was no need for them to participate in the public life in an official way. The various sarcophagi and tombstones from Philippopolis undeniably reflect the high status of the veterans. The latter is apparent from the tombstone of M. Annius Severus, a veteran from the Misene flete whose stele was probably set up by another veteran. The text can be read as follows: *Dis Manibus. M. Annius Seuerus, uetranus* (sic) *ex clas(se) pr(aetoria) Mis(enensi), militauit annos XXVI, uixit annos XXXXVIII. Cur(avit) C(aius) Scenti(us) Celer*[42] As a study has revealed, this stele belonged to a small group of four stelae of this type and style from Philippopolis[43], which clearly points to the wealthy C. Scentius Celer. His name, which was not accompanied by more details as it was the norm for stelae set up in Philippopolis,[44] shows his high status in the city. There was no need for a detailed epigram; the name itself was adequate for public recognition. This is not the only case of this kind. The cases of Αὐρ(ήλιος) Ἀσκληπιόδοτος, who mentioned his father Αἴλ(ιος) Ἰουλιανός in all his epigrams as well as the curator of the Cendrisian tribe in Philippopolis Αὐρ(ήλιος) Ἀπολλωνίδης, son of Aelius Valens, are good examples of high profile sons making use of the prestige of their fathers. The high status of the veterans in Philippopolis can also be seen in an inscription dedicated to Πό(πλιος) Οὐίρ[διος]Ἰουλιανός by his sons whose military background is specified (ἀπὸ στρατείας...)[45]. The lack of references to the military unit or the legion of the veterans in epigrams from Philippopolis is intriguing. The fact that only the personal name or the military rank were thought adequate, I believe, points again to

---

[39] See n. 27.
[40] *CIL* XVI, 45.
[41] See for instance the villa near Chatalka and the examples cited in Gerov 1980, 112-115.
[42] The stela is published in Topalilov 2002, 59-65.
[43] Ivanov 2004, 163-166.
[44] For example, see the case of C. Iulius Gratus, a praetorian veteran, whose stele was set up by his father C. Iulius Gratus in Gerasimova, Martinova 1994, 27-40.
[45] Sharankov 2005, 62.

the Romanisation of the low classes in Philippopolis and to the high status of militiamen regardless of their unit. The public recognition and high status of the veterans must have offered them the opportunity of public involvement. We should also remember that the veterans were assigned to the *honestiores*, making them equal by status to the *ordo decurionum*[46] with the exception that the emperors exempted them from taxes and other responsibilities, typical for the members of the *ordo decurionum*. It has been even proposed that a certain *ordo* of veterans existed despite the absence of epigraphic or other evidence[47]. Their high status, however, is clearly seen in their distinction from the rest of the Roman citizens in the province[48], and therefore, their participation in the public life of the city and the province was not obligatory.

Ivo TOPALILOV
University of Shumen, Bulgaria

Bibliography

Alston 1994 = R. Alston, «Roman Military Pay from Caesar to Diocletian», *JRS* 84 (1994) 113-123.

Alföldy 1966 = G. Alföldy «Notes sur la relation entre le droit de cité et la nomenclature dans l'Empire romain», *Latomus* 25 (1966) 37-57.

Barton 2001 = G. Barton, «The imperial state and its impact on the role and status of local magistrates and councilors in the provinces of the Empire»- In: L. de Blois (ed.) *Administration, prosopography and appointment policies in the Roman Empire,* Impact of Empire (Amsterdam 2001).

Dinchev 1999= V. Dinchev, Римските вили в днешната българска територия [Roman villas in the present-day Bulgarian lands (Sofia 1997).

Garnsey 1970= P. Garnsey, *Social status and legal privilege in the Roman Empire* (Oxford 1970).

Gerasimova 2003= V. Gerasimova, «Към проучването на тракийския койнон» [Toward study of the Thracian koinon], *Numizmatica i Epigraphica* I (2003) 199-208.

Gerasimova, Martinova 1994= V, Gerasimova, M. Martinova, «Нови данни за източния некропол на Филипопол» [New Data about the Eastern necropolis of Philippopolis], *Bulletin des musées de la Bulgarie du Sud* 20 (1994) 27-40.

---

[46] Dig. 49.18.3; on the privileges see Garnsey 1970, 245-251.
[47] On the arguments, see Kolosovskaja 1969, 122-123.
[48] See the inscription from Troesmis: *CIL* III, 6166, where «Veterani et cives romani consistentes» is mentioned. These expressions are quite often found in inscriptions from Lower Moesia.

Gerov 1961 = B. Gerov, «Römische Bürgerrechtsverleihung und Kolonisation in Thrakien vor Trajan», *Studii Clasice* 3 (1961) 107-116.

Gerov 1980 = B. Gerov, *Земевладението в Римска Тракия (I-III в.)* [Der Besitz an Grund und Boden im römischen Thrakien und Mösien (1.-3.Jh) (Sofia 1980).

Haynes 2001 = I.P. Haynes, «The impact of auxiliary recruitment on provincial societies from Augustus to Caracalla»- In: L. de Blois (ed.) *Administration, prosopography and appointment policies in the Roman Empire*, Impact of Empire (Amsterdam 2001) 62-83.

Ivanov 2004 = M. Ivanov, «Наблюдения върху няколко надгробни римски плочи от Philippopolis» [Some observations on several Roman tombstones from Philippopolis], *Annuary of the Archaeological museum- Plovdiv*, 9, 2 (2004) 160-170.

Kadeev & Martemyanov 1996 = V.I. Kadeev, A.P. Martemyanov, «Ветераны римской армии в Нижней Мезии в первых веках н.э.» [Roman army veterans in Lower Moesia and Thrace in the first centuries AD], *Anali* 1-4 (1996) 75-89.

Karadimitrova & Ilieva 2003 = K. Karadimitrova, P. Ilieva, «Колекция от частни печати в античния фонд на Софийския археологически музей» [Private Seals Collection from the Antique Depot of the Archaeological museum in Sofia], *Numismatica & Epigraphica* 1 (2003) 209-224.

Kolosovskaya 1969 = J. Kolosovskaya, «К вопросу о социальной структуре римскаго общества I-III вв. н. э. (collegia veteranorum) [On the structure of Roman society in the first three centuries A.D. (Collegia veteranorum)]», *Vestnik Drevnej Istorii* 4 (1969) 123-129.

Le Bohec 1994 = Y. Le Bohec, *The Imperial Roman Army* (London 1994).

Mann 2002 = J. Mann, «Name Forms of the Recipients of Diploma», *ZPE* 139 (2002) 227-232.

Mócsy 1986 = A. Mócsy, «Die Namen der Diplomempfänger», dans W. Eck, H. Wollf (eds.) *Heer und Integrationsplitik. Die römischen Militärdiplome als historische Quelle* (Köln-Wien 1986) 437-466.

Mroszewicz 1989 = L. Mroszewicz, «Die Veteranen in den Munizipalräten an Rheine und Donau zur hohen Kaiserzeit (1.-3.Jh.)», *Eos* 77 (1989) 65-80.

Sharankov 1999 = N. Sharankov, «Два надписа с името на Аврелий Асклепиодот (*IGBulg*. V, 5463 и *IGBulg*. III, 1, № 1150+ № 1151)» [Two inscriptions with the name of

Aurelius Asklepiodotus (*IGBulg.* V, № 5463 and *IGBulg.* III, 1, № 1150+ 1151)], *Archeologia* (Sofia) 3-4 (1999) 84-85.

Sharankov 2005 = N. Sharankov, «Statue-bases with honorific inscriptions from Philippopolis», *Archaeologia Bulgarica* 2 (2005) 55-71.

Speidel 1965 = M. Speidel, *Die equites singulares Augusti. Begleittruppe der römischen Kaiser des zweiten und dritten Jahrhunderts* (Bonn 1965).

Speidel 1992= M. Speidel, «Roman Army Pay Scales», *JRS* 82 (1992) 87-106.

Topalilov 2002= I. Topalilov, «A Roman veteran's tombstone from Philippopolis», *Archaeologia Bulgarica* 1 (2002) 59-65.

Topalilov 2011= I. Topalilov, «Една група преторианци от Филипопол» [A group of praetorians from Philippopolis], *Istorikii* 4 (2011) 257-268.

Topalilov 2011a = I. Topalilov, «Roman veterans and the city institutions of Philippopolis, Thrace», dans O.Picards, A. Dumitru (éds.), *Travaux du Symposium international Le livre, La Roumanie. L'Europe, tome IV. Routes et frontières au Sud-Est européen- relations économiques, militaires et culturelles* (Bucarest 2011) 536-581.

Tsontchev 1941 = D. Tsontchev, *Le sanctuaire thrace près du village de Batkoun* (Sofia 1941).

Tsontchev 1960 = D. Tsontchev, «Les sarcophages romains en pierre à Philippopolis et aux environs», *Latomus* 19 (1960) 340-349, Pl. XIV-XVI.

Venedikov 1960 = I. Venedikov, *Тракийската колесница* [The Thracian chariot] (Sofia 1960).

ETHNIC AND SOCIAL COMPOSITION OF THE ROMAN ARMY IN MOESIA INFERIOR : SOLDIERS FROM ASIA MINOR AND THE EASTERN PROVINCES OF THE ROMAN EMPIRE

Oleg ALEXANDROV

The ethnic composition of the Roman army is a problematic topic that has attracted much attention. However, most current views do not process or even take account of collected data from monuments, while in other cases the dissociation or over-intellectualisation of historical and epigraphic data has led to doubtful conclusions[1]. During the last decades, a few scholars have considered the problem in their studies on the Roman culture in Lower Moesia province[2].

In this paper, I will attempt to answer a few recurring questions about the ethnic composition of the Roman army in Lower Moesia. Since relevant studies require much space as well as use of diverse sources, I will only review here the problems concerning the numbers, religion and social composition of the soldiers with eastern origin[3].

First of all it has to be noted that the ethnic composition of the Roman army was constantly changing. In the first century BC, legions were recruited from Roman citizens only, i.e. mostly natives of the Apennine Peninsula, while during the third century the army was mainly barbarian. Following the introduction of local recruitment by Emperor Hadrian, the ethnic composition of the army was normally related to the territories, within which the legions moved. Yet, it must be taken into account that legionnaires were continually drawn even after the mid second century not only from the neighbouring and eastern provinces, but also from the provinces where the *vexillationes* were temporarily located.

The fact that the preserved epigraphic monuments are only a part of those actually made by the Roman soldiers must also be considered together with the inconsistent or incomplete investigation into the *limes*. Therefore, all conclusions regarding the ethnic composition of the dedicators and hence the composition of the Roman army in the province as a whole would be more or less questionable.

Having in mind that the limited historical sources give only general information without specifics, I have used only written monuments, which were left by soldiers and found in the region. In this study, I present a different approach to the matter using the evidence from Roman votive dedications. The votive dedications give us information on the name, military rank and unit of the dedicator as well as the name and epithets of the worshipped deity. In comparison with funerary stelae, the votive dedications help us in reaching more valid estimations about the ethnic origin of the person named in the inscription. Having in mind the conventional names during the

---

[1] Gerov 1949, 3–91; Gerov 1950/52, 17–121; Gerov 1952/53, 307–415; Todorov 1928.
[2] Alexandrov 2010; Boyanov 2008; Matei-Popescu 2010; Sarnowski 1988.
[3] In this paper, the term «eastern» stands for Asia Minor and the eastern provinces of the Empire. Where possible, the region or Roman province are specified.

Principate and the fact that notwithstanding the official religion, soldiers worshipped mainly their native deities, I think that this method could lead to interesting results[4]. I note in advance that the thesis maintained by certain scholars that the wide diffusion of eastern cults in the Roman army contrasts with the actual scarcity of dedications from Lower Moesia as well as their minor role compared to other cults[5].

I consider two aspects here: a) what portion of the soldiers who dedicated to eastern deities were of actual eastern origin, and b) what portion of the soldiers who dedicated to other deities were likely to originate from Asia Minor and the Eastern provinces of the Roman Empire.

Dedication of high rank officers

A number of intriguing monuments can be connected with high rank officers. A dedication to Serapis was made by the most prominent military man in the province – the governor (*legatus Augusti pro praetore*) of Lower Moesia, who was also the commander of the provincial army (*exercitus provinciae*)[6]. However, the dedicator Marcus Iallius Bassus was not of eastern origin. At the same time, another former provincial governor of Lower Moesia – L. Statilius Iulius Severus was known to be a priest of Mithras in Istros[7].

An inscription from the late third century refers to a dedication to the Great Mother of the Gods (Mater Deum Magna), which was made by the military governor (*dux*) of Scythia Minor, Aurelius Firmianus[8]. He also did not originate from the East. At the beginning of the fourth century, a dedication to Sol was made by another military governor (Valerius Romulus) in Salsovia[9]. However, any connection with an eastern cult is unlikely. It is probably connected with Aurelius' heliolatry, not with

---

[4] About two hundred monuments with references to the religion in the Roman army have been discovered within the territory of *Moesia Inferior*. A study of all military dedications from the region can be found in Alexandrov 2010.

[5] The inscriptions related to this group of deities constitute about 15 % of all dedications made by soldiers within the province.

[6] *CIL* III, 12387; Tacheva-Hitova 1982, 13, N 1: *[Iovi Optimo Maximo Soli?] / [Sar]apidi pro sa[l(ute) imperator]/ [rum] Caesarum Aug[g(ustorum)] M. Aureli An]/[to]nini et L. Aureli Veri [et Faustinae] / [Au]g(ustae) liber(orum) q(ue) eorum t[emplum cum sig]/[ni]s M. Ialli(us) Bass(us) le[g(atus) Aug(usti) pr(o) pr(aetore) / in]/[ch]oavit, consummavit ... / [...]eg(atus) Aug(usti) pr(o) pr(aetore)*. Marble slab originate (probably) from Oescus. Date: AD 164–166.

[7] *CIMRM* II, 2296; *ISM*, I 137: Τύχηι ἀγαθῆι / Ἡλίωι Μίθρᾳ ἀνεικήτῳ / Ἐπὶ ἱε[ρ]έω Ἰουλίου Σεουήρο[υ] ὑπατικοῦ / οἴδε συνεισήνεγ[κα]ν εἰς τ[ὴν] / [ο]ἰκοδομίαν τοῦ ἱεροῦ / σπηλέου καί [θεο]σέβει/αν ὑπη[ρ] ετοῦ[ντ]ος πατρὸς / [ε]ὐσεβοῦς Μ[εν]ίσκου Νουμηνί[ου] / Μ(ᾶρκος) Οὔλπ(ιος) Ἀρτεμίδωρος ποντάρ[χης] / [Ἱ]ππόλοχος Πυθίωνος / [Κ]άρπος Ἀ[π]ολλοδώρου / [Κ]αλλίστρατος Ἀπολλοδώρου / [Α]ἴλ(ιος). Διονύσιος Δημοκράτου[ς] / Ἰούλ(ιος) . Βάσσος β(ενεφικιάριος) ὑπατικοῦ / [Αὐ]ρήλιος Αἰμιλιανός / [Αἴ]λ(ιος) Φίρμος Διονύσιος Διονυσοδ[ώρου]. Limestone slab found in Istros. Date: late second century.

[8] *CIL* III, 764; *ISM* II, 144: *Matri deum / magnae / pro salute adq(ue) / incolumitate / D(ominorum) n(ostrorum) Aug(ustorum) et Caes(arum) / Aur(elius) Firmianus, / v(ir) p(erfectissimus) dux limit(is) prov(inciae) Scyt(hiae) / bonis auspiciis / consecravit*. Altar found in Tomis. Date: AD 293–294.

[9] *ISM* V, 290: *Dei Sancti Solis / Simulacrum consecr(atum) / die XIV kal(endis) Decemb(ribus) / debet singulis annis / iusso sacro D(ominorum) N(ostrorum) / Licini Aug(usti) et Licini Caes(aris) / ture cereis et profu/sionibus eodem die / a praep(ositis) et vexillat(ionibus) / in Cast(ris) Salsoviensib(us) / agentib(us) exorari. / Val(erius) Romulus v(ir) p(erfectissimus) dux / secutus iussionem / describsit*. Marble slab found in Salsovia. Date: AD 322–323.

Mithras, as it has been noted by certain scholars. Another dedication connected with the same cult refers to the prefect of the camp (*praefectus castrorum*) of Legio I Italica to Sol Augustus[10]. In any case, the name of the dedicator (Titus Flavius Sammius Terentianus) was Italic and for this reason cannot be used as proof of his eastern origins. The early Romanised name «Caius Iulius Maximus» of another prefect from the camp of the same legion probably marks a person of eastern origin. An eastern origin is also likely on the basis of the reference to *Deus Invictus*, who has been commonly connected with Mithraism[11]. At the end of the third and the beginning of the fourth century, a dedication to Dea Placida in Novae was made by Aurelius Saturninus, who was *praefectus Augusti legionis I Italicae*[12].

The only high rank officer in service who made a dedication to an eastern deity, in this case Luna, and who was undisputedly of eastern origin as noted in the inscription itself, was Caius Tullius from Scythopolis, Palestina. The dedicator was *primus pilus* of Legio I Italica and he made the dedication as a gift to the Eagle (Aquila) of the legion[13].

Other names that reveal eastern origin are the ones of the provincial governor Domitius Antigonus, who had sanctified a dedication made by the cohort at Sostra to the emperor's numen (*numen imperatoris*) in AD 235[14]. He also made in person the dedications to «Deities of the Eternal Rome (Roma Aeterna)» and to «The Genius of Province Lower Moesia (Genius provinciae Moesiae Inferioris)» in Durostorum in the same year[15]. Other names of similar origins are Iulius Asclepiodotus and Afranius Hannibalianus (the last one of African origin) – praetorian prefects (*praefecti praetorio*), who manifested their loyalty to Diocletian's *numen* at Oescus in AD 285[16].

There are some patterns observed in the inscriptions of high rank officers from the province: a great number of the dedications to eastern deities were not made by people of shared origin; on the other hand, people whose names were clearly of eastern

---

[10] Naidenova 1990, 606–607; Naidenova 1994, 225–228: Inscription on two altars: *1. Soli / Aug(usto); 2. T(itus) Fl(avius) Sam/mius Te/rentianus / praef(ectus) kastr(orum) (sic)*. Limestone altars found in shrine of Sol Augustus in the vicinity of Novae. Date: late third century.

[11] *CIMRM* II, 2271; *IGLN*, 36: *[Deo] / Invict[o] / C(aius) Iulius / Maximus / praef(ectus) castr(orum) / leg(ionis) I Ital(icae)*. Limestone altar found in the vicinity of Novae. Date: early 3rd century.

[12] *IGLN*, 40: *[P]lacidae [A]u[r(eliius)] / [S]aturninus / [p]raef(ectus) Au[g(usti)] leg(ionis) / [I Ita]l(icae) et Aur[elia] / [...Q]uieta S[...] / [...e]t coniux / [...]PE[...]*. Limestone altar found in Novae. Date: late third– early forth century.

[13] *ILBulg*, 293; *IGLN*, 31: *Lunae sac(rum) / C(aius) Tullius C(ai) f(ilius) / Col(onia) Apollina/ris Scythop(olis) p(rimus) p(ilus) / Aquil(ae) leg(ionis) I Ital(icae) d(onum) d(edit)*. Marble altar found in Novae. Date: second century.

[14] *CIL* III, 14429; *ILBulg*, 261: *Imp(eratori) Caesar[i] / [[Gaio Iulio Vero]] / [[Maximino]] Aug(usto) / [p]ontifici [max(imo)] / [t]ribunici[ae po]/[t]est(atis) co(n)s(uli), p(atri) [p(atriae)] / coh(ors) I C[isipad(ensium)] / [[Maximiniana]] / devot[a numini] / maiest[atiq(ue) eius.] / D(e) p(ecunia) questur(ae) de/dicante Domitio An/[t]igono cl(arissimo) v(iro) leg(ato) Aug(usti) pr(o) p[r(aetore)]*. Limestone altar found in Sostra. Date: AD 235.

[15] Donevski 1976, 61–63: *Divinib[u]s Ro/mae Aeternae / Ge[ni]o provin/ciae Moes(iae) Inf(erioris) / Dom(itius) Antigo/nus vir c(larissimus) leg(atus) Aug(usti) / pr(o) pr(aetore) cum Pompeia / Apa c(larissima) f(emina) coniuge / et Domitiis An/tigon(us) et Ant(igonus)*. Limestone slab found in Durostorum. Date: AD 235–236.

[16] *ILBulg*, 8: *Imp(eratori) Caes(ari) C(aio) Aurel(io) / Val(erio) Diocletiano / p(io) f(elici) invic(to) Aug(usto), pont(ifici) / max(imo), Germanico / max(imo) trib(uniciae) potest(atis) / p(atri) p(atriae), proco(n)s(uli) / Afranius Hanni/balianus Iul(ius) As/clepiodotus v(iri) / em(inentissimi) praef(fecti) pr(aetorio)] / d(evoti) n(umini) m(aiestati)[que eius]*. Limestone altar found in Oescus. Date: AD 285.

origin, made dedications complacent with the official cults of the empire – mostly the cult of the Emperor, Roma Aeterna and Genius provinciae, which represented the power and importance of the state. The reasons were mostly political. The provincial governors were of great local significance to Rome and for this reason they were personally nominated by the emperor. That is why we discover mostly official dedications: the purpose was to satisfy all the locals. Of similar importance within the legions were their *legatus, praefectus castrorum* and especially the *primus pilus*. These were the people with the task of ensuring that the Roman imperial policy and consequently the official religion were complied with in the army. Totally different was the dedication to *Luna*, but it was a deed of a high rank officer, who was promoted after a long career in the army and not because he was hired by Roman politicians.

Dedications of centurions

The dedications made by centurions in honour of eastern deities are more numerous. Even in this military group, the dedicators with a certain eastern origin were not many. Dedications to Mithras were made by Marcus Ulpius Modinus[17], Cornelius Faustus[18], L. Valerius Fuscus[19] and Q. Lucilius Piscinus[20]. All of the listed centurions had Italic names. Only Annius Saturninus[21] made a dedication to Deus Invictus noting a person of eastern origin. Another one of certain eastern origin was the centurion Marcus Aurelius Iason[22], who made a dedication to Deus Aeternus. Eastern were also the names of the centurions Caius Iulius Africanus[23] and Aelius Artemidorus[24], who made dedications to Diana and Apollo in the sanctuary in Montana between the years 157 and 160.

The centurions were the spine of the Roman army and largely Romanised. Even though they were only fifty nine in each legion, they were important to the army

---

[17] *ILBulg*, 343: *Invicto / M(arcus) Ulpius / Modianu(s?) / [(centurio)] leg(ionis) I Ital(icae) / [v(otum)] s(olvit) l(ibens) m(erito)*. Limestone altar found in Iatrus. Date: second century.

[18] *CIL III*, 7475; *CIMRM*, II 2273: *[In]vict(o) / Mit(h)r(ae) Cor/neli(us) Faus/tu(s) centurio l(e)g(ionis) XI Cl(audiae)*. Limestone altar found in Durostorum. Date: late second century.

[19] *CIMRM* II, 2286; *ISM* V, 221: *Invicto Mi/thrae sac(rum) / L. Valerius / Fuscus (centurio) / leg(ionis) V M(a)c(edonicae) / v(otum) l(ibens) s(olvit)*. Limestone altar found in Troesmis. Date: mid-second century.

[20] *CIMRM* II, 2312: *In hon(orem) d(omus) d(ivinae) / So[l]i Invicto / sacrum / Q. Lucilius / Pis[ci]nus (centurio) / leg(ionis) I Ital(icae) / v(otum) s(olvit) l(ibens) m(erito)*. Altar found in Tropaeum Traiani. Date: third century.

[21] *CIL III*, 7483; *CIMRM* II, 2311: *Deo / Invicto / pro salu(te) imp(eratoris) M. Ant(onini) / Veri Annius / Saturninus / (centurio) leg(ionis) XI Cl(audiae) / v(otum) s(olvit) l(ibens) m(erito)*. Altar found in Tropaeum Traiani. Date: late second century.

[22] *CIL III*, 12388: *Aetern[o] / M(arcus) Aur(elius) Iaso[n] / (centurio) leg(ionis) I Ital(icae) [et] / Ulp(ius) Lucre/tius et Au[r(elius) Ia]/son et Au[r(elius) Lu]/cretia[nus] / Eq(uites) [Romani] / pro su[is a]/ram po[suerunt] / A[n]toni[no et ... co(n)s(ulibus)]*. Marble altar found in the vicinity of Byala Slatina (near Oescus). Date: early third century.

[23] Velkov Alexandrov 1994, N 47: *Dianae Regi/nae et Apolli/ni sacrum / pro sal(ute) Vitra/si Pollionis / v(iri) c(larissimi) leg(ati) Aug(usti) / pr(o) pr(aetore) / C(aius) Iul(ius) Afric[a]/nus (centurio) leg(ionis) XI / Cl(audiae) / v(otum) s(olvit) l(ibens) m(erito)*. Marble slab found in Montana. Date: AD 157–158.

[24] *CIL III*, 12371; Velkov Alexandrov 1994, N 51: *Dianae / Reginae et Apol/lini, pro salute / L(uci) Iuli Statili Se/veri leg(ati) Aug(usti) pr(o) / pr(aetore) et li[bero]rum ei/us Aelius / Artem(i)dorus / (centurio) leg(ionis) I Ital(icae) r(apacis?)*. Marble altar found in Montana. Date: AD 159–160.

organization, because they were the link between commanders and common soldiers. That is why only loyal candidates, who were familiar with the Latin language and traditions, were hired for these posts. This is the reason why this position was available not only to soldiers from the Wwest, but also to persons of eastern origin, who were heirs of Roman pioneers in the East or members of early Romanised families from the local elites.

Dedications of non-commissioned officers

Higher is the number of soldiers of eastern origin (mostly from Asia Minor) in the establishment of the non-commissioned officers (*principales*). Most probably a dedication to Mithras (Deus Invictus) was made by Ti(berios) Claudios Zenodotos[25]. The dedicator was a standard-bearer (*signifer*) from Legio I Italica and the inscription was found in Iatrus. The soldier kept his Greek name as a *cognomen* since his family had probably been already romanised in the first century AD.

A Greek *cognomen* was also kept by Ulpius Demetrius[26], who made a dedication to the same deity. The inscription has been found in Carsium. The dedicator was a guardsman (*singularis consularis*) from Ala II Aravacorum. This monument alone testifies to the spread of eastern cults among auxiliaries.

With respect to dedications to eastern deities by dedicators with common names, the eastern origin of the soldiers is open to question: Flavius Valens[27], (...)ninus[28], Μᾶρκος Πομπέιος Λούκιος[29], Caius Lucius Domitianus[30].

In other dedications to eastern deities by *principales*, the eastern origin of the dedicators is dubious – Q(uintus) Samicius Serenus[31], Iulius Bassus[32], Numisius Rufinus[33].

In some cases, soldiers (from the group of the *principales*) of a certain eastern origin worshipped other deities; for example the legion clerk (*librarius legionis*) – Ulpius

---

[25] Vahtel Naidenova 1984, 41: *Invicto / Ti(iberios?) Claudios (sic) / Zηnodotos (sic) / sig(nifer) (centuriae) Iuni Pac/ati leg(ionis) I Ital(icae) / v(otum) s(olvit) l(ibens) m(erito)*. Limestone altar found in Iatrus. Date: second century.

[26] ISM V, 102: *Deo inv(icto) / Ulpius / Demetri/us L ^ P s(ingularis) c(onsularis) a/lae II Ara(vacorum) / v(otum) s(olvit) l(ibens) m(erito)*. Limestone altar found in Carsium. Date: late second–early third century.

[27] Radoslavova, Dzanev 2003, 120, fig. 20: *I(ovi) O(ptimo) M(aximo) Dol(icheno) / Fl(avius) Valens / b(ene)f(iciarius) leg(ati) (legionis) / v(otum) s(olvit) l(ibens) m(erito)*. Altar found in Abritus. Date: late second–early third century.

[28] ILBulg, 276; IGLN, 26: *[D]olic(heno) pro salu[te...] / [...Anto]nini Pii Felicis Au[g(usti)...] / [...]ninus a questionari[is ...] / ex v(oto) p(osuit)*. Marble altar found in Novae. Date: late second–early third century.

[29] IGBulg, I 24: Ἀγαθῆι τύχηι. / Διὶ Δολιχαίῳ / Μ(ᾶρκος) Πομπ[ἐϊ]ος Λού/κιος βενε[φ]ικιά/ριος ὑπατικοῦ / λεγ(ιῶνος) αʹ Ἰταλικῆς / Ἀντωνεινιανῆς / βουλευτὴς Διονυ/σοπολειτῶν Καλ/λατιανῶν Μαρ/κιανοπολειτῶν / εὐχαριστήριον/ ὑπὲρ σωτηρίας τοῦ κυρίου αὐτοκράτορος. Limestone altar found in Dionysopolis. Date: AD 214–217.

[30] Naidenova 1990, 606–607; Naidenova 1994, 225–228: *Soli Invicto / C(aius) Iul(ius) Domi/tianus imm(unis) / libr(arius) ex voto*. Limestone altar found in the vicinity of Novae. Date: 3rd century.

[31] CIMRM II, 2313: *Invicto Mithrae / Q. Samicius Serenus archite[c]/tus salariarius leg(ionis) XI Cl(audiae) posuit*. Fragmented relief of Mithras found in Durostorum. Date: late second century.

[32] See not. 5.

[33] ILBulg, 275; IGLN, 27: *I(ovi) O(ptimo) M(aximo) D(licheno) / Numisius Ru/finus opt(io) leg(ionis) / I Ital(icae) / votum sol/vit l(ibens) m(erito)*. Limestone altar found in Novae. Date: late second–early third century.

Dionysius was a follower of the cult of Dionysus[34]; Σεβαζιανὸς Ἀλεξάνδρου *(beneficiaries)* dedicated a statue of Asclepius in the sanctuary near Glava Panega[35].

As a whole, the *principales* in the Roman Army of Lower Moesia were of various origins. Those from the western provinces were fewer. According to the principle of local recruitment of soldiers, the *principales* of Lower Moesia were mostly of Balkan origin. Recruits from Asia Minor, Greek or Hellenic populations were not excluded. It makes more sense to assume that the surviving dedications by the *principales* were made by soldiers of mainly local origin, even if their names were eastern – Thracians, Greeks, Hellenic or Romanised populations from Lower Moesia and her nearby provinces.

Dedications of common soldiers

The only dedication by a common soldier (*miles*) to an eastern deity was made by a member of Legio V Macedonica. Caius Tironius Alexander made a dedication to *Dea Suria* in Oescus in the late third-early fourth century[36].

The reason for the lack of such monuments lies with the ethnic origin of the common soldiers (*milites*). After Hadrian (117–138), the auxiliaries and then the legions were mostly recruited from local populations. This is confirmed by the preserved epigraphic material. The nature of the monuments (location, iconography and epigraphic data) testifies to the Thracian origin of the soldiers. In most cases, it concerned the poor rural population, who came from the slightly Romanised Thracian lands. This population joined the army without adhering to the Roman traditions, language and culture. The lack of familiarity by most Thracians with Latin, which was the formal language of the army, precluded their promotion to higher ranks. Being on the lowest position in the army and not familiar with Roman culture, the Thracians remained devoted to their native divinities.

Positive evidence for the followers of eastern cults with Thracian origin is not preserved to date. Therefore it is acceptable to assume that eastern cults remained foreign to the natives. Dedications to eastern deities were only found in *Oescus* and the vicinity, Novae, Iatrus, Durostorum, Abritus, Tropaeum Traiani, Carsium, Troesmis, Salsovia, Istros, Dionysopolis and the province capital – Tomis, i.e. in the major military and Romanising centers in the province of Lower Moesia. The lack of monuments, which were left by the local population, is because of two facts: either most of the followers of eastern cults were their worshippers of eastern origin or they were military men with a higher social status affected by the mode.

---

[34] CIL III, 6150 = 7437 = 12346; ILBulg, 438: Q(uod) b(onum) f(elix) f(austum) / Albino et Maximo co(n)s(ulibus) / Nomina Bacchi vernaculorum: l. 6 ... frater: Ulp(ius) Dionysius lib(rarius) leg(ionis) .... Slab found between villages of Butovo and Nedan (near Nicopolis ad Istrum). Date: AD 227.

[35] IGBulg II, 513: Σεβαζιανὸς Ἀλεξάνδρου β(ενε)[φ(ικιάριος)] / εὐχαστήριον. Marble statue of Asclepius found in the sanctuary of Glava Panega. Date: late second–early third century.

[36] ILBulg, 41: G(aius) Tironius Al[exand]/er mil(es) leg(ionis) V Ma[cedon(icae)] / v(otum) s(olvit) Dia Suriae. Slab found in Oescus. Date: late third, early forth century.

During the second and third centuries, the Roman army in Lower Moesia was ethnically heterogeneous. Among the dedicators, there were individuals from almost all the Empire – the western provinces, the Apennine peninsula, the Balkans, Asia Minor, Africa, etc. The surviving dedications from Lower Moesia, which were made by soldiers from Asia Minor and the Eastern provinces of the Empire, testify that during the second and third centuries a part of the soldiers in the region were of Eastern origin. In most cases, these were Romanised individuals. The military rank and the social status of the dedicators were relatively high. The worshipped deities were mostly Mithras and Iuppiter Dolichenus, which matches well with the fact that the soldiers perceived deities as warrior-gods against evil. The dedicators marked in the inscriptions were high officers, direct representatives of the imperial authority, centurions and principals, who worshipped their native gods [comma] or those with a long service in the army.

In conclusion, an examination of the above written monuments has shown that it is possible to answer, if only approximately, the main question of this paper, i.e. what the number of soldiers of eastern origin (from Asia Minor and the eastern provinces) in Lower Moesia was.

Firstly, I have to point the overall number garrisons in Lower Moesia. It is appropriate to pay special attention to the date of most written monuments, i.e. the second half of the second century and the first half of the third century. During that time, two legions – Legio I Italica and Legio XI Claudia, numbering twelve thousand soldiers, were permanently stationed in the region. Auxiliary units with the same number of soldiers were assigned to each legion in the province. However for reasons noted above, eastern cults were not mentioned with respect to military personnel in the *auxilia* in Lower Moesia.

An interesting fact is the lack of dedications made by common soldiers (*milites*) from the noted two legions to eastern deities. The group of *milites* composed 80 % of the general number of the legionaries in a legion. On the other hand, the groups of the *immunes, principales* and the *centuriones*, within which worshippers of eastern cults were found, consisted of thousand soldiers in total. The preserved dedications to the eastern gods were no more than 15% of all the dedication made by soldiers in the province. Hence, it is logical to assume that the soldiers of eastern origin (both from Asia Minor and the eastern provinces of the Roman Empire) in the province were barely a few hundreds. Their number was not constant, since it depended on a number of factors, such as the progress of the Roman expansion in this part of the Balkans, the economic and political situation on the peninsula and the whole Empire, the degree of Romanisation in Lower Moesia and the nearby provinces, the official politics of the Roman empire with regard to the recruitment of legions and auxiliaries, the participation of the Thracian population in the Roman army and the *vexillationes* of the Lower Moesia's legions in the East and etc.

Finally, it is important to underline that most inscriptions testify to a Greek or Hellenized population from the provinces of the Balkans and western Asia Minor. The soldiers, who came from the eastern Asia Minor, Middle East and the African provinces, such as Cilicia, Cappadocia, Pontus, Armenia, Commagene, Syria, Iudaea, Aegyptus etc., were not numerous. However in most cases, the above inscriptions are important evidence not only for the movement of people within the cosmopolitan Empire, but also for the cultural relations and interaction between the Balkans, the eastern provinces and Asia Minor.

Oleg ALEXANDROV
University St. Cyril and Methodius, Veliko Tărnovo, Bulgaria

Abbreviations non given in the *Guide de l'épigraphiste*

IGLN = J. Kolendo, V. Božilova, *Inscriptions Grecques et Latines de Novae* (Mésie Inférieure) (Bordeaux 1997).

ISM I = M. Pippidi, *Inscriptiones Daciae et Scythiae Minoris Antiquae. Series altera: Inscriptiones Scythiae Minoris graecae et latinae. Vol. 1. Inscriptiones Histriae et vicinia* (București 1983).

ISM II = I. Stoian. *Inscriptiones Daciae et Scythiae Minoris Antiquae. Series altera: Inscriptiones Scythiae Minoris graecae et latinae. Vol. 2. Tomis et territorium* (București 1987).

ISM V = E. Doruțiu-Boilă. *Inscriptiones Daciae et Scythiae Minoris Antiquae. Series altera: Inscriptiones Scythiae Minoris graecae et latinae Vol. 2. Capidava, Troemis, Noviodunum* (București 1980).

CIMRM II = M. J. Vermaseren, *Corpus Inscriptionum et Monumentorum Religionis Mithraicae. Vol. 2* (Hague Comitis 1960).

Bibliography

Alexandrov 2010 = O. Alexandrov, *Религията в римската армия в провинция Долна мизия I–IV век* (Veliko Tărnovo 2010).

Boyanov 2008 = I. Boyanov, *Римските ветерани в Долна Мизия и Тракия I–IV век* (Sofia 2008).

Donevski 1976 = P. Donevski, «Латински надписи от Дуросторум», *Arheologia* 4 (Sofia 1976) 61-64.

Gerov 1949 = B. Gerov, «La romanisation entre le Danube et les Balkans (première partie – d'Auguste à Hadrien)», *Annuaire de l'Université de Sofia, Faculté Historico-Philologique* 45 (1949) 3-91.

Gerov 1950/52 = B. Gerov, «La romanisation entre le Danube et les Balkans (deuxième partie – d'Hadrien à Constantin le Grand, 1)», *Annuaire de l'Université de Sofia, Faculté des Lettres* 47 (1950/1952) 17-121.

Gerov 1952/53 = B. Gerov, «La romanisation entre le Danube et les Balkans (deuxième partie – d'Hadrien à Constantin le Grand, 2)», *Annuaire de l'Université de Sofia, Faculté des Lettres* 48 (1952/53) 307-415.

Matei–Popescu 2010 = Fl. Matei–Popescu, *The Roman Army in Moesia Inferior* (Bucharest 2010).

Naidenova 1988 = V. Naidenova, «Le mithraeum récemment découvert à Novae» *Akten des XIII Internationalen Kongresses für Klassische Arhäologie* (Mainz 1988) 601-606.

Naidenova 1994 = V. Naidenova, «Un sanctuaire syncrétique de Mithra et de Sol Augustus découvert à Novae» *Studies in Mithraism. Storia delle regioni, 9* (Roma 1994) 225-228.

Radoslavova Dzanev 2003 = G. Radoslavova, G. Dzanev, «Abritus», in R. Ivanov (ed.) *Roman and Early Byzantine Settlements in Bulgaria* (Sofia 2003) 110-148.

Sarnowski 1988 = T. Sarnowski, *Wojsko rzymskie w Mezji Dolnej i na połnocnym wybrzeżu morza czarnego* (Warszawa 1988).

Tatcheva–Hitova 1982 = M. Tatcheva, *История на източните култове в Долна Мизия и Тракия V в. н. е. – IV в. от н. е.* (Sofia 1982).

Todorov 1928 = Y. Todorov, *Паганизмът в Долна Мизия през първите три века след Христа* (Sofia 1928).

Vahtel & Naidenova 1984 = K. Vahtel, V. Naidenova, «Monuments du culte de Liber et Mithra de Iatrus (Mésie Inférieure)», *Arheologia* 4 (Sofia 1984) 39-45.

Velkov & Alexandrov 1994 = V. Velkov, G. Alexandrov, *Монтана. Vol. 2.* (Montana 1994).

ROMAN ARMY AND THE MONETISATION OF DACIA

Constantina KATSARI

Dacia was annexed by the Romans, more than a century after the Principate was well established in Europe and around the Mediterranean. As it was usually the norm, the Romans imposed their political rule in the area, but allowed for some independence in some sectors as culture and administration. Back then, Dacia exhibited certain particular characteristics that gave her a unique character which distinguished her from the rest of the empire. Even though politically it was part of a strong state and geographically part of the Balkans, some of its characteristics find their roots in local traditions. Of course, other aspects were influenced by the central administration of Rome or its location on the northeastern frontier. In addition, Dacia stood unique among other provinces because it was highly militarised; in fact, it was considered to host the highest number of Roman soldiers. In this article we are about to see whether these influences are visible also in the patterns of the coin circulation within the province.

There is no doubt that coinage is one of the most important indicators of regional economic growth, interregional connections and movements of population. The study of the monetization of Dacia, the circulation of coins within this region and their quantification could give us clues with regard to the economic development of the frontier province. All aspects of gold, silver and bronze coinages may have influenced the monetisation and, consequently, the economy of this region. By studying the mint they came from, the years they remained in circulation, and the areas where they have been found we could get clues about the specific type of financial transactions in which coins were involved. However, instead of embarking on a complete study of the coinage of Dacia during the Principate, I intend to focus only on some of its unique characteristics. In this article I would like to emphasise on the substantial monetary differences between the province of Dacia and its neighbouring provinces in the south of Balkans and in Asia Minor, while I will pay attention to the extent of the intervention of the Roman administration on the economic and political development of the region.

Patterns of Coins

Upon Dacia's annexation, we notice that the nature of coinages that started circulating there changed. This should have been expected, since the the area withstood profound political changes. Let us not forget that political authorities guarantee the value of money within their controlled territories. The Roman empire was not different. In fact, according to chartalist theory, the Roman State produced fiat money that circulated within its territory and became immediately acceptable means of transactions[1]. Therefore, the official silver denarii became the main currency for larger transactions, as soon as the Roman emperor became the acknowledged leader of the province. Also, we cannot exclude the possibility that gold aurei were used in substantial quantities, even if their presence among archaeological finds is limited. If a gold coin goes astray usually its owner will not rest until he recovers it. And yet, gold aurei are plentiful in museum collections, which means that adequate numbers have been initially produced. The reason that denarii are more prominent as archaeological finds or as part of hoards (by comparison to gold) is that we tend to lose coins of smaller denominations. Accordingly, we notice an abundance of bronze coins minted in Rome and circulating throughout the province. Bronze coins are found in large numbers in excavations, but also in hoards (depending on the financial capacity of the owner). These were probably used in smaller transactions, on a daily basis. In all likelyhood, bronze currencies usually are the best indicators of the levels of the monetisation of a region. Dacia is no different in that respect[2].

Even if Rumania is a significant part of the Balkan region, there is a sharp contrast between coinages found in Dacia and the coinages encountered in the Southern Balkans. The southern provinces seem to have followed Hellenistic traditions that emphasised on the minting of local coinages. Civic coinages were abundant and they circulated widely. Specifically, more than 500 civic mints were in operation in the eastern provinces at some point or another during the Principate, reaching a peak during the Severan period[3]. Cities sometimes sought permission from the emperor to found a mint, while other times they decided to do so independently[4]. In all cases they produced bronze coins which were used as small denominations in the local markets. Such coins circulated normally within a range of around 200 km, although we do find some of them that travelled longer distances[5]. It is an acknowledged fact that the Roman emperor was not especially interested in controlling the production and distribution of these smaller denominations. Although they were extremely important for the conduct of local trade, the central authorities would not have made any substantial profits from their issuing. Hence the emperor left the task to civic or in a few cases to other local magistrates. In fact, he probably would have considered it a great hassle to coordinate production in hundreds of small cities and to implement centrally controlled weight standards.

---

[1] Chartalist theory first became known at the beginning of the twentieth century when G. F. Knapp published his book on *The State Theory of Money* (1924), 32.
[2] For a detailed account of the coins found in Dacia after its annexation both as excavation finds and as part of hoards see Gazdac 2002.
[3] Jones 1963, 308-347; Jones 1965, 295-301. The exact number of mints remains unknown according to Heuchert 2007, 33.
[4] For the civic authorisation to issue coins see selectively Howgego 1985, 85; Burnett, Amandry & Carradice 1999, 4-5.
[5] Kraft 1972, 275.

Despite the imperial preference for the decentralisation of minting, Dacia followed a distinctly different path. Only a handful of these civic coins appear in coin hoards and excavation finds in Rumania. Their number is low and insignificant by comparison to the bronze coins that were issued from the official mint of Rome and have been found in the area. Archaeological finds clearly indicate the predominance of bronze coins minted in the capital. According to Gazdac, we can notice an initial increase of 5.2 % in the number of civic issues during the period 193-218 AD. The circulation of these coinages reached the highest peak at 13.3 % in 218-238 AD. After that their production as well as circulation declined until they were terminated during the reign of Philip I[6]. It is evident that they relied heavily on the importation of smaller denominations from the mint of Rome, instead of the local southern Balkans or Asia Minor mints. Also, there have never been any interest from local cities to issue their own coinages. They were either not interested in the profits they would have made from the conversion of raw metal into coins or they considered the process troublesome and not cost effective.

Additionally, in the East we find that some of the silver coins did not follow the Roman weight standard but previous Hellenistic standards. Such coins were a) the cistophori of Pergamum, b) the quarter drachms, hemidrachms, drachms, didrachms, tridrachms, tetradrachms from Caesarea of Cappadocia, Antioch, Crete, Cyprus, Amisus, Lycia, Tarsus, Tyre, Egypt[7]. Cistophori and all denominations of drachms are regularly found across Asia Minor provinces, but we do not encounter them with the same density in the southern Balkans[8]. The Antiochene tetradrachms were very popular and they circulated within the province of Syria. The Syrian people used both denarii and tetradrachms simultaneously, as the excavations of Dura Europos and other cities of this frontier province indicate[9]. Both of these currencies have been in circulation until the collapse of the monetary system at some point after the third century AD, when they were all replaced by billon antoniniani[10].

The use of multiple currencies in Syria, which happened to be also a frontier province, is in sharp contrast to the use of only one silver currency in Dacia. The mint of Rome was the only mint represented in the excavation finds of this province for over two centuries[11]. In that respect Dacia resembles the other western provinces that looked at Rome for the importation of larger denominations. Numismatically speaking, the province belonged to the west and not to the Balkans. This develop-

---

[6] Gazdac 2002, 203.
[7] Burnett, Amandry & Ripolles 1992, 26-30.
[8] This result is based on personal observation of coin hoards and excavation finds from Asia Minor and Greece.
[9] Bellinger 1949.
[10] The replacement of denarii and other silver coinages by antoniniani is a phenomenon we encounter across the empire, in the eastern as well as the western provinces, according to Katsari 2011, 129-131.
[11] Gazdac 2002, 190.

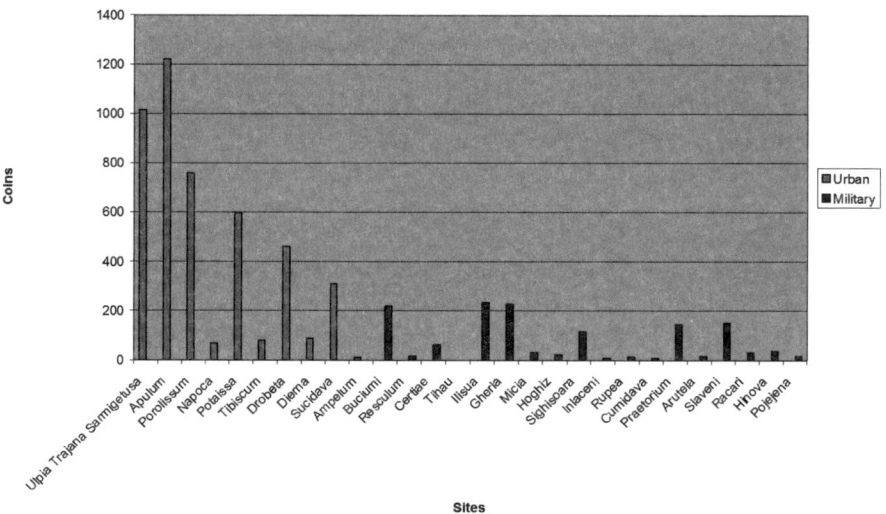

Chart 1
Dacia Excavations

ment would have simplified currency exchange in the area, since they would have used only currencies that belonged to a single weight standard, unlike the eastern provinces that used multiple standards. It is also possible that trading activities with the western provinces were more frequent than those with the East. Nevertheless, numismatic evidence alone cannot prove this assumption. Other indicators, one of which may be pottery, should by studied in order to give as a complete picture of commercial movements.

The above pattern was disrupted only when the decentralisation of minting occurred before the middle of the third century AD. By then, a number of new official mints made their appearance. The emperor Valerian continued the production of 'official' issues at Antioch and also opened a second eastern mint at Cyzicus, while Gallienus opened a third mint at Trier in the western provinces. Other mints were then founded in Milan and Siscia, whilst Postumus established one at Cologne. By 274 the official mints were eight and by 300 AD they became 15[12]. In accordance to this trend, the mint of Viminacium started its operations in 239 AD and it provided bronze coins in the entire Balkan area until 255 AD. Hence it fulfilled its purpose, since it was established in order to supplement the irregular supply of the mint of Rome. By 246 the province of Dacia was also granted the right, for the first time, to issue its own bronze coinage. For the entire reign of Philip the Arab this mint provided the province with the necessary for minor transactions small denominations.

---

[12] Harl 1996, 138-144.

However, its operation was short lived and lasted until 257 AD[13]. Also in this case the pattern of minting resembles that of the western provinces. After all, by that time the mints of Asia Minor and Syria were reducing their production of coins until they ceased completely after the middle of the third century AD[14]. Several centrally controlled mints took over the entire production of bronze coins across the empire, until this one also stopped by the reign of Aurelian[15].

Army, urbanisation, and trade

It is evident that the province relied almost exclusively upon the mint of Rome for its provision with the necessary coins. What would be the reason for such a reliance? Why would they not have used the coins issued from civic mints in the Southern Balkans? After all, geographically the mints in the southern Balkans were easier to access than the mint of Rome. One possible reason for the distinct monetary character of this province could have been the large number of Roman troops residing in the area. We know that these troops were paid directly from the State probably in silver denarii, although their salary was estimated in aurei[16]. It is also possible that part of this salary was given in Roman sestertii after the appropriate deductions in food, clothing, weapons and fodder were made[17]. Regular shipments of coins from Rome towards Dacia could justify the almost exclusive use of official issues in this province, according to a widely held view reagarding coin circulation in the western provinces[18]. Such reasoning used to be especially popular amongst ancient historians who followed substantivists' ideas on the importance of army payments in the economy of the Roman empire[19]. According to this school of thought, the presence of the army in a specific region could greatly alter the economic parameters in a way that would have also affected the production and distribution of coinages. The central authorities would have played a pivotal role in that respect. They would have issued coins specifically for the payment of the legions and they would have transferred them for this purpose in the area. Subsequently, the money would have purchased services and goods locally. This way, they would have entered the wider economy.

On the whole, scholars believe to date that the army played a significant role in both the urbanisation and the establishment of new emporia in Dacia. There is no doubt that the annexation of this province to the Roman empire radically changed

---

[13] Gazdac 2004, 73.
[14] Salamon 1970, 146-162.
[15] Watson 1999, 127-132.
[16] Alston 1994, 113-123.
[17] Van Berchem 1977, 331-334; Pollard 2000, 182.
[18] Selectively see Hobley 1998. However, in this book there seem to be no correlation between the supply of bronze coins and military activities in the area.
[19] Among others see Crawford 1970, 40-48.

the development of cities and trading centers. Traditionally, the settlement pattern of Roman Dacia consisted of urban centres (municipia, coloniae) and rural centres, such as villas or villages (vici)[20]. Archaeologically speaking, the permanent or temporary nature of these settlements is yet to be defined. What is certain, though, is the fact that some of these settlements had a military character. As in the neighbouring Moesia where many municipia evolved out of vici and canabae[21], similar developments took place in Dacia. The army was undoubtedly partly responsible for local economic growth and the eventual rise of military settlements. Specifically, canabae were a gathering of buildings - tabernae, workshops, warehouses etc - located close to legionary and auxilliary camps. Even though these communities were more or less permanent, they were also unplanned. They were considered military property and they could disappear if the commander wished so. Vici were a bit further from army land and of a more permanent nature. They were legally independent and hosted several merchants as well as veterans. Some of these places were eventually promoted to coloniae, especially in Dacia such a development was centrally encouraged. In other cases abandoned legionary fortresses were given the status of colonia. These coloniae turned eventually into major urban centres and emporia[22].

We cannot doubt that the army had a substantial impact on the urbanisation of the region. The reason for its increased influence was the sheer volume of the military in the area. The northeastern frontier became one of the strongest (or the strongest) in terms of army enforcements as early as its consolidation took place under the reign of Trajan[23]. The numbers of soldiers residing in the area were added to the local population and this way affected local trading activities. The number of active trading agents boomed under the Roman empire in the region. These agents could have belonged to the military as well as the civilian population. Since more services and more commodities were necessary, more transactions took place and, since the economy was already monetised, more money changed hands. Nevertheless, the number of active soldiers remained small comparatively to the population of the Roman empire. Let us not forget that the Roman army never included more than 500.000 thousand soldiers, while the population of the empire exceeded 50.000.000 people. Even in areas such as Dacia, where large number of troops were stationed, their presence did not always justify a significant impact on the local economies[24]. Therefore, it is possible that the role of the army in the economy has been inexcusably overrated. Instead, we should assess its impact in combination with the local development of trade and the building of cities by the locals.

---

[20] Oltean 2007, 119.
[21] Hanson & Haynes 2004, 80.
[22] Watkins 1983, 15-16.
[23] Webster 1998, 58-64.
[24] Katsari 2011, 39.

In an article I published recently[25], I tried to show that the reliance of the frontier markets on «official» issues was not necessarily connected to the military character of the area or the needs of the army troops. Instead, the monetisation of the limes relied mostly on processes of urbanisation and extensive trading activities within a specific area. Specifically, you can see in the following chart that the number of coins increased in excavations of cities, while it declined in the cases of fortresses. For this purpose I used coin finds from urban sites in Dacia[26], coin finds from fortress-cities in Dacia[27] and coin finds from military sites in Dacia[28]. A closer look at the evidence indicates that the urban sites were more monetised than the military sites. The fortress-cities, however, indicate an even higher use of coins in the area. The evidence, without a doubt, suggest that urbanisation and not militarisation was responsible for the heavy use of coinage. The impact of the army was only indirect and became visible only when the soldiers were mixing with the local urban population, as in the case of fortress-cities.

Local tradition

So, if the needs of the army were not the predominant reason for the similarities of Dacia to the western provinces, where should we turn for a solution? In this case, I would like to suggest that the patterns of minting and the distribution of coinage in the province follow local traditions. Before the annexation of Dacia to the Roman empire there has been a centralised production of gold (Koson), silver or billon Geto-Dacian coins. Especially during the Hellenistic period, coins from Macedonia and Thasos circulated in the area alongside local issues. Drachms from Dyrrhachium

---

[25] Katsari 2008, 242-266.
[26] Ulpia: Winkler 1974-5, 117-136; Chirilă 1978, 60; Alicu 1997; 1992-1993; Gazdac 2002, 729-732. Napoca: Vlassa 1964, 139-141; Protase 1966, 96; Mitrea 1967, 198, no. 47; Mitrea 1968, 177, no. 51; Chirilă 1978, 53-57; Chirilă 1974, 136; Mitrea 1988, 217, no. 19; Boenaru Bordea & Mitrea 1994-1995, 466, no. 37. Sucidava = Celei : Mitrea 1964, 575, no. 44; Tudor, 'Sucidava 1937-1940, 393-399; Tudor 1945-1947, 202; Preda 1975, 441-486; Duncan 1993; Gazdac 2002, 743-744.
[27] Apulum = Alba Julia: Csermi 1987, 35-45; Winkler 1965, 213-256; Ocheşanu 1974, 617-619; Moga 1981, 79-82; Pavel-Popa 1981, 127; Blajan 1984, 93-112; Chirilă & Blajan 1988, 191; Pavel & Moga 1994, 251-256; Suciu, 1995, 123-132; Nicolae, 1998, 270; Poenaru Bordea & Mitrea, 465, no. 21; Moga 1998, 110-235; Gazdac, 2002, 732-734. Porolissum = Moigrad: Winkler 1974, 215-23; Muzeul Zalău, Catalogul colecţiei de monete antice 1968; Gudea, 1997; Gazdac 2002, 734-736. Potaissa = Turda: Winkler and Hopârtean 1973; Chirilă et al., «Descoperiri monetare», 60; Poenaru Bordea and Mitrea 1992, 205, no. 51; Barbulescu 1994, 134. Drobeta Turnu-Severin: Protase 1966, 182, no. 149; Stânga 1998.
[28] Buciumi: Gazdac 2002, 744-745. Resculum: Gazdac 2002, 745. Certiae: Matei 1997. Tihau: Protase 1995, 235. Ilisua: Protase, Gaiu, and Marinescu 1997. Gherla: Gazdac 2002, 747-748. Micia = Vetel: Gazdac 2002, 749. Hoghiz: Gazdac 2002, 750. Sighisoara: Munzen aus der Sammlung des Museums der Stadt Sighisoara 1972, 17 and passim; Mitrofan and Moldovan 1968, 99-109. Inlaceni: Gudea 1979, 232. Rupea: Munzen... Sighi soara 1972, 16 and passim. Cumidava = Raˆsnov: Gudea and Popescu, 1971, 60. Praetorium = Mehadia: Gudea 1975, 147-151; Macrea, Gudea, and Motu, 1993. Arutela = Calimanesti: Gazdac, 2002, 756. Slaveni: Gazdac 2002, 757. Racari: Protase 1966, 94, 181, no. 144; Tudor 1965, 233-257. Hinova: Davidescu and Stângă 1985, 75-89; Davidescu 1989, 87-95. Pojejena: Chirilă and Gudea 1972, 713-717; Mitrea 1972, esp. 145, no. 80; Bălănescu 1984, 131, no. 10.

and Apollonia were another type of imitation coins circulating especially in Transylvania[29]. This practice continued and, in fact, expanded during the Roman Republic. Dacians imported Republican denarii firstly around 75-65 BC[30] and later around the late 40s BC. The locals were so familiar with Roman coins that they even attempted to create copies that circulated widely in Iron Age Dacia[31]. Michael Crawford suggested that these were used almost exclusively for the slave trade[32]. However, the longevity of this numismatic habit and the extended use of fake denarii may indicate that they had a more variable use. Indeed, most Romanian scholars reject Crawford's idea[33].

The numismatic habits of this province did not change significantly when it was annexed into the Roman empire. In fact, the practice of copying official silver coinages continued well into the Empire, during which time we notice large numbers of fake Roman coins circulating up until the third century AD. According to Gazdac, despite the strict laws that prohibited the production of counterfeited gold and silver coins in the empire, 6.8% of silver coin finds from Apulum are plated, at Potaissa 4.8% of denarii and 2.7% of antoniniani are plated, at Drobeta 29.1% of denarii are plated, at Napoca, Tibiscum and Dierna the plated denarii represent 20%, 21.6% and 11.1% respectively of the total number of coins. Most importantly the plated coins that have been recovered from a custom's house (statio portorii) reach 63%. It is possible that in this case the Roman authorities withdrew the plated denarii from circulation and they hoarded them in this house. On the other hand, no law prohibited the production and circulation of fake bronze coins[34]. The importation of gold, silver and bronze issues from the mint of Rome supplemented by the local production of fake types were nothing less than the continuation of the tradition that saw the importation of Republican denarii and their copying several decades earlier. It is obvious that the local population were used to conducting their transactions with official denarii and sestertii instead of the variety of coins from eastern Greco-Roman cities, which were based on the Hellenistic standards. In fact, they showed such a strong preference for denarii that they did not hesitate to use copies.

With regard to the uninhibited continuation of the long existing situation, I am convinced that the central government could not have found adequate reasons to change an already established system. To the best of my knowledge the Roman emperors did not interfere in the newly annexed areas unless there was a strategic or political reason. This way, they avoided the administrative costs of implementing a new system, while they escaped the hassle of persuading the local population to

---

[29] Preda 1976.
[30] Lockyear 1995, 85-102; Lockyear 1996, 165-178.
[31] Lockyear 2008, 147-176.
[32] Crawford 1977, 117-124.
[33] Chiţescu 1981.
[34] Gazdac 2001.

follow it. After all, whether the inhabitants decided to use civic issues from Greece and Asia Minor or chose to mint their own bronzes, they would have had to be trained in recognising their value. Let us not forget that civic coinages followed a variety of weight standards. If anything, the information costs that such an operation involved would have been substantial. In the case of silver coins based on the denarial standard, it was certainly easier and definitely more cost effective to continue using them in local transactions, as they did since the Republican period. The local population did not seem to have been accustomed to the use of hellenistic weight standards after the collapse of the Hellenistic states in the East. Even before the annexation of Dacia to the Roman empire, the Dacians were numismatically part of the western regions of the Roman world. Therefore, there was no reason to change their orientation after they have been politically annexed.

Constantina KATSARI
University of Leicester

Bibliography

Muzeul Zalău, Catalogul colecției de monete antice (Cluj-Napoca 1968).

Munzen aus der Sammlung des Museums der Stadt Sighisoara (Sighisoara 1972).

Alicu 1992-3 = Alicu, D. et al., *Cercetări arheologice la Sarmizegetusa* (Campania 1992-3).

Alicu 1997 = Alicu D., *Ulpia Trajana Sarmizegetusa. Amfiteatrul* (Cluj-Napoca 1997).

Alston 1994 = Alston, R.«Roman military pay from Caesar to Diocletian», *Journal of Roman Studies* 84 (1994) 113-123.

Bălănescu 1984 = D. Bălănescu, «Descoperiri monetare din sudul Banatului (I)», *Studii si Cercetari de Numismatică 8* (1984), 129–36.

Bărbulescu 1994 = M. Bărbulescu, *Potaissa* (Cluj-Napoca 1994).

Bellinger 1949 = A. Bellinger, «The Coins», in M.I. Rostovtzeff, A.R. Bellinger, F.E. Brown, N.P. Toll and C.B. Welles (eds.), *Excavations at Dura, Final Report*, vol. 6 (New Haven 1949).

Blajan 1984 = M. Blajan, «Circulația monetară în județul Alba, argument al continuității populației romanice în Dacia postromana», *Apulum* 22 (1984), 93–112.

Burnett, Amandry & Carradice 1999 = A. Burnett, M. Amandry and I. Carradice, *Roman Provincial Coinage*, vol. 2, part 1 (London/Paris 1999).

Burnett, Amandry & Ripolles 1992 = A. Burnett, M. Amandry and P.P. Ripolles, *Roman Provincial Coinage : From the Death of Caesar to the Death of Vitellius (44 BC to AD 69)*, vol. 1 (London, Paris 1992).

Chirilă et al. 1978 = E. Chirilă et al., «Descoperiri monetare antice în Transilvania (XII)», *Acta Musei Porolissensis 2* (1978), 53–7.

Chirilă 1974 = E. Chirilă, «Descoperiri monetare antice în Transilvania (XI)», *Studii si Comunicari Sibiu 18* (1974), 136.

Chirilă & Gudea 1972 = E. Chirilă and N. Gudea, «Descoperiri monetare antice în Banat», *Apulum 10* (1972), 713–17.

Chirilă & Blajan 1988 = Chirilă, E. and M. Blajan, «Descoperiri monetare antice în Transilvania», *Acta Musei Porolissensis 12* (1988), 191.

Chiţescu 1981 = M. Chiţescu, *Numismatic Aspects of the History of the Dacian State*, BAR International Series (Oxford 1981).

Crawford 1970 = M.H. Crawford, «Money and exchange in the Roman world», *Journal of Roman Studies* 60 (1970) 40-48.

Crawford 1977 = M.H. Crawford, «Republican denarii in Romania: The suppression of piracy and the slave trade», *Journal of Roman Studies* 67 (1977) 117-124.

Csermi 1987 = B. Csermi, «Apulumi maradványok», *Az Alsófehérmegyei Történelmi Évkönyve 9* (1987), 35–45.

Davidescu 1989 = M. Davidescu, *Cetatea romană de la Hinova* (Bucharest 1989).

Davidescu & Stânga 1985 = M. Davidescu and I. Stângă, «Monedele din castelul roman târziu de la Hinova», *Drobeta 6* (1985), 75–89.

Duncan 1993 = G. Duncan, *Coin Circulation in the Danubian and Balkan Provinces of the Roman Empire, AD 294-578* (London 1993).

Gazdac 2004= C. Gazdac, «Center and periphery. The Roman monetary policy regarding the Lower Danube provinces, at the mid third century AD', in C. Gaiu and H. Bodale (eds.), *Centru si Perifer*» (Accent 2004) 71-76.

Gazdac 2002 = C. Gazdac, *Circulaţia monetară în Dacia şi provinciile învecinate de la Traian la Constantin I*, 2 vols. (Cluj Napoca 2002).

Gudea 1997 = N. Gudea, *Porolissum. Un complex daco-roman la marginea de nord a Imperiului Roman* (Zalău 1997).

Gudea 1979 = N. Gudea, «Inlăceni. Incercare de monografie», *Acta Musei Porolissensis* 3 (1979), 232.

Gudea 1975 = N. Gudea, «Monedele din castrul roman de la Mehadia», *SCIVA* 26/1 (1975), 147–51.

Gudea & Popescu 1971 = N. Gudea and I. Popescu, *Castrul roman de la Risnov, Cumidava*, (Brasov 1971).

Hanson & Haynes 2004 = W.S. Hanson and I. Haynes, *Roman Dacia: The Making of a Provincial Society*, Journal of Roman Archaeology (London 2004).

Harl 1996 = K.W. Harl, *Coinage and the Roman Economy, 300 BC to AD 700* (Baltimore/London 1996).

Heuchert 2007 = V. Heuchert, «The chronological development of Roman provincial coin iconography», in C. Howgego, V. Heuchert and A. Burnett (eds.), *Coinage and Identity in the Roman Provinces* (Oxford 2007) 29-56.

Hobley 1998 = A.S. Hobley, *An Examination of Roman Bronze Coin Distribution in the Western Empire, AD 81-192*, BAR International Series (Oxford 1998).

Howgego 1985 = C. Howgego, *Greek Imperial Countermarks* (London 1985).

Jones 1965 = T.B. Jones, «Greek Imperial coins», *The Voice of the Turtle* 4 (1965) 295-301.

Jones 1963 = T.B. Jones, «A numismatic riddle: The so-called Greek imperials», *Proceedings of the American Philosophical Society* 107 (1963) 308-347.

Katsari 2011 = C. Katsari, *The Roman Monetary System: The Eastern Provinces from the First to the Third Century AD* (Cambridge 2011).

Katsari 2008 = C. Katsari, «The monetization of the Roman frontier provinces», in W. V. Harris (ed.), *The Monetary Systems of the Greeks and Romans* (Oxford 2008) 242-266.

Knapp 1924 = G.F. Knapp, *The State Theory of Money* (New York 1924).

Kraft 1972 = K. Kraft, *Das System der kaiserzeitlichen Munzpragung in Kleinasien* (Berlin 1972).

Lockyear 2008 = K. Lockyear, «Aspects of Roman Republican Coins found in Late Iron Age Dacia», in V. Spinei and L. Munteanu (eds) *Miscellanea numismatica Antiquitatis. In honorem septagenarii magistri Virgilii Mihailescu-Bîrliba oblata* (Bucharest 2008) 147-176.

Lockyear 1996 = K. Lockyear, «Dmax based cluster analysis and the supply of coinage to Iron Age Dacia», in H. Kamermans and K. Fennema (eds.), Computer Applications and Quantitative Methods in Archaeology CAA95 (Leiden 1996) 165–178.

Lockyear 1995 = K. Lockyear, «The supply of Roman Republican Denarii to Romania», *Studii si Cercetari de Numismatică* 11 (1995), 85-102.

Macrea, Gudea & Motu 1993 = M. Macrea, N. Gudea and I. Motu, *Praetorium. Castrul și asezarea romana de la Mehadia* (Bucharest 1993).

Matei 1997 = I.B. Matei, *Castrul roman de la Romita-Certiae* (Zalau 1997).

Mitrea 1988 = B. Mitrea, «Découvertes monétaires en Roumanie -1987 (XXXI)», *Dacia* ns 32 (1988) 217.

Mitrea 1972 = B. Mitrea, «Descoperiri de monede antice si bizantine în Republica Socialista România (XV)», *SCIVA* 23/1 (1972), 133–47.

Mitrea 1968 = B. Mitrea, «Descoperiri recente şi mai vechi de monede antice şi bizantine în Republica Socialistă România», *SCIVA* 19/1 (1968), 169–82.

Mitrea 1967 = B. Mitrea, «Descoperiri recente si mai vechi de monede antice si bizantine in Republica Socialistă România», *SCIVA* 18/1 (1967), 188–202.

Mitrea 1964 = B. Mitrea, «Descoperiri recente si mai vechi de monede antice si bizantine in Republica Populară Româna», *SCIVA* 15/4 (1964), 568–82.

Mitrofan & Moldovan 1968 = I. Mitrofan and and G. Moldovan, «Castrul roman de la Sighisoara», *AMN* 5 (1968), 99–109.

Moga 1998 = V. Moga, *Castrul roman de la Apulum* (Cluj- Napoca 1998).

Moga 1981 = V. Moga, «Notițe arheologice apulense», *Apulum* 19 (1981), 79–82.

Nicolae 1998 = E. Nicolae, «Descoperiri de monede antice şi bizantine», *Buletinul Societății Numismatice Romane* 142–3 (1998), 270.

Ocheşanu 1974 = R. Ocheşanu, «Monede romane din secolul IV e.n. descoperite la Alba Iulia», *Apulum* 12 (1974), 617–19.

Oltean 2007 = I.A. Oltean, *Dacia: Landscape, Colonisation and Romanisation* (London/New York 2007).

Pavel & Moga 1994 = V. Pavel and V. Moga, «Descoperiri monetare romane în castrul de la Apulum», *Apulum* 32 (1994), 251-6.

Pavel-Popa 1981 = V. Pavel-Popa, «Descoperiri monetare romane imperiale la Alba Iulia între anii 1957–1980», *Apulum* 19 (1981), 127.

Ponearu Bordea & Mitrea 1994-1995 = G. Boenaru Bordea and B. Mitrea, «Decouvertes monetaires en Roumanie—1993 (XXXVII)», *Dacia* 38–39 (1994-1995) 459–477.

Poenaru Bordea & Mitrea 1994-1995 = G. Poenaru Bordea and B. Mitrea, «Découvertes monétaires en Roumanie - 1993», *Dacia* 38-9 (1994-1995), 459-77.

Poenaru Bordea & Mitrea 1994-1995 = G. Poenaru Bordea and B. Mitrea, «Découvertes monétaires en Roumanie - 1991», *Dacia* ns 36 (1992), 205, no. 51.

Pollard 2000 = N. Pollard, *Soldiers, Cities and Civilians in Roman Syria* (Ann Arbor 2000).

Preda 1973 = C. Preda, *Monedele Geto-Dacilor*, Editura Academie Republicii Socialiste România (Bucharest 1973).

Preda 1975 = C. Preda, «Circulația monedelor romane postaureliene în Dacia», *SCIVA* 26/4 (1975), 441–86.

Protase 1966 = D. Protase, *Problema continuității în Dacia în lumina arheologiei și numismaticii* (Bucharest 1966).

Protase 1995 = D. Protase, *Orizonturi daco-romane* (Cluj-Napoca 1995).

Protase, Gaiu & Marinescu 1997 = D. Protase, C. Gaiu and G. Marinescu, *Castrul roman de la Ilisua* (Bistrita 1997).

Salamon 1970 = M. Salamon, «Causes of disappearance of city-mints in Asia Minor in the second half of the third century AD», *Wiadomosci Munizmatyczne* 14 (1970) 146-162.

Stângă 1998 = I. Stângă, *Viata economică la Drobeta în secolele II-VI p.-Ch.* (Bucharest 1998).

Suciu 1995 = V. Suciu, «Descoperiri monetare romane aflate în colectii din judetul Alba», *Apulum* 33 (1995) 123–32.

Tudor 1965 = D. Tudor, «Castra Daciae Inferioris (VIII)», *Apulum* 5 (1965) 233–57.

Tudor 1945-1947 = D. Tudor «Sucidava (III)», *Dacia* 11–12 (1945-1947) 145–208.

Tudor 1937-1940 = D. Tudor «Sucidava (II)», *Dacia* 7–8 (1937-1940) 359–400.

Van Berchem 1977 = D. Van Berchem, «L'annone militaire est-elle un mythe?», in A. Castagnol, C. Nicolet and H. van Effenterre (eds.), *Armées et Fiscalité dans le Monde Antique: Colloque National du Centre National de la Recherche Scientifique, au Centre Universitaire Tolbiac de Paris I, 14-16 Octobre 1976* (Paris 1977) 331-334.

Vlassa 1964 = N., «Două descoperiri monetare post-aureliene în Transilvania», *SCIVA* 15/1 (1964) 139–41.

Watkins 1983 = T.H. Watkins, «Roman legionary fortresses and the cities of modern Europe», *Military Affairs* 47.1 (1983) 15–25.

Watson 1999 = A. Watson, *Aurelian and the Third Century* (London/ New York 1999).

Webster 1998 = G. Webster, *The Roman Imperial Army of the First and Second Centuries AD* (Oklahoma 1998).

Winkler 1964 = I. Winkler, «Despre circulatia monetară la Porolissum», *AMN* 1 (1964), 215–23.

Winkler 1965 = I. Winkler, «Circulatia monetară la Apulum», *AMN* 2 (1965), 213–56.

Winkler 1974-1975 = I. Winkler, «Descoperiri monetare în Ulpia Traiana Sarmizegetusa», *Sargetia* 11–12 (1974-1975), 117–36.

Winkler & Hopârtean 1973 = I. Winkler & A. Hopârtean, *Moneda antica la Potaissa* (Cluj 1973).

Index

Le présent index répertorie les noms géographiques, ethniques et de personnages historiques du nord des Balkans, ainsi que des autres parties du monde antique lorsqu'ils ont une importance significative dans les articles de ce volume (à l'exception des termes «Grèce, Grecs» et «Rome, Romains» et de leurs équivalents anglais, qui apparaissent trop fréquemment). Les mots inventoriés sous leur forme anglaise apparaissent en italique.

Termes géographiques et ethniques

Augusta Trajana, *Augusta Traiana* 184
Abdère, *Abdera* 37, 94, 103, 106
Abritus 199, 200, 203
Acontisma 106
Adriatique, *Adriatic* 5, 94, 120, 123, 126, 129, 130, 131, 133, 134, 136, 138, 139, 141, 142, 144, 145, 146, 147, 150, 151, 152, 157, 160, 163, 164
Ainos, *Aenus* 68, 103
Agighiol 33, 36, 40
Agrianes 68
Amphipolis 17, 89
Antigoneia 137
Apollonia (d'Illyrie) 113
Apulum 123, 125, 211, 212, 213, 214, 216, 217, 218
Archontiko 14, 15
Ariarathes 89, 90
Ardiéens 113, 121
Arges 113
Arutela 211
Asparagium 135
Astai, Astaean 105, 106, 107
Aruvium 146
Athènes, Athéniens 6, 25, 40, 41, 42, 43, 44, 113, 138
Atintanes 130, 131
Autariatai 51, 55
Axios 11, 12, 14, 16, 17, 87
Bessi, Bessoi 88, 107
Beroe 101

Bessarabie 117
Bisaltai 11, 19
Borovo 26, 28, 30, 33, 36, 42
Bosna 147, 148
Bosnia 144, 145, 147, 148, 150, 157, 162
Boullinoi 143
Bouthrotos 134, 135, 137, 138
Breuques, *Breuci* 133, 147, 148
Buciumi 221
Budoi-Marghita 117
Bugojno 148
Bylazora 61
Byllis 135
Cabyle 101
Caenice, Caenic 103, 104
Carsium 199, 200
Cendrisian (tribe) 187, 189
Celtes, Gaulois, Galates, *Celts, Gauls, Gaulish, Gallic, Galatae* 5, 37, 69, 70, 76, 87, 92, 98, 146, 159, 160, 173, 174, 175,
Certiae 211, 216
Chaonie 134
Chatalka 189
Chersonese 103
Coelaletae 107, 172
Craiova 26
Crénidès 31, 36
Daces, Dacie, dace, *Dacia, Dacians* 3, 5, 6, 29, 40, 43, 113, 114, 118, 119, 121, 123, 125, 126, 161, 187, 205, 206, 207, 208, 209, 210, 211, 212, 213, 214, 215, 216, 217, 218

Dalmates 121
Dalmion/Delmion 143
Dalmatia 91, 139, 141, 142, 144, 145, 147, 149, 150, 151, 153, 164
Danube, *Danube*, *Danubian* 5, 7, 26, 37, 38, 87, 92, 95, 96, 109, 113, 119, 126, 133, 141, 182, 202, 203, 214
Daorsi 145
Dardanians 88, 91, 92, 94, 95, 96, 98, 110, 161
Debelo Brdo-Sarajevo 148
Delphes 7, 97, 98, 99, 221
Delmatae, Delmatean 142, 143, 144, 145, 146, 150, 151, 153, 154, 221
Dentheletae 89, 91
Derrones 11, 12, 22, 221
Désidiates, *Daesitiates, Daisoi* 133, 142, 147, 148 221
Desilo 145, 221
Dessarètes 221
Détroits 25, 36, 69, 74, 78, 221
Dieci 115, 116, 221
Dierna 212, 221
Dii 107, 125, 172, 221
Dimale 131, 221
Dioclétien 190, 197, 213, 221
Dionysopolis 199, 200, 221
Dolj 117, 123, 221
Donja Dolina 145, 147, 148, 150, 158, 160, 221
Drabeskos 17, 221
Drave, *Drava* 87, 96, 113, 147, 148, 221
Drin, *Drilo* 133, 150, 221
Drobeta 211, 212, 214, 217, 221
Durostrum 221
Dürres 136, 221
Duvanjsko 143, 144, 156, 221
Dyrrachion, *Dyrrhachium* 3, 6, 113, 114, 115, 116, 117, 118, 119, 120, 121, 122, 123, 124, 125, 126, 127, 130, 131, 133, 134, 135, 136, 137, 138, 150
Epire 124, 130, 133, 134, 135, 136, 137, 138, 139, 158, 221
Eneti 91, 221

Gabiène, *Gabiene* 53, 54, 55, 56, 57, 58, 61, 67, 75
Gacka 146, 221
Gaugamela 51, 55, 59, 221
Genusus 131, 221
Gètes 35, 38, 66, 114, 118, 119, 121, 221
Gherla 211, 221
Glamoko 221
Glasinac 142, 144, 147, 149
Glava Panega 200, 221
Golyama Kosmatka 25, 31, 32, 33, 221
Grozesti 117, 125, 221
Hebrus 101, 103, 221
Hellespont 36, 91, 104, 221
Herzegovina 144, 157, 221
Hiéron Oros 35, 221
Hinova 211, 214, 221
Histri 141, 162, 221
Hoghiz 211, 221
Hutovo Blato 145, 221
Hvar 142, 150, 221
Hylloi 143, 221
Iader 152, 221
Iatrus 198, 199, 200, 203, 221
Ialomita 113, 221
Iapodes, Iapodean 141, 142, 145, 146, 151, 153, 154, 146, 150
Ichnaioi 11, 221
Ilisua 211, 217, 221
Illyricum 126, 133, 142, 143, 159, 160, 161, 163
Illyrie, Illyriens, illyrien, Illyrians, Illyrian 3, 5, 8, 110, 113, 114, 118, 119, 121, 122, 124, 129, 130, 131, 132, 133, 134, 135, 136, 137, 138, 139, 141, 157, 158, 159, 161, 163, 164
Imotsko 144, 221
Inlaceni 211, 215, 221
Issa 130, 131, 221
Istros (cité) 5, 196, 200
Istros (fleuve), *Istrus*, Danube 5, 7, 26, 37, 38, 87, 92, 95, 96, 104, 109, 113, 119, 126, 133, 141, 202, 203, 214, 221

Italy, Italian 43, 94, 124, 150, 151, 221
Judée, *Iudaea* 71, 72, 73, 78, 79
Kamenjača 148, 162, 221
Kaptol 148, 149, 221
Kavala 106, 221
Kouroupédion 65, 76, 77, 78
Korčula 150, 221
Krajina 147, 221
Krka 144, 145, 151, 221
Kypséla 67, 79, 221
Lete 11, 87, 92, 97, 102
Livanjsko 144, 156, 221
Labéates 221
Laeaei 11, 12
Lašva 147
Lekane 106
Liburnes, *Liburni, Liburnian* 121, 141, 145, 146, 150
Lissus 119, 133, 134, 136, 152
Ljubljanica 146
Loveč 37
Lukovit 26
Lychnides 131
Lysimacheia 65, 67, 68, 69, 79
Macédoine, Macédoniens, macédonien, *Macedonia, Macedonians, Macedonian* 3, 6, 11, 13, 14, 15, 16, 18, 19, 20, 21, 22, 23, 30, 31, 35, 37, 38, 39, 42, 45, 46, 50, 51, 52, 53, 54, 55, 56, 57, 58, 59, 60, 61, 62, 63, 70, 71, 72, 74, 79, 82, 85, 87, 88, 89, 90, 91, 92, 93, 94, 95, 98, 99, 102, 103, 104, 106, 107, 108, 109, 110, 113, 114, 116, 118, 119, 120, 122, 124, 126, 129, 130, 131, 132, 133, 134, 135, 139, 142, 145, 150, 151, 152, 172, 211, 224
Maedi 87, 88, 89, 91, 92, 94, 95, 96
Maedica 91, 101
Magnésie 68, 69, 77
Mandina Gradina 144
Manioi 143
Maritsa 27
Maronée, *Maronea* 68, 103, 106, 113, 114, 116, 124
Mezaei 142, 147, 148

Metulum 146
Micia 211
Mihailovgrad 37
Moesie inférieure, *Lower Moesia* 7, 181, 182, 190, 191, 195, 196, 197, 200, 201
Montana 198, 203
Morava 87, 119
Mosses 11
Mureş 119
Napoca 211, 212, 213, 214, 216, 217
Narona 152
Neretva 113, 115, 143, 144, 150, 151
Nestoi 143
Nestus 103, 106
Nicopolis ad Istrum 209
Novae 197, 199, 200, 202, 203
Odryses, odryse, *Odrusae, Odrysians* 25, 27, 29, 33, 34, 35, 36, 37, 38, 39, 45, 89, 103, 172
Olcinitae 133
Oreskioi 11
Orjahovo 26
Panade 116, 117, 123, 125
Panagjurište 25, 26, 28, 32, 33, 36, 37, 44
Pangée 6, 31
Paraitakene 53, 55, 56, 57, 58, 60, 61
Parthia, *Parthians* 167, 169, 171, 172, 177
Parthiniens 122, 131
Paionians, Péoniens, péonien 5, 6, 12, 51, 55
Paionios 55
Pannoniens, *Pannonia, Pannonii, Pannonian* 121, 125, 141, 142, 143, 146, 147, 148, 153, 154, 169, 170
Parorbelia 101
Perinthos 106, 110
Perses, perse, *Persians, Persian* 11, 13, 14, 15, 17, 18, 19, 22, 28, 29, 30, 45, 51, 52, 53, 54, 55, 58, 59, 60, 61, 6368, 74, 75
Perside 75, 79
Perushtitza 189
Philippes, *Philippoi* 104, 106, 122
Philippopolis, *Philippopolis* 8, 101, 107, 109, 172, 181, 182, 183, 184, 185, 186, 192
Phoinikè 130, 137

Pleven 37
Pod 148
Pojejena 211
Pont-Euxin, mer Noire 5, 42, 80, 87, 109
Porolissum 211, 215, 218,
Potaissa 211, 212, 213, 218
Požega 148
Prateorium
Promona 145
Propontide 5, 34
Raphia 67, 68, 70, 75, 81
Resculum 211
Rhizonitae 133
Rhodope 44, 88, 104, 106
Rogozen 26, 27, 28, 29, 30, 32, 33, 34, 35, 37, 41, 42, 43, 44, 45
Rupci 116
Rupea 211
Salona 145, 151, 152
Salsovia 196, 200
Sanski Most 145, 147, 148, 158
Sapaioi, Sapaean 104, 105, 106, 107
Save, *Sava* 66, 87, 96, 113, 142, 146, 147, 148, 149
Segestani 147
Selepitani 132
Serdica 188
Scardona 145
Scodra
Scordisques, *Scordisci* 7, 87, 88, 91, 92, 94, 95, 96, 97, 98, 110, 113, 114, 118, 119, 161
Scythes, *Scythia* 29, 35, 37, 38, 41, 196, 202
Séleucides 7, 42, 65, 67, 68, 69, 70, 71, 75, 78, 79, 80, 85
Seron 72, 73
Seuthopolis 29, 66
Sieu-Odorhei 116
Sighisoara 211, 213, 216
Sinjsko 144
Sinti 91
Šipka 25
Sofia 11, 28
Sostra 197
Sredna Gora 25, 28

Stojanovo 26
Strymon 12, 19, 21, 27, 91, 101, 103
Sucidava 211, 218
Syrie, syrien, *Syria, Syrian* 37, 41, 70, 71, 72, 79, 81, 82, 181, 202, 207, 209, 217
Thasos 6, 45, 113, 114, 115, 116, 126, 211
Thrace, Thraces, thrace, *Thrace, Thracians, Thracian* 5, 6, 7, 8, 11, 13, 14, 15, 16, 18, 1920, 21, 22, 23, 24, 25, 26, 27, 28, 29, 30, 31, 32, 33, 34, 35, 36, 37, 38, 39, 40, 41, 42, 43, 44, 45, 46, 65, 66, 67, 68, 69, 70, 71, 72, 73, 74, 75, 76, 77, 78, 79, 81, 82, 84, 85, 88, 89, 90, 91, 93, 97, 98, 99, 101, 102, 103, 104, 110, 113, 114, 118, 119, 121, 126, 167, 168, 169, 172, 173, 174, 175, 176, 177, 181, 182, 184, 186, 187. 188, 189, 191, 192
Tiberius 143, 167, 168, 169, 170, 171, 172, 173, 174, 176
Tibiscum 212
Tihau 211
Tileagd 117, 125
Tomis 196, 200, 202
Tomislavgrad 143, 144
Toundja 25
Troesmis 190, 198, 200
Tropaeum Traiani 198, 200
Tylis 101
Triballes, *Triballoi* 35, 37, 101
Ulpia 211, 213, 218
Una 146
Via Egnatia 36, 90, 103, 110, 120, 136
Viişoara 117, 125
Viminacium 119, 208
Vis 142, 150
Vladinja 26
Vodovrati 87
Voivodeni 117, 123
Vratsa 37, 43
Vulchitran 32
Zagora (Dalmatian) 81, 141, 144, 150, 151
Zaklopaca 116

Noms de personnages historiques

Agron 103, 131, 139
Alexandre Ier (de Macédoine), *Alexander I* 6, 14, 20, 22, 23
Alexandre (le Grand) 41, 42, 75
Amadokos 89
Anaximenes of Lampsakos 14
Andriscus 101
Anicius 132
Antiochos Ier 65
Antiochos II 65, 66, 67, 79, 80
Antiochos III 65, 66, 67, 68, 69, 71, 77
Antipatros 54
Antigonos Monophtalmos
Athéas 36
Audoleon 51, 55
Augustus, voir s.v. Octavian
Aurelian 209, 219
Bato 133
Bastareus 12, 22
Brutus 122, 133, 173
Burebista 119
Caecilius Metellus Caprarius 88
Calpurnius Pison (L.), *Calpurnius Piso (L.)* 89, 102, 134
Cassius 89, 106, 129, 131, 145, 173
Cornelius Scipio Asiagenus / Asiaticus 94, 95
Cosconius (M.) 87
Démétrios de Pharos, *Demetrios of Pharos* 130, 131, 153
Didius (T.) 88, 103
Diegylis 103
Dokimos 12
Eumenes of Kardia
Gaius Cassius Longinus 145
Genthios, *Genthius* 122, 135, 139
Germanicus 167, 169, 170, 171, 172, 174, 176, 177
Hadrian 195, 200
Hortensius 90, 91, 94, 95, 96

Jugurtha 170, 171
Julius Civilis 173, 175
Kassandros 51, 54, 55
Kimon 15, 18
Kendebaios 73, 74
Kersebleptès 34
Kotys (nom de plusieurs princes ou rois thraces) 34, 35, 89, 103, 104, 105, 168, 169, 170, 171, 172
Lucullus (L.) 88, 89, 104
Lysimaque 37, 65, 66, 76, 77, 79
Manlius Vulso 68, 69, 83, 88
Marius 90
Marcus Minucius Rufus 88
Mark Antony 169
Mithridate, *Mithridates* (Eupator) 89, 91, 94, 96, 97, 98, 99, 108, 109, 119, 124
Ménas 76, 77, 78, 84
Octavian, Augustus 107, 109, 143, 145, 148, 163, 168, 169, 170, 172, 174, 191, 197, 203
Patraos 6, 49, 51, 53, 54, 55, 56, 57, 58, 60, 61
Perseus 101, 103
Philippe II de Macédoine 22, 27, 31, 35, 36, 37, 39
Philip V (king of Macedon) 101
Philip the Arab 208
Pleuratos 130, 131, 132
Porcius Cato (C.) 87, 92
Publius Vellaeus 172
Rhaskos 106
Rhaskuporis 104, 106, 167, 168, 170, 171, 172, 175, 176
Rhoemetalkes 105, 107, 168, 172, 173, 175
Sadalas 89, 104
Sejanus 167, 168, 173, 174
Séleucos Ier 65, 67, 75, 76, 77, 78
Séleucos II 66, 75
Séleucos III
Sentius Saturnus (C.)
Seuthès 30, 33, 34, 43, 66

Sextus Pompeius 87
Skerdilaïdes 131
Sitalkès 39
Sothimus 89
Sparadokos 23
Sulla 89, 90, 91, 93, 94, 95, 96
Tarquinius Superbus 174
Térès, *Teres* 33, 66, 89
Teuta 130
Tiberius 143, 167, 168, 169, 170, 171, 172, 173, 174, 176
Timasion de Dardanos
Trajan, *Trajan* 30, 134, 168, 182, 191, 210, 213
Trebellenus 172
Valerian 208
Valerius Flaccus (L.) 90, 91
Vonones 169, 172